# Classical Hindu Mythology

*A Reader in the Sanskrit Purāṇas*

## Hindu Tradition Series

*The Hindu Tradition Series aims to bring together books of the highest academic standard that critically interrogate Hindu tradition in the widest sense. Its focus is on cultural and religious history, including relevant political and social developments. The interaction with other traditions, whether originally from inside or outside the Indian subcontinent, will figure prominently among its volumes.*



**Number 3**

# Classical Hindu Mythology

Edited and Translated by
CORNELIA DIMMITT
J.A.B. VAN BUITENEN

## *A Reader in the Sanskrit Purāṇas*

MOTILAL BANARSIDASS PUBLISHERS
PRIVATE LIMITED • DELHI (INDIA)

*Classical Hindu Mythology*
*A Reader in the Sanskrit Purāṇas*
Hindu Tradition Series,
Number 3

ISBN: 978-81-208-3972-4

**First Indian Edition: Delhi, 2015**
Earlier published in 1978 by Temple University Press



MOTILAL BANARSIDASS
41 U.A. Bungalow Road, Jawahar Nagar, Delhi 110 007
8 Mahalaxmi Chamber, 22 Bhulabhai Desai Road, Mumbai 400 026
203 Royapettah High Road, Mylapore, Chennai 600 004
236, 9th Main III Block, Jayanagar, Bengaluru 560 011
Sanas Plaza, 1302 Baji Rao Road, Pune 411 002
8 Camac Street, Kolkata 700 017
Ashok Rajpath, Patna 800 004
Chowk, Varanasi 221 001

LIBRARY OF CONGRESS CATALOGUING-IN-PUBLICATION DATA
Puranas. English. Selections.
Classical Hindu mythology.
Includes Bibliography,
Glossary and Index.
1. Dommitt, Cornelia, 1938— II. Buitenen,
Johannes Adrianus Bernardus van. III. Title.
BL 1135. P6213 294.5'925 77-92643
ISBN 978-81-208-3972-4

*Printed in India*
by Avantika Printers Private Limited
New Delhi-110065 and published by JP Jain
for Motilal Banarsidass Publishers Private Limited,
41 U.A. Bungalow Road, Jawahar Nagar, Delhi-110007

to H. H. Vibhuti Narain Singh Kashiraj
for his princely contribution to
Purāṇa scholarship

# Foreword by the General Editor

Of all genres of Sanskrit texts, the Purāṇas is the most extensive; their combined size is enormous. The amount of academic study they receive is yet not commensurate with this size. Fortunately recent years have seen increasing academic concern with this textual corpus, and we may be confident that a better understanding of its origin and development will become available in years to come. In spite of this, the Reader prepared by Cornelia Dimmit and J.A.B. Van Buitenen already more than 35 years ago has lost none of its value and utility today. It contains, in English traslation, a representative sample of passages from various Purāṇas, dealing with topics repeatedly dealt with in these texts. An Indian reprint of this work is timely and welcome.

—JOHANNES BRONKHORST

# Contents

# Preface

There has been a clear need since Heinrich Zimmer's *Myths and Symbols in Indian Art and Civilization** for a textbook that would incorporate the classical statements of Hindu mythology, a comprehensive, if not exhaustive, selection of Indian accounts of their own cherished stories. This need has been felt and variously responded to. In recent years R. K. Narayan, in *Gods, Demons and Others,*† has given an excellent version of his own beloved lore. James Kirk, also with a southern Indian emphasis, has retold some very fine tales in his *Stories of the Hindus.*‡ In her *Hindu Myths,*§ Wendy O'Flaherty has dug more ambitiously into Veda, Epic and Purāṇa with an historical perspective on the vagaries of Hindu mythography In addition, cultural anthropologists have shown more and more interest in the ways little communities relate to a larger network of cultures and even civilizations ("Great Traditions"), but their large knowledge about small societies has often found pause before their unfamiliarity with the larger traditions. The historians of Indian art, on the other hand, have built up an architecture of Hindu mythology so magisterial that it has become almost a closed world to the non-specialist.

The authors felt it might be useful to present those who are intrigued by the myths of Indian civilization with representative classical texts. We did not expect to find a single origin for Hindu mythology since sources abound in a variety of media. The Sanskrit Purāṇas proved particularly useful for our purposes. If their very multitude suggests that there is no single original text for Hindu myths, their common language confirms that there is a single tongue

*Heinrich Zimmer, *Myths and Symbols in Indian Art and Civilization* (New York: Pantheon Books, 1946).

†R. K. Narayan, *Gods, Demons and Others* (New York: Viking Press, 1964).

‡James A. Kirk, *Stories of the Hindus* (New York: Macmillan, 1972).

§Wendy Doniger O'Flaherty, *Hindu Myths* (Penguin Books, 1975); in her appendices O'Flaherty has assembled an invaluable collection of bibliographical material concerning Purāṇic mythology which we saw no need to duplicate in this volume.

in which their variety was collected. They are not original texts: with every vocative they make clear that they are told by teachers speaking to students who want to listen. And the very substance of this teaching consists of stories about the gods, or mythology as we understand it.

Of course the Purāṇas themselves had their teachers too. The influence of the epics, the *Mahābhārata* and the *Rāmāyaṇa*, has been profound; and on those teachers, the influence of the Veda is clear, though not always transparent. But we wanted to present the mythology of the Hindu tradition from a period later than the epics, much as it has been received ever since, too often told, perhaps, but miraculously still fresh.

Moreover the the authors saw no need to duplicate materials that are already available in other translations, notably the *Mahābhārata* and the *Rāmāyaṇa.* A Purāṇa reader besides being justifiable in itself, has the value of presenting texts not readily available to most people. While tradition ascribed to the *Mahābhārata a lakh* of couplets, or one hundred thousand, to the Purāṇas it assigns a crore, or ten million. There are translations of some of this material, but not of all the eighteen Grreat Purāṇas, let alone the Minor Purāṇas. Thanks to the generosity of the Kashiraj Trust founded by the Mahārāja of Vārāṇasi (Banaras) there are good editions of some of the Purāṇas; the *Viṣṇu* and *Bhāgavata,* and to a lesser extent the *Mārkaṇḍeya* are also well edited. But it cannot be said that the Purāṇas are an open book even for the specialist.

The sheer mass of the materials imposed limitations on us. We had no intention of reproducing the contents of any single Purāṇa, because each one includes, in addition to mythology a wealth of didactic, legal and moralistic material. In fact, their encyclopedic aspirations cover the breadth of human knowledge for their place and time. In making our selections, we have used the Purāṇas most popular in the Hindu tradition itself; our chief sources have been the *Viṣṇu, Mārkaṇḍeya, Bhāgavata, Matsya, Vāmana* and *Kūrma,* and to a lesser extent the *Brahmavaivarta, Śiva* and *Garuḍa.* With such an abundance of riches to choose from, the choice on occasion became simply a matter of balance. We could have used the *Bhāgavata* more extensively on Kṛṣṇa, for example, but since that text has been translated and anthologized often, the *Viṣṇu* and *Brahmavaivarta* accounts seemed preferable.

We intend this book as a reader. Hence we have felt our responsibility to its readers quite strongly Even though tempted, we have tried not to interpose a private interpretation between the text and its users. The introductions before each section seek mostly to describe and give guidance to the reader, whom, oratorically, we presume to know very little. We hope to be forgiven for stating the obvious.

There are some cautions. Some of the Sanskrit text editions used are quite good; some are very poor. While we have attempted to render our texts accurately, there were times when the texts failed us, and emendation was necessary. The specialist will readily discern the course we have chosen. At the beginning of certain selections we have sometimes extended the sense of the text in the translation, to facilitate transitions between fragments. And although pleading the exigencies of space is poor justice, at times we have shortened stories because the alternative was to select a shorter but poorer version; the couplets omitted are indicated in the Notes on Sources. Contrariwise, we have not stinted on the variety of names attributed to a single deity, for homogenization here would have impoverished the rich fabric of identities in which each one is clothed. A Glossary of names will, we hope, assist the reader

Practically all the Purāṇas are composed in a meter called *śloka* which consists of thirty-two syllables, half of which are free. It is a very easy meter that is best translated into English prose. In the case of a number of cultural terms the English translations can only be approximations. Where even approximations would not do we have kept the Sanskrit word and have explained it either in a footnote or in the Glossary.

While both authors stand behind the whole book, the reader needs to know the division of labor between them. The initiative for the book was taken by Cornelia Dimmitt, who located and selected the texts, and who is largely responsible for the content of the introductions. The translation itself has been wholly collaborative.

Cornelia Dimmitt
Washington, 1977

Boston, 2014

# Classical Hindu Mythology

*A Reader in the Sanskrit Purāṇas*

# The Purāṇas: An Introduction

India, extraordinarily rich in myth, has no special word for it. Closest perhaps is *purāṇa,* "a story of the old days," but the word encompasses a great deal more than what we nowadays understand by "myth." The word has become the broad term for a Sanskrit genre of works which profess to record these stories of antiquity, the Purāṇas. These Purāṇas are the principal sources for our knowledge of Hindu mythology.

There is no exact parallel to the Purāṇas in Western literatures, although the chronicles of medieval Europe come to mind. Both share in common the celebration of religion, the glorification of saints and kings, and the edification of readers, whose faith is to be strengthened. Like those chronicles the Purāṇas are prolix, repetitive, derivative from earlier models, with a good deal of borrowing and conflation. But the Purāṇas lack even the slender thread of history that runs through the chronicles.

From one point of view it is irrelevant to date the Purāṇas, for by definition they never contain novel materials; they merely repeat the stories of the old days. But broadly speaking one can say that the genre begins when the composition of the *Mahābhārata* is concluded in about 300 A.D. While the *Mahābhārata* in its final form already exhibits Purāṇic features, it is traditionally set apart from the Purāṇas as *itihāsa,* a story about events. But how fluid this distinction was is shown by an old collective *itihāsapurāṇam,* which in the Upaniṣads is occasionally mentioned as a sort of "fifth" Veda. The transition between *Mahābhārata* and Purāṇas is illustrated by the *Harivaṃśa,* in intention an appendix to the *Mahābhārata* supplementing the epic's treatment of Kṛṣṇa and his family, in practice the earliest Purāṇa.

Spanning the period from 300 to 1000 A.D., the Purāṇas document the triumph of Hinduism in India, and the ascendancy of this or that main god in the evolving pantheon. Although normally not too sectarian in tone, they tend to be dedicated to one god or another—

usually Viṣṇu or Śiva—around whom the old stories are retold, frequently by the god himself. Although they greatly overlap in content, eighteen specific Purāṇas are distinguished; these are the Great Purāṇas. But there are an equal number of minor Purāṇas, while numerous others claim the title.

In spite of their early title of "fifth Veda," the Purāṇas do not in fact carry the authority of scripture. But this is not saying much. The scholastics of Hindu orthodoxy, the Mīmāṃsakas, had refined the notion of scriptural authority to the point of evanescence. According to their doctrine only those passages in the Veda itself which enjoined a certain rite to be performed for a specific end were authoritative. The collections of the earliest Vedas were dismissed as mere *mantra*, while the numerous narrative passages in the later literature of Brāhmaṇa, Āraṇyaka and Upaniṣad were allowed a derivative validity in so far—and only in so far—as they could be construed as being either laudatory or condemnatory of certain actions enjoined or prohibited. Yet despite its severely limited authoritativeness, the "Veda" had a lofty, though vague, authority as *śruti*—the learning that had come down from the beginning of creation from teacher to pupil by "hearing."

As this *śruti* bore exclusively on ritual and this ritual itself had pretty much spent its force by the late centuries B.C. (and even before had touched only a small class of the population), there was room, and indeed a need, from early on for a broader, more popular, less exclusive body of "revelations" that responded to the actual beliefs and concerns of the orthodox. By its nature ill defined and of uncertain authority, it acquired the title of *smṛti*, "recollections," supplementary to *śruti* but validated by its acceptance among the same class in society who were the source of the knowledge of *śruti*, the brahmin class. It is to this category of texts that the Purāṇas are assigned by the Indian tradition itself.

## The Eighteen Purāṇas

Among the large mass of Purāṇic texts, eighteen have been singled out as Great Purāṇas, great in the sense that they have an all-Indian acceptance. Each of these provides a list of all eighteen, including itself, but while these lists overwhelmingly agree, there are minor discrepancies. The result is a list of twenty:

| | | |
|---|---|---|
| *Agni* | *Brahmā* | *Garuḍa* |
| *Bhāgavata* | *Brahmāṇḍa* | *Harivaṃśa* |
| *Bhaviṣya* | *Brahmavaivarta* | *Kūrma* |

| | | |
|---|---|---|
| *Linga* | *Padma* | *Varāha* |
| *Mārkaṇḍeya* | *Skanda* | *Vāyu* |
| *Matsya* | *Śiva* | *Viṣṇu* |
| *Nārada* | *Vāmana* | |

In some of the texts an attempt is made to divide these eighteen into three neat sets of six each; it is said that they divide either according to their inspiration by one of the triad of Gods (Brahmā, Viṣṇu or Śiva), or according to the particular "quality" (*guṇa*) that informs them (*sattva, rajas* or *tamas*). However, neither title nor classification of the individual Purāṇas gives an accurate description of their contents.

The Purāṇas do share certain characteristics which mark them as a distinct genre of literature. They are all composed in Sanskrit of a mediocre quality, usually in *śloka* meter, occasionally in *triṣṭubh* or prose. They are all told in question and answer form. Their contents consist principally of stories about the Hindu gods, goddesses and supernatural beings, with a sprinkling of tales about men, women and famous seers. And their mode is epigonic, as if the narrator himself were retelling a story whose details he at times imperfectly remembered, or as if the narrator were providing only the outline of a tale requiring living imagination to amplify the details. Precisely when, where, why and by whom these old stories were edited into discrete collections is not easy to determine. As they exist today, the Purāṇas are a stratified literature. Each titled work consists of material that has grown by numerous accretions in successive historical eras. Thus no Purāṇa has a single date of composition. The most that can be done is to determine a chronology of strata, and even that is a difficult task, given the encyclopedic nature of the contents of each Purāṇa. It is as if they were libraries to which new volumes have been continuously added, not necessarily at the end of the shelf, but randomly. Thus dating these works with any accuracy must await the discrimination of the strata, a large task as yet to be begun.

The criteria by which such stratification of contents may be discerned will be both internal and external. The subject matter of different sections of Purāṇas must be correlated with phases of Indian tradition as known from other literature. On this basis, certain speculations may be hazarded. The oldest material in the Purāṇas is contemporaneous with the Vedas, but was recited either in a different milieu than the brahminic ritual or by persons other than the brahmin priests. This alternate milieu would be the source of the *smṛti* tradition that gave rise eventually to both epic and Purāṇic collections. Thus the Purāṇas, which share many stories with the epics, the

*Mahābhārata* in particular, do not derive from that epic, but from the same body of oral tradition, or *smṛti,* whose origins may be as old as the period of the Vedas.

A more precise clue to the dating of the Purāṇas is found in the genealogical lists that are offered in a number of Purāṇas, the dynasties of kings. While frustratingly incomplete, Purāṇic genealogies appear to provide indications of two different eras in which these old stories were collected and edited: about 1000 B.C., the time after the putative *Mahābhārata* war; and about the fourth to sixth centuries A.D., the period of the Gupta Dynasty. In both eras, political events were particularly significant in the formation of social consciousness for the early inhabitants of northern India.

The first series of genealogies, beginning with the original ruler, the semi-legendary Manu, ends shortly after the *Mahābhārata* war, variously with Parikṣit or his son Janamejaya, whose lineage is more clearly given in the *Mahābhārata.* Subsequent genealogies are depicted as prophecies of the future, as if added to already established texts at a later time. This second set of genealogies ends either with one of the Gupta rulers, or with one of the foreign tribes who succeeded the Guptas in northwest India, the Śakas, Yavanas or Hūṇas. No Purāṇa mentions Harṣa, who ruled in the seventh century, while the poet Bāṇa's *Harṣacarita,* about 625 A.D., which tells the story of Harṣa's reign, knows the Purāṇas and even cites a public recitation of the *Vāyu*.

If we can accept that some of the Purāṇic material was in fact collected and edited in these two eras, there is still no clear way to know what, other than the genealogies themselves, was included in each edition, for there has been no final closing date for the Purāṇas. Alterations in the texts continued gradually after the sixth century A.D. by a variety of means, including adding chapters, replacing chapters, rewriting old stories to a new purpose, and using old titles for wholly new material.

In this manner, these old stories, whatever their original provenance, have become encyclopedic repositories of successive waves of development within the Hindu tradition. Repeating stories and legends as old as 1000 B.C., they have continued to accrue material of various kinds in every era of the Hindu tradition, a tradition which continues even now to sponsor a lively and vigorous oral literature. Today these old Purāṇic stories still thrive, taking on a life of their own appropriate to the modern world.

Other clues to their origin occur in the Purāṇas, however. Romaharṣaṇa, variously spelled Lomaharṣaṇa, is called *sūta,* or bard.

If we presume that old stories were recited by another class of poets than the brahmin priests who knew the Veda, then this was the title of their office. What exactly did *sūta* mean? Several apparently conflicting definitions have been given: a bardic reciter, a charioteer, and the son of a cross-caste marriage between a brahmin father and kṣatriya mother. If we ask how all three of these definitions coalesce, it may not be entirely far afield to suggest the following: that it was the duty of a charioteer to report on the actions of his master, to celebrate his victory in battle, to eulogize his bravery, in short to recite heroic events (perhaps enhanced by poetic imagination), to an audience at home. That this was less than a high-class office, the *sūta* being lower in status than the warrior himself, is apparent. Perhaps the designation of *sūta* as the offspring of a cross-caste marriage conveyed a kind of truth, that the bard's office eventually came to include the recitation not only of kṣatriya heroics but also of brahminic traditions as well.

In any case, two sources of oral tradition are found in Purāṇic lore; the ritual practices and social values of the brahmin class of priests, and the heroic deeds and social values of the kṣatriya class of kings and warriors. Their values were not always the same. Were these originally two entirely separate oral traditions in which brahmin reciters and kṣatriya reciters addressed two wholly different classes, each with its own literature? Or were they two strata of a composite society whose oral tradition included both components, and perhaps others as well? It seems likely that these two traditions were never entirely distinct, for Vedic literature includes numerous stories of kings, and the epics and Purāṇas both promote the social and religious preeminence of brahmins and their values. Thus the Purāṇas represent an amalgam of two somewhat different but never entirely separate oral literatures: the brahmin tradition stemming from the reciters of the Vedas, and the bardic poetry recited by *sūtas* that was handed down in kṣatriya circles. Both traditions are equally ancient, *śruti* emphasizing Vedic ritual practices and gods, *smṛti* emphasizing the acts of kings and the deities of the lower classes.

If these are the two traditions from which the "old stories" that comprise the Purāṇas were drawn, what was the occasion of their compilation into separate books, the famous eighteen? And who was responsible? The first impetus was provided by the record of the *Mahābhārata* war, about 1000 B.C. For it was after this war that the earliest form of the *Mahābhārata* as epic was compiled and, from the testimony of Purāṇic genealogies, that the original Purāṇas were first collected. It was the first self-definition of the Sanskrit-speaking people of northern India, and this self-definition was expressed in literary form, by telling the story of the war. To recall their history was to state their cultural identity as a distinct people.

By the evidence of the genealogies, the Purāṇas were collected a second time between the fourth and sixth centuries A.D. under the rule of the Gupta kings. This period has been called a Hindu "renaissance" with some justification, for it appears that the synthesis of religious beliefs and practices called Hinduism began to take shape during this time, after almost a millennium in which the power and influence of the Vedic cult, and by consequence, the religious and political power of the brahmin class, had become seriously eroded. Among the several reasons for this decline, two are prominent: the growth and popularity of Buddhism, virtually classless at least in its ideals, and the invasion of a succession of foreign tribes, each of whom held temporary control over parts of northwest India. The Gupta dynasty reestablished native Hindu traditions, and this amounted in the history of India to a second self-definition, this one attested to by the final editing of the *Mahābhārata* and the second edition, so to speak, of the major Purāṇas.

But the story of the Purāṇas does not end in the Gupta period, for their contents continued to grow for another five hundred or a thousand years. At whose hands? From their sometimes unstylish use of Sanskrit, epigonic style, unoriginal theology, and abundance of repetitive prayers and hymns, it seems plausible that after the decay of the Gupta dynasty, the Purāṇas were preserved by a class of variously educated priests who tended temples and pilgrimage sites, and who used the old stories as sectarian vehicles to promote the worship of their own particular deities. This took place in both north and south India, as the texts indicate by the wide geographical spread of shrines and sacred rivers mentioned. Perhaps these post-Gupta preservers of the Purāṇic traditions can be identified with the *smārta* brahmins, those brahmins who observed the *smṛti* and who also began to incorporate the devotional practices of non-brahmins into their own rituals, slowly transforming Vedic ritual tradition into the devotional system of later Hinduism. It is likely that the original Purāṇas were preserved in the local literature of certain temples and shrines, and that under the *bhakti*, or devotional influence of these places, the collection grew to include the vast quantities of devotional material that characterize the extant Purāṇas today.

In the course of their long history the Purāṇas have become truly encyclopedic in content. They contain four principal types of material which, in accordance with the approximate chronology outlined so far, have accrued in an identifiable, if not precisely datable, order: the *pañcalakṣaṇa,* or "five characteristics"; *bhakti,* or devotional theism; *dharma,* or social duty; and practical matters, derived from both arts and sciences.

The earliest mention of the contents of the major Purāṇas is found in the lexicon of Amarasiṃha, the *Amarakoṣa,* dated variously in the fifth or sixth century A.D. Here Purāṇas are said to treat of five topics, namely: world creation; world recreation after each periodic dissolution; Manus, or legendary primal kings in each new era; genealogies of kings and seers; and stories about these famous kings and seers. While these five items do occur in some of the Purāṇas, their length comprises only about 2 percent of the total volume today, and some Purāṇas omit some of this material. If the *pañcalakṣaṇa* comprise in fact the earliest stratum of the texts, the Purāṇas have since swollen beyond recognition into something else entirely.

By far the major component of today's Purāṇas is devotional material from the *bhakti* tradition, of two distinct but interrelated kinds: stories about the gods who are the objects of people's loyalty, and practices of various kinds appropriate to the worship of these gods.

Who are the gods of these old stories? Even the gods are stratified, for there appear both Vedic and post-Vedic deities together. Of the Vedic gods, Indra, Agni, Soma, Vāyu and Sūrya reappear in Purāṇic lore, but they are no longer central, as they were to Vedic ritual, and some of their functions have changed. It is as if they have been demoted in favor of the famous Hindu "triad" of Brahmā the creator, Viṣṇu the preserver, and Śiva the destroyer, who dominate Purāṇic literature, displaying the characteristic divine personalities they still bear in modern Hindu tradition. Each of the three has a goddess as consort; Brahmā's wife is Sarasvatī, patroness of music and learning; Viṣṇu's wife is Lakṣmī, goddess of fortune, sometimes beneficent and sometimes not; and Śiva's wife is Pārvatī, daughter of the Himālaya mountain. Other goddesses appear as well, but rarely and briefly; one notable exception is to be found in the *Devī-māhātmya* section of the *Mārkaṇḍeya* Purāṇa, in which the ferocious Durgā and the black Kālī, created spouseless out of the combined energy of the gods, become manifest to do combat with demons. And while some lesser deities appear, the main actors in most Purāṇic stories are the three major gods, almost to the exclusion of heroic kings and noble seers, who appear as narrators and devotees but play a relatively minor role in the Purāṇic literature as a whole.

The divine population of the Purāṇas also includes a host of supernatural beings who provide a background to the *gestes* of gods, men and seers. These include the *pitṛs,* or Fathers, the dead ancestors who inhabit the lower heavens and require periodic worship by their descendents; and the *mātṛkās,* or Mothers, who resemble the ferocious goddesses in their ability to bring disease and wreak havoc among the living. There are also the inhabitants of the heavens who shower flowers on earth at auspicious moments, the Gandharva musicians, who are male, and the female Apsarases, who are celestial dancers. Also inhabiting the heavens are the *devas,* or gods, as a collective, who are marginally concerned with the affairs of mankind, but not very influential; the older Vedic gods have been consigned to this rank. The denizens of the lower regions, the netherworlds, in a mirror image to the gods in heavens, are the *asuras,* the demons, whose numbers include the Daityas, Dānavas and Rākṣasas, who harass human beings in the woods and oppress them as wicked rulers. Finally there are the Yakṣas and Guhyakas, beneficent beings inhabiting mountains and other auspicious spots, who make up the retinue of Kubera, the demi-god of good fortune.

It can be seen that there are at least two orders of deities in the Purāṇic universe. First there are the *devas* and *asuras,* who live in the heavens and netherworlds respectively, and interact with human beings and belong to the socio-cosmic realm. These deities are destroyed and reborn in the periodic dissolutions of the universe, along with human beings and all other elements of the material universe. The exalted deities of the cosmic realm, Brahmā, Viṣṇu and Śiva, are beyond the limits of space and time. They in fact execute the periodic creation and destruction of the universe, as they dream, breathe, or dance out their mighty deeds. Even among the gods, then, a clear stratification can be discerned in these old stories. The Vedic gods and the Hindu deities are assigned different places and functions within the Purāṇic universe, one socio-cosmic, the other cosmic.*

A second component of the devotional tradition that makes up a large part of the extant Purāṇas is people's response to their gods, the religious practices of *bhakti.* These include prayers and ceremonial hymns reciting the virtues of a deity; gifts to be given to brahmins and gods; vows to be undertaken in the service of a god; *śrāddhas* or ritual practices of devotion to *pitṛs;* and of greatest importance, *tīrthas,* those shrines at sacred fords of holy rivers to which pilgrimages are made.

The *tīrthas* cited in the extant Purāṇas are many and various. They include not only the famous northern sites along the Ganges River of Kāśī (Banaras), Prayāga (Allahabad), as well as the holy Himālaya

*This distinction has been carefully noted and described by Madeleine Biardeau in "Étude de Mythologie Hindoue: Cosmogoniques Purāniques," *Bulletin de l'École Française d'Extrème Orient,* LIV (1968), 19–45; LV, 59–60.

mountains, and Gayā, but also rivers, hills and fords of southern India as well, for example along the Kāverī and the Godāvarī and others in the Vindhya mountains. An allegory in the *Padma* Purāṇa points to a southern origin for *bhakti,* and provides a clue to the geographical location of some Purāṇic traditions as well.

> *Bhakti* was born in Drāviḍa, grew up in Karṇātaka, became worn out in Maharāṣṭra and Gurjara, sought refuge with her two sons Knowledge and Dispassion in Vṛndāvana, and regained her vigor there. . . . Enough of vows, sacred fords, disciplines, sacrifices, and discourses about knowledge; faith alone bestows release!
> (*Padma* 6.189.51–56; 190.22)

After the Gupta era, the Purāṇas were kept alive as sectarian documents by recitation at various shrines and *tīrthas* throughout the whole sub-continent of India—hence the prominence of such shrines, and lists of shrines, within Purāṇic literature.

A third stratum found in the major Purāṇas treats of *dharma,* or social duty. The same rules of caste and stage in life as found in the Hindu law codes and epics are taught in the Purāṇas, both by example in illustrative stories, and in lecture form. The social values are predominantly brahminic, presenting as they do an orderly view of a caste society in which brahmins are the privileged upper class, to whom gifts and homage are always due. Duties and practices of kings are also mentioned, but far less frequently, as well as the appropriate behavior for women and the lower classes. It is in fact the morality of the *Bhagavad Gītā* that prevails in the Purāṇas. But whereas *mokṣa,* or release from rebirth, is the loftiest aim of life taught in other Hindu literature, and whereas a central issue of the *Bhagavad Gītā* is to resolve certain intellectual and existential problems engendered by the juxtaposition of the two value systems of *mokṣa* and *dharma,* the Purāṇas, while not denying the possibility of a synthesis, emphasize the importance of *dharma* over *mokṣa*. The traditional four aims of man, the *puruṣārthas,* are represented in Purāṇic morality: *artha,* worldly success; *kāma,* love; *dharma,* social duty; and *mokṣa,* release. But release is in fact downplayed in favor of social duty and the love of god. It appears that the value of life on earth, rather than release from it, is a principal theme of importance in Purāṇic thought. So the reward of a virtuous life, lived according to one's *dharma,* and/or the reward of a life of *bhakti,* devotion of loyalty to one's god, is repeatedly said to be "whatever one desires." This may signify rebirth on earth into more prosperous circumstances, ascension to the heaven of one's chosen god, or final liberation from rebirth. The reward for virtue or loyalty is depicted in somewhat ambiguous terms, perhaps intentionally permitting a choice among these alternatives on the part of the listener.

Just as there are two strata of antiquity and two strata of deities in the Purāṇas, so in similar fashion are *dharma* and *bhakti* stratified. They are directed toward alternative goals, each of which offers two further alternatives of its own. In the socio-cosmic realm there is the possibility of either rebirth on earth into better or worse social circumstances, or translation into an appropriate heaven or hell. There are also two kinds of cosmic rewards. Either one ascends after death to an endless existence in the heavenly city of one's chosen deity, for example in Viṣṇu's paradise named Vaikuṇṭha, or in Śiva's magnificent city called Kailāsa, or else one finds *mokṣa,* the final release from rebirth in any form, liberation from the conditions of existence of any kind whatsoever.

The most recent layer of material added to the Purāṇas consists of a miscellaneous collection of material from various arts and sciences that provides descriptions of the techniques and principles of numerous crafts and occupations. Some of these, however, are fragmentarily represented while others are described with considerable thoroughness. The most clearly developed include, for example, the arts of drama, dance, icon-making and the sciences of rhetoric, grammar, astrology and medicine. From descriptions of the emergence of the universe into being at the beginning of time, through the genealogies and deeds of kings and seers, including stories of the actions of the gods, to lessons on social duty for all castes, and descriptions of a variety of arts and sciences, the Puranas must be regarded as veritable encyclopedias, or even as entire libraries of Hindu lore, to which volumes of new material have been added in age after age of a continuous tradition, and which even now are being emended in the ongoing oral literary tradition of contemporary India.

Finally, we must ask if there is any overall plan, theme or structure to these collections of old stories as they now exist. Whether intended by a compiler, or unintentional, can we discern a central thread, an inner coherence, a guiding principle to the contents of these eighteen major Purāṇas? Granting that they have been multiply edited and added to numerous times in their history, it nevertheless appears that a guarded yes can be given to the question of intention. One principle guiding every accretion to a received text of these old stories is the principle of exotericism by which less esoteric, more popular religious beliefs and practises were dignified by acceptance into the loftier Sanskritic oral tradition maintained by the class of brahmin priests. The Purāṇas, as *smṛti,* became one means of expanding, widening and transforming the more exclusive Vedic tradition or *śruti,* one means by which a narrow orthodox brahmanism grew to become the all-inclusive Hindu tradition whose chief characteristic is the continuous synthetic amalgamation of new ideas and practices.

Let us be specific. Prior to the epics and Purāṇas, two distinct esoteric traditions dominated religion in the Indian subcontinent, at least in so far as religious practice was recorded and preserved in the Sanskritic literary tradition. These were the Vedic ritual as mediated by educated brahmins, and the traditions of Yoga, practiced by carefully disciplined ascetics who remained outside the mainstream of society. In the Purāṇas, two wholly exoteric, or popular forms of belief and practice, are wedded to these prior two in a variety of ingenious ways. Thus *bhakti,* or devotion to a chosen deity, apparently a common practice among lower classes, and *dharma,* the social duties of caste and stage in life, are both accepted as religious pursuits leading to an ultimate reward, and form the principal subject matter of the Purāṇas. This double vision which includes the exoteric alongside the esoteric, the wedding of *bhakti* and *dharma* to Vedic ritualism and Yogic askesis, the valuation of worldly life held in balance with the teaching of release, this dual thrust, seems to have been a recurrent purpose among Paurāṇikas, whenever and however they told and retold the ancient tales. These are the people's stories, mediated and recited by brahmins, idealizing *mokṣa* or release, but also alive with the earthly needs of ordinary people for whom both the love of god and social duty are the most important values of all. As such, the Purāṇas have been the scriptures of Hinduism for the past thousand years, and their values, sermons, prayers and stories are still a main foundation of Hindu religion in the present day.

# 1 Origins

## To OṂ

*When a Yogin pronounces the syllable OṂ, it reaches the crown of his head.*

*When a Yogin is absorbed in the syllable OṂ, he becomes eternal.*

*When Brahman, the incomparable target, is pierced as with an arrow by a vigilant Yogin, his breath the bow and his self the arrow, he becomes one with Brahman.*

*OṂ is the three Vedas, the Ṛk, the Sāman and the Yajus.*

*OṂ is the three worlds.*

*OṂ is the three fires.*

*OṂ is the three gods, Viṣṇu, Brahmā and Hara.*

*A Yogin who is yoked to OṂ will gain absorption in it.*

*OṂ lasts three and a half* mātrās* *when pronounced aloud; in reality this is to be known.*

A *is called Bhūrloka;* U *is called Bhuvarloka; and the consonant* Ṃ *is called Svarloka.*

*The first* mātrā *is the manifest world; the second is the unmanifest world; the third is the power of thought and the last half-*mātrā *is the ultimate goal; these stages of Yoga are to be known in this order.*

*The first* mātra *is short; the second extends the length; the third extends it further; and the last one called a half-*mātrā *is silent, beyond the range of speech; thus is the eternal supreme Brahman expressed as OṂ.*

*Everything existent and non-existent will be grasped by pronouncing OṂ.*

*Shortest metrical quantity in prosody.

*A man who knows this completely, who meditates on it repeatedly, escapes the round of rebirth, his three-fold fetters loosed.*

*He wins absorption in Brahman, in the supreme ultimate Self.*

# Introduction

An ordered universe is established in the cosmogonic and cosmological myths of the Purāṇas. Symmetrical in space and time, it supports the social order and values of early Indian society. It is a grand and complex vision, assembled in the course of a lengthy oral tradition, and it synthesizes an entire collection of stories about the origin of the world. As presented in the Purāṇas, this vision is the foundation of what has become, in the years since their compilation, the Hindu view of the origins and nature of the world in space and time.

There is no single creation myth to be found in the Purāṇas, but rather a blend of several alternative views of the origins of the cosmos. From the interweaving of various themes there has been fashioned a complex and almost wholly integrated vision of the primal emergence of phenomenal forms from formless potential. The blending together of different creation myths has been ingeniously and creatively, if not always consistently, accomplished. And the attempt to reconcile apparently different views of the creative process reveals a distinguishing feature of Purāṇic style as a whole, perhaps of Hindu thought as a whole: a preference for the synthesis of disparate views into a larger whole rather than the rejection of apparently dissident elements in favor of a single view considered to be exclusively true.

What are the major themes so interwoven in Purāṇic accounts of world creation? The awakening of Viṣṇu that starts the creative process; a primal egg that contains the universe; the dual principles of Prakṛti and Puruṣa, whose interaction brings about the emergence of phenomena; and the pouring forth of forms from the various parts of the body of an anthropomorphically conceived deity, either Brahmā, Puruṣa or Viṣṇu.

Perhaps the most prominent creation motif centers on the god Viṣṇu in the form called Nārāyaṇa (often interpreted to mean "lying in the waters"). In the waters, or cosmic ocean which conceals all phenomena in potential, sleeps the god resting on a serpent named Ananta, "endless," or Śeṣa, "remainder," in the positive sense of survivor. The deity is understood to be represented in all three elements of the myth: waters, snake and sleeping god. It is his substance and power that lie at the source of all creation. How then does creative activity proceed from this somnolent scene? The active agent in creation is identified as the god Brahmā, who himself derives from Viṣṇu.

In a process reminiscent in a peculiar way of human birth, perhaps a masculine image of bodily reproduction, a lotus grows out of the sleeping Viṣṇu's navel, a lotus that holds within it the god Brahmā from whose body subsequently pour forth all the elements of creation as emanations from his own substance. Creation is presented in this myth as the successive appearance of phenomenal forms from within the body of a god, first Viṣṇu, then Brahmā, in whom they have lain previously in potentiality.

A second significant motif is that of a golden egg sometimes depicted as self-existent, sometimes the product of Prakṛti and Puruṣa, and sometimes itself the abode of Brahmā, the active creator god. This egg rests on the waters of the universal ocean "swollen with beings" (*Mārk.* 42.64), all phenomena contained within it, awaiting birth. An analogy with birth from the egg is drawn in various descriptive passages. In "The Cosmic Egg" it is the human (or animal) fetal sac that is identified with the mountains, the amniotic fluid with the oceans and rivers of earth. From this self-arisen egg the world is produced. And the active agency of its production is identified as the god Brahmā, who effects creation by breaking open the egg in the beginning.

A third creation theme involves the cooperation of two eternal elements, Prakṛti and Puruṣa. While these terms take on a philosophical significance elsewhere in Indian tradition, in numerous Purāṇic passages their creative function is more mythologically pictured. It is hard to avoid the impression (in "Prakṛti and Puruṣa," for example) that the two together produce the egg whose contents are the universe, and that they do so in a process like the coming together of sperm (Puruṣa) and egg (Prakṛti) in the conception of human or animal life. In this passage the egg so produced is not broken open to reveal emergent life; instead, it appears that the physical universe of seven concentric spheres of material is located within the unbroken egg, whose invisible motivation is Puruṣa and whose material substance is Prakṛti, both eternal. The whole creation as man knows it, with "gods, demons, men, islands and so forth, oceans and the entire aggregate of celestial lights" (*Mārk.* 42.67), i.e., man's perceptual world, continues to exist to within this surrounding egg.

A complex synthesis of the notions of Brahmā as active creative agent along with Prakṛti and Puruṣa as cooperative creators is found in "The Origin and Nature of Time." And here we also find another recurrent theme or major premise of these creation myths: that creation is always recreation, that the cosmos which emerges into existence periodically dissolves into potentiality, and then reemerges into actuality in a cycle that has no beginning and will have no end. The process of the pouring forth of forms eventually reverses itself, and all phenomona are reabsorbed into potentiality: the dissolution of all forms is the inevitable consequence of their manifestation.

Each of these creation themes, then, finds resolution in a corresponding mode of dissolution. Two major modes of such dissolution are implied. As Viṣṇu, via Brahmā, ceases his inactivity and arises to create, or more literally, to pour forth forms, so Viṣṇu as Rudra or Śiva in an excess of activity brings about the furious destruction of all forms and their dissolution back again into the cosmic sea.

In different terms, Prakṛti and Puruṣa, who in cooperation produce the world, also permit the quiescence and reabsorption of all forms. "When this whole world goes to dissolution in Prakṛti, then it is said by the learned to be reabsorbed into its original nature" (*Mārk.* 43.3). Just as Brahmā is the creative agent for Viṣṇu, so the three *guṇas*, or qualities, like the interwoven strands of a cord, are the agents by which the material world of forms and activity comes forth from the primal interactions of Prakṛti and Puruṣa. In "The Origin and Nature of Time" these two themes are combined with each other. Prakṛti is agitated, aroused to creative activity through Puruṣa; then *rajas*, the quality of passion, in the form of the god Brahmā creates the world; *sattva*, the quality of tranquility, in the form of the god Viṣṇu supports and protects creation; and *tamas*, or darkness, in the form of the god Śiva (Rudra or Hara) destroys the world. And these three strands of the created web of the world hold within themselves the inevitability of their own dissolution. When they separate once again into their constituent threads, the world no longer hangs together. Note that in both the myth involving Viṣṇu and that which involves Prakṛti and Puruṣa, creation and the created world are pictured in terms of activity; dissolution and the reabsorption of forms are depicted in terms of sleep, or complete inactivity.

Another motif that forms a contributing part of all of the foregoing themes is the literal emergence from, or identification of the forms of the material world with, the body of a god. Both Brahmā and Puruṣa, in different passages, perform this function of substantial cause. In both cases the human body is the model for creative emanation.

In "The Origin of the World from Brahmā," Brahmā's breath, head, heart and so forth give rise to the famous seven seers variously identified with the promulgators of the Veda and with the stars of the

Little Dipper; demons arise from his buttocks, gods from his face, sheep come from his breast, goats from his mouth, cows from his stomach, horses from his feet and so on; from his four mouths arise the meters, hymns and prayers of the Vedic sacrifices. In "Puruṣa, the Cosmic Person" the four castes derive from Puruṣa's body; the seven levels of heaven are located in his upper body; and the seven netherworlds in his lower parts. In both cases it appears that, in a manner similar to that of the cosmic egg, the body of the god continually supports these elements of the universe. This is an ongoing creative activity, not one effected and completed in a past primal scene. Evidently continuing the view of the *Ṛg Vedic* hymn X.90, where the cosmos in all its parts is arranged in the body of a deity, this vision remains a powerful image throughout Purāṇic times.

What specific phenomena emerge from these various creations? Three categories of things are described at length: the shape of physical space including heavenly, underworldly and earthly geography, the divisions of time, and the conditions of social and ritual life.

**Time**

An extraordinary vision of the passage of time, from the smallest wink of an eye to the vast length of the lifetime of the creator god Brahmā—12,000 thousands of divine years, each of which equals 360 human years, for a total of 4,320,000,000 human years—is depicted in the Purāṇas. Cosmic existence is equated not only with the body of the god spatially, but temporally as well. The universe endures as long as the god lives,then dies as he dies; a periodic dissolution of all forms coincides with the ending of Brahmā's life. "Brahmā, the golden embryo, origin of the gods, without beginning so to speak, resting in the calyx of the world lotus, was born in the beginning. His life-span is one hundred years . . ." (*Mārk.* 43.22). The reckoning of this life-span, however, is exceedingly complex; it amounts to a series of superimposed calendars including daily, weekly, yearly and cosmically patterned calculations. This complicated scheme comprises the temporal conditions under which all created beings (gods, demons, humankind and others) live. And within this scheme can be discerned at least three distinct organizing principles. Just as various discrete creation motifs have been superimposed on the mythical vision of original creation, so have several temporal systems been more or less effectively harmonized with each other.

The simplest system appears to be a yearly calendar derived from the visual observation of the alternation of day and night, the monthly phases of the moon, and the solstices and equinoxes of the solar year. Another system is that of the four Ages Kṛta, Tretā, Dvāpara and Kali, which diminish in length and virtue in a continuous cycle punctuated by cosmic dissolutions and recreations. A third is the confusing scheme of fourteen successive Manvantaras or ages of ruling Manus, semi-mythical kings.

In "The Four Ages" the daily alternation of light and dark is attributed to the activity of Brahmā, a consequence of the emanation of gods and demons from his several bodies. The dark form which he abandons after emitting demons therefrom, identified with *tamas*, becomes the night; the light form he abandons, or *sattva*, becomes the day. That which lies between these two, identified with *rajas*, is the twilight. Much more frequently found, however, is a sort of yearly calender which gives no divine or supernatural source for the divisions of time, but lists them in order of length from the eye-blink through the lifetime of Brahmā of one hundred years of 360 divine days.

The first system, the yearly calendar, appears to derive from simple human observation of the actions of sun and moon. Characteristic of this calendar is the way in which day, month and year are each subdivided into analogous pairs of halves. The 24-hour day is denominated by *ahorātra,* day-night, a composite of two opposite halves, reminiscent of the pairing of gods and demons, and of *tamas* and *sattva* in Brahmā's creation given above. The lunar month also has two halves, comprised of the waxing and waning moon. So does the solar year; in its northern half, or *ayana*, the sun moves from solstice to solstice in a northerly course from December to June, and in its southern half the sun moves in a southerly course from June to December. This polar model takes on mythological significance when it is identified with the days, years and finally the entire length of Brahmā's life. Creation is said to occur and persist in existence during the light of his day; the dissolution endures the length of his night. One human year, of two halves, is equivalent to a day and night of Brahmā's life, which lasts one hundred divine years. Note that each divine year is equivalent to 360 human years, for a divine day equals a human year and a year is held to be 360 days. This lifetime also is divided into two halves, one half of which has passed already, the second half of which remains ahead, as yet unlived. In this manner the relatively simple observations of day, lunar month and solar year are given divine and universal significance; the existence of the created world is thoroughly identified in time with the life of the god Brahmā.

However, this is by no means the only scheme of time. A second system of temporal organization is superimposed on this one, that of the four Ages. Comprising a total of 12,000 divine years, equal to 4,320,000 human years, the four Ages appear to be wholly imaginative, corresponding to no known observable phenomenon. They last 4,000, 3,000, 2,000 and 1,000 years respectively. Each also includes two twilights of one-tenth the length of the Ages itself; this adds 800 (or two twilights of 400 years each), 600, 400 and 200 years to each Age for an overall total of 12,000 years. The names of the four Ages, Kṛta, Tretā, Dvāpara and Kali, correspond roughly to the numbers 4, 3, 2 and 1; they may refer to the rolls of a now-forgotten dice game, or perhaps to phases of the moon, but they fail in any satisfactory way to explain the meaning of the Ages themselves.

Most significant in this numerical scheme of Ages is the progressively decreasing lengths of years, which corresponds to a decrease in excellence and virtue among men and in the quality of human life. Moreover, like day, month and year, the four Ages as a unit are understood to repeat in a continual and endless cycle. Every world creation begins in the perfection of the Kṛta Age, progressively deteriorates throughout the Tretā and Dvāpara until the final destruction comes at the end of every Kali—only to give way once more to a recreation in a new Kṛta, and so on. As we shall see below, the most important function of the notion of these four Ages seems to lie in the negative moral judgment leveled on present society, for we are always living in the Kali Age, in the time just before the coming dissolution of the universe, when men are both weak and evil.

One day and night of Brahmā is said to comprise a thousand units of four Ages. So there ensue mini-dissolutions of the cosmos after each Kali, intermediate dissolutions after each day and night of Brahmā, and a complete dissolution at the end of his lifetime; then the god is presumably reborn once again out of the lotus arising from Viṣṇu's navel as he sleeps in the cosmic sea.

The characteristics of human life in each of the four Ages are carefully described against a background of decreasing felicity in all aspects of life. These descriptive passages also offer clues about the actual conditions of society among the writers of the Purāṇas. A number of hierarchies are constructed, using the device of the four deteriorating ages, that effectively catalogue the evils of the present day (which is in the Kali age, of course). For example, meditation, virtue of the Kṛta, surpasses gift-giving, virtue of the Kali; Dharma stands solidly on four feet in the Kṛta, wobbles on one in the Kali—the implication is that men no longer possess the power to do good. That power was complete in the Kṛta, but only a quarter remains in the Kali. In the Kṛta no one suffers. There is no judgment made among things as to better or worse, and everyone is always self-sufficiently content. All needs, shelter, food and so on are supplied by magical trees which arise in both Kṛta and Tretā. But this idyllic situation changes in Dvāpara and Kali due to human greed, which somehow spontaneously arises as men seize and apparently hoard the bounty of these trees. Because of human avarice the trees vanish of their own accord, after which men without shelter and food begin to suffer severely. The message of this passage appears to be that human greed lies at the root of human suffering, and that men bring suffering upon themselves. In subsequent ages, then, the laws of caste arise as measures of organization among men. The Veda and the rest of the respected literature that outlines ritual and social behavior also come into being to provide the necessary guidelines for human behavior. In their absence, presumably, human selfishness leads inevitably to war, disease and death: "In the first Age, the Kṛta, there was virtue; it continued throughout the Tretā; becoming confused in the Dvāpara, it is lost altogether in the Kali" (*Kūrma* 1.27.57).

This decay is pictured as a natural process, and the laws of society arise in response to the loss of spontaneous order among men and in nature. The final cataclysm of the Kali Age also comes in the course of time as part of a natural process of continual decay. Evil among men arises in the Kali, even brahmins are untrustworthy, the Vedas are forgotten, classes mix with each other, trickery and murder prevail, and hunger, fear and war occur. As is almost lovingly described in "The Kali Age," when even the kings themselves are corrupt, nobility and virtue among men are nowhere to be found. People hide from evil rulers in the mountains and revert to living on gathered food. Due to this hard life they die young, and this grim state of affairs is clearly the prelude to a complete destruction of the cosmos destined to occur at the close of the Kali Age.

The dissolution described in "The Dissolution of the World in Viṣṇu" is a model for all three sorts of dissolutions noted above. After a thousand four Age periods, Brahmā's life comes to a close. A marvellously ghastly vision describes the destruction of the universe. As the earth becomes bare of vegetation, all beings die for lack of sustenance. Viṣṇu as Rudra (Śiva) finishes the destruction. At his agency, the fiery sun scorches the earth, drying up all oceans and rivers. Due to the intense heat, the world catches fire and burns until it is as "bare as a turtle's back." Next the lord produces huge rain-bearing clouds that pour for a hundred years, quenching the fire and covering the earth with a vast flood. When nothing exists but this ocean, which has absorbed into itself all created beings, Viṣṇu, the lord, rests in "meditative sleep." His night begins. It lasts as long as his day, and when it is over he arises to issue forth in the form of Brahmā to fashion the cosmos once again.

Underlying this scheme of continuous creations and dissolutions appears to be a pulsating view of the universe in which matter and energy are periodically transformed into each other. In the cosmic sea all phenomena lie in potentiality and wait for emergence. Once emerged into manifestation through the creative activity of a deity, all conditions of life gradually decline until they are once more completely dissolved. It is the continual, inevitable process itself that is prime; even the gods appear to be only the successive agents in these continual transformations.

A third temporal scheme also exists, that of the Manvantaras, and it is the most difficult to understand. Whereas the four Ages blend more or less adequately with the day, month, year calendar, both fitting into the lifetime of Brahmā, the Manvantaras do not fit so well. Nor is it evident what their origin was or what they signify as they appear in the literature.

Of principal importance appears to be the fact that there are fourteen Manvantaras, or periods of time in which an original ruler of earth is called a Manu. In each of these ages arise the same sorts of powerful beings: "the gods, the seven seers together with Indra, Manu and the kings who are his sons . . . " (*Mārk.* 43.35). Interestingly enough, just as Brahmā's life has two halves (in the middle of which we are now living), so are the fourteen Manus divided into two groups of seven; seven are past and seven are yet to come in the future. These Manus are given names, but only one of them, the first, called Svāyambhuva (the "self-existent"), appears to have a significant existence as the original law-giver, primal human, first ruler among men. The others, in particular the future seven, lack flesh almost entirely.

The numerical calculations associated with the fourteen Manus are simply an attempt to correlate them with the other temporal systems. In a day of Brahmā occur a thousand periods of four Ages. If there must also be fourteen Manus in Brahmā's day, then there will be roughly seventy-one Manvantaras, for 71 times 14 is 994, or almost 1000. In some accounts, in fact, the number of Manvantaras is given as seventy-two, for 72 times 14 is 1,008. The evident attempt to resolve numerically these disparate temporal systems fails, for the numbers obviously do not quite fit together. In any case, the single common denominator of the three systems of time reckoning is a day of Brahmā, at the end of which all created things are destroyed.

Whereas the day, month, year scheme appears to have arisen from visual astronomy, and the four-Age system reveals an ethical concern with the decline of goodness, the Manvantaras perhaps make connection with actual human kings. Fictional as it seems, it is possible that the purpose of listing a reigning Manu for each era is to identify the source of kingship. Each Manu is a semi-divine being whose sons become the rulers of society. And he is also known to be the originator or original upholder of Dharma in each age. Here perhaps we can see the final step in the creative process, in which the origins of the universe are related to society. After time and space are established, and the order of human society is fixed, then human existence under the leadership of kings takes shape.

**Space**

The configuration of space given in the Purāṇas is as complex as the categorization of time, if not more so. The cosmic egg of seven concentric spheres appears to be the usual framework within which all space is located. There are seven successively higher heavens (*lokas*), realms of the gods and immortal beings, and seven successively lower netherworlds (*pātālas*) where demons and chthonic beings dwell. In the middle lies the earth on which human beings live. This symmetrical picture is somewhat complicated by the fact that there are also a number of hells (*narakas*) which are found in a downward direction of no clear spatial location. That the hells are different from the netherworlds is clear, for the hells, which to begin with number more than seven, are the locations of gruesome punishments for human sinners, whereas the netherworlds are described in glowing terms, with the demons inhabiting most pleasant houses and gardens. As the sage Nārada says, they are even more delightful than the third heaven, Svarloka itself. Furthermore, Śeṣa is said to lie below the netherworlds, holding the universe above like a crown on his head. It may be possible to discern two or three different imaginative visions in these passages: Śeṣa and the netherworlds are associated with the sleeping Viṣṇu; the fourteen levels of heavens and netherworlds correspond to the divisions within the cosmic egg and its seven concentric spheres of Prakṛti; and there are numerous hells in which moral and ritual lapses are punished.

*Heavens.* Upwards from earth extend seven heavens, layered spheres of space. The first three, Bhūrloka, Bhuvarloka and Svarloka correspond to the three spatial levels identified in the Vedas: earth, atmosphere, heaven. And it is these three that comprise the "triple world" or "three worlds," the usual term for the world inhabited by people. The other four heavens are the realms of the gods and immortal beings where the heavenly bodies also move. These levels of heavens become a means of locating sun and moon, the stars and planets in space. The range of the light that radiates from sun and moon determines the extent of Bhūrloka; Bhuvarloka extends the same distance to the pole star, Dhruva, whose realm is Svarloka. Ranged in the higher heavens are the six planets, the Little Dipper (the Seven Seers) and the *nakṣatras*, the so-called lunar mansions, which are configurations of stars marking 27 or 28 points on the ecliptic in which the moon rises in the course of a lunar month. All these heavenly bodies are understood to be attached by invisible ropes made of winds to Dhruva, who lies in their center. As they circle in the heavens they turn him around like a millstone or "potter's wheel" (*Kūrma* I.39.39).

Sun and moon are both likened to or pulled by huge heavenly chariots. One end of the sun chariot's axle rests on the pole star around which it continually circles. Directly beneath the pole star on earth rises the central mountain, Meru. On any part of earth, therefore, night comes when the sun is concealed behind the huge mountain, and day dawns when in its continual circling the sun comes around the side of the mountain once again. Noon and midnight occur on directly opposite sides of Meru. As we will see in more detail below, this vision of space amounts to a huge sphere of many concentric levels. Balanced symmetrically both above and below the central earth are the heavens and the netherworlds; the various continents and oceans of Bhūrloka symmetrically ring Mt. Meru. The whole resembles a three-dimensional *maṇḍala*, a completely balanced vision of the physical cosmos in space. Its center, Mt. Meru, lies in the exact middle of the central continent of Jambūdvīpa, the southern subcontinent of which is the land of Bhārata, India itself.

Like the alternation of night and day, the waxing and waning of the moon are imaginatively explained. The immortal beings in the heavens, which include both gods and deceased ancestors, the "Fathers," continually drink the moon which is filled with nectar/ambrosia by the sun. As it is drunk it gradually wanes. When completely empty it is replenished by the sun, and hence waxes. Like the sun, the moon has a chariot drawn by marvelous horses. When it is eclipsed it has been suddenly devoured by the ravenous demon Rāhu, who has no body, only a greedy head. Eclipse ends as the moon reappears out of his bodiless neck.

The sun is called the support of creatures because of its nourishing properties; through the moon's nectar it nurtures gods and ancestors in the heavens; through nourishing the plants it feeds animals and men on earth. And it has its support in the pole star Dhruva.

*Netherworlds.* The seven netherworlds offer a clear symmetry with the seven heavens. As gods and immortal beings inhabit the heavens, demons and chthonic beings inhabit the netherworlds, and they do so in elegant style. These beings are not necessarily malevolent, but they are sometimes encountered on earth by men in dangerous places like forests and wildernesses. These fearful beings include Dānavas, Daityas and Yakṣas, who are vaguely described as demonic beings, and "classes of great snakes," chthonic underworld beings of whom Śeṣa is the nethermost and most respected. Śeṣa, who elsewhere is depicted as a manifestation of Viṣṇu, is himself depicted in "The Seven Netherworlds" as the creator, sustainer and destroyer of the universe. Most delightful is the description of Śeṣa as he holds earth, or the triple world, on his head; his eyes flashing, his hoods covered with sparkling jewels, he lies below the seven netherworlds, continually sustaining the universe by his support, shaking the world of beings to its foundations whenever he yawns.

*Hells*. The hells are given no particular spatial location. Nor is there a fixed number, as in the case of heavens and netherworlds. Our text announces that there are twenty-one, but several more than this number are either listed or described. Their purpose is to provide retribution for social transgressions; they are the domains of Yama, god of death, whose servants carry out the various forms of punishment. Interestingly enough, the corresponding notion that the heavens are the rewards of good actions is not elaborated upon; these texts primarily describe the hells where human beings go after death, reaping the ill effects of their evil acts on earth. They are a moral rather than a physical space, their function analogous to that of the four Ages, whose purpose is not simply to depict a temporal calendar, but to outline the moral condition of man, to identify social transgressions, and to threaten people with the dreadful consequences thereof. In the case of the Ages, the ultimate result of unrighteousness is cosmic dissolution. In the case of the hells, it is individual pain after death.

It is interesting to see not only what sorts of actions merit punishment, but what sorts of punishments are most feared. A significant number of sins in our passage involve three sorts of behavior: neglect of family obligations, lack of respect for teachers and brahmins, and the abuse of traditional rituals. Incorrect bodily habits are also criticized: eating and eliminating improperly, touching cows and brahmins with the foot, and so on. Of utmost importance is the maintenance of bodily purity both for one's own benefit and for the benefit of one's associates. A final group of sins involves social relations in general: ingratitude, dishonesty, stealing and murder are also to be punished, but these sorts of faults seem less significant than those relating to family, to ritual and to brahminhood. A strictly ordered, hierarchical society with clearly defined relationships appears to lie behind these injunctions, one in which mutual obligations, respect for elders and superiors, and bodily purity are of supreme importance.

A survey of the sorts of punishments meted out also reveals a concern for bodily purity and integrity, for to violate the body amounts to the worst sort of punishment. There are two principal sorts of hells: those that abuse the body by external means and those that cause internal pollution of the body. The former include, for example, burning vats, pincers, razor-sharp leaves, the flaying of skin, the crushing by a mortar, and the most grotesque punishment of all, having the intestines pulled out by the sharp beaks of birds. The second sort of punishment requires the wicked to eat a variety of dreadful things: dogs, wolves, scorpions, spit, pus, feces and urine. All these tortures are understood to be the natural consequences of one's acts. There is no external judging agent; Yama, god of death, along with his nameless servants, is merely the executor. It is hard to know from the text precisely what place this grotesque vision of hells played in the minds of those who told and heard of the ghastly prospects of sin. There is no indication that these hells are of eternal duration, and it is clear in other Purāṇic passages that after death rebirth on earth of some sort is anticipated for all beings. It is probable that the notion of retributive hells and the expectation of rebirth were originally two different views of what would follow after death, and that some sort of compromise was eventually effected between them. The simplest resolution would be that tenure in the hells is of temporary duration, to be succeeded by inevitable rebirth. The function of this vision, of course, would be a social one, that the fear of reprisal would compel the living to avoid the sins as depicted out of fear of eventual punishment. How literally, or how spatially these hells were viewed, we simply cannot know.

*Earth.* Bhūrloka is the realm in which humankind lives at the center of the cosmic egg. Again there is a symmetrical design to what appears to be basically a two-dimensional picture. Jambūdvīpa is the central continent, surrounded concentrically by six other circular lands separated by seven seas of different liquids. Holy Mt. Meru rises in the center of Jambūdvīpa, shaped like "the calyx of the lotus flower which is this earth" (*Kūrma* I.43.9), and wider at the top than at its base. Viṣṇu's navel-lotus here becomes the earth itself, Mt. Meru its central seed-cup, and the surrounding lands its petals. Four lesser mountains, like buttresses, support Meru from the four directions: Mandara from the east, Gandhamādana from the south, Vipula from the west and Supārśva from the north, each with its own characteristic fruit-bearing tree. A godly city sits on the top of Meru where Brahmā, Viṣṇu and Śiva dwell, worshiped by mortals and lesser gods. On the sides of the great mountain in the four major and the four intermediate directions lie the cities of the lesser gods, most of whom are of Vedic origin, apparently having been replaced at the top of the divine hierarchy by Brahmā, Viṣṇu and Śiva. These cities form a directional symmetry:

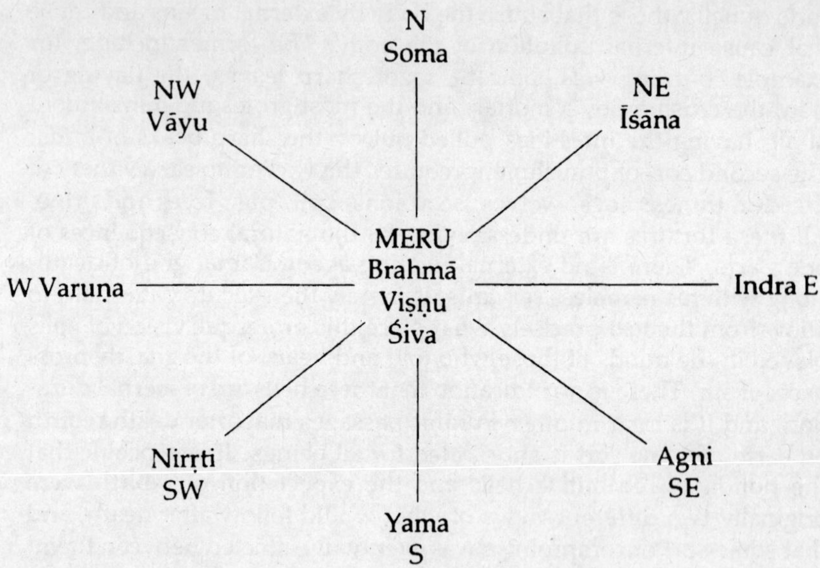


The river Ganges falls from the heavens directly above Meru and flows around the city of the gods. It continues down the sides of the mountain in four directions and passes through the four lands of Jambūdvīpa, which are inhabited by four peoples, and thence to the surrounding sea. One of these lands is Bhāratavarṣa, ancient name for the land of India, home of the Bhāratas, named for the legendary progenitor of the Indian people. The conditions of existence differ from land to land among these four as to length of life, customary food, occupations and gods worshiped. But it is only in Bhāratavarṣa where proper ritual is performed, where suffering and sorrow persist, and where the four Ages leading to dissolution and recreation prevail.

The Purāṇic picture of space is complex, highly organized and symmetrical. Envisioned is a three-dimensional *maṇḍala* with the land of Bhārata near the center. This center is identified as the huge Mt. Meru on which the gods dwell, and over which hangs the pole star in the heavens. As Meru is the center of the continents and seas, lying also in the middle of the heavens and the netherworlds, so the pole star is situated in the center of the circular courses of all the heavenly bodies, which are fastened to him by ropes of wind. The whole is an imaginative vision of the shape of the cosmos which clearly locates the land of India in the center of the universe.

The result of this harmonizing process in which various visions of space, time and society have been blended together in Purāṇic mythology is a grand, almost symmetrical scheme in four dimensions, three of space and one of time, in which up and down, gods and demons, the four directions and all the other elements of the cosmos are effectively held in balance. It almost wholly succeeds in its attempt to image an entire universe within a single spatial and temporal vision.

# Texts

## The Origin of Brahmā from the Lotus in Viṣṇu's Navel

At the end of the last Eon* when the three worlds were in darkness there was nothing but a solitary sea, no gods and so forth, no seers. In that undisturbed desolation slept the god Nārāyaṇa,† supreme person, lying on the bed that was the serpent Śeṣa. The all-knowing one who is contemplated by wise men had 1,000 heads, 1,000 eyes, 1,000 feet and 1,000 arms. Wearing a yellow robe, he was large-eyed, of vast dominion like a dark cloud, the soul of Yoga whose dwelling is the heart of *yogins*. Once during his sleep there arose in play from his navel a pure lotus, wondrous and divine, core of the three worlds. Spreading out 100 leagues, bright as the morning sun, it had a heavenly fragrance, with auspicious calyx and stamen. The lord Hiraṇyagarbha‡ approached that place where the Archer§ had been lying for a long time. The universal soul,‖ having made the eternal one# arise with his hand and infatuated by the other's illusion, spoke these sweet words: "Tell me, who are you, lying hidden here in darkness in this dreadful, desolate, solitary sea?" Hearing his words and smiling, the one whose banner bears Garuḍa** spoke to lord Brahmā with a voice deep as the rumbling of a cloud. "*Bhoḥ! Bhoḥ!* Know me to be the god Nārāyaṇa, origin and dissolution of the worlds, great lord of Yoga, the supreme person. See inside me the entire world, the continents with their mountains, the oceans and the seven seas, and also yourself, the grandfather of the worlds."

When he had said this, the universal soul, Hari,†† although he recognized the great *yogin*, asked Puruṣa, the creator,‡‡ "Who are

*"Eon" will translate *kalpa*. †Viṣṇu. ‡Brahmā. §Viṣṇu. ‖Brahmā. #Viṣṇu. **Viṣṇu. ††Viṣṇu. ‡‡Brahmā.

you?" Beginning to laugh, the lord Brahmā, keeper of the Vedas, with lotus eyes, replied in these polished words, "I am creator and ordainer, the self-existent great-grandfather; in me is everything established; I am Brahmā who faces in all directions." Hearing this, Viṣṇu, whose power is his truth, took his leave and entered into the body of Brahmā by Yoga. Seeing all three worlds with gods, demons and men in the belly of the god, he was astonished. Then the lord whose emblem is the Lord of the Birds,* emerging from his mouth, spoke thus to the Grandfather,† "Now in the same way you must enter my eternal belly and see these wonderful worlds, O bull of men." Hearing his encouraging words and saluting him, Kuśadhvaja‡ entered the Lord's great belly in turn. He, whose power is his truth, saw these worlds in the womb; roaming around inside the god, he saw no end or limit. All doors being shut by the great-souled Janārdana,§ Brahmā found passage through the navel. Then the one born from a golden egg, the four-faced Brahmā who had entered therein by the power of Yoga, displayed himself on the lotus. Lord Brahmā, self-existent, the Grandfather, womb of creation, lustrous as the inside of a flower, shone there radiantly, resting on the lotus.

## Prakṛti and Puruṣa

By the direction of Puruṣa and through the favor of the unmanifest Prakṛti, the principles from Mahat through the distinct elements produced an egg, gradually swelling out of those elements like a water-bubble. Swollen with beings, O sage, this huge egg was lying in the water. The knower-of-the-field|| called Brahmā grew inside the egg made of Prakṛti. The first embodied being is called Purusa and in the beginning arose as Brahmā, creator of creatures. By him is this triple world pervaded, all things moving and unmoving. Meru and the other mountains were the afterbirth. The womb water of this great-souled egg was the ocean. In this egg is the whole creation: gods, demons, men, islands and so forth, oceans and the entire aggregation of celestial lights. This egg was encompassed by the principle Bhūtādi, enveloped one by one in water, wind, fire and ether, each of which is ten-fold. By Mahat was it so surrounded. Mahat was concealed in the unmanifest Prakṛti by means of all these elements. By these seven layers of Prakṛti was the egg hidden. And these eight Prakṛtis# persisted, covering one another. This Prakṛti is eternal and inside it is Puruṣa.

*Viṣṇu. †Brahmā. ‡Brahmā. §Viṣṇu. ||Embodied soul.
#The previous seven plus the original Prakṛti.

# The Cosmic Egg

Long ago when all things animate and inanimate were lost in one dreadful ocean there appeared a large egg, source of the seed of all creatures. Lying in this egg, Brahmā went to sleep. At the end of a thousand Ages* he awoke.

Awake and knowing creation to be lost in this flood, the lord broke open the egg. From it *OṂ* was born; then arose Bhūḥ, matchless Bhuvaḥ and third, the sound Svaḥ. Together they are known as Bhūr-Bhuvaḥ-Svaḥ. From this arose *tejas* (which is *tat savitur vareṇyam*).† *Tejas,* escaping from the egg, evaporated the water. When the residue had been dried up by *tejas* it became an embryo. The embryo, called a bubble, became solid. It is known as *dhāraṇī*‡ because of its hardness and because it is the sustainer of all creatures. The place where the egg rested is lake Saṃnihita. That which first came forth from *tejas* they call Āditya. Brahmā, Grandfather of the world, arose in the middle of the egg. The placenta is known as Mt. Meru, the afterbirth is the mountains, and the waters of the womb are the oceans and the thousand rivers. The water which surrounds the navel of Brahmā is Mahat, and by this choice pure water is the great lake filled. In the middle of it, O great-minded one, a banyan tree stood like a pillar. From it sprang the classes: brahmins, kṣatriyas, vaiśyas and śūdras, who thus arose to do reverence to the twice-born.

# The Origin of the World from Brahmā

The lotus-born god poured forth all things, representatives of their realms. Hear me speak of them. Having given forth the waters, fire and atmosphere, the sky, wind and earth, rivers, oceans, mountains and budded trees, instants, moments, minutes, hours, days and nights, fortnights and months, half-years, years, ages and so on, all delegates of their domains, again he poured forth the accomplished seers: Marīci, Bhṛgu, Aṅgiras, Pulastya, Pulaha and Kratu. From his breath the god Brahmā emitted Dakṣa, Marīci from his eye, Aṅgiras

*"Age" will translate *yuga*.

†Beginning words of Ṛg Veda III.62.10, which with the other *mantras* constitute one often used invocation.

‡Literally, "that which supports," also a word for "earth."

from his head, Bhṛgu from his heart and the one named Atri from his ears. Dharma, having taken human form in these seers, was set in motion. Brahmā wished to create in those waters these four: gods, demons, Fathers and men, and he yoked his mind to this task. *Tamas* was the quality of the self-controlled Prajāpati that predominated first. So the demons, his sons, originated first from his buttocks. The supreme person abandoned this body after emitting the demons. That body was cast off; thereby night was instantaneously born. Because night is filled with darkness, creatures sleep in it. The god took another form having the quality of *sattva;* thereupon gods were brought forth from his face. This body too was abandoned and from it arose day, which is made of light. Therefore the divinities, united with Dharma, worship the day. He took still another form of *sattva* nature; to him, thinking like a father, were born the Fathers. When he had poured forth the Fathers, the all-creator cast off that body too; then twilight immediately arose. Therefore the day belongs to the gods and the night belongs to the enemies of the gods. Between these two lies the venerable twilight, manifestation of the Fathers. Therefore all the gods, and demons, Manus and mankind, self-controlled, continually honor the form which is the midpoint of day and night (twilight). Then Brahmā took another body, of the quality of *rajas.* Human beings arose from this as his passion-ridden sons. At the instant that Prajāpati abandoned this form, O brahmins, the light appeared that is called morning twilight. Then, O bulls among the twice-born, lord Brahmā again took on material form. Once more yoked, he adopted a body made mostly of *tamas* and *rajas.* Hungry Rākṣasas arose from him in this darkness as his sons, powerful night-rangers whose nature was predominantly darkness and passion. Together with these there came forth snakes, Yakṣas, Gandharvas and other creatures. So did the lord pour forth other beings possessed by darkness and passion. Having emitted birds from his vigor, he sent forth sheep from his breast, goats from his mouth and he fashioned cows from his stomach, horses from his feet. Likewise from his limbs were formed donkeys, along with elephants, buffalo, antelope, camels, mules and others. Herbs which have fruits and roots were born from his body hair. From his eastern mouth, the *gāyatra* meter, the Ṛg, the Sāman melody, the *rathantara* laud, and of the sacrifices the *agniṣṭoma.* From his southern mouth he sent forth the Yajus, the pleasing *triṣṭubh* meter, the fifteen-verse *stoma* and the *bṛhatsāman* melody. He emitted from his western mouth the *sāmans,* the *jagatī* meter, the seventeen-verse *stoma,* the *vairūpa* and the *atirātra;* from his northern mouth the twenty-one verses of the

Atharva, the *āptoryāman,* and *anuṣṭubh* meter and the *vairāja.** From his limbs were engendered creatures of all kinds. In this manner proceeded the pouring forth of beings from the creating Brahmā Prajāpati.

# The Four Heads of Brahmā

Manu asked, "Why did Brahmā, the Grandfather of the worlds, have four heads? And how did he pour forth the worlds?" And Matsya, the Fish, replied, "First the Grandfather of the gods did *tapas,* and from this appeared the Vedas with their limbs, branches, and methods of recitation. The first of the sciences that Brahmā called to mind was the Purāṇa, which is holy, eternal, made of sound, comprising ten million verses. Immediately thereafter he emitted the Vedas from his mouths, the Mīmāṃsā, the knowledge of Nyāya, and the eight means of proof.

Beings were born from Brahmā's mind while he was immersed in the Vedas, wishing for offspring. Due to this, they are called his mind-born sons. First there appeared Marīci, then the holy seer Atri, next Aṅgiras, and after him, Pulastya. Then came the seer called Pulaha, and after him was born Kratu, then Pracetas. Next Vasiṣṭha appeared, followed at once by Bhṛgu and Nārada. Thus Brahmā produced the ten mind-born seers as his sons.

Now I shall relate what sprang from the body of Prajāpati without benefit of mothers. The progenitor Dakṣa came from his right thumb, Dharma from his nipple, Kāma, the flower-armed god of love, from his heart, Anger from between his eyebrows and Greed from his lower parts. Delusion came from his mind, Lust from his egotism, Joy from his throat, Death from his eyes, O king, and Bharata from the palm of his hand. These are his nine sons, O king, and the tenth child of Brahmā was a girl called Aṅgajā, the limb-born. . . .

Then, cleaving his pure body in two, the universal creator put the goddess Sāvitrī in his heart in order to create the world. One half of himself he made into a woman's body, the other half into a man. The woman he called Śatarūpā and celebrated her as Sāvitrī, Sarasvatī, Gāyatrī and Brahmāṇī, O enemy-burner. And so he made the goddess out of himself, from his own body.

*Ṛg, Sāman, Yajus and Atharva are names of vedas. *Gāyatra, triṣṭubh, jagatī* and *anuṣṭubh* are names of meters. *Rathantara, bṛhatsāman,* the 15-verse stoma, and the 17 verse stoma, *vairūpa* and *vairāja* are names of *sāmans. Agniṣṭoma, atirātra,* and *āptoryāman* are names of sacrifices.

When he looked at her, the lord Prajāpati was smitten with the arrows of love. Disturbed, he cried out, "Oh what beauty! Oh what loveliness!" And the seers, led by Vasiṣṭha, protested that she was their sister, his daughter, but Brahmā saw nothing but the sight of her face. "How lovely! How beautiful!" he exclaimed over and over again, as he watched her bowing humbly before him.

Then that lovely woman circumambulated her father, but he was ashamed of his desire to stare at her beauty in the presence of his sons. So a face appeared on his right side, with pale cheeks. And another sprang up in back, its lip quivering in wonder. Then another face appeared due to his love-sickness, and then a fourth one too, on his left side, wounded by love's arrows. And because Brahmā still craved the sight of her as she sprang up into the air, a fifth face came out of the top of that wise one's head, which the lord hid in his matted hair. The tremendous *tapas* which Brahmā had practised for the purpose of creation was entirely annihilated through his desire to unite with his own daughter.

So Brahmā spoke to those sons who had sprung from him, saying, "From now on *you* must produce all the creatures, as well as the gods, demons and human beings." And at his command, they began to pour forth all manner of beings.

When the seers had left in order to create, the universal soul married that virtuous Śatarūpā who was prostrate before him, and coupled with her, lost in love. Out of modesty, just like an ordinary man, he made love with her inside the pavilion within the lotus for as long as a hundred years. And after a long time she bore a son, a Manu called Svāyambhuva, and also Virāj, so we have heard. He is said to be the Primal Person because he shares the qualities of Brahmā. From him were born many Vairajās of intense vows, the seven eminent Manus. All these Manus, Svārociṣa and the rest, resemble Brahmā in nature. And there are seven more, of which Auttami was the first, and you, at present, are the seventh.

# Puruṣa, the Cosmic Person

At the end of a thousand periods of years that egg was lying in the water. Puruṣa, having come to abide in Prakṛti by the workings of time, made lifeless matter come to life. Having broken the egg, this Puruṣa emerged from it, with a thousand thighs, ankles, arms and eyes, a thousand faces and heads. From his limbs the wise ones fashioned the worlds, seven downwards from his buttocks and so forth, seven upwards from his hips and so on. The head of Puruṣa is the brahmin, the kṣatriya his arms; of the lord's two thighs are born the vaiśya, the śūdra from his feet. Bhūrloka* was made from his feet, Bhuvarloka from his navel, Svarloka from his heart and from the breast of the great-souled one, Maharloka. Janarloka came from his neck, Taparloka from his two nipples, and from his heads Satyaloka, which is the eternal Brahmaloka. Bhūrloka was made from his feet, Bhuvarloka from his navel, Svarloka from his head; thus runs an alternative belief of the people. And from his hips was made Atala;† Vitala came from the lord's thighs, from his knees bright Sutala and Talātala from his shins. Mahātala came from his ankles, Rasātala from his instep and Pātāla from the soles of his feet. Thus the Puruṣa consists of the worlds.

# The Origin and Nature of Time

When this whole world goes to dissolution in Prakṛti, then it is said by the learned to be reabsorbed into its original nature. When the unmanifest abides in its own self, when the created world is annihilated, Prakṛti and Puruṣa exist with the same nature. Then the two qualities, *tamas* and *sattva*, rest in balance, interwoven, with nothing lacking and nothing to spare. Like sesamum oil in seeds, like ghee in milk, so does *rajas* reside in *tamas* and *sattva*.

A day of the supreme lord is as long as a life-span from the birth of Brahmā, namely two *parārdhas*. Of equal length is the night of the world's dissolution. This supreme one, whose work is unequalled, whose nature is inconceivable, the cause of everything, first beginning of creation, wakes up at the start of the day. As soon as the lord of creation has penetrated Prakṛti and Puruṣa he agitates them by intense Yoga. Just as a spring-breeze invades the mind of a young woman to excite her, so does he in yogic form enter into Prakṛti and Puruṣa. When Pradhāna is aroused, the god called Brahmā who is lying in the egg arises, as I have already told you. So the lord of Prakṛti is first the agitator; then he is what is to be agitated by means of expansion and contraction, even while he rests in the state of Pradhāna. This womb of the world, born possessing *rajas* but without qualities, proceeds to create as Brahmā. Then he, in the form of Brahmā, having an excess of *sattva*, pours forth humankind; having become Viṣṇu, he

*The seven successive heavens.
†The seven netherworlds.

protects them with Dharma. And when, in the shape of Rudra, abounding in *tamas,* he has destroyed the whole creation, the three worlds, he—of three qualities and without qualities, both—lies down to sleep. As he is first the purveyor of the field of existence, then the protector and the destroyer, he gets this name: the one composed of Brahmā, Viṣṇu and Hara. As Brahmā he pours forth the worlds; as Rudra he destroys; and he is also in between as Viṣṇu: these are the three conditions of the self-existent. *Rajas* is Brahmā; *tamas* is Rudra; Viṣṇu, lord of creation, is *sattva*. These are the three gods (and these are the three qualities). All three are paired, each joined to his quality. Not for an instant's separation do they abandon each other. Thus Brahmā, four-faced god of gods, is first in the world. Having assumed the quality of *rajas* he exists as creator. Brahmā, the golden embryo, origin of the gods, without beginning so to speak, resting in the calyx of the world lotus, was born in the beginning. His life-span is one hundred years according to the Brahmā count. Hear me relate its length. A *kāṣṭhā* is said to equal fifteen *nimeṣas;** thirty *kāṣṭhās,* one *kalā;* and thirty *kalās,* one *muhūrta*. A day and a night are known by men to be thirty *muhūrtas;* an *ahorātra,* a day and a night; and a month is said to consist of two fortnights, with thirty days and nights. A half-year *(ayana)* is made up of six such months; a year is two *ayanas:* southern and northern. This year is a day and night of the gods; its day is the *ayana* called northern.† The four Ages known as Kṛta, Tretā, Dvāpara and Kali comprise 12,000 divine years. Hear from me their distribution.

Kṛta is said to last 4,000 years, the morning twilight, 400 and the evening twilight the same. There are reckoned 3,000 divine years in the Tretā, 300 in its morning twilight and the same allotted to the evening twilight. 2,000 years are counted in the Dvāpara with 200 years in each twilight. And in the Kali there are 1,000 divine years, O best of the twice-born; its morning and evening twilights are said to be 100 years each. These 12,000 year counts of the Ages are made by the sages. This period multiplied by 1,000 is called a day and night of Brahmā. In a day of Brahmā there should be 14 Manus. 1,000 periods of four Ages are allotted to these Manus, according to their distribution. The gods, the seven seers together with Indra, Manu and the kings who are his sons are poured forth together with Manu and annihilated as in the past. Seventy-one Manvantaras plus some additional years are distributed over 1,000 periods of four Ages. Hear me tell the length of the Manvantara in human years: one Manvantara

*Eye blink.

†The period from the winter solstice to the summer solstice.

numbers 367,020,000 years in all. Hear me recount the aforementioned Manvantara by divine years: one such Manvantara is 852,000 years. Fourteen of these are said to constitute a day of Brahmā. The occasional dissolution* is said by the wise to come at the end of it. Bhūrloka, Bhuvarloka, Svarloka and their inhabitants then proceed to destruction while Maharloka survives. Consumed by heat, its residents retreat to Janaloka. And when the three worlds are one great ocean, Brahmā sleeps in the night. That night is the same length as his day; at the end of the night the world is poured forth again. And so passes one Brahmā year; his life lasts one hundred years. One hundred of his years is called *para;* fifty years is termed *parārdha* (half a *para*). One half of his life has passed, O best of the twice-born, at the end of which is the final great Eon known as Pādma. The present one, O twice-born, is the first Eon of the second half of Brahmā's life, called Vārāha.

# The Four Ages

The first Age is called Kṛta by the wise, the next Tretā. The third is said to be Dvāpara, O Pārtha, and Kali the fourth. The highest virtue is said to be meditation in the Kṛta, knowledge in the Tretā, sacrifice, they say, in the Dvāpara and gift-giving in the Kali. Brahmā is god in the Kṛta Age, lord Sun in the Tretā, in the Dvāpara the divine Viṣṇu and great lord Rudra in the Kali. Brahmā, Viṣṇu and the Sun are all worshipped in the Kali. Lord Rudra, who carries the Pināka,† is honored in all four Ages. Eternal Dharma is four-footed in the Kṛta Age, three-footed in the Tretā Yuga, and stands two-footed in the Dvāpara. In Tiṣya,‡ missing three feet, it barely survives. In the Kṛta, birth occurs through sexual intercourse. All creatures are continually content, with their livelihood spontaneously arising out of their pleasure in doing it. In this Kṛta Age there is no distinction between the best and the worst of them, O city-conqueror; their life, happiness and beauty are equal. They are free from sorrow, full of goodness, much given to solitude; devoted to meditation, intent upon *tapas,* their final end is Mahādeva. They act without self-interest; their minds are always joyful; they have no permanent home; they live in the mountains or by the oceans.

*I.e., the intermediary dissolutions after each Eon before the final dissolution at the end of Brahmā's life.

†Name of Śiva's bow.

‡Kali.

In the course of time the spontaneous arising of pleasure came to an end in the Tretā. When the natural propensity for pleasure was lost, another perfection came into being. When the subtleness of waters [their spontaneous welling forth] had ceased, then rain in the shape of clouds poured forth from thunderheads. As soon as earth's surface was covered by the fallen rain there appeared trees called homes. All food came from these trees; indeed, at the beginning of the Tretā Age all creatures subsisted entirely on them. Then, after a long period of degeneration, their disposition became unexpectedly passionate and greedy. Because of their decadence, in the course of time all these trees known as homes disappeared. After they had vanished, those who were born from intercourse became confused. They set their hearts on success, but yet paid attention to truthfulness. The trees they called homes then reappeared and brought forth clothing, fruit and ornaments. In their holes was potent honey not collected by bees, with sweet smell, color and taste. In fact, at the start of the Tretā Age all beings lived on this honey and were happy, well-fed and free from trouble. Then, after a time, they once again turned to greed, forcibly seizing these trees whose honey was not gathered by bees. And once more, because of their misdeeds, through their fault, the wishing-trees abounding in honey everywhere disappeared. Suffering acutely through intense rain and oppressed by the opposites of cold and heat, they made shelters. After the wishing-trees with their copious honey were lost, those who were hiding from the opposing elements pondered how to make a living. So success came again to them in the Tretā Age: another type of rain, conducive to their livelihood, fell in accordance with their desire. Then a continual succession of supernal rains flowed down the valleys, bore the waters downward, and thus became rivers. The drops of water which once again covered the earth's surface then became herbs through the commingling of earth and water. Fourteen kinds of trees—both flowering and fruit-bearing—took root, some appropriate to barren soil, some to untilled land, some to unsowed soil, and some to village and forest. Then greed and passion arose again everywhere, inevitably, due to the predestined purpose of the Tretā Age. And people seized the rivers, fields, mountains, clumps of trees and herbs, overcoming them by their strength. Because of their perversity, the herbs reentered earth. Pṛthu milked the earth by command of the Fathers. Then all the people, insensate with anger, due to the influence of the times, captured each other's land, wives and wealth by their own power. Knowing this, the unborn lord Brahmā emitted the kṣatriyas for the purpose of setting limits and for the benefit of the brahmins. In the Tretā the lord instituted the rules of class and stage in life and also the performance of sacrifice without injury to cattle.

In the Dvāpara, however, differences of opinion continually occured among men, as did passion, greed and war, and a lack of firm resolve regarding truth. In the Tretā the four-footed Veda was laid down as a unit whereas in the Dvāpara and the others it was divided into four parts by Vyāsa. They were re-divided by the sons of the seer who commited errors in judgment by way of distinctive divisions of *mantra* and *brāhmaṇa;** the errors were due to changes in accents and phonemes. Because of certain differences of opinion here and there, the collections of Ṛg, Yajus and Sāma Vedas were compiled by the seers of *śruti* according to their various characteristics; also the Brāhmaṇa, the Kalpasūtras, the recitations and mantras; Itihāsa and Purāṇa, and the Dharmaśāstras, O one of strong vow. Disgust with existence arose among mankind along with death, calamity and disease through suffering born in speech, mind and body. From disgust there arose among human beings reflections on liberation from suffering, and from such reflection arose indifference to worldly desires, and from indifference the perception of fault. In the Dvāpara, then, wisdom arose from the observation of error. This behavior, along with *rajas* and *tamas,* is remembered of the Dvāpara. In the first age, the Kṛta, there was virtue; it continued throughout the Tretā, became confused in the Dvāpara, and is lost altogether in the Kali.

In Tiṣya, men confounded by *tamas* continually perpetrate trickery, envy and the murder of ascetics. In the Kali there is fatal disease, continuous hunger and fear, awful dread of drought and revolution in the lands. Evil creatures born in the Tiṣya—wicked, unprincipled, weak in wit and strong in anger—speak lies. Fear arises among people because of brahmin errors in behavior: crimes, lack of knowledge, evil conduct and ill-gotten gains. In the Kali the twice-born are ignorant of the Vedas. Nor do they perform sacrifice; others of inferior intellect do the sacrifice, and they recite the Vedas incorrectly. In this Kali age there will occur the association of śūdras with brahmins through *mantras,* marriages and the practice of sleeping and sitting together. Kings who are mostly śūdras will have brahmins killed; abortion and hero-murder will prevail in this age, O king!

**Mantra* is a Vedic verse; *brāhmaṇa* is a prose text or ritual; *śruti* is "revelation;" Kalpasūtra is a ritual manual; Itihāsa is epic; Purāṇa is "traditional lore"; Dharmaśāstra is a manual of Dharma.

# The Kali Age

All kings occupying the earth in the Kali Age will be wanting in tranquillity, strong in anger, taking pleasure at all times in lying and dishonesty, inflicting death on women, children and cows, prone to take the paltry possessions of others, with character that is mostly *tamas,* rising to power and soon falling. They will be short-lived, ambitious, of little virtue and greedy. People will follow the customs of others and be adulterated with them; peculiar, undisciplined barbarians will be vigorously supported by the rulers. Because they go on living with perversion, they will be ruined. The destruction of the world will occur because of the departure from virtue and profit, little by little, day by day. Money alone will confer nobility. Power will be the sole definition of virtue. Pleasure will be the only reason for marriage. Lust will be the only reason for womanhood. Falsehood will win out in disputes. Being dry of water will be the only definition of land. The sacred thread alone will distinguish brahmins. Praiseworthiness will be measured by accumulated wealth. Wearing the *linga* will be sufficient cause for religious retreat. Impropriety will be considered good conduct, and only feebleness will be the reason for unemployment. Boldness and arrogance will become equivalent to scholarship. Only those without wealth will show honesty. Just a bath will amount to purification, and charity will be the only virtue. Abduction will be marriage. Simply to be well-dressed will signify propriety. And any water hard to reach will be deemed a pilgrimage site. The pretense of greatness will be the proof of it, and powerful men with many severe faults will rule over all the classes on earth. Oppressed by their excessively greedy rulers, people will hide in valleys between mountains where they will gather honey, vegetables, roots, fruits, birds, flowers and so forth. Suffering from cold, wind, heat and rain, they will put on clothes made of tree-bark and leaves. And no one will live as long as twenty-three years. Thus in the Kali Age humankind will be utterly destroyed.

# The Dissolution of the World in Viṣṇu

At the end of a thousand periods of four Ages, when the earth's surface is for the most part wasted, there arises a dreadful drought that lasts for a hundred years. Then all these earthly beings whose strength has declined perish completely through oppression. And so the imperishable lord Viṣṇu, who abides in himself, adopts the form of Rudra, and exerts himself to act in order to destroy all creatures. Permeating the seven rays of the sun, the lord Viṣṇu then drinks up all the waters, O excellent sage. When he has consumed all the waters that had gone to the world of creatures, he dries up the earth's surface. Oceans, rivers and flowing mountain streams as well as whatever water lies in the Pātālas*—all this he leads to dissolution. Then due to his power, those same seven rays become seven suns, invigorated by the absorption of water. These seven blazing suns ignite all three worlds, above and below, along with the surface of the Netherworld, O twice-born. The three worlds, O twice-born one, consumed by these fiery suns, complete with mountains, rivers and the expanse of the ocean, become arid. Then the whole triple world whose water and trees are burned away, and this earth as well, become as bare as a turtle's back. Likewise, when the monstrous fire has burned up these Pātālas, it rises to the earth and utterly devours its surface. And a frightful tornado of flame rolls through the entire Bhuvarloka and Svarloka. The three worlds then blaze like a frying-pan; all things moving and unmoving are consumed by the surrounding flames. The inhabitants of these two worlds, overcome by heat, their duties done, retreat to Maharloka, O great seer. Still seared by the heat they flee again; seeking safety in a different place, they hurry thence to Janaloka. So when Janārdana in Rudra's form has consumed all creation, he produces clouds from the breath of his mouth that look like a herd of elephants, emitting lightning, roaring loudly. Thus do dreadful clouds arise in the sky. Some are dark like the blossom of the blue lotus; some look like the white water-lily; some are the color of smoke; and others are yellow. Some resemble a donkey's hue; others are like red lacquer; some have the appearance of a cat's-eye gem; and some are like sapphire. Still others are white as a conch shell or jasmine, or similar to collyrium; some are like fireflies, while others resemble peacocks. Huge clouds arise resembling red or yellow arsenic, and others look like a blue-jay's wing. Some of these clouds are like fine towns, and some like mountains; others resemble houses, and still others, mounds of earth. These dense, elephantine clouds fill up the surface of the sky, roaring loudly. Pouring down rain they completely extinguish this dreadful fire which has overtaken the three worlds. And when the fire is thoroughly quenched, the clouds raining day and night overwhelm

*Netherworlds.

the entire world with water, O excellent seer. When they have completely inundated the atmosphere with copious streams of water, then, O twice-born, they flood Bhuvarloka on high. When everything movable and immovable in the world has perished in the watery darkness, these vast clouds pour down rain for another one hundred years. So is it at the end of every Eon, O excellent seer, by the majesty of the eternal Vāsudeva, the supreme lord.

When the waters come to rest, having reached the realm of the seven seers, then this single ocean completely covers the three worlds. Wind blown out of Viṣṇu's mouth makes the clouds disappear in a hundred years. When the eternal lord, fashioner of all creatures, inconceivable, the condition of creation, the beginning of everything who has no beginning himself, has entirely consumed the wind, then, reposing on Śeṣa in the single ocean, the lord, first creator, rests in the form of Brahmā, praised by Sanaka and others, the seers who went to Janaloka, and also meditated upon by those who went to Brahmaloka seeking freedom. Resting in meditative sleep, in the divine form of his own illusive power, Viṣṇu, destroyer of Madhu, concentrates on the form of himself called Vāsudeva. This is the dissolution called occasional, O Maitreya;* the occasion is that Hari rests in the form of Brahmā. When the soul of all awakens, then the world stirs; when the imperishable one has gone to his bed of illusion, it falls completely asleep. A day of Brahmā, born from the lotus, lasts a thousand periods of four Ages; a night, when the world is destroyed and made into a vast ocean, is of the same length. At the end of the night, Viṣṇu, unborn, having awakened, takes the form of Brahmā in order to create, as it has already been told to you.

## The Dissolution into Prakṛti and Puruṣa

Next I shall relate in brief summary the incomparable, supreme dissolution of Prakṛti. Hear what I say. After the second half of Brahmā's life-span, Time, counting down the world, makes up his mind to reduce everything to ashes as the Fire of Time. Putting the self in the Self, becoming the god Maheśvara, he burns up the entire egg of Brahmā with its gods, demons and people. The blessed blue and red god Mahādeva assumes a horrible shape and enters the

*Sage to whom this text is narrated.

world to destroy it all. He penetrates the orb of the sun and multiplies it seventy-seven times in order to burn up the whole world. When he has ignited everything, he hurls his mighty Brahmaśiras weapon into the bodies of the gods, thereby incinerating the universe.

When all the gods are consumed by fire, the mountain-born goddess Pārvatī, she who is the Vedic revelation, stands alone, sole witness of Śaṃbhu. Adorned with a choice necklace, made of the skulls of the heads of the gods, he fills the orb of heaven with its hosts, the sun, moon and other celestial bodies. The god with a thousand hands and feet, with a thousand flames, huge arms, gaping mouth and fangs, fiery eyes ablaze, carrying a trident, clothed in an animal skin, resorting to divine Yoga, drinking by himself the supreme, blissful, abundant nectar—the supreme lord looks at the goddess as he dances the Tāṇḍava dance.

This goddess of supernal felicity in turn drinks in the nectar of the dance of her husband while she herself, abiding in Yoga, enters the body of the trident-wielding god. Quitting his Tāṇḍava dance as he pleases, the blessed Pināka-bearer whose nature is light burns up the orb of the egg of Brahmā. Then, while the gods Brahmā, Viṣṇu and the Pināka-bearer alone remain, the earth, with all her properties, dissolves into the waters.

Fire devours the element of water along with its qualities, and the Fire itself, with its attributes, is absorbed into Wind. Wind that sustains everything, with its properties, is absorbed into Space, and Space, with its qualities, is dissolved into Bhūtādi. All the faculties of sense are received into Taijasa, and the hosts of gods are dissolved into Vaikārika, O excellent ones. The three-fold Ahaṃkāra, namely Vaikārika, Taijasa and Bhūtādi, O fine ones, is absorbed into Mahat. The single, unmanifest, eternal womb of the world which is the most brilliant Brahman absorbs Mahat with its three modes.

After dissolving the beings and the elements in this manner, Maheśvara separates Pradhāna and the supreme Puruṣa from each other. This dissolution of the unborn Pradhāna and Puruṣa is said to be engendered by the desire of Maheśvara. This distinction does not occur spontaneously. The unmanifest equilibrium of the *guṇas* is renowned as Prakṛti. Pradhāna is the womb of the world, without consciousness, the element of Māyā, or illusion. The Self, consisting of consciousness, stands at the summit, separate, as the twenty-fifth.* Celebrated as the Witness by the seers, it is the only one, the Grandfather. Thus, according to *śruti,* does the everlasting *śakti* power of Maheśvara consume everything in fire, from the primordial matter of Pradhāna down to the atoms.

*In the Sāmkhya system twenty-four principles are listed such as elements and senses, to which the self is the twenty-fifth.

# The Shape of Space

The heavenly form of the mighty lord Hari is made of stars and shaped like a porpoise with Dhruva* in its tail. This constellation makes the planets, moon, sun and so on revolve, and the *nakṣatras* circle him like a wheel. The sun, moon, stars, and *nakṣatras* together with the planets are bound to Dhruva with fetters made up of a series of winds. The porpoise-shaped constellation, which is Nārāyaṇa, is the pathway of the stars' fixed abodes. Its hub lies in his heart. Dhruva, the son of Uttānapāda, having propitiated this lord of creation, now sits in the tail of the starry porpoise. Janārdana, superintendent of everything, is the support of the porpoise; the porpoise, the foundation of Dhruva; and on Dhruva rests the sun, upholder of the world with its gods, demons and human beings. Hear from me, attentively, the regulation by which the sun rules.

The sun, source of day and night, revolves, O twice-born, regularly nourishing fathers, gods, humankind and so forth. The moon is nourished by the *suṣumnā* ray of the sun. In the dark half of the month the moon, made of nectar, is continually drunk by the immortals. Among them, then, the Fathers drink refreshment from the sun, two digits of the moon being consumed in the dark half of the month, O twice-born. With his beams the sun absorbs the juice remaining on earth; as rain he pours it forth for the nourishment of creatures. The holy sun pleases all the immortal beings by doing this. Thus does he nurture Fathers, gods, human beings and others. Each fortnight, O Maitreya, the sun gives sustenance to the gods, each month to the Fathers, and daily to mortals.

The three-wheeled chariot of the moon runs on, drawn by ten horses, light as jasmine, yoked to left and right. The Bear† constitutes the pathway with the swift chariot upheld by Dhruva. The moon has a rhythm of decrease and increase like the rays of the sun. Thus these horses, arisen from the womb of the sea, draw the chariot of the moon for the span of one Eon, O excellent seer. When the moon, consumed by the gods, is only a single digit wide, O Maitreya, the brilliant sun makes it grow with a single ray. Every day the bright sun nourishes the moon, which has been gradually drunk by the gods. And the deathless gods, O Maitreya, having drawn forth the liquor, drink the nectar remaining in the moon, which has accumulated every half-month. Thirty-three thousand, thirty-three hundred and thirty-three gods drink the maker of the night. When the exalted moon has two digits, it enters the orb of the sun called Amā, and so it

*The pole star. †The Pleiades.

is named Amāvāsya.* Each night and day the moon first enters the water, then dwells in the plants, eventually going to the sun. So he who cuts down plants or destroys one leaf in which the moon lives incurs the murder of a brahmin. Whatever portion of the moon is left on the fifteenth day of the month, the hosts of Fathers share in this last part during the afternoon. The gods drink up two digits, but the Fathers drink its remaining digit, which consists of nectar and ambrosia, O hermit. On new-moon day that elixir pours forth from the moon-beams, and for a month the fathers, having obtained great satisfaction, are content. Thus the moon nourishes the gods in the bright fortnight, the fathers in the dark fortnight and the plants, with cool drops of water made of nectar. And it nurtures men, earth and insects through the growth of plants and herbs, and with the joy of its light.

Eight bee-black horses, yoked once for all time, ceaselessly pull this gray chariot of Rāhu, O Maitreya. Going forth from the sun, Rāhu travels to the moon on the lunar eclipse days and from the moon to the sun on the solar eclipse days. The horses of the chariot of Ketu (Rāhu) are eight, fleet as the wind, dark as the color of straw smoke and red like lac juice. These nine chariots of the planets about which I have told you, O illustrious one, are bound to Dhruva by the cords of the winds—all the planets, constellations, stars and meteors are without exception tied to Dhruva with wind cords and move in their proper courses, O Maitreya.

There are as many cords of wind as there are heavenly bodies; all of them, bound to Dhruva, moving make him spin. Just as oil pressers make the wheel turn as they move so do the luminaries all move by influence of the wind. Because the wind pulls the stars, which are propelled in a windy circle like a fiery wheel, it is known as the Pravaha.

# The Seven Heavens

Next I will relate in brief, O best ones among the twice-born, the size of the triple world, for it is not possible to do so at length. Bhūrloka, Bhuvarloka, Svarloka, Maharloka, Janaloka, Taparloka and Satyaloka are the worlds thought to have their origin in the egg. In the old stories Bhūrloka is said to stretch out as far as sun and moon radiate their beams of light, O bulls of the twice-born. As far as Bhūr-

*New-moon day.

loka extends in width and circumference, so does Bhuvarloka spread out from the sphere of the sun, from which sphere the firmament extends upward as far as Dhruva is located. This region is called Svarloka; in it are fellies of wind. The seven fellies of wind are: Āvaha, Pravaha, Anuvaha, Saṃvaha and Vivaha; above this the Parāvaha and higher still the Parivaha. The sphere of the sun lies 100,000 leagues from earth. The orb of the moon is also said to be 100,000 leagues from the sun. The whole circle of *nakṣatras* appears the same distance from the moon. Twice this distance beyond the *nakṣatras*, O wise ones, is the planet Budha (Mercury), and Uśanas (Venus) dwells the same distance from Budha. Aṅgāraka (Mars) too is the same distance from Śukra (Venus). The priest of the gods (Bṛhaspati/Jupiter) resides 200,000 leagues from Bhauma (Mars), while Sauri (Saturn) is the same distance from the *guru* (Jupiter). This is the sphere of the planets. The sphere of the Seven Seers* shines 100,000 leagues' distance from that. Dhruva dwells the same number of leagues above the sphere of the seers. Dhruva is the central point of this entire wheel of luminaries in which resides the lord Dharma, Viṣṇu Nārāyaṇa.

The chariot of the sun is 9,000 leagues in length, O best ones of the twice-born, and its staff is twice that. The axle on which its wheel rests is 22,000,000 leagues long—the wheel of time, which is based completely on the year, is made up of three hubs, five spokes and six fellies. The second axle of the sun's chariot, O best ones of the twice-born, is 45,000 leagues. The length of both axles equals the length of both half-yokes; the short axle, the half-yoke of the chariot, rests on the support of Dhruva. The wheel in the second axle is fixed on Mt. Mānasa, and the seven horses are the seven meters. Hear their names: Gāyatrī, Bṛhatī, Uṣṇij, Jagatī and Paṅkti, Anuṣṭubh and Triṣṭubh—these are the seven horse-meters of Hari. The great city of Indra lies to the East, on the top of Mt. Mānasa; Yama's is to the South, that of Varuṇa to the West and Soma's to the North. Hear their names one by one: Amarāvatī, Saṃyamanī, Sukhā and Vibhā. Going around the post† to the South, Prajāpati, god of gods, curves like a shot arrow, along with the circle of the *nakṣatras*. The sun is stationed in the middle of the sky at all times, O noble seers, directly opposite to midnight in the seven continents. The sun's rising and setting are always opposite to the midnight point in all directions and intermediate directions. So like a turning potter's wheel does the lord

*The Little Dipper.

†After the winter solstice the sun rises increasingly further north until the summer solstice; then it turns around to rise further to the south, like a race-horse rounding the midway post in the hippodrome.

make day and also night when he leaves earth, O twice-born ones. This triple world is pervaded by the sun's ray called Trailokya by the wise ones of the worlds, O bulls of seers. The three worlds are wholly rooted in the sun, without a doubt; from it proceeds the entire universe, complete with gods, demons and humankind. They all give praise to the sun of a thousand rays—Gandharvas, gods, serpents, Kinnaras and so forth. With various sacrifices do the twice born honor him who consists of sacred hymns, who is the ancient form of Brahmā.

## The Seven Netherworlds

The width of the earth as I have told you is 70,000 leagues, O twice-born; so also is its height. The seven Pātālas are each 10,000 leagues deep, O best of sages, and are the following: Atala, Vitala, Nitala, Gabhastimat, Mahākhya, Sutala and the seventh, Agrya. They are white, black, red, yellow, tan, gray and gold. In them there are palaces decorated in choice style, O Maitreya. Dānavas, Daityas and Yakṣas live in them by the hundreds, O great seer, and classes of great Snakes. Nārada, amid the heaven-dwellers, having gone to heaven from the Pātālas, said they were even more delightful than Svarloka! This Pātāla, where radiant jewels on the ornaments borne by the Snakes bring delight, their luster radiating forth—to what is it equal? And whose pleasure is not aroused—even if he has gained release—in this beautiful Pātāla by the daughters of the Daityas and Dānavas moving to and fro? Here by day the sun's rays diffuse light, not heat, and moonbeams by night are luminous, not cold. Here the Snakes as well as the Dānavas and others, merry with good food, fine provisions and excellent drinks forget where the time has gone. Here there are forests, rivers, masses of lotuses in beautiful pools, the voices of male cuckoos and garments delighting the mind, brilliant ornaments, sweet-smelling oils and the harmonious sound of lute, pipe and drum, O twice-born! These and other most happy delights, O noble one, are enjoyed by the Dānavas, Daityas and Snakes whose range is inside the Pātālas.

Below the Pātālas lies the obscure form of Viṣṇu, named Śeṣa, whose qualities neither Daityas nor Dānavas are able to describe. He is called Ananta by the wise, a deity honored by divine seers. This thousand-headed form whose pure diadem is a clearly visible *svastika*, who illuminating space with the thousand gems of his hood makes all demons powerless for the good of the world, who, eyes roving to and fro in agitation, always wears a single earring, is crowned with a garland of jewels and shines forth like the white mountain on fire.* Puffed up with excitement, dressed in dark blue, adorned with a white necklace like another Kailāsa circled by the stream of the celestial Ganges, holding in his hands the powerful plough and the great mace, he is attended by Kānti herself and by Vāruṇī embodied. Emerging from his mouth at the end of the Eon, Rudra, as Saṃkarṣaṇa, ablaze with poisonous crests of flame, devours the three worlds—he is Śeṣa, who bearing the whole earth like a chaplet on his head, lies at the bottom of the Pātālas, revered by all the gods. Furthermore, the strength and power of his own form can neither be told nor known even by the thirty gods—Śeṣa, of whom this material earth is but a tuft of hair on his jewelled hood, like a crown of flowers. What more can be said about his manly power? When Ananta yawns and stretches, his eyes rolling with lust, then this earth along with its oceans and forests trembles. Various creatures come forth: Gandharvas, Apsarases, Siddhas, Kinnaras, Snakes and Cāraṇas—there is no end to the forms that proceed from this imperishable, endless one. . . . So is this great earth upheld by the head of the most excellent serpent. He wears the three worlds with their gods, demons and humankind like a tiara on his head.

# The Hells

Hear, O great demon, the size and features of all of these hells called Raurava and so forth, which number twenty-one. The first notorious hell is named Raurava (Horrifying); it is 2,000 leagues in extent, strewn with blazing coals. Twice the size of this is the second level, therefore called Mahāraurava (Most Horrifying), consisting of melted copper and heated by fire below it. Next is the one called Tāmiśra (Dark), twice the size of the last one, and the fourth is named Andhatāmisraka (Utter Dark), doubling that. Kālacakra (Wheel of Time) is reported to be the fifth. The next is Apratiṣṭha (Foundationless) and the seventh, Ghaṭīyantra (Diarrhea). And another, Asipatravana (Forest of Sword-Blades), said to be 72,000 leagues, is the eighth and a most important hell. The ninth is called Taptakumbha (Burning Vat), the tenth, Kūtaśālmali (Thorny); Karapatra (Saw-Toothed) is the next, and another is Śvānabhojana (Dog-Eating). And also Saṃdaṃsa (Pincers), Lohapiṇḍa (Red Hot Iron Balls), Kar-

*Himālaya.

ambhasikatā (Groat-Gravel), Ghorā (Horrible), Kṣāranadī (Ash-River), and Kṛmi-bhojana (Worm-Eating). The eighteenth is said to be the dreadful river Vaitaraṇī. Also there is Śoṇitapūyabhojana (Blood and Pus-Eating), Kṣurāgradhāro (Razor-Edge Sharp), Niśita (Sharp) and Cakraka (Wheel); then one named Samśoṣaṇa (Drying Up) and Ananta (Endless). Thus are the hells described to you, O Sukeśin.*

Those sinners who have constantly condemned Vedas, gods or brahmins, those who have ignored the beneficial teachings of Purāṇa and Itihāsa, those who find fault with their teacher, who obstruct sacred feasts, who hinder donors, all these fall into these hells. Wicked people who provoke dissension between friends, between husband and wife, between brothers, between master and servant, father and son, sacrificer and teacher, and those dishonorable men who give their daughter to one man having already given her to another—all these are split in two by Yama's servants with a saw. People who make trouble for others, thieves of sandal-wood, or *usīra*† and yak-tail fans go to the Karambhasikatā (Groat-Gravel) Hell. The foolish man who refuses food, eating elsewhere when invited to the *śrāddha* for gods and ancestors, is bitten in two by large sharp-beaked birds. Battering them with their beaks, birds alight on those who strike good men in vulnerable spots and abuse them with words. One who is hypocritically slanderous to good men suffers huge birds with horny beaks and claws who pull out his tongue. Those haughty people who treat their mothers, fathers and teachers with contempt go to hell where they lie with their faces downward in pus, feces and urine. Those who eat when gods, guests and servants as well as children, fathers, Fire and the mothers have not eaten, these disgraceful hosts will eat spoiled blood, pus and urine. They will become pointy-faced, always ravenous and mountainous in size. Those who serve a row of seated guests unequally travel to the Vibhojana Hell, O Indra of demons. They go to the Śleṣmabhojana (Slime-Eating) Hell traveling in the same caravan. The hands of those who, while defiled, have touched fire, cow or a brahmin, O demon, are thrust into the Taptakumbha (Burning Vat) Hell. After they have wantonly looked at sun, moon and stars in an impure condition the fire of their eyes will be blown out by the servants of Yama. People who have touched a friend's wife, an elder brother, father, sister, female relatives, teachers or elders with their foot have their ankles bound with fiery hot iron shackles; burning with fire up to the knees they are thrown into the dreadful Hell Raurava. Hot iron balls are

*Demon to whom this text is narrated.
†Kind of plant.

thrust into the mouths of those who have frivolously eaten milk, sesamum and meat. Those who listen to the reviling of teachers, gods, brahmins and Vedas by wicked men are pierced in the ears over and over by the servants of the king of Dharma with red-hot iron spikes. The skin of those who cause the ruin of cisterns, groves of trees, cloisters, halls and brahmins' houses, wells, ponds and tanks is sliced off with sharp knives by the horrible servants of Yama, while they moan. Crows rip out the intestines through the anus of men who urinate in front of cows, brahmins, the sun or fire. In times of confusion or famine, those men who, feeding only themselves, forsake sons, servants, wives and kinsmen, men who abandon those who have gone to them for shelter and those who are jail-keepers, all these fall into the Yantrapīḍa (Pressing Machine) Hell, beaten by Yama's servants. Evil-doers with no good work of their own who torment brahmins and others are crushed in a mortar and evaporated by desiccators. Dishonest men who appropriate deposits are bound with iron fetters and, emaciated with hunger, with dry palates and lips, are hurled into the Vṛsicikāsana (Scorpion-Eating) Hell. Sinners who copulate on holy days and those who have sexual intercourse with another's wife must embrace a red-hot spike with a pointed top. The lowest brahmin who puts his learned teacher below himself while he studies with him, and his teacher too, will carry millstones around their necks. Those who pass urine, mucus or feces in water are thrown into the Viṇmūtra (Feces and Urine) Hell which is stinking, filled with pus. Those fools who eat each other's *śrāddha* offerings on earth are made to devour each other's flesh in hell. He who forsakes the Vedas, the Fire, his teacher, wife or parents is thrown from a mountain top by the servants of Yama. Also those who remarry widows, those who violate virgins, and one who partakes of the *śrāddha* of such a son must eat ants and worms. Both the patron and the sacrificing priest who accept payment from a low caste person or a *caṇḍāla* become gross insects inside a rock. Stupid back-biters and men who take bribes are thrown into the Vṛkabhakṣa (Wolf-Eating) Hell, O night-wanderer. A gold-thief, a brahmin-slayer, a drunkard, a man who violates his teacher's bed, those who steal cattle and land, those who murder cows, women and children, these as well as twice-born men who become vendors of cows, Soma and the Veda, and those who indulge in trickery, who give up cleanliness and both regular and occasional rites, and those who give false testimony—all these inhabit the Mahāraurava Hell. They stay in Tāmiśra for 10,000 years, for just as long in Andhatāmiśra and in Asipatravana, and equally long in Ghaṭiyantra and in Taptakumbha. So do those people who have done evil fall into hell.

The river Vaitaraṇī, downfall of men, surpasses in horror all these unbearable, impenetrable and dreadful hells, O lord of the demons. Likewise ungrateful people are the worst of sinners and ingratitude the worst of sins. Expiation is possible for the evil-doer who kills brahmins, cows and so on, but for those ingrates who are ungrateful to a friend, there is no expiation for tens of millions of years.

## The Regions of Earth

This great egg of Brahmā with fourteen parts has been described. Now I shall relate the true lore about Bhūrloka. Jambūdvīpa (Rose-Apple Land) is the principal continent, along with Plakṣa (Fig Tree), Śālmala (Silk-Cotton Tree), Kuśa (Grass), Krauñca (Curlew), Śāka (Teak Tree) and Puṣkara (Blue Lotus), the seventh. These seven continents are circled by seven seas. Each continent is said to be greater than the next, likewise each sea. The oceans are called Kṣāra (Salt), Ikṣurasa (Sugarcane Juice), Surā (Wine), Ghṛta (Ghee), Dadhi (Curds), Kṣīra (Milk) and Svādu (Sweet Water). Earth, composed of seven continents, together with the oceans extends 500,000,000 leagues across. Holy Jambūdvīpa lies in the middle of all the continents; in its center is said to be lofty Mt. Meru, bright as gold. Its height is 84,000 leagues, and it extends 16,000 leagues below the earth; its width at the top is 32,000 leagues, and its diameter at the base is 16,000 leagues. This mountain stands as the calyx of the lotus-flower which is this earth. The mountain ranges are Himavat, Hemakūṭa and Niṣadha to the south and to the north, Nīla, Śveta and Śṛṅgī. The two in the middle are 100,000 leagues long; the others are 10,000 leagues less. They are 2,000 leagues in height and width. The range to the south is called Bhārata; next is Kiṃpuruṣa, then Hari. These lie to the south of Mt. Meru, O twice-born ones. To the north is Ramyaka; next to this lies Anuhira and then Kurava. They are the same size as Bhārata. Each of them extends 9,000 leagues, O best of the twice-born. In the center lies Ilāvṛta and in the middle of it rises Meru. Ilāvṛta spreads out 9,000 leagues from Meru in all four directions; on it are the supports of Meru, four eminent mountains which rise a thousand leagues high. To the east lies the mountain called Mandara; to the south, Gandhamādana. Vipula is nearby to the west, and on the Northern side is Supārśva. On these grow *kadamba*, rose apple, fig and banyan trees. This, O great seers, is the reason for the name Jambū (rose apple) of Jambūdvīpa (Rose-Apple Land). Fruits of the Jambū tree, big as elephants, fall crushed on all sides of the mountain top. From the juice of these fruits is formed the celebrated

Jambū river. And as the river flows by it is drunk by the inhabitants of this land. Here, due to the drinking of this river, there arises among men whose minds are at peace neither sweat nor foul smell, neither old age nor deterioration of the senses. Soil gathered from its bank and dried by the wind becomes the gold called Jāmbūnada, adornment of the Siddhas.

On Meru there is a great city belonging to the god of gods, noble and renowned, 14,000 leagues wide. There lord Brahmā, soul of all, creator of everything, is worshipped by great *yogins,* great hermits, and by Upendra (Viṣṇu) and Śankara (Śiva). There the blessed lord Sanatkumāra continually honors Prajāpati, soul of everything, the lordly lord of the gods. Engaged in Yoga, having drunk the peerless nectar of immortality, he sits there honored by accomplished seers, Gandharvas and gods as well. In front of Brahmā stands the brilliant, white, shining abode of the first god among gods, Śambhu of infinite luster—radiant with four doors, possessing divine beauty, occupied by hosts of great seers and cherished by those who know Brahmā. Along with the goddess, Mahādeva, lord of the universe, leader of the tormentors, with eyes of moon, sun and fire, enjoys himself with his demons. There tranquil seers, wise in the Veda, celibate students and ascetics speaking truth, worship the great god Mahādeva. He, highest lord, along with Pārvatī, receives in person the offering of these Brahmā-following sages with his head. On the eminent mountain to the east lies the beautiful city of Śakra; replete with splendors, it is named Amarāvatī. Crowds of Apsarases and Gandharvas bent upon song—thousands of deities—worship Indra of a thousand eyes. This exalted spot, difficult to attain even for these gods, is the dwelling place of those virtuous ones, versed in the Veda, whose aim is making sacrifice and oblation. To the south of this lies a city of immeasurably splendid fire, full of divine wonders, named Tejovatī. There dwells the blessed god of fire, shining forth with his own flame, inaccessible to Dānavas, and this city is the refuge of those who recite prayers and make *homa** offerings. To the south of the lofty mountain lies the great heavenly city of Yama named Sāṃyamanī, inhabited by Siddhas and Gandharvas. Here deities and so on attend the god Vaivasvata. The refuge of faithful, meritorious men on earth is in this place. In the west lies the city of the great-souled Nirṛti† named Rakṣovatī, which is completely inhabited by Rākṣasas. Here Rākṣasas worship the god Nirṛti; people devoted to duty whose lives are characterized by *tamas* go here. On the great western mountain

*Oblation into the fire. †Originally a goddess, here the god of revenge for *homa* transgressions.

sits the grand city of Varuṇa named Śuddhavatī, filled with all objects of desire and opulence. Here dwells king Varuṇa, lord of immortals, served by troops of Apsarases and Siddhas. There go clouds, those who repeatedly make pilgrimages and those whose sins are effaced in the world. The great city of Vāyu, too, is to the north of the above city. This holy city is named Gandhavatī; here lives the god of the storm, and here the lord of the immortals is attended by Gandharvas and groups of Apsarases. Mortals who practise breath control go to this eternal place. To the east of it stands the great lustrous city of Soma called Kāntimatī in which the moon god shines. This place, which is filled with all sorts of delights, appeals to people who follow their own duty while devoted to pleasure.

The great city of Śankara called Yaśovatī lies to the east of this, and is most difficult for anyone to attain. Here stands the huge magnificent palace of Īśāna, who is composed of the bodies of Rudra and Viṣṇu and the lord of the *gaṇas*, who surround him. A dwelling was created there by the trident-wielding god of gods for those devotees of Parameṣṭhin who are desirous of pleasure. Gangā, the heavenly river flowing from the feet of Viṣṇu and inundating the orb of the moon, falls all around the city of Brahmā. Falling on the four regions, O twice-born ones, she subdivides into four rivers, namely Sītā, Alakanandā, Sucakṣus and Bhadrā. The river Sītā flows from the atmosphere east of Mt. Meru and then through the eastern range called Bhadrāśva to the sea. And each of the others does likewise: Alakanandā to the South enters Bhāratavarṣa; Sucakṣus to the West falls on Ketumāla, and Bhadrā to the North flows through Uttarakuru. The lands of the Bhāratas, Ketumālas, Bhadras and the northern Kurus are the leaves of the world-lotus outside the mountain boundaries.

In the subcontinent of Ketumāla dwell dark-skinned men and women whose sheen is like that of lotus leaves; they eat breadfruit and live 10,000 years. On Bhadrāśva men are white-skinned, the women complexioned like moon-beams; eating mango fruit they live 10,000 years. Men and women light as silver enjoy 11,500 years on Ramyaka; they exhibit goodness and eat the fruit of the banyan tree. On Hiraṇmaya they are all bright as gold, eating bread-fruit; men and women live 12,500 years as if dwelling in the realm of the gods. 14,500 years do they live in the land of Kuru, dark-bodied people subsisting on milk. All beings are born of sexual intercourse and enjoy continual pleasure in Candradvīpa. Here they constantly worship the great god Śiva. Likewise in Kiṃpuruṣa, O twice-born ones, people are golden, live 10,000 years and subsist on figs. Unceasingly they worship the four-bodied, four-faced god with minds composed in meditation, reverentially, immersed in devotion. Next, in Harivarṣa they resemble gold, live 10,000 years and eat sugarcane. Here men, given being by Viṣṇu, worship the god Viṣṇu, lord Nārāyaṇa, eternal womb of all creation. There, shining like the moon, made of purest crystal, stands the shrine of Vāsudeva in a grove of Pārijāta trees.* It is incomparable, with four doors and four towered gates, invincible and insurmountable, with ten surrounding walls. With crystal pavilions, decorated on all sides by thousands of golden pillars, it looks like the house of the king of the gods. Complete with gold staircases, adorned by all sorts of jewels, appointed with a divine throne, it is embellished with all splendors. Adorned with pools and streams of sweet water, the palace is filled with the pure devotees of Nārāyaṇa engrossed in learning the Vedas, by *yogins* uninterruptedly meditating on Hari, the Puruṣa, praising him with *mantras* and giving reverence to Mādhava. There at all times the kings celebrate the brilliant, deathless Viṣṇu, first god of gods. Women—charming, radiant and youthful—sing and dance without ceasing, fond of their ornaments. On Ilāvṛta people are the color of the lotus, eating rose apple fruit they live as long as 13,000 years. In Bhāratavarṣa women and men display diverse colors, worship various gods and perform many different duties. The full length of their lives is said to be a hundred years, O virtuous ones. They consume all kinds of food and live their lives according to virtue or vice. This country extends 9,000 leagues. It is the land of ritual, O brahmins, for men so qualified. In these eight subcontinents, Kiṃpuruṣa and the others, O great seers, there is neither sorrow nor weariness, and no anxiety, hunger or fear. And the people, healthy, unoppressed, free from all cares, ever youthful, all enjoy themselves in various ways. Only in Bhāratavarṣa, the wise say, and nowhere else, occur the four Ages: Kṛta, Tretā, Dvāpara and Kali.

# The Origin of the Seers and the Manus

Then as Brahmā thought about them, human beings arose from his mind together with their duties to be done and the means to do them, which were both produced from his body. Embodied souls endowed with intelligence originated from his limbs; all those which have al-

*Trees of paradise.

ready been described by me came into being. Creatures poured forth, animate and inanimate, from the gods and so on down to inorganic matter known to belong to the realm of the three *guṇas*. When all this wise one's creatures grew up he released from himself other mind-born sons. Those conceived in his mind are Bhṛgu, Pulastya, Pulaha, Kratu, Aṅgiras, Marīci, Dakṣa, Atri and Vasiṣṭha. These then are the nine sons of Brahmā which are recognized in the ancient lore. Once more Brahmā poured forth Rudra, who arose from his angry self, and Saṃkalpa* and Dharma, who was born first, even before these others. Those who first came forth from Svāyambhuva, with their sons and so on, were composed and indifferent, having no attachment to the world. All of them, their passion gone, being without jealousies, had foreknowledge of the future. Mighty anger mounted in the great-souled Brahmā at their indifference toward the world. From this arose Puruṣa, resembling the sun, having a super-body which was half-man, half-woman. Having said, "Divide youself!" Brahmā disappeared. Thus admonished, he effected the separation of male and female natures and split the male into eleven parts. The lord god then divided both maleness and femaleness in various different ways, into countless souls that were good and bad, mild and sharp. Next lord Brahmā produced from himself the first Manu Svāyambhuva, similar to himself, to be the protector of the people, O brahmin. The god Manu Svāyambhuva took as wife the woman Śatarūpā, whose stains had been purified by *tapas*. By her husband Śatarūpā gave birth to two sons renowned as Priyavrata and Uttānapāda because of their deeds, and also two daughters, Ākūti and Prasūti. And then, in time past, the father gave Prasūti to Dakṣa and Ākūti to Rici. Prajāpati† accepted his wife; from these two was born a son, Yajña and also Dakṣiṇā,‡ O illustrious one, from the union of the couple.

The number of *manvantaras* is seventy-one periods of four Ages plus a fraction. First comes Svāyambhuva Manu and then the Manu Svārocisa. Next Auttami and Tāmasa, Raivata and Cākṣuṣa. These are the six past Manus. At present it is Vaivasvata; the five Sāvarṇas, Raucya and Bhautya are yet to come. The earth belonged to the great-spirited sons of Manu Svāyambhuva; to them were born ten sons like themselves.

In the beginning and in the Tretā Yuga the entire earth, the seven

*The formal intention to perform a ritual for a specified purpose.

†Dakṣa.

‡Usually a fire sacrifice for whom the performer engaged professional priests who are recompensed with a *dakṣiṇā*, a "stipend, fee."

continents with their mountains, oceans and mines was inhabited, land by land, by the sons of Priyavrata, the grandsons of Svāyambhuva.

# The Manvantaras

Saṃjñā, daughter of Viśvakarman, was the wife of the sun. Their children were Manu, Yama and Yamī, O sage. Unable to endure her husband's radiance, she offered Chāyā in attendance to her lord and herself hastened to the forest for *tapas*. Then the sun, taking Chāyā for Saṃjñā, generated three more children: Śanaiścara, Manu and Tapatī. When Chāyā in the guise of Saṃjñā, angered, uttered a curse on Yama, the realization came to Yama and Sūrya that she was a different woman. When Vivasvat was told by her that Saṃjñā was living in the forest, he looked with his inner eye and saw her as a mare, sitting in *tapas*. Taking the form of a stallion the sun discharged seed into her, and she gave birth to Revanta and the two Aśvins. Once again lord Sun took Saṃjñā to his home, whereupon Viśvakarman tempered his brilliance. Fixing the sun on his wheel he pared his radiance, shaving off an imperishable one-eighth. That splendor of Viṣṇu which was sliced off from him by Viśvakarman fell in flames to the earth, O excellent sage. From its brilliance Tvaṣṭar fashioned Viṣṇu's discus, Śarva's trident, the wealth-giver Kubera's palanquin, the power of Guha and the weapons of the other gods as well. All this Viśvakarman made to happen from the sun's flame. The second child of Chāyā disguised as Saṃjñā was the Manu named Sāvarṇi, who was the same color as her first-born.* His is the eighth Manvantara, the Sāvarṇika. Hear the future divisions of the Manvantaras; I will relate them. The future Manus will be Dakṣa-Sāvarṇi, Brahma-Sāvarṇi, Dharma-Sāvarṇi, Rudrá-Sāvarṇi, Raucya and Bhautya.

At the end of each period of four Ages comes to pass the dispersion of the Vedas. The Seven Seers descending from the sky to the earth initiate them once again. In Kṛta after Kṛta there arises a Manu, promulgator of *smṛti,* O twice-born; likewise in each Manvantara arise gods who enjoy the sacrifice. For the length of a Manvantara the earth is protected by these sons of Manu who come forth in succession. The powerful authorities in a Manvantara are these: Manu, the Seven Seers, gods and kings, the sons of Manu and Indra. A full Eon is said

**Savarṇa* means "of the same color."

to be a thousand Ages long, measured by the passage of fourteen Manvantaras, O brahmin. Of the same length, O wise one, is the following night. When he has devoured the three worlds in the flood, the lord Janārdana, creator of everything, subsisting by his own illusion, reposes on the snake Śesa in the midst of the watery deluge in the form of Brahmā. As it was in the beginning, so is it every time; Age after Age the imperishable lord, endowed with the quality of *rajas,* awakens and pours forth creation. Charged with *sattva,* the lord, along with the Manus, kings, Indra, gods and the Seven Seers, sustains creation, O most excellent among the twice-born!

# 2 Viṣṇu

## To Viṣṇu

*OṂ! Praise be to the blessed Vāsudeva!*

*May you be purified by Hari's lotus feet*
*That became manifest when they bestrode earth, atmosphere and heaven!*

*May you be purified by Hari's lotus feet*
*That have the power to annihilate the sorrow and fear of existence!*

*May you be purified by Hari's lotus feet*
*That are approached by* yogins *whose minds discern the truth!*

*May he whose form lies on the serpent's coils within the milky ocean's depths protect you!*

*May he protect you at whose touch the sea with froth of foam tossed upward by his breath seems to begin to dance.*

## Introduction

Viṣṇu is one of the most popular deities in Purāṇic mythology. While Brahmā is regarded as the agent of creation, and Śiva that of destruction, Viṣṇu is worshiped as the preserver of the created world during the periods of time between each successive emergence and dissolution of the universe. Viṣṇu is called the all-pervader, but he is also said to be the primal person and the first-born of creation, who has neither beginning nor end. In fact, Viṣṇu appears to be regarded by his devotees as the sole source of the universe, active in all three of its phases: creation, preservation and dissolution. Epithets similar to those given to Viṣṇu are elsewhere in the Purāṇas offered both to Śiva and to the Goddess in some of her forms, no doubt assigned to them by their particular devotees. It appears that a generalized view of deity as the monistic source of the birth, growth and death of all universal phenomena dominates Purāṇic thought and that various deities, no doubt the gods of different cults or shrines, are regarded as the sole divine source of the world in different passages composed by their devotees. Thus many of the epithets attributed to Viṣṇu are applied as well to other gods.

Unique to Viṣṇu, however, are a number of names derived from his own particular divine deeds, some of which are described in the Purāṇas, and some of which are not. In fact, in the Purāṇas Viṣṇu is most often called by some other name, because Viṣṇu as high god includes a collection of various other deities, each of whom originally bore his own name, signaling his own deeds, and only later was absorbed into the one universal lord who is the author of all action, Viṣṇu.

The name Viṣṇu itself is usually understood to mean "pervader," in the sense of an unseen divine force or spirit that pervades and motivates the entire universe. A deity of this name plays a minor role in the *Ṛg Veda,* where he is renowned for his three strides, the purpose of which is never clearly revealed:

> We celebrate that very manhood of [Viṣṇu] the savior who gives not harm but bounty,
> Who with three strides bestrode in width the wide spaces to bestow wide-ranging scope and life itself.
> The mortal who watches two of the strides of him who gazes on heaven bestirs himself,
> But no one dares to conquer his third, not even the winged sky-going birds.
> (*Ṛg Veda* I.155.4, 5)

Another ancient title of Viṣṇu is Nārāyaṇa, traditionally understood as "he whose abode is the waters." Viṣṇu is known by this name when he sleeps on the cosmic ocean between successive periods of dissolution and creation. (See Ch. 1, "The Origin of Brahmā in the Lotus.") The name Vāsudeva connotes his incarnation as Kṛṣṇa, son of the mortal Vasudeva (see Ch. 3), and the name Govinda, "cow-finder," refers to his occupation as the youth Kṛṣṇa. Most common of all names for Viṣṇu is Hari, whose origin is unclear. Signifying the color yellow, it may refer to the lord's customary yellow garb. It may also connote the taking away of evil, and is sometimes coupled with Hara, which means the same, and which is a popular name for Śiva. (See Ch. 4, "Hari-Hara.")

In sum, Viṣṇu is known by a variety of names and epithets in the Puraṇas, among which the name Viṣṇu itself is the least frequently used. Most of these names refer to some specific event in the god's divine career, like Nārāyaṇa, and may have originally been the names of other deities absorbed by Viṣṇu in the course of time. Others define an attribute of his personality, as for example, Acyuta, "imperishable." And still others, such as Kṛṣṇa, designate an incarnation of the god in human or animal form. In all his forms, however, Viṣṇu is the preserver and protector of the universe. His divine personality is one of kindness and beneficence. He is always the destroyer of the enemies of the good, the preserver of the welfare of the world.

As is the case with each prominent Purāṇic deity, Viṣṇu is accompanied by a collection of distinguishing accoutrements that serve to identify his own personal symbolism. These include his weapons, jewels, animals, spouse, and mount. So formulaic are these attributed items that they often resemble descriptions of an icon to be worshiped rather than the appurtenances of an active being. In fact, stories explaining the origins of most of these items are for the most part missing or vestigial in the Purāṇas. They simply appear as the god's collection of personal goods, which distinguish him from other deities, and always unmistakably identify who he is.

Viṣṇu wields four distinctive weapons, one in each of his four hands: the mace, conch, lotus and the discus Sudarśana. The heaven where he resides, and which his devotees attain, full of wonders most pleasing to the senses, is called Vaikuṇṭha and floats somewhere in the sky above the seven heavens. On his body are identifying marks: a whorl of hair on his chest called the Śrīvatsa, a jewel on his breast called Kaustubha, and sometimes also the wealth-giving gem called Syamantaka. The particular animal on which he rides through space is always Garuḍa, the giant eagle. Closely associated with him, often said to be identical with Viṣṇu himself, is the cosmic serpent called Ananta, "endless," or Śeṣa, "remainder." The names connote that the snake is immortal, for when all else in the universe has perished, he remains, coiled up as the god's bed in the ocean of milk.

Viṣṇu's spouse is Lakṣmī, or Śrī, the goddess of good fortune and prosperity, who may also bring bad luck if she is displeased. In the Purāṇas she has no independent identity of her own, but always appears as consort and counterpart of Viṣṇu, the supreme lord. She is born, according to one story, at the Churning of the Ocean, solely to adorn lord Viṣṇu:

> The goddess Śrī of vibrant beauty rose from this milk, standing in a blossoming lotus with a lotus in her hand. . . . Wearing celestial garlands and garments, bathed and adorned with ornaments, with all the gods looking on, she went to Hari's chest. While resting on Hari's chest, Lakṣmī made the gods know immediate supreme bliss, O Maitreya, just by looking at them.
> (Viṣṇu 1.9.100; 106; 107)

Viṣṇu and Lakṣmī sometimes appear to be a single divinity, the lord god and the ever-devoted lady who is inseparable from himself.

As preserver and protector of the universe, the most important feature of lord Viṣṇu lies in his *avatāras*, or "descents." Often called "incarnations," these *avatāras* are descents of a portion of the lord into animal or human form in order to redress the balance of good and evil in the world by supporting the forces of good:

> When the end of an Age rolls around and time has lost its strength, then lord Viṣṇu is born among men. When the gods and demons go to war, then Hari is born.
> (*Matsya* 47.32)

> For the protection of his creation, the unborn, undying Vāsudeva made various *avatāras*.
> (*Garuḍa* 1.13)

> When lord Hari descended in order to annihilate the law of the demons and to preserve the law of the Vedas and other laws, . . . the unborn god assumed *avatāras*.
> (*Garuḍa* 142.2)

From as early as Ṛg Vedic times there is a story told in Indian literature about a battle, or battles, between the gods and demons, raging periodically in the heavens or on earth, in which, despite desperate struggles, neither side ever succeeds in totally vanquishing the other. Such a contest forms the backdrop for many Purāṇic stories about the gods (as, for example, "The Churning of the Ocean," Ch. 2 below). This scenario allows the major deities to intercede on behalf of the gods or of mankind, who are time and again oppressed by the demons. And it is often, if not always, in such a context, that Viṣṇu intercedes in one or another of his *avatāras*.

The idea of the god's descent into animal or human form powerfully pervades the Purāṇas, but the number, occasion and sequence of these descents varies widely. Today it is common to list ten famous *avatāras* as the foundation of an evolutionary Vaiṣṇavite theology, but in the Purāṇas this meaning of the *avatāras* is by no means so clear as it has become in recent times. Sometimes the *avatāras* occur singly, and sometimes they are enumerated in lists of twenty or more. Sometimes they are related to the four Ages, the Kṛta, Tretā, Dvāpara and Kali, sometimes to the Manvantaras, and sometimes they stand alone. Sometimes they are listed in apparent evolutionary order, from the fish, to the amphibian, to the hybrid, and to the human heroes, while at other times they occur in apparently random order. Each *avatāra*, however, does perform some heroic act on behalf of the welfare of mankind, and it is this unity of purpose that ties them all together as the work of Viṣṇu.

As with the epithets of Viṣṇu, the many *avatāras* in the Purāṇas may well have been originally separate deities, each with its own deeds, devotees and cult, who in the course of time became subsumed under a single god. United by the beneficent heroism of their feats, they were absorbed into a single, over-arching deity, Viṣṇu, the protector, who pervades the world. This Vaiṣṇava expansionism is evident in a variety of other ways throughout the Purāṇas. For example, stories that feature Śiva or a goddess may depict Viṣṇu at the start or finish, taking both credit and praise for the feats of another god. It should be noted that Śiva and the Goddess also show similar expansionist tendencies, but it is only Viṣṇu who descends in *avatāras*.

The currently famous "ten descents" include some of the most frequently repeated stories known to Hindu tradition. Matsya, the Fish, rescuer of earth and the Vedas, inhabits the cosmic ocean between successive creations. Kūrma, the Tortoise, provides support for the churning stick as the gods and demons churn the ocean of milk for the nectar of immortality. Varāha, the Boar, rescues the globe of earth from beneath the cosmic sea where she has been lost. Vāmana, the Dwarf, who takes three famous strides, as does the Viṣṇu of the Ṛg Veda, defeats the demon Bali with a trick and regains earth for the gods' dominion. Narasiṃha, the Man-Lion, also defeats the demon Hiraṇyakaśipu with a trick, then rips his body to shreds in a gory killing. Paraśurāma, with his axe, rids the earth of kṣatriyas twenty-one times because they persecuted brahmins. Rāma defeats King Rāvaṇa of Lankā to rescue his kidnaped wife and regain his throne. Kṛṣṇa, of several personalities himself, defeats his wicked uncle Kaṃsa for the benefit of his family and clan. Buddha, in the Kali Age, leads mankind astray with false teaching, though sometimes he is depicted more positively as a model of compassion; and Kalkin, riding a white horse, waits in the future, an *avatāra* yet to come.

This familiar systematization of the *avatāras* of Viṣṇu does not occur in this clear and tidy form anywhere in the great Purāṇas, although each one is mentioned at least once. The stories of Matsya, Kūrma, Varāha, Vāmana, Narasiṃha and Kṛṣṇa are repeatedly told, sometimes at great length. Paraśurāma and Rāma are occasionally recalled, but only rarely described. Buddha and Kalkin occur once or twice in lists, but have no significant stories of their own at all. The *avatāra* doctrine so clearly defined today appears to have been somewhat in flux at the time of the compilation of the Purāṇas. The meaning of *avatāra* is consistent; the lists and functions of the *avatāras* are not.

The animal descents in the Purāṇas may represent remnants of animal worship, or they may simply be the fruits of religious imagination. The same might be said for the semi-human *avatāras* of Vāmana, the Dwarf, and Narasiṃha, the Man-Lion. But the heroes Rāma and Kṛṣṇa stand out as potentially historical figures, first transformed by legend into deities, then later subsumed under the personality of Viṣṇu. Rāma is found to be the hero of Vālmīki's epic, the *Rāmāyaṇa*, and the battle in which he defeats his foe has been given (outside of the Purāṇas) a legendary date: the juncture of the most recent Tretā and Dvāpara Ages (see Ch. 1, "The Four Ages"). The site of much of the activity of the Rāmāyaṇa is the Deccan plateau of southern India, and the fortress Rāma breaches is called Lankā, presumed to be the ancient, and now the newly restored, name of Ceylon. It is likely that Rāma was a hero whose heroism and exploits were deified and then absorbed by Viṣṇu, the guardian of mankind.

Kṛṣṇa, too, has historical personality, one even more thoroughly documented than that of Rāma. In the *Mahābhārata* he is a prince of the Yādava clan, and he plays an important part in the war at the epic's climax. It seems plausible that the miraculous stories of the childhood and youth of the divine child Kṛṣṇa sprang up at a later date out of religious elaboration, and were fused with the more mundane biography of an actual hero to create a god. The *Mahābhārata* war may well have occurred in history, and like Rāma's battle, it has been given a legendary date: the transition between the most recent Dvāpara and Kali Ages, the Kali being the Age in which we are now living, which began according to Indian tradition in 3102 B.C. Once again, it is likely that Kṛṣṇa was first a hero, advanced to become a minor deity, and finally became absorbed into the godhead of the eternal and supreme lord of the universe, Viṣṇu. In any event, in the years since the compilation of the Purāṇas, Kṛṣṇa has become the best-loved, most enchanting *avatāra* of them all.

By the time the Purāṇas were compiled, Viṣṇu, a minor deity in early Vedic times, had had a long and complex history, in the course of which he grew to be regarded as the source, goal, and sole deity of the universe by his devotees. He absorbed other deities into himself along the way, perhaps at the price of specific details of his own career, which had faded in human memory before the Purāṇas took their final form. Most characteristic of Viṣṇu in all his forms, however, is his nature as a benevolent, protective deity who pervades the universe in all its multitudinous phenomena, and who takes shape as animal or man to assist the forces of good in the world whenever evil threatens to prevail. Despite the often confusing testimony of the Purāṇas about the *avatāras* and exploits of Viṣṇu, his central character as guardian, protector and preserver of the world remains consistent wherever and whenever he appears. And further, it is through the symbolism of Viṣṇu that the complete identity of god and universe, a theme of continuing importance to Hindu thought, is made abundantly clear. This identity also implies the full identity of god and man, so evident in the *avatāras* of Rāma and Kṛṣṇa, but also experienced personally by Viṣṇu's famous devotee Prahlāda, who exclaims after a period of intense meditation on the lord:

> Viṣṇu is omnipresent. Because of this he exists even as myself. I am the source of everything! I am all things. Everything exists in me. I am eternal. I am undecaying. I am immortal. I am the Supreme Self! I am the refuge of all souls. I am known as Brahman, and at the end, I am the Supreme Person!
> (*Viṣṇu* 1.19.86)

# Texts

## The Four Forms of Viṣṇu

Lord Nārāyaṇa, the blessed god who pervades the universe, is fourfold, O brahmin. He exists both with and without characteristics. One form is beyond description; the wise see it as white. Its limbs are obscured by wreaths of flame. It is the ultimate foundation of *yogins*. Being both far and near, this form is beyond the three *guṇas*. Called Vāsudeva, he is said to be indifferent to possessions. The color, shape and other attributes of this first form are not without existence, but they exist in imagination. This form does exist. It is always pure, single in form, and a fine foundation. The second form, called Śeṣa, lies below, carrying the earth on its head. Said to be full of *tamas*, it stretches out horizontally. The third form performs action. Its aim is the maintenance of creatures. It abounds in *sattva* and upholds Dharma. The fourth form, lying in the middle of the water, rests on a serpent bed. Its characteristic is *rajas* and it continually produces creation.

In his third form Hari protects creatures and constantly sustains Dharma on earth. He destroys the demon Asuras, who arise to obstruct Dharma, and he protects the gods and virtuous men whose aim is the defense of Dharma. Whenever Dharma declines and non-Dharma rises to power, O Jaimini, then the lord pours himself forth.

Long ago, after dispelling the water with his snout while in the form of a boar, the lord dug up the earth like a lotus. Taking the form of a man-lion, he slew Hiraṇyakaśipu and other Dānavas led by Vipracitti. I cannot here enumerate all his *avatāras*, the dwarf and the rest, but now he has appeared as a man in Mathurā. In this way does the *sāttvika* form of Hari produce *avatāras*. Called Pradyumna, this form is bent upon acts of protection. It adopts a variety of natures—divine, human and animal—always according to the desire of Vāsudeva.

# The Twelve *Avatāras* of Viṣṇu

When the end of an Age rolls around and time has lost its strength, then lord Viṣṇu abandons his divine form to be born among men. When the gods and demons go to war, then Hari is born.

Long ago when the Daitya Hiraṇyakásipu ruled the triple world, and later when the three worlds were governed by Bali, there was real friendship between the gods and demons, who equally abided by the orders of these two rulers. But then the world became disordered, overrun with demons, and grievous and ferocious death-dealing war began between the demons and the gods who sought Bali's destruction.

When Bhṛgu cast his curse on both the gods and demons, Viṣṇu was born among men for the maintenance of Dharma. . . . There were in all twelve ferocious battles fought between the gods and demons over the shares of the sacrifice, from the battle of the Boar to the battle of Ṣaṇḍa and Marka. Hear now their designations.

First was the Man-Lion, second was the Dwarf, third was the Boar and fourth was the Churning of the Nectar. Fifth there was the battle of Tāraka, and the sixth was called Āḍīvaka, the Heron and the Crane. The seventh was over Tripura, the eighth dealt with Andhaka and the ninth was the killing of Vṛtra. Tenth came the battle of the Creator, eleventh, the Halāhala poison, and twelfth, the dreadful Kolāhala.

The demon Hiraṇyakaśipu was felled by the Man-Lion and Bali was captured by the Dwarf who traversed the triple world so long ago. Hiraṇyākṣa was slain in a duel when he fought with the celestials, and the Boar parted the ocean with his tusks. Prahlāda was defeated in battle by Indra at the churning of the ocean, and Virocana, Prahlāda's son, who was always trying to kill Indra, was slain in the Tāraka war when Indra attacked him with great courage. This Tāraka could never tolerate anything about the gods.

In the Andhaka battle, all the Dānavas in the triple world were slain by Tryambaka, and the demons and Piśācas were also destroyed. When the gods, humans and the Fathers were utterly annihilated, the awful Vṛtra was murdered in the Hālāhala battle, along with the demons. Vṛtra was checked by the mighty Indra who, accompanied by Viṣṇu and Vipracitta (who knew Yoga), and concealed by Māyā, penetrated the emblem on his flag during the Dhvaja battle, then killed him along with his younger brothers.

The bull and both Ṣaṇḍa and Marka were killed in the Kolāhala war at the concluding ceremony of the sacrifice after being surrounded by the gods, who were victorious over all the assembled Daityas and Dānavas. These are the twelve wars that took place between the gods and demons, wreaking havoc on gods and demons alike, for the benefit of creation.

# The Twenty-Two *Avatāras* of Viṣṇu

Nārāyaṇa is the only god, overlord of the gods, supreme soul and unequalled Brahman, "source of this world and everything in it."* For the protection of his creation, the unborn, undying Vāsudeva made various *avatāras,* such as the tortoise Kumāra and other forms.

The god Hari, first undertaking the tortoise creation, performed the difficult *brahmacarya* vow without interruption, O brahmin. Second, for the prosperity of the world, the lord of sacrifices took the form of a boar to raise up the earth, which had sunk to the netherworld Rasātala. Third, he poured forth the sages; becoming a divine seer himself, he produced the Sātvata doctrine, by virtue of which actions become free of their consequences. Fourth, worshiped by the gods and the demons, Hari performed *tapas,* having become Naranārāyaṇa for the protection of Dharma.

Fifth, as the lord of the Siddhas named Kapila, he proclaimed Sāṃkhya to the gods; this definitive account of the true principles of existence had been lost in the course of time. Sixth, as Atri, born of Anasūyā, he taught the school of Logic to Ālarka, Prahlāda and others. Then seventh, he was born in the Svāyambhuva Manvantara as the Sacrifice, son of Ruci and Ākūṭī, sacrificing with his truthful counselors, the hosts of the gods. Eighth, born of Nābhi and Merudevī, he was Urukrama, who showed the way to women that is honored in all stages of life. Solicited by the sages, ninth, he adopted the form of Pṛthu who milked from the earth the great herbs that strengthened the brahmins and other creatures.

Tenth, he took the form of a fish during the flood in the Cākṣusa Manvantara, rescuing Manu Vaivasvata from the waters with a boat which was earth. Eleventh, the lord in the form of a tortoise carried Mt. Mandara on his back to help the gods and demons who were churning the ocean. Twelfth, he took the form of Dhanvantari and, thirteenth, he nourished the gods by adopting the body of the

*Brahmasūtra I. i. 2.

woman Mohinī, who deluded the demons. Becoming Narasiṃha in the fourteenth *avatāra* he ripped apart the mighty Daitya chief as a plaiter of straw mats shreds his reeds. Fifteenth, as a little dwarf, he went to Bali's sacrifice and asked for three steps, planning to take the three worlds in return. In the sixteenth descent, angry at seeing kings hostile to brahmins, he rid the earth of kṣatriyas twenty-one times.

Then, in the seventeenth, he was born to Satyavatī and Parāśara; seeing the ignorance of mankind, he made branches on the tree which is the Veda. Having next become a man-god, out of desire to do a task for the gods, he subdued the ocean and did other chores as well. In the nineteenth and twentieth *avatāras,* he was born twice among the Vṛṣṇis as Rāma and Kṛṣṇa and in these forms he removed the burden from earth. Next, at the close of time's twilight, he will become the son of a Jina among the non-Āryans, named Buddha, in order to delude the foes of the gods. In the future, in the eighth twilight, when the kings have largely disappeared from earth, he will be born the son of Viṣṇuyaśas, as the lord of creation called Kalkin.

Innumerable are the *avatāras* of Hari, who contains the ocean of being, O twice-born ones! Those who know the Veda, the Manus and all the others are said to be portions of this same Viṣṇu. From them the various creatures are born; they are to be honored by means of vows and other observances.

# The *Avatāras* of Viṣṇu and the Story of Anasūyā

When lord Hari descended in order to annihilate the law of the Daityas and to preserve the law of the Vedas and other laws, he defended his own lineage and others as well. The unborn god assumed *avatāras,* or descents, in the form of the fish and other incarnations.

After becoming a fish and after killing the demon Hayagrīva, a thorn in battle, he brought forth the Vedas and protected the Manus and others. Becoming a tortoise for the well-being of the world, he held Mt. Mandara on his back. At the churning of the milk ocean he became Dhanvantari, the physician, who emerged carrying a jar filled with nectar. After relating the eight-limbed Āyurveda to Suśruta, he disguised himself as a woman and gave the nectar to the gods. Then, descending as a boar, he slew Hiraṇyākṣa, bore up the earth and rescued the deities. After killing the deceitful Hiraṇyakaśipu in the Man-

Lion *avatāra,* he protected the law of the Vedas and the other laws. Then the lord of creation became Paraśurāma, son of Jamadagni, in which form he rid the earth of kṣatriyas thrice seven times. Next he killed Kārtavīrya in battle and gave the earth to Kaśyapa. Having made a sacrifice, this long-armed Rāma retired to Mt. Mahendra.

Then, when Viṣṇu became the second Rāma, destroyer of the wicked, he was born four-fold from Daśaratha as Rāma, and as Rāma's younger brothers Bharata, Lakṣmaṇa and Śatrughna; Rāma's wife was Jānakī. Acting to preserve his father's honor and for the welfare of his mother, he went to Śṛngavera, Citrakūṭa, and the Daṇḍaka forest, where he cut off Śūrpanakhā's nose and slew the demon Kharadūṣaṇa, the night-ranger who had abducted Sītā. After making Rāvaṇa's younger brother Vibhīṣaṇa ruler over the city of Lankā, he left with the monkeys headed by Sugrīva and Hanumān. Riding on his chariot Puṣpaka and accompanied by the faithful Sītā, who was utterly devoted to her husband, Rāma returned to his own city Ayodhyā. There he ruled over gods and men, protected all creatures, upheld Dharma and performed the Horse Sacrifice and other great sacrifices. Rāma and his sweet wife, who was devoted to her lord, amused themselves there as they pleased. While Sītā stayed in Rāvaṇa's house without Rāghava, not in deed, thought or word did she turn to Rāvaṇa. She was as faithful to her husband as Anasūyā.

I will now relate the glorification of the faithful Sītā. Long ago in Pratiṣṭhāna there lived a leprous brahmin named Kauśika. Afflicted with disease, he was nevertheless treated like a god by his wife. Even when rebuked by her husband, she regarded him as a divinity. Once this faithful wife was ordered by her husband to take him to a prostitute and to bring along plenty of money. Meanwhile, a certain Māṇḍavya, mistaken for a thief, had been impaled on a stick for punishment and was in extreme pain. Jostled by the brahmin Kauśika, who was going on his way in the dark mounted on his wife's shoulders, and furious at being touched by someone's foot, Māṇḍavya cursed him, "Whoever has shoved me with his foot will die at sunrise!" When she heard this, his wife said, "Then the sun shall not rise!" And continuous night ensued because there was no dawn.

After many years had passed, the gods grew afraid and went to Brahma for help. The lotus-born god said to them, "*Tapas* is appeased by *tejas,* and *tejas* by *tapas.* The sun has not risen because of the majesty of this devoted wife! Because of this there will be continual privation among mortals and yourselves, the gods. Therefore you should placate the ascetic Anasūyā, the devoted wife of Atri!" Desiring dawn, the gods duly appeased the faithful Anasūyā who then made the sun rise again and revived her husband as well. And Sītā was a wife even more faithful than Anasūyā!

# Matsya, the Fish

Now hear, O brahmins, the ancient tale of Matsya, the Fish, which is holy, purifying and life-bestowing, as it was sung by the mace-bearer, Viṣṇu.

Long ago there was a patient king named Manu, son of the sun, practising abundant *tapas,* who gave his kingdom to his son. In a particular place in Malaya that hero, possessed of all the fine qualities of the self, to whom grief and joy were the same, attained supreme Yoga. After a million years had passed, the boon-giving Brahmā, whose seat is a lotus, was pleased with him and said, "Choose a boon!"

Thus addressed, the king bowed to the Grandfather and replied, "I want only one thing from you, the ultimate boon: make me the protector of all standing and moving creatures when the dissolution comes."

"So be it!" said the universal soul. And then and there he disappeared, while abundant showers of flowers thrown by the gods fell from the sky.

Once while that king was making water offerings to the Fathers in his hermitage, there fell into his hands along with the water a tiny fish. When he saw the little fish, that compassionate lord of earth carefully looked after it, trying to protect it in his bowl of water. In only one day and night that fish's body grew to the length of sixteen finger-breadths, and it cried out, "Save me! Rescue me!"

So the king took the fish and put it into a large pitcher, but even there it grew to the length of three hands overnight. Once again the fish cried out in anguish to the son of the thousand-rayed sun, "Save me! Save me! I have come to you for refuge!" So that son of the sun put the fish into a well, and when that also grew too small, he put it into a pond where it grew still larger until it was a league in length. The miserable fish cried out again, "Save me, save me, excellent king!"

But even after it was tossed into the Ganges river it continued to grow, so the king threw it into the sea where it filled the entire ocean. Then Manu became alarmed, and asked, "Are you some sort of demon, or are you Vāsudeva? How could you be anyone else, such as you are? Now I recognize you, the lord, in the form of a fish! O Keśava, you have fooled me indeed; O Hṛṣīkeśa, Jagannātha, Jagaddhāma, praise be to you!"

Thus praised, the lord Janārdana in the form of a fish said, "*Sādhu, sādhu!* O faultless one, you have recognized me. Soon, O king, the earth shall be flooded with water, with its mountains, trees and forests. A boat has been constructed by a group of all the gods in order to rescue the great aggregate of creatures, O lord of earth, those who are sweat-born, egg-born, plant-born and live-born. Put all these helpless creatures into the boat, O faithful one, and save them! When the boat is battered by the wind at the end of the Age, O king, fasten it to my horn, O chief of kings. Thus at the end of the dissolution of the world with its standing and moving beings you shall be Prajāpati, master of creatures on earth, O king. You shall be the all-knowing wise king at the start of the Kṛta Age, and you shall rule the Manvantara, worshiped by all the gods."

Thus addressed by Madhusūdana, Manu asked him, "O blessed one, how soon will this intermediary dissolution occur? And how, O guardian, shall I protect the creatures? And when shall we meet again, you and I, O Madhusūdana?"

"Beginning then," said the Fish, "there will be a drought on the surface of the earth lasting a full hundred years, and a brutal famine. Seven cruel rays of the sun will deal death to the weak, and there will be seven times seventy solar rays the color of fiery coals. At the close of the Age the submarine fire will blaze forth, and burning poison will flow from the mouth of Saṃkarṣaṇa in the netherworld, and also from the third eye of Bhava. The three worlds, aflame, will crumble, great seer, and the entire earth will be burned to ashes. Space will be scorched by the heat, O enemy-burner, and the world with its gods and constellations will be utterly annihilated.

"Seven rain clouds will bring destruction: Bhīmanāda (Awful Roar), Droṇa (Bucket), Caṇḍa (Cruel), Balāhaka (Thundercloud), Vidyutpatāka (Lightning Banner) and Śoṇa (Crimson). And as they flood the earth, clouds will form because of the fire, like sweat, and the turbulent oceans will merge together into a single sea. They will turn the entire triple world into one vast sheet of water.

"Then you must take the seeds of life from everywhere and load them into the boat of the Vedas. Fasten to it the rope I shall give you, O well-vowed one, and tie the boat to my horn. When even all the gods have been burned up, O enemy-burner, you alone shall survive, by my power, along with Soma, Sūrya, Brahmā and myself, and the four directions, the holy river Narmadā, the great seer Mārkaṇḍeya, Bhava, the Vedas, the Purāṇas and all the sciences. All of these, along with yourself, shall be saved when that vast ocean is all that is left in the dissolution at the end of the Cākṣusa Manvantara. At the start of the next creation, which you shall rule, I shall again promulgate the Vedas, O lord of earth." So speaking, the lord vanished on the spot.

Manu resorted to Yoga, by the grace of Vāsudeva, until the flood began, as prophesied. When the aforementioned time came, as Vāsudeva had said, Janārdana appeared in the form of a horned fish, and a serpent in the form of a rope approached Manu's side. The virtuous king collected all the creatures and loaded them into the boat, by Yoga. Then he fastened the boat to the fish's horn with the rope made of the snake. And prostrating himself before Janārdana, he stepped into the ship. . . .

Then in the midst of that vast flood, Manu asked Keśava, "Tell me at length the whole of Dharma, about the origin and dissolution of the world, about the lineages, genealogies and the Manvantaras, and the extent of the earth, about gifts, Dharma, rules, the eternal rituals of *śrāddha*, the divisions of caste and stage of life, the rites called *iṣṭa*, and *pūrta*, the fashioning of statues, about the gods and so on, and anything else found on earth. Tell me all this!"

So Vāsudeva replied, "At the end of the time of the great dissolution, the universe consisted of darkness, as if it were asleep, inconceivable, unknowable, without characteristics of any kind. The world with its standing and moving creatures was unknown and unknowable. Then the unmanifest, self-existent Svayambhū, the origin of good deeds, appeared in order to make manifest all this, by dispelling the darkness. He who is beyond what is manifest, both infinite and infinitesimal, eternal, known by the name of Nārāyaṇa, appeared alone, all by himself. Desiring to pour forth the manifold world from his body, he set his mind on the task. He emitted the waters and put his seed into them. Then a huge golden egg appeared that shone like ten thousand suns for a thousand years. That splendid being who was himself his own origin entered inside the egg and became Viṣṇu, pervading it by virtue of his own power. Inside the egg the lord became the sun, which is called Āditya, because it was first, long ago. And then he became Brahmā because he recited the Brahman, the Veda. He made heaven and earth from the two halves of the egg, made all the directions, and put the sky in the middle for all time. The after-birth became the mountains, with Mt. Meru as the chief mountain. The membrane became the clouds, and the umbilical cord, the lightning. Rivers, called eggs, appeared, as well as the Fathers and the Manus. The seven seas flowed from the water inside the egg: Lavaṇa (Salt), Ikṣu (Sugar cane), Surā (Wine) and the rest, filled with various jewels.

"O foe-conqueror, the god Prajāpati desired to create, and so Mārtaṇḍa, the sun-god, arose from his brilliance. Because he was born as the egg died, he is called Mārtaṇḍa, the Dead Egg. The body of this great-souled being, which consists of the *guṇa* called *rajas*, became the four-faced lord Brahmā, Grandfather of the world. Know that this *rajas* body, from which the whole world was poured forth, with its gods, demons and human beings, is called the Great Being."

# Kūrma, the Tortoise

I shall relate the tortoise *avatāra* that destroys the sins of those who hear it. Long ago, in the battle between the gods and the Asuras, the gods were defeated by the Daityas. Because of Durvaśas' curse they became bereft of good fortune. Praising Viṣṇu who had gone to the ocean of milk, they said, "Protect us from the demons!"

Hari replied to Brahmā and the other gods, "Make a compact with the Asuras to churn the milky ocean for the nectar that will restore your good fortune, O gods. One should treat with one's enemies when something important is to be done. I shall see to it that *you* drink the nectar, not the Dānavas. Using Mt. Mandara as a churning stick and the snake Vāsuki as a rope, unflaggingly churn the milk ocean, with my help."

After making the agreement with the Daityas that Viṣṇu had advised, the gods went to the ocean of milk and taking Vāsuki's tail, began to churn. When heated by the serpent's breath, the gods were invigorated by Hari. Because the unsupported mountain sank down into the water as they stirred up the sea, Viṣṇu took the form of a tortoise and held Mt. Mandara on his back. From the milky ocean that was being churned in this way arose the poison Halāhala. Hara took it into his throat, and because of this his throat turned blue. Then the goddess Vāruṇī came forth, followed by the coral tree Pārijāta, the jewel Kaustubha, cows, celestial Apsarases and the goddess Lakṣmī, who went to Hari. Seeing and praising her, all the gods regained their good fortune.

Then Viṣṇu arose as Dhanvantari, the promulgator of the Āyurveda, holding a jar filled with nectar. The Daityas took the nectar from his grasp and gave half of it to the gods. When Jambha and the other demons had taken it, Viṣṇu assumed a female form.

When they saw a beautiful woman appear, the deluded Daityas said, "Please be our wife, fair-faced one! Bring the nectar and give it to us to drink!" Agreeing to this, Hari took the nectar from the demons and gave it to the gods to drink instead.

Pretending to be the moon, one demon, Rāhu, was exposed by the sun and the moon while he drank the nectar; whereupon Hari cut off his head. This head, now separate, became immortal through the nectar's grace. So Rāhu spoke to boon-granting Hari, "Let the sun and the moon undergo eclipses because of me!" Thus Rāhu became the cause of eclipses; gifts given at such times are inexhaustible.

"So be it," said Viṣṇu with all the immortals as he left the woman's body. Then when Hara said "Show it to me!" lord Hari exhibited his female form to Rudra. Fooled by this trick and abandoning Gaurī, Śaṃbhu went after the woman. Naked and crazy-looking, he grabbed the woman's hair. She shook herself loose and fled, with Hara in pursuit. Wherever Hara's semen spilled on the earth there appeared a sacred place of *lingas* which are as good as gold. After Hara had recognized her to be an illusion and had resumed his own form, Hari said to Śiva, "Rudra, you have seen through my deception. There is no other person on earth but you who can conquer it!"

Then the Daityas who had been deprived of the nectar were felled by the gods in battle and the deities went to live in heaven. Whoever recites this story will also go to heaven.

# Varāha, the Boar

At the end of the last Eon when the tempest of time began, the forest trees were uprooted, the fire god burned the three worlds as if they were straw, the earth was flooded with rain and the oceans overflowed. While all the regions were sunk in vast sheets of water and the waters of destruction had begun their ferocious dances, leaping with fish and undulating with circular, arm-like waves, Brahmā as Nārāyaṇa slept peacefully in the sea. . . .

The Siddhas who lived in Janaloka, folding their hands in prayer and singing hymns, awoke the lord of the thirty gods who lay in Yogic sleep as he concentrated on Śiva, just as the Śrutis awoke the lord at the beginning of creation, long ago. Waking up and rising from his bed in the middle of the water, his eyes cloudy with Yogic sleep, the lord looked in all directions. He saw nothing whatsoever but himself! Sitting up like one bewildered, he grew deeply concerned, thinking, "Where is that lovely lady, the broad earth, with her many lofty mountains, her streams, towns and forests?" Worrying this way, Brahmā could nowhere spy the earth.

Then he called to mind his father, the lord with three eyes. Because he remembered Bhava, the god of gods with infinite splendor, the lord of the world realized that the earth was immersed in the sea. Wanting to rescue earth, Prajāpati thought of the heavenly form of the boar with a body like a mighty mountain, who delighted in water-play. This boar was terrifying, making a hissing noise like a big black cloud, booming forth with a dreadful sound. His trunk was round, fat and firm, his hips high and full, his shank-ends short and rounded, his snout sharply pointed. Red as a ruby were his horrible round eyes; his body was long and tubular with shining stiff little ears, curvaceous in trunk and cheek; he was covered with a fine, waving mane of hair.

The ocean of Doomsday was roiled up by the heavy panting of this boar, who was adorned with gems, ornaments and glittering jewelry, shining like lofty piles of clouds filled with lightning. Having assumed this vast, infinite, boar-like shape, the lord entered the netherworld in order to raise up the earth. There this mountainous boar blazed forth as radiantly as if he had gone to the foot of Maheśa's mountain, which is shaped like the *linga*.

Then the earth-upholder dug up the earth which was sunk in the sea and emerged from the netherworld holding it on his tusks. When they saw him, the inhabitants of Janaloka, the seers and Siddhas, rejoiced and danced, showering his head with flowers. The mighty boar's body covered with flowers was as beautiful as a mountain of antimony alive with fireflies on the wing.

When the boar had brought the great earth to its proper place, he returned to his own form and stabilized it. Aligning the earth, the lord piled up the mountains and fashioned the four worlds and all the rest, just as it had been before. Thus having rescued the great earth from the middle of the vast ocean of dissolution, Viśvakarman once more poured forth creation with its moving and unmoving beings.

## Narasiṃha, the Man-Lion

Hiraṇyakaśipu was overcome with rage and grief when his brother was killed by Hari in the form of a boar, O Vyāsa. Happily feuding with Hari, he directed the heroic Asuras, who themselves loved bloodshed, to sow destruction among creatures. When they received on their heads the command of their master, these murderous demons began to slaughter creatures and gods. When earth herself was wounded by these evil-minded Asuras, the gods left heaven and roamed the earth unseen. Mourning his dead brother, Hiraṇyakaśipu performed the water offerings for him and comforted his wife and family.

This leader of the kings of the Daityas wanted to make himself the only sovereign, unconquerable, immortal, undecaying, without an equal. In order to do so he performed the highest degree of *tapas* with only his big toe touching the ground, his arms raised aloft, his eyes on the sky. While he was doing this *tapas,* the powerful gods defeated all the other Daityas and resumed their proper places in heaven. Then a smoking fire born of Hiraṇyakaśipu's *tapas* arose from his head and spread in all directions, burning the worlds across, above and below. Scorched by this fire, their faces grimacing from the heat, the gods abandoned heaven and went to Brahmaloka, where they reported to the creator. Then, O Vyāsa, instructed by these gods, the self-existent creator went to the hermitage of the Daitya lord, accompanied by Bhṛgu, Dakṣa and the other seers. Having set fire to all the worlds, the demon saw the lotus-born god approaching. To reward him for his *tapas,* the Grandfather said, "Choose a boon." Hearing the gracious words of the creator, the Daitya replied, his mind clear, "O god, lord, lord of creatures, Grandfather, let me never be killed by these means: the striking and throwing weapons of my enemies, thunderbolts, dried tree-trunks, high mountains, by water or fire. Let me be free from the threat of death from gods, Daityas, seers, Siddhas and whatever other beings you have created. But why go on? Let me not be slain in heaven, on earth, in the daytime, at night, from neither above nor below, O lord of creatures!"

When he heard this speech, the god whose womb is the lotus mentally praised Viṣṇu and replied with compassion, "I am indeed pleased with you, lord of the Daityas. You shall have all this. Enough of *tapas!* For 96,000 years your desires will be fully satisfied. Arise and resume your sovereignty of the Dānavas!" When he heard these words, Hiraṇyakaśipu's face grew content. Consecrated as king by the Grandfather, he put his mind to the destruction of the three worlds. Having destroyed all Dharmas, the wanton demon likewise conquered all the gods in battle. Then, out of fear, all the gods led by Indra who were oppressed by the Daitya chief conferred with the wise Grandfather and went to the ocean of milk where Hari lay. After propitiating Viṣṇu effusively with laudatory speech, thinking of him as a savior, they all told the gracious god of their great unhappiness. Satisfied that he had heard the full extent of their suffering, Lakṣmī's husband granted their wish. Arising from his bed, Upendra whose splendor equals Vaiśvānara's, comforted all the gods and seers and spoke at length to them with words befitting his nature, "I will kill the Daitya by force, O lords of gods. You may return home satisfied!"

When they heard what Lakṣmī's consort had said, the lords of gods, Indra and the others, were all very pleased. They went to their homes, lord of seers, thinking that Hiraṇyanetra's younger brother was already dead.

Viṣṇu then assumed a hairy form like both man and lion. It had widely gaping jaws, ferocious fangs, sharp claws, a fine snout, shining most horribly like a *koṭi* of suns, blazing forth like the fire of time at the end of the Age—but why go on? At sunset the great-souled lord went to the city of the Asuras. Doing battle with the mighty Daityas, he seized the demon hosts and killed them. This Man-Lion roamed about the city showing supernatural valor and shattering demons. When the Daityas saw his matchless might, they all panicked. Observing that lion of universal form, Prahlāda, the son of the Daitya lord, said to the king, "Why has this cosmic king of beasts come here? The everlasting lord god in the shape of a man-lion has entered your city. Turn back from battle and seek refuge in him! I see the gaping mouth of this lion whom no one can oppose in the three worlds! Act like a king and bow down to this lord of beasts!"

Hearing his son's speech, the evil-souled king replied, "Why are you so afraid, my son?" So speaking, the eminent hero among the bulls of the Daityas cried out, "Heroes, seize that lion with the contorted grimacing face!" So at his command, the best of the Daityas approached the beast in order to capture it. But they were instantly scorched, like moths nearing fire, attracted by its beauty. After the Daityas has been burned, their king himself entered the battle against the lord of beasts using all manner of striking and throwing weapons: spears, javelins, nooses, elephant hooks, fire and other means. While the two of them fought, sword in hand, with heroic outcries, most virile, their minds fixed in fury at each other, a day of Brahmā passed.

Suddenly the Daitya sprouted multiple arms, each with a sword, and attacked the Man-Lion who was fighting ferociously with him. Engaging in an unendurable battle with various striking and throwing weapons, the chief of the Daityas, carrying a spear, swiftly rushed at the Man-Lion after the weapons he threw had come to naught. Seizing the demon Hiraṇyakaśipu with his many arms hard as mountains, he threw him across his knees, and with his shoot-like claws ripped apart the tender belly of the Dānava between his arms. When the lion's claws had rent the lotus of his heart, the demon instantly dropped dead, like a log, his limbs thoroughly mangled.

After the enemy of the gods had been destroyed, the gracious Viṣṇu welcomed Prahlāda, who bowed before him. The wonderful heroic Viṣṇu consecrated him king of the Daityas and went on his incomprehensible way. All the lords of gods, the Grandfather and the others, were very happy, O brahmin. Bowing there to Viṣṇu, the blessed lord most worthy of praise who had accomplished his task, they went home.

# Aditi and the Birth of Vāmana, the Dwarf

Aditi said: "O god, if you who are loyal to your followers look with favor upon me, your devotee, then restore my son Vāsava as lord of the three worlds! He has been deprived of his kingdom and of his share of the sacrifice by the demons; now let my son regain all this through your kindness, O giver of boons."

The lord replied: "The favor you wish shall be granted, O goddess. After the tortoise *avatāra* I will enter your womb with a portion of myself that will be fathered by Kaśyapa. After growing in your womb, I will destroy your enemies. Be happy again!"

Aditi replied: "Have mercy on me, lord of the gods of gods! Praise be to you, creator of all things! I will not be able to bear you, lord, upholder of the universe, in my belly. You yourself, O lord, are the womb of the world." The blessed one answered: "I will carry both you and myself, O happy woman, and I will do you no injury. Good luck to you; I am now leaving." So speaking, the god disappeared, and Aditi conceived.

While Kṛṣṇa lay in her womb, the entire earth trembled, the mountains quaked and the mighty oceans roiled. Wherever Aditi walked, wherever she put her fine footstep, there the earth shrank in pain, O bulls of the twice-born. While Madhusūdana lay in her womb, all the Daityas lost their power, as had been predicted by Parameṣṭhin.

When he saw the Asuras deprived of their strength, the Lord of the demons, Bali himself, asked his grandfather Prahlāda, "Why have these Daityas lost their vigor, as though consumed by fire or struck down by Brahmā's staff? What curse is upon the Daityas? What hex has been laid by fate upon the demons for their destruction so that they have been made powerless?" Thus questioned by his grandson, the foremost Asura pondered for a long time, O brahmins, and then said this to the demon Bali: "The mountains sway, the earth has suddenly lost its firmness and at the same time the oceans are stirred up and the Daityas are deprived of their strength. What can be the cause of this?" . . .

Putting his mind on the path of meditation, the demon Prahlāda concentrated on the god Janārdana. He saw the shape of Vāmana in Aditi's belly, and inside him, the Vasus, Rudras, Aśvins and Maruts; the Sādhyas, the Viśvedevas and the Ādityas; the Gandharvas, Snakes and Rākṣasas. He saw Virocana and his son Bali, chief of the demons; Jambha, Kujambha, Naraka, Bāṇa and the other Asuras; himself, earth, sky, wind, rain, fire, oceans, mountains, rivers, continents, pools, animals and land; birds, creeping creatures and all mankind. He saw the creation of the whole world, Brahmā and Bhava, the planets, constellations and the Prajāpatis, Dakṣa and the others.

Filled with wonder at seeing this, Prahlāda returned at once to normal and spoke to the Daitya lord Bali, Virocana's son: "I know now why your power was lost. Hear all about it! The god of gods, the womb of the world who himself comes from no womb, the first-born of creation who himself has no beginning, the first of everything, the desirable, boon-granting Hari, most excellent of all beings far and near, goal of the high and low, measure of measures, teacher of teachers in the seven worlds, Jagannātha, the unknowable, has become an embryo to uphold the world and support it. . . . This great-souled god, O mighty demon, is the womb of the world. With a sixteenth part of himself he has entered the womb of the mother of the chief of the gods and by doing this has stolen the strength from your bodies." . . .

Aditi got her wish, the fruit of all she desired, as the famous god grew gradually in her belly. Then in the tenth month when the time for his birth had come, lord Govinda was born in the form of the dwarf Vāmana. When this lord of the universe, Jagannātha, descended, the gods were freed from suffering as was Aditi, mother of the gods. Breezes blew, pleasant to the touch; the sky grew clear of dust, and mindfulness of Dharma was born in all beings.

# Vāmana, the Dwarf, and Bali

When Bali saw the earth with its mountains and forests shaking, he prostrated himself before Śukra-Uśanas with folded hands and said, "O teacher, the earth covered with oceans and mountains is trembling! Why do the Fires refuse the Asuras' offerings?" The great-minded Kāvya, best among these who know the Veda, pondered Bali's question for a long time before he answered the foremost Daitya lord. "The eternal Hari, the supreme soul, womb of the world, has descended in the form of a dwarf into the house of Kaśyapa.

Surely he is coming to your sacrifice, bull of the Dānavas! The earth quakes with the tread of his feet, the mountains shake and the dwelling places of the great fish are disturbed. The earth cannot support the lord, the master of creatures! Gods, demons, Gandharvas, Yakṣas, Rākṣasas and Snakes, the earth, waters, fire, wind and sky are all held up by him alone. He supports all the gods, demons and human beings. Because he is nearby, the god's enemies, the demons, are not entitled to their shares of the sacrifice. Because of him the three fires refuse the Asuras' offerings." . . .

After a while Janārdana, who consists of all the gods, assumed the body of a dwarf by illusion and arrived at Bali's sacrifice. When they saw the lord enter the sacrificial enclosure, the Asuras were shaken by his appearance, their splendor overshadowed by his. Those who had gathered at the great sacrificial site, Vasiṣṭha, Gadhi's son Viśvāmitra, Garga and the other excellent seers, began to say prayers under their breath. Bali thought that his whole life had suddenly borne fruit and none of the trembling seers dared to say a thing. One by one they worshiped the overlord of the gods with all their might. When he saw the master of the demons and the finest seers bowing before him, Viṣṇu, lord god of the gods, in the form of a dwarf, himself praised the sacrifice, the Fire, the sacrificer, the ritual acts, the officiants, the celebrants and all the offerings. The brahmin sacrificial attendants cried out, "*Sādhu! Sādhu!*" to Vāmana, who had appeared before them in the sacrificial enclosure, a vessel wholly worthy of their honor. Holding out the hospitality gift of water, the great Asura Bali thrilled to the worship of Govinda and said, "I shall give you this pile of gold and jewels, these herds of elephants and horses, women, clothes, ornaments, cows and many villages. All these and the entire earth as well I shall give to you. Take whatever you desire; my dearest possessions are yours!"

Thus addressed by the Daitya chief, lord Viṣṇu in the form of a dwarf spoke words filled with affection in a deep, smiling voice, "Give me three paces of land for a fire-altar, O king. Give the gold, villages, jewels and the rest to others who want them."

"What good are only three steps, best of striders? You should ask for a hundred or a hundred thousand steps!"

"I am content with only this much, lord of the Daityas. Give your wealth to other supplicants as you see fit."

When he heard this reply, Bali ordered recitations for the great-souled dwarf. As the hospitality water fell into his hand, Vāmana shed his dwarf-life shape. In the twinkling of an eye he manifested the form which consists of all the gods. His eyes were the moon and the sun; the sky was his head and the earth his feet. His toes were the Piśācas and his fingers the Guhyakas. The Viśvedevas were in his knees and the excellent deities, the Sādhyas, were in his shins. In his nails appeared the Yakṣas and in the contours of his body, the Apsarases. All the Pleiades were the lord's eyes, the rays of the sun the hairs of his head, the stars the pores of his skin and the great seers the hairs of his body. His arms were the intermediate directions, and the principal directions were in the great-souled one's two ears. In his hearing lay the Aśvins, and the wind was in the nose of that great-souled god. . . . All the luminaries and supreme *tapas* appeared as the splendor of this foremost god of gods. In the cavities of his body lay the Vedas, and his knees were the great sacrifices, the offerings, the cattle and the ritual acts of the brahmins. When they saw the divine form of the great-souled Viṣṇu, the Daityas crept closer like moths approaching a flame. The great demon Cikṣusa bit him on the big toe, and Hari kicked him in the neck with it. When the lord had driven off all the demons with the palms of his hands and soles of his feet, assuming a gigantic body, he quickly made off with the earth. As he stepped across the earth, the sun and moon were in the center of his chest. As he bestrode the sky, they sank to the region of his thighs. When he took his ultimate step, the sun and moon lay at the base of his knees. Thus Viṣṇu performed the task of protecting the gods.

After he had won the three worlds and had slain the bulls of demons, the masterful, blessed lord, wide-striding Viṣṇu, gave the triple world to Indra, sacker of cities, and to Bali, the netherworld named Sutala, below the surface of the earth. . . . When he had given this boon to Bali and given Śakra his heaven, Hari vanished from sight in his form as all-pervader. And so Indra ruled the three worlds as of old and Bali remained in the netherworld for all time. . . .

> The brahmin learns the Veda;
> The kṣatriya conquers earth;
> The vaiśya wins wealth and prosperity;
> The śūdra gains happiness.

Whoever hears the glory of Vāmana is released from all evil.

## Paraśurāma, Rāma with the Axe

What was that trouble that the lord had with the rājanyas* who had not mastered themselves, so that he repeatedly destroyed the race of

*Kṣatriyas.

kṣatriyas? Arjuna, overlord of the Haihayas, bull of the kṣatriyas, propitiated Dattātreya, a portion of Nārāyaṇa, along with his attendants. In return he received a thousand arms, invincibility before his foes, the force of invincible strength, unflagging faculties, wealth, brilliance, heroism, fame, strength, and mastery of Yoga, the power that includes the ability to become infinitesmal and so on. With these gifts he moved through the world, his way unhindered like the wind. . . .

Once while ranging in a forest grove on a hunt he happened to enter the hermitage of Jamadagni. The seer, whose wealth was *tapas,* respectfully offered hospitality to that god among men, along with his army, his counsellors and their mounts, using the products of his sacrificial cow. Covetous of that cow, which he judged to exceed his own fortune in value, that Haihaya hero thought disparagingly of his own wealth. Out of arrogance he ordered his men to capture the sage's sacrificial cow, and they led her forcibly away with her calf to Mahiṣmatī, while she bellowed piteously.

When the king had gone, Rāma arrived at his father's hermitage. When he heard about this wickedness he became as mad as a stepped-on snake. Taking up his dreadful battle-axe, bow, quiver and shield, that invincible hero pursued the king like a lion on the trail of a bull-elephant. As he was entering his own city, the king saw Rāma, best of the Bhṛgus, approaching with his bow, arrows and axe, clothed in deer-skin, with matted hair that shone like the splendor of the sun. At this the king sent out seventeen formidable battalions complete with elephants, chariots, horses, and infantry carrying clubs, swords, arrows, javelins, iron-spiked missiles and spears. But lord Rāma butchered them all by himself. Wherever he attacked—that battle-axe wielding killer, destroyer of the army of his foes, with strength swift as the speed of thought or the wind—there did his enemies fall to earth, their mounts and charioteers slain, their arms, thighs and necks severed.

When he saw his own army felled, the battlefield mired in rivers of their gore, their shields, banners, bows and bodies sundered by the axe and missiles of Rāma, the Haihaya himself attacked in fury. With his thousand arms Arjuna nocked to his bows five hundred arrows simultaneously, but Rāma, chief of the arms-bearers, cut them all off at the same time with his single bow and arrow. Further, uprooting mountains and trees with his own hands in the fray, he cut off with his sharp axe the arms of his enemy who was attacking violently, as if they were the heads of a many-hooded cobra, and cut off the head of that armless trunk like the top of a mountain. When their father died, his myriad sons fled in terror.

Rescuing the aggrieved cow with her calf, the foe-killing Rāma returned to the hermitage and restored her to his father, describing to his father and brothers the feat he had accomplished. When he had heard the story, Jamadagni spoke, "O Rāma, well-armed Rāma, you have committed a sin! You have willfully killed the man-god who consists of all the gods! We brahmins have become meritorious by dint of our forbearance; by this too has the god who is the *guru* of the world achieved his position as Parameṣṭhin. It is through forbearance that Brahmā's good fortune shines forth like the sun, and the blessed lord Hari is soon pleased with the forgiving. Now the murder of a consecrated king is graver even than the killing of a brahmin! Come now! Expiate your guilt by making a tour of the sacred fords with unflagging spirit! Thus admonished by his father, O delight of the Kurus, Rāma said "So be it!" and made a year's pilgrimage, after which he returned to the hermitage.

Reṇukā, who had gone to the river Ganges, happened to see the king of the Gandharvas, wreathed in lotuses, cavorting with the Apsarases. Watching their sport, Reṇukā, who had gone to the river for water, became rather enamored of King Citraratha and forgot the time for sacrifice. Noticing the lapse of time and afraid of the seer's curse, she returned home. Putting the water-jar before her husband, she stood there with folded hands. The angry seer, knowing of his wife's lapse, said "Children, kill this wicked woman!" Though ordered, they did not do so. But Rāma, fully aware of the power of the *tapas* and *samādhi** of that seer, killed both his mother and his brothers when commanded by his father. Well pleased, the son of Satyavatī gratified him in turn with a boon. Rāma chose that his dead kin return to life and that he forget having killed them. At once they rose up, alert as though waking from sleep. Thus did Rāma slay his beloved relatives, knowing the might of his father's *tapas*.

Meanwhile the sons of Arjuna who had been humbled by Rāma could find no rest, remembering their father's murder. Once, finding an opportunity when Rāma had gone into the forest with his brothers, they arrived at the hermitage intent on revenge. They saw the seer sitting in the hut of the sacrificial fire, with his mind fixed on the blessed lord whose honor is supreme. Bent on evil, they killed him. Although implored by the pitiable mother of Rāma, the cruel kṣatriyas forcibly cut off his head and carried it away. The noble Reṇukā, smitten with sorrow and anguish, beat herself and cried aloud, "O Rāma, Rāma, my son!" When he heard this sorrowful cry, "Woe, Rāma!" from some distance in the woods, he hastily made for

*Concentration on the supreme spirit.

the hermitage where he saw his father dead. Distraught with sorrow, anger, impatience, pain, grief and shock, he too cried out, "Alas, my father, *sādhu*, most noble one! You have gone to heaven, abandoning us here!" Lamenting thus and having laid out his father in the presence of his brothers, Rāma took up his battle-axe, determined to put an end to the kṣatriyas.

Rāma then went to Mahiṣmatī, whose prosperity had been ruined by the brahmin-killers, O king, and raised in the middle of the city a huge mountain of their heads. Making the river run red with their blood, terrifying those brahmin-haters, he used his father's murder as motivation for wreaking havoc on the kṣatriyas. Expunging the kṣatriyas from the earth twenty-one times, the lord filled nine lakes in Samantapañcaka with their blood.

Joining his father's head to his body, he placed it on sacrificial grass and offered up sacrifices to himself as the god who consists of all gods. He gave the east to the *hotar* priest; the south to the *brahman*, the west to the *adhvaryu* and the north to the *udgātar*. The intermediate directions he gave to the other priests; to Kaśyapa the center, Āryāvarta to the *upadraṣṭar** and other places to the *sadasyas*. Thereafter, all his guilts washed away by the *avabhṛtha* ceremony in Brahmā's river (the Sarasvatī), he shone forth like the radiant sun in a cloudless sky.

Thus worshiped by Rāma, Jamadagni regained his well-marked body and became the seventh in the circle of the Seven Seers. And in the forthcoming Manvantara, Jamadagni's son, the blessed lotus-eyed Paraśurāma, will accomplish a mighty deed. At present, having relinquished his weapons, he sits on Mt. Mahendra with mind composed, his feats hymned by the Siddhas, Gandharvas and Cāraṇas. Thus the blessed lord Hari, soul of the universe, descended among the Bhṛgus, repeatedly slew the kings, and lifted earth's ultimate burden.

## Rāma in the Rāmāyaṇa

Now I shall relate the Rāmāyaṇa, the hearing of which effaces evil.

Brahmā arose in the lotus which sprang from Viṣṇu's navel; his son was Marīci. From Marīci was born Kaśyapa, whose son was Ravi. From Ravi came Manu, so it is remembered, and from Manu,

*Lit. "spectator," an attendant brahmin who watches but does not participate in the ritual.

Ikṣvāku, in whose lineage was born a king called Raghu. Aja was Raghu's son and the father of Daśaratha, who had four mighty and courageous sons. To his wife Kausalyā was born Rāma; Bharata was the son of Kaikeyī; and sons Lakṣmaṇa and Śatrughna were both born to Sumitrā.

Devoted to his father and mother, Rāma was given a store of weapons by Viśvāmitra, with which he slew the Yakṣī called Tāḍaka, a murderess. During Viśvāmitra's sacrifice the mighty Rāma killed Subāhu. Going to Janaka's sacrifice, he took his daughter Jānakī for his wife. The hero Lakṣmaṇa wed Urmilā; Bhārata and Śatrughna married the two daughters of Kuśadhvaja, Māṇḍavī and Kīrtimatī. Rāma and others went to Ayodhyā to be near their fathers and kin while Śatrughna and Bhārata went to live with their maternal uncle, Yudhajit.

During the absence of these two brothers, the eminent king Daśaratha prepared to give the kingdom to his noble son Rāma. But the king's wife Kaikeyī demanded that Rāma spend fourteen years in the forest instead, and that her son Bharata be put on the throne. For his father's welfare Rāma abandoned his reign as if it were straw, and went to Śṛngavera accompanied by his brother Lakṣmaṇa and his wife Sītā. Leaving behind his chariot, he went to Prayāga and Mt. Citrakūṭa. Meanwhile, grieving over the loss of Rāma, king Daśaratha went to heaven. After performing his father's funeral rites, the powerful Bharata went to Rāma and said, "Return to Ayodhyā, great-minded one, and be king!" Declining this request, Rāma departed, giving his sandals to Bhārata as a sign of his sovereignty. Thus dismissed, Bharata protected Rāma's kingdom in his stead. Remaining in Nandīgrāma and keeping his vow, the devoted Bharata did not return to Ayodhyā.

Meanwhile, Rāma went from Citrakūṭa to the hermitage of Atri. Bowing to Sutīkṣṇa and Agastya, he went next to the Daṇḍaka forest where a demoness named Śūrpanakhā had come to feed. Rejecting her advances, Rāma cut off her ears and nose and sent her away. In retaliation she sent the demons Kharadūṣana and Triśiras who appeared with a company of Rākṣasas 14,000 strong. But Rāma sent them to Yama's city with his arrows. Then Rāvaṇa himself came to the forest, sent by the demoness, to abduct Sītā. After having first transformed Marīci into a deer, he himself appeared in the guise of a beggar carrying a triple staff. Urged by Sītā, Rāma killed Marīci who cried out in Rāma's voice as he died, "O Sītā, O Lakṣmaṇa!" Implored by Sītā, Lakṣmaṇa then went to his brother's rescue. When Rāma saw his brother, he cried out, "This is a demon's trick! Sītā has been kidnapped!" The mighty Rāvaṇa lying in wait nearby took Jānakī on his lap, stabbed the bird Jaṭāyu and sped off to Lankā where he kept her guarded in a grove of *aśoka* trees. When Rāma returned, he found his leaf hut empty.

After performing the funeral rites for Jaṭāyu, Rāma went south as the bird had directed, searching for Jānakī in sorrow. There Rāghava* made friends with the monkey Sugrīva. After piercing seven palm trees with his smoothed arrow, and after killing Sugrīva's enemy, his brother Bali, he made Sugrīva king of the monkeys in Kiṣkindhyā and he himself went to live on Mt. Ṛśyamūka. Sugrīva summoned the great and mighty mountain monkeys to look for Sītā in all directions. After searching fruitlessly in the west, north and east, they returned and set off toward the south, seeking Jānakī. Scouring the forests, mountains, continents, rivers and seashores without finding her, the monkeys resolved to die.

Hanumān, however, elephant among monkeys, knowing what the bird Saṃpāti had said, jumped across the hundred-league-wide abode of the great fish to Lankā. There he spied Jānakī lying in a grove of *aśoka* trees, abused by the Rākṣasīs† and the demon Rāvaṇa who kept saying, "Be my wife!" Giving to Sītā, who thought only of her husband, a finger ring of Rāghava's, the monkey asked after her welfare.

"I am Rāma's messenger, Maithilī; grieve no more! Give me some token of yours by which Rāma will remember you."

Hearing this, Sītā gave Hanumān an ornament from her hair, saying, "Tell Rāma to fetch me quickly!" Saying "So be it!", Hanumān demolished that enchanting grove of trees, killed Akṣa and other demons, and broke up that captivating divine grove of trees. Captured in turn by the many arrows of Indrajit, the monkey faced Rāvaṇa and said, "I am Rāma's messenger Hanumān. Give Maithilī back to Rāma!" Enraged at hearing this, Rāvaṇa set Hanumān's tail on fire. Tail ablaze, the mighty monkey then set fire to the city. When he had burned up Lankā, and after stopping to eat fruit in a honey forest, Hanumān returned to Rāma's side to report, "Sītā has been found!" And he gave Rāma her hair ornament.

So Rāma set off for the city of Lankā with Sugrīva, Hanumān, Angada and the other monkeys, and his brother Lakṣmaṇa. Rāvaṇa's younger brother Vibhīṣaṇa, however, took refuge with Rāghava, who consecrated him king of Lankā. With Nala's help, Rāma built a causeway in the sea to carry him across the water. Sitting down on the shore, he observed the city of Lankā. Then these monkey heroes

*Patronymic of Rāma.
†Female Rākṣasas.

Nīla, Angada, Nala and others, Dhūmra, Dhūmrākṣa and Vīrendra led by Jambavat, Maindra and Dvivida—all these attacked the city of Lankā and its demons, who had huge bodies like mountains of black collyrium.

Rāma, along with Lakṣmaṇa and the monkeys, killed all the Rākṣasas: Vidyujjihva (Lightning-Tongue), Dhūmrākṣa (Smoke-Eye), Narāntaka (Death-to-Men), Mahodara (Big-Belly), Mahāpārśva (Great-Flank), the powerful Atikāya (Giant), Kumbha (Water-Jar) and Nikumbha, Matta (Crazy), Makarākṣa (Fish-Eye) and Akampana (Never-Trembling), the mad hero Prahasta (Fore-Arm) and the mighty Kumbhakarṇa (Pot-Ear). Lakṣmaṇa and the powerful Rāghava cut down Rāvaṇa's son with throwing weapons and others. Splitting the protecting circle of arms, Rāma felled Rāvaṇa. Recapturing the pure Sītā, Rāma took off in the chariot Puṣpaka for the fine city of Ayodhyā, along with the monkeys, where he became king at last, protecting all creatures as though they were his sons.

After performing ten Horse Sacrifices, having ceremonially dropped the *piṇḍas* for his ancestors at Gayaśiras and having liberally given gifts, Rāghava found his two sons Kuśa and Lava in the hermitage and consecrated their sovereignty. So Rāma ruled in this way for 11,000 years. . . . Thus accomplishing his purpose, he went to heaven along with all the citizens of Ayodhyā.

# Kṛṣṇa in the Mahābhārata

Now I shall relate the Bhārata story that describes how Kṛṣṇa removed earth's burden by fighting for the cause of the Pāṇḍavas and others.

Brahmā was born from the lotus navel of Viṣṇu. Brahmā's son was Atri, whose son was Soma. Budha was Soma's son, and from him by his wife Urvaśī was born Purūravas, whose son was Āyus. Yayāti, Bharata, Kuru and Śantanu were born in the lineage of Āyus, and the son of Śantanu by Gangā was Bhīṣma, full of virtues, learned in the various manifestations of Brahmā. To Śantanu and Satyavatī were born two sons, Citrāngada, who was killed by a Gandharva of the same name, and Vicitravīrya, who was the husband of the daughters of the king of Kāśī. When Vicitravīrya went to heaven, Vyāsa sowed his field by fathering Dhṛtarāṣṭra on Ambikā, Pāṇḍu on Ambālikā, and on a servant girl, Vidura. There were born to Dhṛtarāṣṭra by his wife Gāndhārī one hundred mighty sons, the eldest of whom was Duryodhana. Five sons were born to Pāṇḍu by Kuntī and Mādrī: the courageous heroes Yudhiṣṭhira, Bhīmasena, Arjuna, Nakula and Sahadeva.

Because of fate, enmity arose between the Kurus and the Pāṇḍavas, who were harassed by the foolish Duryodhana. When the house of lac burned,* these innocent young men escaped by their own wits. Then in the house of a brahmin, who lived in Ekacakra, the great-souled heroes disguised as brahmins killed the demon Baka. Next, having learned of Draupadī's *svayaṃvara* in the country of Pāñcāla, the Pāṇḍavas married that girl whose bride-price was valor. With the permission of Droṇa and Bhīṣma, Dhṛtarāṣṭra called them together and gave them sovereignty over half the kingdom in the excellent city of Indraprastha. Calling an assembly, the five brothers, firm in their vows, performed a Rājasūya.

In Dvārakā, Arjuna won Subhadrā, beloved sister of Vāsudeva, as a wife, and Kṛṣṇa himself won Devakī's son as a friend. And from Fire he acquired the celestial chariot Nandighoṣa, the peerless divine bow Gāṇḍīva, famous in the three worlds, as well as an inexhaustible supply of arrows and impenetrable armor. With that bow, the virile, awe-inspiring hero Arjuna, seconded by Kṛṣṇa, fed the fire god.† Defeating the kings at the conquest of the world and seizing their treasures, he gave them with pleasure to his brother, the great Yudhiṣṭhira, wise in leadership. However, Yudhiṣṭhira, whose soul is Dharma, was defeated along with his brothers in a rigged gambling match by the wicked Duryodhana, who was obeying the wishes of Karṇa, Duḥśāsana and Śakuni.

After this defeat, the Pāṇḍavas performed great *tapas* in the forest for twelve years, living there with Dhaumya‡ and Draupadī and a group of seers. After this sojourn, those wise heroes went to the city of Virāṭa in disguise, where they found protection herding cows and doing other menial tasks for another year. When they were recognized, the reverent Pāṇḍavas asked King Duryodhana for their own kingdom: five villages from half the realm. When he refused to grant this, the mighty heroes made war in Kurukṣetra. They had seven divine armies, while Duryodhana and the others stood ready, armed with eleven. A violent battle ensued, like the one between the gods and the demons. At the start, Bhīṣma was the chief of Duryodhana's forces and Śikhaṇḍin commanded the Pāṇḍavas'. A most ferocious battle was joined between the two armies; sword to sword and arrow to arrow it lasted ten nights. Bhīṣma, pierced by hundreds of arrows loosed by Śikhaṇḍin and Arjuna, waited to die throughout

*A fire trap built to burn the five Pāṇḍavas and their mother alive.

†At the burning of the Khāṇḍava forest.

‡The priest of the Pāṇḍavas.

the sun's northern course while concentrating on Viṣṇu, the mace-bearing god. After recounting many Dharmas and feeding the numerous Fathers he entered the pure abode of bliss, his sins released.

After Bhīṣma's death, the heroic Droṇa went to battle with Dhṛṣṭadyumna; in this most dreadful conflict, which lasted five days, many lords of earth died in the ocean that was Pārṣata.* After he had met that ocean of sorrow, Droṇa too gained heaven. Then Karṇa entered the fray against the great-souled Arjuna; having fought a mighty two-day battle and submerged in a flood of arrows shot by Pārtha,† this hero also died and attained the realm of the sun. Then Śalya joined the war against the wise king Dharma and was slain by flaming arrows after half a day. Next the fierce, heroic Duryodhana suddenly took up a club and attacked Bhīma, destructive as Time, Death and Yama. But he was slain by Bhīma's own club instead. Then Droṇa's son Aśvatthāman, remembering his father's murder, went to the sleeping army at night and slew Dhṛṣṭadyumna with his bare hands, after which he slaughtered the heroic sons of Draupadī. While Draupadī was weeping over the loss of her children, the noble Arjuna seized the jewel in Aśvatthāman's head and killed him with the Aiṣīka weapon. After consoling Yudhiṣṭhira and the women who were overcome with grief, he took a ritual bath and propitiated the gods, Fathers and Grandfathers. After this Arjuna ruled the mighty kingdom, supported by Bhīṣma, worshiping Viṣṇu with the Horse Sacrifice, according to the rule, with full stipends for the priests.

After hearing about the annihilation of the Yādavas at the club-fight,‡ he established Parikṣit as ruler of the kingdom. Repeating the thousand names of Viṣṇu, he went to heaven along with his brothers. Thus did Vāsudeva awaken once again to delude the enemies of the gods, to protect the gods and virtuous men, and to destroy lawlessness.

# Vaikuṇṭha, Viṣṇu's Celestial City

There is a city named Nārāyaṇa, which is inaccessible and unsurpassable, complete with subdivisions and so forth, furnished with golden walls, filled with crystal pavilions, covered with thousands of lights, invincible and brilliant, replete with watchtowers, halls, ramparts and palaces. With thousands of golden gateways adorned with various jewels, it is equipped with shining awnings decorated in brilliant colors, and with amusements of all kinds, rich in rivers, filled

*Patronymic of Dhṛṣṭadyumna.
†Metronymic of Arjuna.
‡A battle with clubs in which the Yādavas killed off one another in a drunken brawl.

with ponds on all sides, and resonant with lutes and flutes. It is embellished with numerous colored banners, with avenues running in all directions and with stairways set with gems.

Enriched by the presence of hundreds of thousands of women and full of celestial bards, strewn with geese and ducks, adorned with Cakravāka birds, this city with its four incomparable gates is impregnable to the foes of the gods. It is beautified everywhere by throngs of Apsarases who know the composition of all sorts of songs and whom even the gods find hard to win. They are adept in various coquetries, amorous and most charming. With faces like the full moon and with the tinkling of anklets, slightly smiling, with lips full and red like the Bimba fruit, young, naive and doe-eyed, blessed with slender waists, they move like fine flamingos, beautifully dressed, with sweet voices, clever in conversation, adorned with lovely, heavenly ornaments. Stooping from the weight of their breasts, their eyes rolling from intoxication, with bodies of various bright colors, they delight in a variety of sexual pleasures.

Decorated everywhere with gardens of blossoming flowers, the city is spotless, possessing countless fine qualities, unattainable even by the thirty gods. In the middle of it is the splendid sacred seat of Viṣṇu, husband of Śrī, hard to win even for *yogins,* resplendent with lofty ramparts and towers. In its center, on the serpent Śeṣa as his bed, lies Hari, the sole lord, lustrous as a lotus petal, origin of all the worlds. Contemplated by the leaders of the *yogins* led by Sanandana who had drunk the nectar of the bliss of the Self, that long-armed one is himself beyond darkness, the practiser of great illusion, eternal, clothed in yellow, whose feet are embraced continuously by the daughter of the milk ocean. And this goddess, the beloved of Hari, who is to be honored in the world, sits at his feet with her mind perpetually devoted to him, having drunk the nectar of Nārāyaṇa. The lawless do not go there, nor do those whose goal is other gods.

This place, celebrated even by the thirty gods, is called Vaikuṇṭha. My wit cannot picture it all; only this much can be said: this is the city of Nārāyana! So sits the supreme Brahmā, the eternal Vāsudeva, the glorious Nārāyaṇa, deluding the world with his illusion. This world is born out of Nārāyaṇa; in him is it stationed; so does it return to him at the end of the Eon. He is the supreme goal!

# Sudarśana, Viṣṇu's Discus

Long ago there was a mighty demon lord called Śrīdāman who attacked the whole world and put Śrī under his own control. When this powerful demon had robbed the three worlds of good fortune, he wanted to capture Vāsudeva's *śrīvatsa.** Learning of his wicked plan and desiring his death, lord Janārdana sought out Maheśvara.

Meanwhile, the imperishable Śaṃbhu, in his *yogic* form, had found refuge where the ground was flat and was living on the Himālaya plateau. Approaching Jagannātha, the thousand-headed lord, Hari himself propitiated him who was the Self. He stood on his big toe for an entire millennium, invoking the supreme Brahman who is without characteristics, knowable only to *yogins.* Then the glorious lord, well pleased, bestowed on Viṣṇu a most excellent boon—the divine, splendid discus Sudarśana, in visible form.

After giving him the discus which inspires fear in all creatures, resembling as it does the wheel of time, Śankara said to Viṣṇu: "This choice weapon, O lord of gods, that destroys all other weapons is the swift Sudarśana, with twelve spokes, six naves and two yokes.† Located in its spokes are the distant gods, months, divisions of the zodiac and the six seasons, for the protection of the learned. Agni, Soma, Mitra and Varuṇa, Śacī's consort Indra, Indrāgnī, the Viśvedevas and the Prajāpatis, the powerful Hanumān, the god Dhanvantari, Tapas and Tapasya—these twelve are stationed in the spokes of the discus and so also are the months from Caitra to Phālguna. So, mighty one, take this choice weapon and kill the enemy of the gods without delay! It is unerring, praised by the king of the immortals and held in my eye by the power of *tapas.*"

Thus addressed by Śambhu, Viṣṇu spoke these words to Bhava: "O Śambhu, how am I to know whether it is useful or useless? In order to determine if your discus is effective and irresistible everywhere, I will throw it at you. Here, catch it!" Hearing Vāsudeva's words, and Pināka-bearer answered: "Hurl it then; let there be no doubt in your mind!" When he heard Maheśvara's reply, Viṣṇu threw the swift Sudarśana at Śankara in order to find out its power. When the discus thrown by the enemy of Mura struck the trident bearer, the lord of the universe, the lord of sacrifice, the sacrificer of sacrifices, it hit him in three places. Seeing Hara cut in three parts, the longarmed Hari fell at his feet, overcome with shame. When he saw Dāmodara bowing at his feet, Bhava was gratified and said repeatedly, "Arise! This, O great-armed one, is only my created form that is injured. My true being has not been harmed by the edge of the discus, for it can be neither cut nor burned. Without a doubt, Keśava, these three parts cut by the discus will be holy. One will be called Hiraṇyākṣa, the second Suvarṇākṣa, and the third Virūpākṣa.

*Name of the curl in Kṛṣṇa's chest hair.

†The twelve months, six seasons, and the intervals between solstices.

All three will give merit to men. Arise and go, O lord, to attack the slayer of the immortals. When you have killed Śrīdāman, O Viṣṇu, the gods will rejoice!"

Being so addressed by Hara, the lord whose banner bears Garuḍa went to the plateau of the mountain of the gods where he saw Śridāman. Seeing that Daitya who had killed the pride of the gods, Hari, most excellent of the deities, hurled the swift discus while crying out again and again, "You are dead!" The Daitya's head was severed by that irresistible discus; beheaded, he tumbled down the mountain like a mountain top struck by a thunderbolt. After the enemy of the gods had been destroyed, the enemy of Mura propitiated the three-eyed lord, and having received the fine weapon, the incomparable discus, he returned to his resting place in the sea.

## Bali and Sudarśana, the Discus

Descending to Rasātala, the Daitya Bali had a city built that was made colorful with precious jewels and stairways of clear crystal. In the middle of the city a spacious palace was laid out by Viśvakarman with diamond-studded terraces and doors inlaid with pearls. Here Bali enjoyed a variety of pleasures both divine and human. He had a beloved wife named Vindhyāvali. O seer, Virocana's son made love with her, his wife of great splendor who was clothed in virtue, the most outstanding among a thousand young women.

While the Daitya was living in Sutala pursuing pleasure, Sudarśana, destroyer of the demon's splendor, arrived in the netherworld. When the discus invaded Pātāla there arose in the city of the Dānavas a mighty roar as of a storm-tossed ocean. Hearing this great furor, Bali, bull of the demons, seized his sword and cried out, "Aho! What's this?" Whereupon his lawfully wedded wife Vindhyāvali, ever upright in conduct, put the sword back into its sheath and spoke placatingly to her husband: "This is the discus of the lord, of Vāmana, the great-souled one, the destroyer of the circle of the Daityas. You must worship it, O chief of the Daityas!" So saying, the lovely-limbed woman went out with a water pot for the guest.

Then Sudarśana, Viṣṇu's thousand-spoked discus, came near. And the lord of the demons, bowing and offering the gift, his hands cupped, honored the discus with the proper ritual, O seer, and proclaimed this hymn of praise: "I praise the utterly pure discus of Hari with a thousand rays, a thousand colors and a thousand spokes, which cuts down the host of the Daityas. I praise the discus of Hari in whose navel sits the Grandfather, on whose rim rides Śarva bearing the trident, at the root of whose spokes lie the great mountains. The gods dwell in those spokes along with Indra, Sun and Fire; in its swiftness lie wind, water, fire, earth and sky. At the spokes' edges are the clouds, lightning, stars and planets beyond which sit the seers, the Vālakhilyas and others. Devotedly I praise this marvelous weapon of Vāsudeva. Whatever evil arises from my body, speech or mind, O blazing Sudarśana, Viṣṇu's discus, burn up that sin of mine! Whatever sin has come to me from my mother's or father's lineage, destroy it at once! Praise be to you, Acyuta's weapon! Let my ailments be dispelled. Because I sing your name, O discus, let all my troubles cease!"

# The Churning of the Ocean

When the sage Durvāsas, a portion of Śankara, was journeying around this earth, he saw a heavenly garland in the hand of a Vidyādharī. The perfume of its *santānaka* flowers filled the whole woods where the forest-dwellers revelled, O brahmin. When he saw that beautiful wreath, this brahmin who was fulfilling a demented vow asked the full-hipped Vidhyādhara woman for it. At his demand, the slender-limbed, large-eyed Vidhyādharī gave him the garland, prostrating herself respectfully before him. Accepting the ornament he put it on his own head; looking like a madman, O Maitreya, the brahmin roamed the earth.

This lunatic saw Śaci's lord approaching, sitting on Airāvata—Indra, who is first lord of the three worlds—accompanied by the great gods. Lifting from his own head that garland full of frenzied bees, like a crazy man he threw it at the king of the immortals. Indra caught it and put it on Airāvata's head where that wreath shone like the river Ganges on the peak of Kailāsa.

Attracted by the fragrance, the elephant, his eyes clouded with rut, smelled it with his trunk, and threw it on the ground. At this the excellent seer Durvāsas grew angry. Furious, O Maitreya, he said to the king of the gods, "Drunk with power, your soul is corrupted, O Vāsava! You are too arrogant! You have rejected this garland I have given you which is the abode of Śrī! You have not prostrated yourself and exclaimed 'How lucky am I!' Nor have you put it on your head, your cheeks blooming with delight! Because you have not honored this wreath I gave you, fool, your prosperity in the three worlds will come to naught! Thinking that I am like all the other brahmins, Śakra, you have insulted me with your arrogant manner. Because you have thrown the garland I gave you on the ground, you will no longer enjoy good fortune in any of the three worlds. You are treating me haughtily and with contempt, king of the gods, me whose anger when it arises terrifies all creatures moving and unmoving!"

Mahendra,* speedily alighting from the elephant's back, went to pacify the blameless sage Durvāsas. When Indra had prostrated himself before him and placated him, the excellent seer Durvāsas spoke to the Thousand-Eyed god: "I am not a man with a compassionate heart; nor is forgiveness part of my nature as it is for other seers, O Śakra. Know me to be Durvāsas! You have been filled with self-importance by Gautama and others to no purpose. Know that I am Durvāsas, whose sum and substance is implacability. You have been rendered haughty by Vasiṣṭha and others whose core is compassion, who sing your praises on high. Because of this you now treat me, too, with contempt. Who in the three worlds remains unafraid after seeing my glowering face with knitted brow and my blazing knot of hair? Enough said, god of the Hundred Sacrifices, I will not forgive you, however much you try to appease me!" Speaking, the brahmin left, and the king of the gods mounted Airāvata once again, O brahmin, and went to Amarāvatī.

From then on the three worlds, and Śakra too, were bereft of good fortune and desolate with withered plants and herbs. No sacrifices were made, no ascetics practised *tapas*, and people neglected gift-giving and other laws. The worlds were utterly dispirited; people became covetous even of trifles, O excellent twice-born one, their senses afflicted by greed and other weaknesses. . . .

When the three worlds were steeped in misfortune in this way and were without mettle, the Daityas and Dānavas, overcome by greed, turned their power against the gods. The Daityas made war on the luckless, powerless gods. Defeated by the Daityas, Indra and the rest of the thirty gods, led by Fire, fled for refuge to the eminent Grandfather. When the gods told him what had happened, Brahmā said to them: "You should seek shelter with the demon-destroyer, the lord of both higher and lower creation, Viṣṇu, the causeless cause of creation, the lord, the master of Prajāpatis, the eternal, unvanquished god. Go to Viṣṇu, cause of the unborn Prakṛti and Puruṣa, who dispels the suffering of those who bow to him. He will bestow

*Great Indra.

on you supreme good." When he had thus admonished all the gods, Brahmā, Grandfather of the worlds, went with them to the farther shore of the ocean of milk. Having accompanied the thirty gods, the Grandfather extolled the supreme lord Hari with sweet speech. . . .

So praised, the blessed supreme lord appeared before their eyes, bearing conch and discus, O Maitreya. When the gods saw this unprecedented form, carrying conch, discus and mace, radiating a rich aura of splendor, all of them, led by the Grandfather, bowed low, their eyes staring in shock. They praised the lotus-eyed one: "Praise, praise be to you who are without distinctions! You are Brahmā, you are the Pinākа-bearer, you are Indra, Agni, Wind, Varuṇa, Sun, Yama. You are the Vasus, Maruts, Sādhyas, the hosts of Viśvedevas. You are this host of deities who stands before you here. You are he who pours forth the world, pervader of all. You are the sacrifice, you are the cry of *"Vaṣaṭ!"* You are the syllable *OṂ*, you are Prajāpati. You are the knowledge and what is to be known, the soul of the universe. The whole world consists of you. In distress we have come to you for refuge, O Viṣṇu, since we have been defeated by the Daityas. Have mercy on us, O gracious All-Soul! Nourish us with your strength! So long as one does not turn to you for refuge, destroyer of all evil, there is suffering and longing, confusion and unhappiness. O tranquil soul, bestow your favor on us who have come to you for help! Nourish the strength of us all, O protector."

When he had been praised in this manner by the prostrate immortals, the lord Hari with serene aspect, the creator of the universe, said this: "Yes, gods, I will strengthen your power. I shall tell you what you must do. Take all the herbs to the ocean of milk along with the Daityas; then you, together with the Daityas and Dānavas, must throw them all into that ocean in order to make the nectar. Then, using Mt. Mandara as a stirring stick and Vāsuki as a twirling rope, churn the ocean for the nectar while I stand by to help. To enlist the help of the Daityas, tell them diplomatically that they will enjoy the same fruit as you. And then you, the immortals, will become strong from drinking the nectar that arises from the churning of the ocean. I shall arrange it so that the enemies of the thirty gods will not get any nectar, but only the suffering gods themselves."

So directed by the god of gods, all the gods joined with the demons in a compact to produce the nectar. After gathering various herbs, the gods, Daityas and Dānavas threw them into the water of the ocean of milk whose glow was as clear as the sky in autumn. Taking Mt. Mandara as the staff and Vāsuki as the rope, O Maitreya, they began to churn vigorously for the nectar. All the gods gathered with Kṛṣṇa at

Vāsuki's tail while all the Daityas were stationed at his head. Then all the demons of limitless energy lost their power because of the violent blast of fiery heat that came from the hissing mouth of the snake. But the gods were invigorated by the rainclouds blown towards his tail by the wind coming from that hissing mouth.

In the middle of the milky ocean lord Hari himself appeared in the form of a tortoise to support the rotating mountain while it was churned, O great seer. Keśava appeared in one form in the midst of the gods, bearing mace and discus; in another form he pulled the snake-king with the Daityas; and in a third gigantic form, unseen by gods and demons alike, he strode up the mountain, O Maitreya. Hari then infused the serpent-king with strength, and in his original form invigorated the gods with power.

Out of the middle of this ocean of milk that was being churned by gods and demons, there first arose Surabhi, source of the oblation, honored by the deities. Both gods and Dānavas were delighted, great seer, their minds excited, their eyes unblinking. Even as the heavenly Siddhas were thinking "What is this?" the goddess Vāruṇī* appeared, her eyes rolling with intoxication. Next from the whirling milk ocean came the Pārijāta tree, perfuming the world with its fragrance and delighting the wives of the gods. And then, Maitreya, a most marvellous throng of Apsarases, endowed with the virtues of beauty and nobility, sprang up from the milky ocean. Next appeared the cool-rayed moon which Maheśvara took as his own, as the snakes took the poison which arose from the ocean of milk. Finally the god Dhanvantari himself came up, clad in white, carrying a water-jar full of the nectar, whereupon all the mindful Daityas and Dānavas became joyful, Maitreya, along with the seers.

After this, the goddess Śrī of vibrant beauty arose from this milk, standing in a blossoming lotus with a lotus in her hand. With joy the great seers assembled there praised her with the Śrīsūkta;† and the Gandharvas, led by Viśvāvasu, sang before her while the throngs of Apsarases, led by Ghṛtācī, danced. The Ganges and other rivers approached her with their waters for bathing. The elephants of the four quarters holding up golden vessels of pure water bathed the goddess, the great mistress of all the worlds. The ocean in bodily form gave her a wreath of unfading lotuses, while Viśvakarman wrought ornaments for her body. Wearing celestial garlands and garments, bathed and

*The wife of the god Varuṇa, also the name of an intoxicating drink.
†A hymn in the Ṛg Veda devoted to the goddess Śrī.

adorned with decorations, with all the gods looking on, she went to Hari's chest. While resting on Hari's chest, Lakṣmī made the gods know instant supreme bliss just by looking at the two of them, O Maitreya.

But the Daityas led by Vipracitti, forsaken by Lakṣmī, were dismayed. So they stole the jar full of potent nectar that was in Dhanvantari's hand. Whereupon Viṣṇu fooled them with an illusion. Assuming the body of a woman, the lord took the cup from the Dānavas and gave it to the gods. At this, the heavenly host, Śakra and the other gods, drank the nectar. With weapons and swords raised on high, the Daityas attacked the thirty gods. Defeated by the powerful deities who had consumed the nectar, the demons then fled in all directions and entered the netherworld.

After this the gods rejoiced, prostrating themselves before the one who bears conch, discus and mace, and Indra ruled in his heaven once again. The sun, serenely shining, went on his way, and the heavenly bodies followed their paths, excellent seer. The blessed god Fire blazed brightly on high and all creatures put their minds on Dharma. Good Fortune inhabited the three worlds, excellent brahmin, and Indra, chief of the thirty gods, became resplendent once more. Regaining the third heaven, Śakra went to his lion's throne from which he ruled the gods, giving praise to the lotus-bearing goddess.

# Viṣṇu and Śrī

The eternal Śrī, loyal to Viṣṇu, is the mother of the world. Just as Viṣṇu pervades the universe, O excellent brahmin, so does she. Viṣṇu is meaning; Śrī is speech. She is conduct; Hari is behavior. Viṣṇu is knowledge; she is insight. He is Dharma; she is virtuous action.

Viṣṇu is the creator; Śrī is creation. She is the earth and Hari earth's upholder. The eternal Lakṣmī is contentment, O Maitreya; the blessed lord is satisfaction. Śrī is wish, the lord desire. He is the sacrifice, she the fee. The goddesss is the offering of butter, Janārdana the sacrificial cake. At the sacrifice, Lakṣmī is the women's hut, Madhusūdana the sacrificial site. Lakṣmī is the altar, Hari the sacrificial pole. Śrī is the firewood, the lord the sacred grass. The lord has the nature of the Sāma Veda; the lotus-born Śrī is the *udgītha.**

*The principal part of the chant called *sāman*.

Lakṣmī is the *svāhā* cry; Jagannātha Vāsudeva is the oblation-eating fire.

Śauri the lord is Śankara, and Lakṣmī is Gaurī, excellent brahmin. Keśava is the sun, Maitreya, and the lotus-dwelling goddess is its light. Viṣṇu is the host of the Fathers, Padmā the *svadhā* offering of constant nourishment. Śrī is the sky; Viṣṇu, the Self of everything, is wide-open space. Śrī's husband is the moon; its beauty is the constant Śrī. Lakṣmī is fortitude, enacted in the world, Hari the all-pervading wind. Govinda is the ocean, O brahmin; Śrī is the shore, great seer.

Lakṣmī bears the form of Indrāṇī,* while Madhusūdana is Indra, her spouse, among the gods. The discus-bearing Viṣṇu is Yama personified; the lotus-dwelling Lakṣmī is his wife. Śrī is prosperity; the god who possesses Śrī is the lord of wealth himself. Illustrious Lakṣmī is Gaurī; Keśava is Varuṇa himself. Śrī is the host of gods, chief brahmin, and Hari is lord of the host.

He who bears a mace in his right hand is reliability, O excellent twice-born one; Lakṣmī is power. Lakṣmī is the instant, the lord the wink of an eye. He is the hour; she is the second. Lakṣmī is light; he is the lamp. Hari is everything and lord of everything as well. Śrī, mother of the world, is a forest creeper while Viṣṇu is a tree. Śrī is the starry night; the god who carries mace and discus is the day. Viṣṇu, granter of wishes, is the bridegroom; the lotus-dwelling goddess is the bride.

Appearing in the form of a male river is the lord, while Śrī takes form as a female river. The lotus-eyed god is a banner; the lotus-dweller is a flag. Lakṣmī is desire, O Maitreya, and Jagannātha Nārāyaṇa is greed. Together Lakṣmī and Govinda are passion and love.

What more is there to tell? In summary, let it be said that among gods, beasts and human beings, Hari is all that is known as male, and Śrī all that is known as female. There is nothing more beyond these two!

*Indra's wife.

# 3 Kṛṣṇa

## Song of the Cowherd Women to Kṛṣṇa

*Vraja has come to victory by your birth,*
*for here the goddess Lakṣmī dwells forever!*
*O beloved, see your people on all sides,*
*their lives sustained by you, longing for you!*

*O master of the sport of love, do you not slay us with your glance that robs the beauty from within fine, full-blown lotuses?*
*O bestower of boons, we women are your willing slaves,*
*loyal to you!*

*O bull, you have saved us time and again from death by poisoned water,*
*from the demoniac poisonous snake,*
*from the tempest of the rain,*
*from the lightning's fire,*
*from the Bull and the Horse,*
*and from every kind of danger!*

*O friend, delight of all the cowherd women,*
*the inner witness of embodied beings,*
*have you not been born into the Sātvata family,*
*as Brahmā asked, in order to protect the world?*

*O beloved, place on the heads of us who seek your feet out of fear of rebirth your wish-granting, fear-dispelling lotus hand that took the hand of Śrī in marriage!*

*O hero who destroys the suffering of the Vraja folk,*
*whose smile puts to shame the pride of your own kin,*
*O friend, adore us for we are your slaves!*
*Show us women your lovely lotus face!*

*Place on the breasts of us who lie prostrate before you*
*your lotus feet that crush all evil,*
*followed by small creatures,*
*the abode of Śrī,*
*as proffered by the serpents' hoods!*
*O show us love!*

*O hero, grant us the nectar of your lower lip*
*that makes men oblivious to all other passions,*
*increasing our lust,*
*removing our sorrow,*
*and so fondly kissed by the melodious flute!*

# Introduction

The enchanting Kṛṣṇa, the "black" god, has become the most beloved deity in the Hindu pantheon. Of all the *avatāras* of lord Viṣṇu, Kṛṣṇa possesses the lengthiest and most individualized biography. It appears likely that he was first an independent deity, or hero, who was eventually absorbed by Viṣṇu as supreme god. In this way Viṣṇu acquired for himself a number of epithets derived from Kṛṣṇa's exploits. Among these are Govinda, "cow-finder;" Dāmodara, "rope-belly;" Keśava, "fine-hair;" and the like.

Unique among Purāṇic deities, Kṛṣṇa appears to have been a historical hero as well as a god. This is not so evident in the Purāṇas themselves as in the epic, the *Mahābhārata*, where Kṛṣṇa's role is a complex one. He is identified as the ruler of Dvārakā, a descendent of Yayāti and a member of the Yādava clan which lived by the river Yamunā in Gokula and Vṛndāvana. By marriage he is related to the Pāṇḍu heroes of the epic, and as leader of his clan, he manipulates events relating to the *Mahābhārata* war with considerable skill. Crafty and shrewd throughout the epic, he is periodically engaged in subterfuge and deceit. Yet that lengthy sermon on virtue known as the *Bhagavad Gītā*, the Song of God, is put in his mouth. In fact, Kṛṣṇa in the epic appears to be a human hero in the process of becoming a god. This double nature is first revealed when, in the lowly occupation of a charioteer, he recites the *Bhagavad Gītā*, in which he claims for himself all the might and powers attributed elsewhere to the impersonal Brahman, or to the supreme lord Viṣṇu:

> I am the self that dwells in all beings; I am the beginning, the middle and end of all beings.

I am whatever is the seed of all creatures, Arjuna. Not a being, standing or moving, can exist without me.
(*Bhagavad Gītā* 10.20 and 39)

It is this divine Kṛṣṇa, the supreme lord, *avatāra* of Viṣṇu himself, whose life is celebrated in the Purāṇas. The human hero of the epic is scarcely evident in Purāṇic literature. Furthermore, Kṛṣṇa's stories appear in only a few discrete places in the Purāṇas, collected in a carefully wrought and coherent biographical form; they do not appear at random, intermixed with other tales of other gods. It is as if the life of Kṛṣṇa, *avatāra* of Viṣṇu, had been written by a single hand to be included alongside the myth of other gods. This is the clear intention of the *Harivaṃśa*, often called a Purāṇa, and regarded as an appendix to the *Mahābhārata*. And this is the character of the Kṛṣṇa stores in other Purāṇas as well.

The story related at great length in the Purāṇas, utterly different from Kṛṣṇa's exploits in the epic, is that of a cowherd boy who grows from infancy to manhood in the pastoral fields and forests of Gokula and Vṛndāvana on the Yamunā river. In fact, Kṛṣṇa the divine child and Kṛṣṇa the epic hero appear to be two distinct and separate personalities, one human, one divine. If they have anything in common, it is a tendency to trickery and deceit, but always, presumably, in the service of the good.

The comic, clever and heroic events of Kṛṣṇa's rural childhood as retold in the Purāṇas have utterly endeared him to his devotees. The circumstances of his conception and birth are most peculiar. In fact, Viṣṇu's *avatāra* occurs in double form, for Kṛṣṇa and his cousin Balarāma are conceived from two of the hairs of Viṣṇu's head, one black, one white, put in their mothers' wombs. Kṛṣṇa's task on earth is to destroy his wicked uncle Kaṃsa, who, warned of his fate, has murdered each previously born child of Kṛṣṇa's mother shortly after birth. To fool Kaṃsa, Kṛṣṇa is exchanged by his father for another infant, who is killed in his stead. Thus his life is saved, and eventually, as a grown man, he will complete his divine mission to bring down his evil uncle. But as a baby he is simply a beguiling and naughty child. Kṛṣṇa, inseparable from his cousin Balarāma, bedevils the cowherds and their wives by running away, stealing milk and butter, overturning wagons, and felling trees with his prodigious divine strength. It is clear from the start to the narrator, but not to his family, that this bewitching boy is really a god. One day when he has been eating dirt, his mother, angry at the naughty child, opens his mouth to clean it out, and there she sees the universe entire, as if in the mind or belly of a god. She is amazed, but instantly forgets the vision.

Other feats which the child Kṛṣṇa accomplishes are not so easily forgotten, and it gradually becomes apparent that he is no normal child. As he grows up, he kills barehanded numerous threatening demonic enemies, and performs a variety of beneficent feats. Two of the most famous concern Pūtanā, the nursemaid, and Kāliya, the snake. Pūtanā is a witch sent by Kaṃsa to suckle the infant Kṛṣṇa with poisoned milk. But even in his cradle the lord recognizes her to be evil, and destroys the witch by sucking out her milk, unharmed, and then consuming all of her insides until she collapses in hideous agony. In a later incident the snake Kāliya poisons the drinking water of the river Yamunā, threatening the lives of both cows and cowherds. But the child Kṛṣṇa finds out his secret pool and tramples him in a frenzied dance. In our version of the story Kāliya does not die; influenced by the pleading of Kāliya's wives, Kṛṣṇa releases him, converting him to gentility in the process, and making the river water pure. Once again Kṛṣṇa has defeated evil and protected his kin. His other childhood deeds are all of this sort, and the cowherd folk come to regard him with awe and love. Eventually they question him about his extraordinary powers, suspecting that he is a god, but he refuses the claim and insists he is only one of them:

> If you love me, and if I merit your respect, then you must regard me as your kinsman. I am neither god nor Gandharva, neither Yakṣa nor Dānava. I have been born into your family; this is the only way to look at it.
> (*Viṣṇu* 5.13.12)

The irresponsible tricks of Kṛṣṇa's infancy give way to the salvational exploits of the child, then to the amorous adventures of the youth. For when he reaches puberty, Kṛṣṇa's charm takes a sexual turn. Roaming around the woods at night, in amorous mood, he sings and plays his flute to lure the cowherd women to his side. Otherwise loyal wives, they are bewitched by the sound of his song, and leaving their marriage beds at night, they go to dance with the lord by moonlight, lost in love. The climax of this scene comes in the Rāsalīlā, or circular dance, in the course of which Kṛṣṇa appears in multiple form, gratifying the desire of each of the cowherd women that he be her partner in love. Again the trickster, Kṛṣṇa has lured all of them from their homes by the seductive message of his irresistible music. But they are doomed to disappointment in the end, for Kṛṣṇa suddenly departs, leaving them bereft and mystified, ever longing for his return.

Where does he go? To the dismay of the other women Kṛṣṇa has chosen Rādhā as his own, and the two of them go deep into the woods to sport in love-play to their hearts' delight. The act of love, with all its preludes, is described in affectionate detail, as are the arousing and consummation of desire between the youthful Kṛṣṇa and Rādhā. This role of Kṛṣṇa as lover has become one of the most powerful aspects of the god, symbolizing as it does in sexual terms the unity of polarities which that deity always represents in Hindu religious thought.

But there is still one more act to this part of his story. Just as he left the dancing cowherd women to steal off with Rādhā, eventually he leaves her too, to get on with the task of killing Kaṃsa, and she misses him terribly. In this way the story of the love of Kṛṣṇa and Rādhā symbolizes not only the unity of all mundane polarities in god through the metaphor of sex, but also the longing of the human soul to experience spiritual unity with god. The courtship of Kṛṣṇa and Rādhā makes explicit what is only suggested in the Rāsalīlā dance, and serves as a powerful metaphor of man's longing for the ultimate reality.

Kṛṣṇa's story in the Purāṇas does not end here, however. As a man he fulfills his task as *avatāra* of Viṣṇu, which is to destroy his wicked uncle Kaṃsa for the benefit of his people. Kṛṣṇa, with his constant companion Balarāma, sets off on his heroic duty, still working wonders along the way, as when he straightens out a hunch-backed girl, or breaks Kaṃsa's huge bow that no one else can lift. Kaṃsa has constructed an elaborate plot to kill his nephew, staging a wrestling contest in which he expects to trap both boys. But because of their unexpected and divine strength the two defeat the mighty wrestlers in the ring; then Kṛṣṇa springs to the spectators' platform and dispatches Kaṃsa, toppling his crown. The victory is won, evil is overthrown, and the victorious Kṛṣṇa struts around the arena in triumph, with his family looking on.

Kṛṣṇa now assumes the mantle of manhood, the irresponsibility of his childhood apparently left behind. He becomes the guardian of his Yādava clan, defending his people against attacks by the father of Kaṃsa's wives, who is the king of Magadha, and by the Yavanas, or barbarians. Because of these and other threats, he builds the city of Dvārakā as a haven for his people. The enemies of Kṛṣṇa belong to the historical clans of early India, and at this point he seems to become a historical person himself, as in the *Mahābhārata*.

After these heroic deeds, as befits a king, Kṛṣṇa takes an official wife, not one of the cowherd women after all, but Rukmiṇī of Vidarbha, whom he kidnaps. And after her he weds two more, the story goes, and then another 16,000 wives, by all of whom he fathers a vast and nameless horde of sons. His heroic acts continue all the while as he slays demons and human enemies galore. In his last act he arranges (once more by a ruse) the demise of his own family and clan by allowing its members to annihilate each other in a drunken brawl. Soon after, accidentally shot in the foot by the hunter Jaras, he dies. And last of all, the ocean floods and submerges his beloved city Dvārakā; it is as if his life had been a dream which, like Dvārakā, leaves no remains behind. Here, at the end of the story, the epic and Purāṇic Kṛṣṇas merge. Trickster to the end, Kṛṣṇa has become a mortal hero, but one whose family and clan disappears without a trace. Was the flooding of Dvārakā a historical event, the actual termination of the Yādava clan? Or is it a product of religious imagination, describing the moment when the *avatāra* returns to his source in Viṣṇu?

In conclusion, let us consider the clear and consistent features of the personality of Kṛṣṇa. Like Viṣṇu, who has adopted him as his *avatāra*, he is a protector, not of the universe as a whole, but of his family and clan. Like Viṣṇu, he defeats the enemies of the good, both supernatural and human. But as Kṛṣṇa alone he has a unique, original character. He is a trickster and a lover, sometimes both at the same time. As both child and man, he fools people to get his way—during the circumstances of his birth, in the tricks he plays as a child, in the Rāsalīlā, and by the subterfuge with which he tricks the Yādavas into their self-destruction. His apparent irresponsibility, the source of his charm as a child, conceals his other purposes. As god and man he is bound by social custom and the rules of human behavior; as a god he can ignore those rules, and often does, usually for the benefit of his people. This trickster god lays bare, to those who have the eyes to see, the divine dimension of this mundane world. Kṛṣṇa moves easily between two levels of existence, the human and divine. What seems an impossible feat or miracle to men is simply a display of his divine nature. Paradoxically, it is through tricks and miracles that the god Kṛṣṇa continually reveals the ultimate unity of existence.

The unity of all phenomena in god is also shown in Kṛṣṇa's other unique role, that of lover of the cowherd girl Rādhā. Male and female united in the sexual embrace reveal the identity of opposites in divinity. Through Kṛṣṇa's amorous adventures one feels not only the divine embrace, but also, most poignantly, the agony of separation from the lord. And this longing for union, felt so intensely by his devotees, is exquisitely evoked by the stories of Kṛṣṇa, the handsome cowherd who deserts his lovers and leaves them stricken to the heart.

In the Purāṇas, three personalities appear in Kṛṣṇa: the child, the lover and the heroic king. But it is most clearly the trickster child and the irresistible youthful lover who stand as metaphors for the unity of all existence—a divine unity which in these stories bears the name of Kṛṣṇa, the divine lord.

# Texts

## CHILDHOOD

### The Conception of Kṛṣṇa

Once upon a time, great seer, Vasudeva married Devaka's daughter, the august Devakī, who was like a goddess. At the wedding of Vasudeva and Devakī, Kaṃsa, joy of the Bhojas,* drove their coach as charioteer. Respectfully addressing Kaṃsa, a voice in the atmosphere, deep-sounding and rumbling like the clouds, spoke aloud, "Fool! You will be robbed of your life by the eighth embryo of that woman you are carrying in your chariot along with her spouse!" Giving ear to this, the mighty Kaṃsa unsheathed his sword and threatened Devakī, whereupon Vasudeva spoke up, "Don't kill Devakī, O blameless lord! I will deliver over to you each embryo that arises in her womb!"

"So be it!" replied Kaṃsa to Vasudeva, excellent twice-born one, and he ceased his attempt to kill Devakī out of respect for her husband's word.

Meanwhile Earth, oppressed by a heavy burden, went to the assembly for the inhabitants of the triple heaven on Mt. Meru. Prostrating herself before Brahmā and all the gods, she related everything, speaking piteously of her distress:

"Agni is the *guru* of gold, Sūrya the *guru* of cows; my *guru* and that of all the worlds is Nārāyaṇa. He is the lord of the Prajāpatis, of Brahmā, the first-born even of the elder gods. He is Time, consisting of minutes, seconds and instants, his body unmanifest. All of you together, excellent deities, comprise but a portion of him. The

*Name of his tribe.

Ādityas, Maruts, Sādhyas, Rudras, Vasus, Aśvins and Fire, the Fathers who are creators of the world, headed by Atri—all these are the body of the immeasurable great-souled Viṣṇu. Yakṣas, Rākṣasas, Daityas, Piśācas, Uragas and Dānavas, Gandharvas and Apsarases comprise the body of the great-souled Viṣṇu. Space glittering with planets, the Pleiades and the stars, fire, water, wind and I myself as well as the sense objects—all these consist in Viṣṇu. Moreover, these manifold forms of his proceed by night and day in the reciprocal relationship of master and servant, like the waves on the ocean.

"At present the Daityas, led by Kālanemi, have overthrown the world of mortals and oppress all creatures night and day. That great demon Kālanemi, who was once slain by the powerful lord Viṣṇu, has now been born as Kaṃsa, Ugrasena's son! And other mighty evil-souled heroic Asuras have been born in the houses of kings—the impetuous and violent demons Ariṣṭa (Disaster), Dhenuka (Little Cow), Keśin (Flame-Hair), Pralamba (Long-Nose), Naraka (Hell) and the terrible demon Sunda, and Bāṇa, son of Bali—so numerous I cannot count them all. Many such demons with divine shapes and hordes of strong, powerful, arrogant Daitya chiefs roam on top of me. O immortal gods, I tell you that I cannot hold out any longer, so depressed am I by the weight of these demons. O lordly ones, remove my burden lest, so distressed, I plunge into the netherworld!"

Having heard Earth's speech and urged on by the thirty immortals, Brahmā spoke in order to alleviate Earth's burden, "Everything Earth says is true, heaven-dwellers. You and I and Bhava all consist in Nārāyaṇa. . . . Come, let us go to the fine shore of the ocean of milk and worship Hari there; he should hear all about this. When the all-soul who is embodied in the world descends on earth with a portion of himself for the world's benefit, he supports Dharma in every way." So speaking, the Grandfather went to Hari together with the gods, where with attentive mind they hymned him whose banner bears Garuḍa. . . .

"This earth, lord, whose mountains are pressed down by great demons who have arisen on her, comes to you, who are the refuge of the worlds, to lift her burden, O god whose substance is boundless. We stand before you here—Indra, foe of Vṛtra, the wondrous Nāsatyas and Daśra, the Rudras and Vasus with the Sun, headed by Wind and Fire. Tell us, guardian of the gods, what are we all to do? By following your command, we will always remain pure."

Praised in this manner, the supreme lord god pulled two hairs from his head, great seer, one white, one black. And he said to the gods, "These two hairs of mine will descend to earth and remove the painful burden from the world. All the gods should also descend to earth, along with their portions,* in order to do battle with these wild demons that have appeared. Then all the Daityas on earth will most certainly go to perdition, crushed by my glance. One of my hairs, O gods, will become the eighth embryo in the womb of the divine Devakī, Vasudeva's wife. Descending on earth in this form, it will destroy Kālanemi who has been reborn as Kaṃsa." So saying, Hari vanished. Prostrating themselves before the invisible Hari, great seer, the gods went to the top of Mt. Meru and descended to the surface of the earth.

When Kaṃsa heard the god's plan from Nārada, who said, "Devakī's eighth embryo will be Kṛṣṇa, upholder of the earth!" he held both Devakī and Vasudeva captive in their house. As he had previously promised, Vasudeva turned each child over to Kaṃsa, O brahmins. They say that these six sons became the children of Hiraṇyakaśipu, after Sleep,† sent by Viṣṇu, had bestowed the embryos on Devakī, one by one. It is this *yogic* sleep of Viṣṇu, the illusion of which is vast, that deludes all creation with ignorance.

Lord Hari said to her, "Sleep, at my order, go and take the six embryos which are resting on the bottom of the underworld and put them one at a time into Devakī's womb. When these six have been destroyed by Kaṃsa, the seventh in her womb will be an infinitesmal portion of myself called Śesa. In Gokula there lives another wife of Vasudeva, Rohiṇī. During her confinement, which will be at the same time as Devakī's, you are to put Devakī's embryo into her womb. People will say that Devakī's seventh conception has ended in miscarriage, aborted by her fear of the Bhoja king. Because it has been extracted in this way‡ the embryo will be called Saṃkarṣaṇa throughout the world; he will be a hero resembling the peak of the White Mountain.

"Then I myself will take shape in the holy womb of Devakī, while you go without delay into Yaśodā's womb. And in the month of Nabhas, during the rainy season, at night, I will be born as Kṛṣṇa, the eighth embryo, and you will be the ninth. Vasudeva, his mind prompted by my power, will lead me to Yaśodā's bed and you, blameless one, to that of Devakī.

"Now when Kaṃsa discovers you, O goddess, he will dash you against a rocky mountain peak. But you will attain a dwelling place in the sky, where Śakra of a thousand eyes will honor you out of respect for me. His head bowed reverently, he will accept you as his sister.

*That is to say, they should sacrifice a fraction of their personalities to take on human form.

†I.e., Viṣṇu's *yogic* sleep personified.

‡A play on his name, which can be construed as meaning "extraction."

After killing Śumbha, Niśumbha and thousands of other demons, you will adorn the earth with countless shrines. You are prosperity, humility, patience, beauty, fortitude, modesty, wealth, dawn, heaven and earth—and whatever else there is, you are. Those who will praise you with heads bowed in the morning and afternoon, calling you Āryā, Durgā, Ambikā, womb of the Veda, Bhadrā, and Bhadrakālī, the goddess who gives rest and happiness—to those who worship you I will give whatever they desire, by my graciousness. Honored with offerings of wine, meat and other enjoyable things, you will be liberally beneficent toward the desires of all people. By my grace, good mistress, humankind will know no danger. Go, goddess, and do as I have said."

Thus addressed by the god of gods, the midwife of creation then deposited the six embryos in Devakī, as told, and exchanged the seventh. When she put the seventh into Rohiṇī, Hari entered Devakī to benefit the three worlds. On the day that Yoganidrā began to grow in Yaśodā's womb exactly as Parameṣṭhin had directed, all the planets circled in the sky. When Viṣṇu's portion went to earth, O brahmin, all the seasons sparkled. No one could look upon Devakī because of her great brilliance; when they beheld her flaming radiance, their minds trembled. Unseen by men and women, day and night the hosts of gods praised Devakī as she bore Viṣṇu in her body.

# The Birth of Kṛṣṇa

Thus eulogized by the gods, Devakī bore in her womb the god with the lotus eyes, savior of the world. On the day of his birth, the great-souled Acyuta, awakening the lotus which is the world, appeared in the dawn which is Devakī to bring joy to the whole world like the light of the moon. Virtuous people were satisfied, fierce winds grew calm, and rivers ran clear when Janārdana was born. The oceans made sweet music with their waves while the lords of the Gandharvas sang and bevies of Apsarases danced. Gods in the heaven rained showers of flowers upon earth and smokeless fires blazed up afresh when Janārdana was born. Rainclouds rumbled softly, pouring down showers of blossoms, O brahmin, midway through the night when Janārdana, support of all, was born.

When his father, Anakadundubhi,* saw his son born with four arms, pure as the petal of a blue lotus blossom, and with the *śrīvatsa*

*Nickname of Vasudeva.

whorl on his chest, he celebrated him with song. Praising him with gracious words, the great-minded father, who still feared Kaṃsa, said to his son, excellent twice-born ones:

"You have been born, overlord of the gods! O god, abandon, by your grace, this divine form with conch, discus and mace! When Kaṃsa learns, O god, that you have descended this very day into my house, he will kill me outright! Be gracious, lord, you whose form is infinite, complete, embodied in the universe, who bears the worlds within your body even while in the womb. O god of gods, you who bear the form of an infant made visible by illusion, abandon this four-armed form, O universal soul, lest Kaṃsa born of Diti know of your descent!"

"Long ago," said Viṣṇu to Devakī, "out of desire for a son you worshiped me. That propitiation, goddess, has now born fruit for you in that I am born from your own womb!" So speaking, the lord fell silent, excellent seer, and Vasudeva went outside.

As Anakadundubhi carried out his son in the dead of night, the guards were gripped by Sleep, as were the guardians of Mathurā's gate. As they went in the night under cover of the clouds that were raining torrents of water, the serpent Śeṣa followed Anakadundubhi and sheltered him with his hoods. Carrying Viṣṇu, Vasudeva crossed the deep river Yamunā with its hundreds of whirlpools, but it only reached up to his knees.

On the bank of the river he saw the cowherd elders, Nanda and the others, who had come to bring taxes to Kaṃsa. At that time O Maitreya, Yaśodā, too, was fooled by Sleep whom she bore as her daughter, while the people were also deluded. Vasudeva, of infinite splendor, put down the boy, picked up the girl from Yaśodā's bed and quickly left. When she awoke and saw that she had borne a son who was as dark as a blue lotus petal, Yaśodā was ecstatic with joy.

Vasudeva carried the girl to his own house, put her into Devakī's bed and lay down there as before. Hearing the crying of a child, the guards rose up and told Kaṃsa of Devakī's delivery, O brahmin. Going at once to her side, Kaṃsa seized the little girl. Devakī tried to prevent him with strangled cries of "Let go! Let go'" but he dashed the baby onto a rock. When she was thrown down, she rose into the sky where she assumed a vast body with eight weapon-bearing arms. Then she laughed aloud, enraged, and said to Kaṃsa, "Why did you hurl me on the ground, O Kaṃsa? The one who will destroy you is now born! He who himself consists of all the gods has been the cause of your death once before; ponder this and look to your own welfare at once!"

So speaking, the goddess left, with her heavenly garlands and ornaments. Before the eyes of the Bhoja king she sped through the sky, lauded by the Siddhas.

# Pūtanā, the Child-Killer

Vasudeva went to Nanda's wagon where Nanda, overjoyed, exclaimed, "A son has just been born to me!" Vasudeva spoke to him courteously, "Good fortune! Even though you are old, you have had a son! You have paid the king's annual tax, which was the reason you came here. Now there is no further cause for you to remain here with your goods. Why stay now that you have done your duty? Nanda, you should return at once to your own home Gokula. I too have a little son who has been born of Rohiṇī. Please take him with you and protect him as your own." At these words, having paid their taxes, the cowherds led by Nanda put their belongings into their wagons and departed in great numbers.

One night while they were living in Gokula, the child-killer Pūtanā picked up the sleeping Kṛṣṇa and gave him her breast. Every child to whom Pūtanā gives suck at night has his body destroyed. But Kṛṣṇa grabbed her nipple, squeezed it tightly with both hands and furiously sucked out the milk, together with her life. Screeching loudly, the cords of her muscles cut asunder, the ghastly Pūtanā fell dying to the ground.

The inhabitants of Vraja woke up, startled by her screams, and saw Kṛṣṇa on Pūtanā's lap as she lay dead on the ground. Yaśodā too appeared, trembling with fear. Grabbing up Kṛṣṇa, excellent brahmin, she waved a cow's tail over him to ward off evil. And the cowherd Nanda put cow dung on Kṛṣṇa's head to protect him, saying:

"May Hari protect you, he who is the source of all creatures, from whose navel has sprung the lotus which is the origin of the world. May Keśava protect you, the god who raised up earth on the tip of his tusk when he took the form of a boar. May Janārdana protect you on all sides, the lord in the form of Narasiṃha who split asunder his enemy's chest with his claws. May Vāmana always protect you, he who bestrode the three worlds in a wink with weapons flashing. May Govinda guard your head, Keśava your throat, Viṣṇu your genitals and belly, and Janārdana your shins and feet. May the imperishable Nārāyaṇa, whose sovereignty is flawless, watch over your face, arms, forearms, your mind and all your senses. May those ghosts, goblins and demons who oppose you go to perdition when they are struck by the sound of the conch of Viṣṇu, who holds in his hand the bow, discus and mace. May Vaikuṇṭha protect you in the principal quarters, Madhusūdana in the intermediate directions, Hṛṣīkeśa in the sky, and Mahīdhara on earth!"

Wishing him godspeed the cowherd Nanda laid the boy to rest on his little cot under the wagon. And when the cowherds saw the monstrous cadaver of the dead Pūtanā, they were shocked and terrified.

# The Naughty Children Rāma and Kṛṣṇa; the Move to Vṛndāvana

Once when Madhusūdana lay on his cot under the wagon, he threw up his feet and began to cry for the breast. Struck by his kick, the cart tipped over, and all the pots and jars broke. When the cowherd men and women came near, brahmin, crying, "Oh, oh, alas!" they saw the baby lying face-up on his bed.

"Who knocked over this wagon?" asked the cowherds, at which some nearby children said, "We saw that baby do it! He kicked the wagon over with his foot as he was crying; he did it and nobody else." Once again the cowherds were dumfounded. Astonished, the cowherd Nanda picked up the boy while Yaśodā worshiped the wagon and its broken pots and baggage with *ghī*, flowers, fruit and unhusked grain.

Then Vasudeva requested Garga to perform the life passage rites in Gokula for the two boys, his son and his ward, which the seer did in secret from the other cowherds. That great-minded Garga, best among the wise, gave them names; the elder he called Rāma, and the younger Kṛṣṇa. In a short while, brahmin, the two boys were crawling unprotected around Vraja, bruising their knees and covering their bodies with cow dung and ashes.* Neither Yaśodā nor Rohiṇī could restrain them. They played in the middle of the cattle-pen, or else they went to the calf-pen and pulled the tails of the new-born calves, those born that very day. When Yaśodā could not stop the antics of the two children who were constantly together, she tied Kṛṣṇa,

*These are not polluting, but purifying substances.

whose actions are tireless, around the waist with a rope and bound him to a wooden mortar, saying, "You move around too much. Now get loose if you can!" So speaking, the housewife returned to her work.

While she was busy, the lotus-eyed child crawled between two trees, dragging the mortar behind him. Thus pulled, it stuck crosswise between two lofty-branched *yamala* and *arjuna* trees and felled them both. When they heard a crackling sound the people of Vraja came to see. Between the two trees they saw the little child laughing aloud, showing his tiny white newly-budded teeth, the rope tied firmly to his belly. And so he became known as Dāmodara (Rope-Belly), because he had been bound with a rope.

Frightened by these great wonders, all the elder cowherds consulted with their leader Nanda. "We should stay here no longer! Let us move to another great forest, for here we have seen portents that will bring about our ruin: the annihilation of Pūtanā, the overturning of the wagon, the falling of the two trees without benefit of wind, and so on. Therefore, before calamity follows such mighty omens as these on earth, let us leave Vraja and go to Vṛndāvana without delay!"

All the people of Vraja set their minds on going and began to say, each to his own family, "Go at once; don't linger!" And in a moment the inhabitants of Vraja had left with their wagons and cows, driving before them their herds of calves. In an instant, brahmin, the place of Vraja was emptied of every last thing and occupied only by vultures and crows.

Lord Kṛṣṇa, with gracious mind, concentrated on Vṛndāvana, seeing to the welfare of the cows. Because of his meditation, new grass sprang up on all sides as in the rainy season, even though it was arid summer. And all the people from Vraja encamped there in Vṛndāvana, making a half-moon fence with their wagons for a boundary.

There Rāma and Dāmodara became keepers of the calves, and together in the cowpen they played children's games. They made crowns of peacock feathers, earrings of forest flowers, fashioned musical instruments out of the cowherds' reeds, and made music with leaf-instruments. Wearing crow's-wing haircuts, as if they were two princes, the two sons of Fire laughed and enjoyed themselves as they roamed around the great forest. Sometimes they played piggy-back, and other times they played with the cowherd children; they ran around freely driving their calves. As time went on, in greater Vraja, the boys became seven years old. So did the two protectors of the world pass their time as keepers of the calves.

# Kāliya, the Snake

Once Kṛṣṇa went into Vṛndāvana unaccompanied by Rāma. Radiant with a garland of forest flowers, he roved about in the company of cowherds. Then he came upon the river Yamunā, whose waves were tossing about as if she were laughing, throwing patches of foam on the banks. But in the water he saw a dreadful sight—it was the hideous pool of the snake Kāliya, whose water was mixed with a fiery poison! The trees on the bank nearby, splashed by the burning poison, had been scorched while the birds were singed by sprays of that poisoned water tossed aloft in the wind.

Witnessing this sight, horrible as the maw of death, Madhusūdana thought to himself, "This must be the dwelling place of the evil-souled Kāliya, whose weapon is poison, that wicked serpent who abandoned the ocean when I defeated him there once before. Now the entire Yamunā is polluted by him, all the way to the sea, so that neither cows nor men suffering from thirst are able to use it. I must tame this king of snakes so that the inhabitants of Vraja can move around happily, without fear. I have descended into the world for this purpose, to pacify those hard-souled ones whose domain is evil. Let me now climb this broad-branched *kadamba* tree nearby and fall into the pool of this snake who feeds on the wind!" So thinking, and tightly tucking up his garment, Kṛṣṇa dived at once into the pool of the serpent king.

So roiled up by the force of Kṛṣṇa's fall was the vast pool that it flooded even huge trees growing far away. They burst at once into flame, smitten by the wind that carried water burning with that snake's evil fiery poison; and that holocaust filled all of space.

Then, in the serpent's pool, Kṛṣṇa slapped his arm defiantly. Hearing the sound, the serpent king rapidly approached, his eyes coppery-red with rage. He was surrounded by other venomous wind-feeding snakes with mouths full of fiery poison, accompanied by their snake wives by the hundreds adorned with fetching necklaces, who were beautiful with jangling bracelets that trembled when their bodies moved.

Then the snakes encircled Kṛṣṇa, making fetters of their coils, and bit him with their poison-filled mouths. When the cowherds saw that he had fallen into the pool and was being crushed by the serpents' coils, they fled to Vraja. Wholly overcome with grief, they cried aloud, "Kṛṣṇa, distracted, has gone and fallen into Kāliya's pool where he is being eaten alive by the snake king! Come and see him!"

The cowherds and their wives, thunderstruck at these words, hurried immediately to the pool, with Yaśodā ahead of them. "Oh oh, where is he?" cried the agitated crowd of cowherd women as they hastened, confused and stumbling, along with Yaśodā. The cowherds Nanda and Rāma, of wondrous valor, also sped to the Yamunā determined to see Kṛṣṇa. There they saw him at the mercy of the serpent king, rendered powerless, wrapped in the coils of the snake. Staring at the face of his son, the cowherd Nanda was immobilized, excellent seer, and so was the lady Yaśodā. The other cowherds, too, disheartened with grief, looked on weeping while, stammering with fear, they beseeched Keśava with love. . . .

When Kṛṣṇa was called to mind by the cowherds, the petals of his lips blossomed into a smile, and he split open that snake, freeing his own body from the coils. Using his two hands to bend over the middle head of that serpent with curving hoods, the wide-striding Kṛṣṇa mounted that head and began to dance on it. The serpent's hood expanded with his life's breath as it was pounded by Kṛṣṇa's feet. Wherever the snake's head swelled up, Kṛṣṇa trod it down again. Squeezed in this manner by Kṛṣṇa, the snake fainted away with a quiver, vomiting blood because of the blows of Kṛṣṇa's staff.

When his wives saw the serpent king with his neck and head arched over the blood streaming from his mouth, they went to Madhusūdana and said piteously, "Overlord of the gods, you are known to be omniscient, without equal, the ineffable light supernal of which the supreme lord is but a portion. You are he whom the gods themselves are not able to praise. How then can I, a mere woman, describe you? . . . Since silly women and miserable creatures are to be pitied by the virtuous, please forgive this wretched creature, you who are eminent among the forgiving! You are the support of the whole world; this is but a feeble snake. Crushed by your foot, he will soon die! How can this weak, lowly snake compare with you, the refuge of all beings? Both hate and love are within the province of the superior, O imperishable one. Therefore be gracious to this snake who is sinking fast, O master of the world. Our husband is dying! O lord of creation, grant us his life as alms!" . . .

[Then Kāliya himself begged for mercy:] "I am not capable of honoring nor of praising you, overlord of the gods, but please take pity on me, O god whose sole thought is compassion! The race of snakes into which I was born is a cruel one; this is its proper nature. But I am not at fault in this matter, Acyuta, for it is you who pour forth and absorb the whole world; classes, forms and natures have all been assigned by you, the creator. . . . Now I am powerless, having lost my poison. You have subdued me, Acyuta; now spare my life! Tell me what to do!"

"Leave the waters of the Yamunā, snake, and return to the ocean, along with your children and your retinue. And in the sea, O serpent, when Garuḍa, enemy of snakes, sees my footprints on your head, he will not harm you." So speaking, lord Hari released the serpent king, who bowed to Kṛṣṇa and returned to the ocean of milk.

In the sight of all creatures, Kāliya abandoned his pool, along with his dependents, his children and all his wives. When the snake had gone, the cowherds embraced Kṛṣṇa like one returned from the dead and lovingly drenched his head with tears. Other happy cowherds, with minds amazed, sang praises to Kṛṣṇa, who is unwearied by action, when they saw the river water safe. Hymned by the cowherd women and praised by the cowherd men for the fine deed he had done, Kṛṣṇa returned to Vraja.

# Mt. Govardhana

When the cowherds had been persuaded by Kṛṣṇa to make their offerings to the mountain instead of to Indra, Śakra became filled with fury, O Maitreya. He summoned a troop of rainclouds named Saṃvartaka and addressed them, "*Bhoḥ! Bhoḥ*, you clouds, hear what I have to say, and act immediately on my orders! The evil-minded cowherd Nanda, together with the other cowherds, proud of the power of Kṛṣṇa's protection, had disrupted my sacrifice! Harry with rain and wind, according to my command, those cows which are their ultimate livelihood and the cause of their support. Riding on my mountainous elephant I shall assist you in the storm."

At his command, the thunderclouds loosed a horrendous storm in order to destroy the cows, O brahmin. Then in a flash the earth, horizons and sky became one under the mighty downpour of water. A huge flood poured from the clouds as they shook from the blows of whip-like lightning, and the circle of the horizon was filled with thunder. The world was darkened by the incessant raining of the clouds, as if it were nothing but water, above, below and across.

The trembling cows, buffeted by the fierce wind and rain, with shrunken withers, necks and thighs, began to die. Some stood there sheltering their calves under their chests, great seer, while others lost their calves to the flood waters. And the sad-faced calves, their necks shaken by the wind, cried out in feeble voices, "Help! Help!" as if they were sick.

When Hari saw all Gokula, cows, men and women together, so miserable, O Maitreya, he began to ponder, "This has been done by Indra, who is angry because of the loss of his offerings. I must now rescue the entire cowpen! I shall root up this mountain with its broad expanse of rock, and firmly hold it aloft over Gokula like a wide umbrella."

Having made up his mind, Kṛṣṇa lifted Mt. Govardhana with one hand and playfully held it aloft! Then Śauri, holding the uprooted mountain, said to the cowherds with a smile, "Now quickly hide under here where I have stopped the rain. You may stay here contentedly, as in a windless spot, without fear of the mountain falling down."

At Kṛṣṇa's words the cowherds, who were being pelted by the rain, entered under the mountain with their herds, and so did the cowherd women with their belongings piled on carts. And so Kṛṣṇa held that mountain steadily aloft to the delight of the inhabitants of Vraja, their eyes thrilled with wonder. As Kṛṣṇa supported that mountain, his deed was celebrated by the delighted cowherd men and women with eyes wide with joy.

For seven nights huge clouds sent by Indra poured rain on Nanda's Gokula, O brahmin, in order to annihilate the cowherds. But since they were protected by the mighty mountain held on high, that slayer of Bala, his promise proven false, dispersed the clouds. After the sky was free of clouds and Indra's promise had been shown to be empty, the happy people of Gokula came out and returned to their own homes. And Kṛṣṇa then returned Mt. Govardhana to its own place as the inhabitants of Vraja looked on with wonder in their faces.

## Conversation with the Cowherds

After Śakra left, the cowherds who had seen Mt. Govardhana held aloft by Kṛṣṇa spoke to him who is unwearied by action, saying, "O illustrious lord, when you held up the mountain, you rescued both the cows and ourselves from great peril. This child's play of yours has no equal! You are a lowly cowherd but your deeds are godly! What is going on? Tell us, son.

"You subdued Kāliya, felled Dhenuka and bore up Govardhana; at these feats our minds are alarmed! Tell us the truth, you whose strength is infinite. We worship Hari's feet! Having seen your heroism as it is, we don't think you are a mere man. You have the love of all Vraja, along with that of its women and children, yet you have done this deed which is impossible even for the thirty gods. When we consider your childish nature, your great heroism and your humble birth among us, Kṛṣṇa, you whose nature is beyond measure, we are suspicious. Are you a god, a Dānava, a Yakṣa or a Gandharva? Or are you our kinsman after all? Praise be to you!"

Thus addressed by the cowherds, the great-minded Kṛṣṇa grew silent for a moment. Then feigning anger, he replied with affection: "If, cowherds, you are not ashamed to be related to me and if I am worthy of your praise, then why worry about me? If you love me, and if I merit your respect, then you must regard me as your kinsman. I am neither god nor Gandharva, neither Yakṣa nor Dānava. I have been born in your family; this is the only way to look at it."

When they heard Hari speak, the cowherds went from there to the forest wrapped in silence, thinking about Kṛṣṇa who was affectionately angry with them.

# YOUTH

## Kṛṣṇa and Rādhā

One day Nanda went with Kṛṣṇa to Vṛndāvana and let his cattle graze by the banyan tree in the grove. He had them drink the pure water at the ponds, drank himself, and then lay at the foot of the tree with the infant on his chest. Meanwhile, Kṛṣṇa, who had superhuman powers of illusion, cast clouds over the sky with his magic. When Nanda saw the sky overcast and the woods darkening, heard the whistling of the wind, the rumbling of the clouds and the frightening peal of thunder, and observed the heavy rainfall, the shaking and crashing trees, he became afraid. "How can I go to my own shelter," he said, "while abandoning the cows and calves? But if I do not go home, what will happen to the child?" As he was speaking, Kṛṣṇa began to cry and clung to his father's neck out of fear of all the water.

In the midst of this, Rādhā came to Kṛṣṇa with a gait that mocked that of swans and wagtails, a ravishing face that robbed the harvest moon of its splendor, and eyes that stole the loveliness of lotuses blooming at midday in autumn. Her fluttering eyelashes glistened with mascara, her nose put to shame the famed elegance of Garuḍa's beak. Between her eyes shone a large, beautiful pearl, and she wore a fine braid pleated with festoons of jasmine. Her earrings shone brighter than the summer sun at noon, and her lips surpassed the rotund redness of ripe *bimba* berries. The rows of her teeth were luminous like strings of pearls, and when she smiled she eclipsed the whiteness of freshly opened water-lily buds. She was adorned with drops of vermilion mixed with droplets of musk, and she wore a lovely chaplet of jasmine flowers. Her cheeks were perfectly round; her chest was adorned with necklaces of sapphires and other precious stones; and her breasts were as firm as *bilva* fruits.

When Nanda saw her in that desolate spot he was astounded, for she lit up the skies with a brightness greater than a million moons. With tears in his eyes he bowed his head in devotion: "I know from the lips of Garga that you are dearer to Hari than Lakṣmī. And I know that he is the unqualified Acyuta who surpasses the great Viṣṇu; yet, a mere man, I have been dazzled by Viṣṇu's magic. Take the lord of your life and go wherever you please, my dear. Later you will return my son after fulfilling his desires." Speaking thus he gave her the child, who was crying from fear, and Rādhā took him, laughing sweetly with joy.

She said to Nanda, "Be careful not to reveal the secret. You see me as the result of the ripening of the fruits of several lives. You have been enlightened by Garga and know the entire reason. Our ventures are not to be betrayed, but to be kept secret. Go to Gokula. Choose a boon, lord of Vraja, anything you wish in your heart—I shall give you in play what may be rare even to the Gods." Upon hearing Rādhikā's words, the lord of Vraja said, "Grant me love for the feet of you both; I have no other desire. You will grant me the rare boon of dwelling near you two. Grant it to both of us, O Goddess, mother of the worlds!" The Goddess replied to Nanda, "I shall grant you unsurpassed servitude, and you shall now have love. Day and night both of you shall have the rare memory of our lotus feet, which makes your hearts flower. By my boon, illusion shall not ensnare you, and you shall in the end come to us when you have abandoned your human bodies on Gokula."

Speaking thus, she clutched the joyous Kṛṣṇa to her chest and took him far away in her arms, embracing and kissing him as he quiveringly remembered the circle of the Dance. Then Rādhā spied a magic, bejeweled pavilion which was filled with a hundred gem-encrusted pitchers. Inside she saw a handsome youth of a lovely dark hue, adorned with sandal, aglow with the graces of a million love gods. He was lying on a bed of flowers, smiling and most beautiful, clad in a yellow robe, his face and eyes serene.

She found her lap deserted by the infant who was now this youth, and although she was by nature total memory, she was astonished. Seeing that most handsome body she was dazed, and she lovingly drank the moonlight of his face with the *cakora* birds* of her eyes, without blinking, eager for a new union, shivering over her entire body, smiling, love-smitten. Then Hari said to Rādhā, whose lotus face was smiling, ready for a new union, watching him from the corners of her eyes, "Rādhā, you remember what happened in Goloka† in the assembly of the Gods—now I shall fulfill what I promised you before, my darling. You are dearer to me than my life, comely Rādhā. As I am, so are you, there is no difference between us. Just as there is whiteness in milk, and heat in fire, and fragrance in earth, so am I in you always. A potter cannot make a pot without clay, nor a goldsmith an earring without gold. Likewise, I cannot create without you, for you are the soil of creation, and I, invincibly, the seed. Come and lie with me, good woman, take me to your breast; you are my beauty, as an ornament is to the body. When I am separate from you, people call me Kṛṣṇa, but Śrī-Kṛṣṇa when I am united with you. You are Śrī and prosperity; you are the foundation. You are woman, I am man, Rādhā, so it is set forth in the Vedas." . . .

At their wedding the begetter‡ himself had Kṛṣṇa and Rādhā bow to him, perform the ceremony of the marriage thread, and make the seven circumambulations. He also made Rādhā circumambulate the fire, and made Kṛṣṇa bow to him and sit down. The creator made Kṛṣṇa hold her hand and recite the seven *mantras* declared by the Veda. The knower of the Veda had Rādhā place her hand on Hari's chest and placed Kṛṣṇa's hand on Rādhā's back. He let Rādhā recite the three *mantras* and place a garland of *pārijāta* blossoms, which hung to the knees, around Kṛṣṇa's neck. Then the Lotus-Born One made both bow to him once more, and with Hari's hands placed a lovely garland round Rādhā's neck; thereupon he had Kṛṣṇa seat himself once again, with the smiling Rādhā, Kṛṣṇa's heart, beside him on the left. He had them fold their hands and recite the five *mantras* declared by the Veda. After another bow the creator gave away Rādhā to Kṛṣṇa, as a father gives away his daughter, and stood with devotion before Hari.

Meanwhile the gods, thrilled with rapture, played their drums and cymbals, and as a rain of *pārijāta* blossoms fluttered down the Gand-

*Birds that are supposed to feed on moon beams.
†Name of Kṛṣṇa's heaven.
‡The god Brahmā.

harva lords sang and throngs of Apsarases danced. Brahmā lauded Hari and with a smile said to him, "Give me as *dakṣiṇā** that I may adore the lotus feet of you both!" Hari replied to Brahmā's words, "Your love for my feet shall be strong. Go now to your own domain, blessing shall doubtless be on you, and at my behest carry out the task of creation with which I have charged you." When he heard his words, the creator of the worlds bowed before Rādhā and Kṛṣṇa, and went joyously home.

When Brahmā had left, the Goddess smilingly gazed at Hari's face with a crooked glance and covered her face bashfully. Shivering in all her limbs, wounded by the arrows of love, she bowed to him and went to his bed. She placed a *tilaka* of sandal, aloe, musk and saffron on Kṛṣṇa's forehead and chest. Then she handed him lovingly a beautiful gem-encrusted cup filled with nectar and honey, and he drank from it. With a smile she chewed the nectarlike betel that Hari gave her and enjoyed it in front of him. He in turn gave her merrily the betel he had chewed, and she chewed it most lovingly and drank in his lotus face. But when he asked Rādhā for the betel she had chewed, she laughed but did not do it, saying happily, "Forgive me!" Kṛṣṇa then spread an ointment of sandal, aloe, musk and saffron over her limbs, and, for the pleasure he found in Rādhā, he placed himself in the thrall of the very god of love who always contemplates one of his lotus feet, and most willingly, eagerly, submitted himself to the god whom any of his servants' servants could defeat in an instant. Holding Rādhā's hand he pressed her against his chest, loosening her clothes and kissing her the four ways. In this way of love the little bell she was wearing came off, her lip rouge was effaced by kisses, and her body marks by embraces. Her braid and vermilion dot were undone in their love play, and so was the red lac on her soles when positions were inverted.

Her whole body thrilled to the new union, and she was dazed, knowing neither day nor night. Embracing her limb for limb, body to body, Kṛṣṇa played out the eight ways of love as a master of the *Kāmaśāstra*. While he clasped his smiling, sideways glancing bride, he made her whole body tender with his scratches and bites, and her bracelets and anklets tinkled merrily with the music of the battle of love. Once again pulling her to his chest, he placed her on the bed and denuded her playfully of braid and clothes, and she in turn deprived him of his crest jewel and raiment, and so skilled were they at this task that neither suffered a loss. Mādhava then took the jeweled mirror out of Rādhā's hand and she forced the flute from his.

*Sacrificial fee.

Mādhava robbed her of her wits, but Rādhā stole his heart in the Dance.

When the battle of love had been fought, a smiling, sideways glancing Rādhā affectionately gave back the flute to great-spirited Kṛṣṇa, and he returned her mirror and lovely toy lotus. He repleated her beautiful braid and put back on the vermilion dot. Hari dressed her body with such artful skill as not even Viśvakarman possessed, let alone her friends. But when Rādhā was about to dress Kṛṣṇa, he shed his youth and became a child again, and she only saw the infant, crying and hungry, just as Nanda had given her to him. Rādhā sighed and with heavy heart looked everywhere unhappily. Suffering the pain of separation, she said in a wavering voice to Kṛṣṇa, "Why, master of magic, do you play this illusion on your slave?" and she fell to the ground and sobbed, while Kṛṣṇa kept crying. That instant there was a disembodied Voice: "Why do you weep, Rādhā? Remember Kṛṣṇa's lotus feet! As long as the circle of the Dance exists, he will return to it and you shall have all the love play you wish with Hari. Leave your shadow at home and come yourself. Do not weep. Hold the lord of your life in your lap, that master of magic in the form of an infant; rid yourself of your misery, and go home." Thus was she comforted; then she took the child and once more looked at the flower garden, the grove, and that jeweled pavilion.

Quickly Rādhā left Vṛndāvana and went to Nanda's house. With the speed of thought she went in the blink of an eye, her lovely dress wet and sticky, with reddened eyes, and she made ready to hand Yaśodā her baby, saying, "Your husband gave me this heavy child in the pasture, and it has been crying from hunger. I had much trouble on the way; my clothes are wet; it's a dreadful, rainy day, and I was hardly able to carry him on the slippery, muddy road, Yaśodā. Take your child, my dear, give him the breast and calm him down. I have been long gone from home and I must go now. Be at ease, good woman," and she gave her the child and went home. Yaśodā took the baby, kissed and suckled it, and outside, at home, Rādhā did her household chores. But every night she made love with Hari there.

# The Theft of the Clothes

When the month was full, the cowherd women went on the last day to the river to bathe, leaving on the banks all kinds of articles, their jewelry and their lovely clothes of all colors, yellow, red and white. Numerous things adorned the river bank; it looked very gay and was made fragrant by a breeze redolent with sandal, aloe and musk. It was decorated with all kinds of offerings as well, fruits of the season and the region, incense, lamps, vermilion and saffron. The cowherd women, whose hearts were dedicated to Kṛṣṇa, ran merrily in the nude to play in the water and soon were absorbed in their water games.

When Kṛṣṇa saw the clothes and the various articles, he and the other cowherd boys took the clothes and ate the delicacies; then they went some distance away, piling the clothes on their shoulders mischievously. There were twelve of them, and these with Kṛṣṇa and Baladeva* constituted the fourteen principal cowherds, though Kṛṣṇa had other cowherd friends by the millions. They all stood in a group together at some distance, making a heap of the hundreds of garments in eager anticipation. Kṛṣṇa took some of the clothes and gleefully bundled them up. He climbed to the top of a *kadamba* tree and said to the cowherd women, "Ho! little lasses, you have broken your vow! You do what I tell you, then you may play as love commands. This is an auspicious month, fit to keep vows in, so why are you now naked in the water, breaking part of your vow? Your clothes and garlands and articles befitting a vow, which you should be wearing—who has taken them away from you? Varuṇa† himself angers at women who bathe naked during a vow, and his servants take away their clothing and things. How can you go nude? What will become of your vow? Why does she whom you seek to please with your vow not at least protect your clothing? Give some thought to your worshipful Goddess who must be gratified by your offerings. If she cannot even keep your clothes safe, then how can that Goddess of yours reward your vow? For she who can bestow a reward can do anything!"

When they heard Kṛṣṇa's words, the women of Vraja fell to thinking, and they saw the bank of the river empty of clothes and articles. Dejectedly they plunged deep into the water and wept aloud, "Oh where have our clothes gone, where are our things?" Desperate, all the cow maids then and there folded their hands and said, "These servant wenches have to wear clothes, O lord of all that exists. Reveal yourself and allow us to touch you. These articles were meant for the vow and are now the reserved property of gods; they have not yet been given away and are not for the taking. Speak, knower of the Veda. Give us our clean clothes, so we can wear them and conclude our vow, and also the other articles; allow the partaking of the ritual offerings!"

Thereupon Kṛṣṇa showed them all his pile of clothing and ran a short distance in front of them. Seeing the other cowherds with the

*Name of Kṛṣṇa's elder brother, Rāma.
†The god of water.

clothes, Rādhā, the mistress of the women, said angrily, while dripping with water, to her friends, "Get up and tie up that cowherd and bring him to me!" At Rādhā's orders they quickly and indignantly got out of the water and went ahead, covering their shame with their hands. The women all sped after Kṛṣṇa, who ran off with equal speed carrying the pile of clothes. Kṛṣṇa went swiftly to the spot where the other cowherds were with the rest of the clothes, and the girls pursued him in force. They surrounded the clothes' thieves quickly, but the others broke loose and in fear ran to the spot where Kṛṣṇa stood with his clothes. Now the girls surrounded them together with Kṛṣṇa, and in fear of them the cowherds gave the clothes to Kṛṣṇa. He spread them on the limbs of the *kadamba* tree, which sparkled with the many-colored garments. And when he had put all the piles on the branches of the tree, Kṛṣṇa said to the girls in a mocking voice, "Aha, little cow girls, what are you doing, running around naked? Fold your hands at once and beg for your clothes! Go tell your mistress Rādhā to fold her hands at once and beg for her clothes, or else I will not give them back. What can your mistress now do to me? And what can the Goddess you are honoring with your vow now do to me? Tell Rādhā what I have said!"

When they heard Kṛṣṇa's words, all the cowherd maidens peeked at him from the corners of their eyes and went back to Rādhā. They told her what Kṛṣṇa had said, and she laughed and was filled with love. Her body shivered when she heard it, but she did not go to Kṛṣṇa, for she was bashful; yet she smiled. While still in the water she assumed a Yoga posture and meditated on Kṛṣṇa's lotus feet. She praised him and when she opened her eyes, she saw the world filled with Kṛṣṇa. She saw the clothes and offerings lying on the bank of the Yamunā; and Rādhā thought it had all been a dream.

# The Rāsalīlā Dance

When Kṛṣṇa beheld the limpid evening sky by the light of the autumn moon, the air redolent with the perfume of night-blooming lotuses in ponds, the forest grove enchanting with festoons of buzzing bees, he set his mind upon making love with the cowherd women. Unaccompanied by Rāma, Śauri sang a sequence based on the *tālamandra,** most sweetly, in a low voice that was pleasing to the ladies. When

*A musical measure.

they heard the beautiful sound of his song, the cowherd women abandoned their homes and went at once to where Madhusūdana was singing.

One woman sang along very softly, following his tempo. Another heard his song and dreamed of him. One who was bashful whispered, "O Kṛṣṇa, Kṛṣṇa!" while another, blind with love, sprang quickly to his side. One who had stayed at home, after seeing the adorable Govinda outside, meditated on him with eyes closed and thus became one with him. Her store of merit was spent by the pure bliss of thinking about Kṛṣṇa, while all her sins were absorbed in the great sorrow of not obtaining him. Concentrating on the origin of the world whose nature is the supreme Brahman, while holding her breath, another cowherd woman gained release without breathing her last.

Surrounded by the cowherd women, Govinda paid honor to the beautiful moonlit autumn night, eager for the pleasure of beginning the dance. Crowds of women, their bodies carefully following Kṛṣṇa's gestures, moved around Vṛndāvana, looking for the lord who had gone elsewhere. Those cowherd women, their hearts wed to Kṛṣṇa, called aloud to one another, "I am lord Kṛṣṇa! See my amorous movements!"

One spoke up, "Listen to my song, the song of Kṛṣṇa!"

"Stop there, wicked Kāliya! I am Kṛṣṇa!" said another, slapping her arm defiantly in imitation of the lord.

"Stay here without fear, cowherds. Be no longer afraid of the storm!" cried another.

And still another woman, mimicking Kṛṣṇa's sport, spoke up, "I have struck down Dhenuka, so let your cows wander where they will!"

Thus imitating Kṛṣṇa's various exploits did the distracted cowherd women cavort amid delightful Vṛndāvana.

Studying the ground, one lovely cowherd woman spoke, her body half erect, with eyes wide open like blooming lotuses, "I see the footprints of Kṛṣṇa rambling along in amorous play, O friend, with lines longside made by his flag, thunderbolt, elephant-hook and lotus!* Here some intoxicated girl whose merit has ripened has met with him; these are her small footprints, narrow and close together! And here Dāmodara plucked some high-growing flowers because the footprints of the great-souled one show only the toes. And sitting here with him someone was garlanded with flowers, someone who worshiped the great-souled Viṣṇu in another life. And now, casting

*Marks in hand palms or foot soles in which palmists see presages of royalty.

aside the woman who was plaiting wreaths of flowers, the cowherd Nanda's son has gone onward by another path—look!

"Here following him is another woman, slowed by the burden of her buttocks; when she had to run quickly, she stood on tiptoe. Here the lord is walking with a friend, holding her fingers in his hand; I see a trail of stumbling footprints. Treated negligently by the mischievous lord who offered her only a mere touch of his hand, she turned around; here are the footprints of one who moves slowly from despair. Surely Kṛṣṇa said to this woman, 'I must leave, but I'll look for you when I return,' for here his trail of steps is hurried. And now Kṛṣṇa has entered the forest; I can no longer see his footprints. Turn back, for there is no moonlight in the woods!"

The cowherd women then turned back in despair, losing hope of seeing Kṛṣṇa. Reaching the bank of the river Yamunā, they sang his feats. Once there, the women saw Kṛṣṇa himself arrive, the lord who is unwearied by action, the protector of the three worlds, his lotus face abloom. One of them, enraptured at the sight of Govinda, cried out, "Kṛṣṇa, Kṛṣṇa, Kṛṣṇa!" Not another word did she utter. Another knitted her smooth brow into a frown; seeing Hari she drank in the honey of his lotus face with the bees of her eyes. Still another appeared to be in a trance as she observed Govinda with her eyes closed, concentrating on his form. Then Mādhava made each one of them happy—one with kindly words, another with a stern glance, and still another with the touch of his hand. Thus the noble-minded Hari danced courteously with these cowherd women and their minds were pure as they danced the *rāsa* Dance.

But the women failed to form a circle for the Dance; each one was rooted to the spot, not wanting to leave Kṛṣṇa's side. So Hari took each one of them by the hand and completed the circle of the dance with the cowherd women, closing their eyes with the touch of his hand. And so the dance began, with the melodious sound of tinkling bracelets accompanying the seasonal song of autumn.

Kṛṣṇa sang about the harvest moon, the moonlight and the night-blooming lotuses, but the crowd of cowherd women sang only the name of Kṛṣṇa, over and over again. One of them, fatigued from dancing, wound her trembling, creeper-like arm with its jingling bracelet around his shoulder. Another embraced Madhusūdana, her arms fluttering, and using the clever ruse of praising his song, kissed him. Touching her cheek, Hari's arms with their crop of bristling hair, grew moist with clouds of perspiration. While Kṛṣṇa sang in a high voice the song of the dance, the women sang repeatedly, "*Sādhu*, Kṛṣṇa! *Sādhu*, Kṛṣṇa!"

Wherever Kṛṣṇa went, the cowherd women followed. As he

moved around the circle, they danced face to face with him in turn; thus the lovely cowherd women shared lord Hari back and forth among themselves. While Madhusūdana was dancing with the women, a moment without him seemed like a million years. These beautiful wives of the cowherds, although warned off by their husbands, fathers, and brothers, enjoyed Kṛṣṇa, the concupiscent lord, all night long.

Madhusūdana, whose nature is beyond measure, appeared in this way as a young man and sported with the cowherd women day and night. He whose real form is as pervasive as the wind lives as the lord in those women, in their husbands, and in all creatures as well. Just as ether, fire, earth, water and wind are in all beings, so does the lord himself, pervading the universe, dwell in all things.

## Rādhā and the Dance

Then Kṛṣṇa appeared before Rādhā, and she saw the darkly handsome youth, who was clothed in a yellow robe and adorned with bejeweled ornaments. He wore a garland of posies of wild jasmine that hung to his knees, and his face was serene and faintly mocking—a source of grace to his devotees. His whole body was sprinkled with sandal; his eyes were as autumn lotuses; his face was like the harvest moon, and a gem-studded crown sparkled on his head. His teeth had the whiteness of the seeds of ripe pomegranates, and he was most beautiful. He held a toy lotus in his hand, and also his playful flute.

When she saw his wondrous form, Rādhā nervously bowed: she was dazzled by the sight of him, and pained by the arrows of love. The serene-faced lustrous man, joy of Yaśodā, lord of the universe, gave Rādhā his thousand-petaled toy lotus and the jasmine garland, and to the cowherd girls many garlands and flowers. Then he laughed and said with the greatest affection, "In three months time you will play with me in the lovely circle of the Dance in Vṛndāvana. As I am, so are you—the Veda reveals that there is no difference. I am your life, and you are mine. The vow you have kept was for the protection of the world, not to serve your own interests, dear girls. It is from Goloka that you have come with me here. Now hasten home. In every birth you are dearer to me than my life; there is no doubt of it!"

Having spoken, Kṛṣṇa paused on the bank of the Yamunā, and the cowherd girls too all paused, staring at Kṛṣṇa. Faces happy and smiling, they lovingly drank with the *cakora* birds of their eyes the moonlight of Kṛṣṇa's face. Then, after repeated blessings for victory, they hastened home, and Hari too went joyously home with the lads.

After three months Kṛṣṇa came to the woods of Vṛndāvana; it was the night of the thirteenth of the first bright fortnight* of spring, and the moon was full. The wood was redolent with a breeze of jasmine and *mādhavī,* and resonant with the buzzing of bees. The blossoms were fresh, the cuckoos in fine voice. The ground was charmingly covered with many new clothes that suited the Dance, perfumed with sandal, aloe, musk, and saffron. Delicacies of betel leaves seasoned with camphor were at hand, and all sorts of couches stood ready for loveplay along with many ornaments, covered with *campaka* blossoms and scented with musk and sandal. The ground was lit with jeweled lamps, and perfumed with incense; it was many-colored all around, festooned with garlands and all sorts of flowers.

Here lay the circular stage of the Dance, fragrant with sandal, aloe, musk and saffron, which opened upon flowering gardens and ponds that were noisy with the gaggling of geese, ducks, and woodcocks—those ponds for play and the shedding of the fatigue from love were lovely and sparkling with water as clear as crystal. The grounds themselves were lustrated with pots filled with curds, white rice and fried rice; they were graced with fine stands of plantains, with mango blossoms fetchingly strung on strings, with jars filled with vermilion and sandal, and with garlands of jasmine and coconuts.

When Kṛṣṇa saw the circle of the Dance, he laughed and seductively sounded his playful flute to excite the desires of the lusty cowherd maidens. When Rādhā heard the music, she was dazed and love-smitten, and she stood stiff in total absorption. Recovering quickly, she again heard the sound, and she paused and stood there, again totally confused. Deserting her duties she ran out of the house and followed the sound, looking in all directions, while she, luminous with the light of her fine jewelry, pondered upon the lotus feet of the great-spirited Kṛṣṇa. Suśīlā and the other thirty-two dear friends of Rādhā shivered, out of their wits with the music; they deserted their household chores without a thought, for they were crazed with love, and went off, those lovely cowherd women.

Smiling and joyous they assembled in one spot and arranged Rādhā's dress, then went on happily, chanting Kṛṣṇa's name all the way, on to Vṛndāvana, where they saw the enticing circle of the Dance, more beautiful then heaven, bathed in the light of the moon.

*The Indian lunar month is divided into two fortnights, that of the waxing and that of the waning moon. Dates are numbered within these fortnights.

At a propitious moment Rādhā, thinking of Kṛṣṇa's lotus feet, entered the circle with all her friends; Kṛṣṇa, watching her from a distance, was filled with joy.

Bashfully but smilingly she covered her face and swooned from the pain of the arrows of love; she quivered in all her limbs and took leave of her senses. Similarly pierced by her glances which were like the darts of Kāma, god of love, Kṛṣṇa, eager for the pleasure of loveplay, was himself overcome, though he did not fall but stood still like a stick. His flute and bright toy lotus fell from his hands, and his yellow robe and peacock feather from his body. Recovering instantly, he went joyfully up to Rādhā and lovingly took her to his chest, embraced and kissed her. His mere touch revived her, and she embraced and kissed the lord of her life, dearer than her life. Filled with lust he slept with Rādhā on a lovely bed of love, and made love to her in the eight postures, inversion and so on, attacked her with nails, teeth and hands as suited his mood. Expertly he kissed her in the eight ways set forth in the *Kāmaśāstras** which enrapture loving women. And with other bodies he embraced all the lusty women, limb for limb, bringing them joy.

He played on the lovely bank of a pond or in an empty flower garden, and then once more he returned to the circle of the Dance. There the master of the Dance performed the full Dance in the circle, over which the moon had risen outside. It was bestrewn with flowers and sandal and made fragrant by a breeze anointed with aloe and sandal, while bees were buzzing and cuckoos sang. Assuming many forms, that supreme teacher of *yogins* again made love to the cowherd women, stealing their hearts, amidst the merry tinkling of bracelets, armlets and anklets. From the climaxing of love rose a beautiful outcry, and all the women fainted no sooner than they were united. They fell still and motionless, while goose bumps covered their limbs. When loveplay had scarcely ceased and they had recovered their senses, they assailed one another with tooth and nail, while Kṛṣṇa left his mark on their breasts and firm buttocks. Waist-knots were loosened, braids disheveled, little bells undone, fine garments discarded. That master of the tasteful merrily performed the nine embraces, the eight kisses, the sixteen postures of love with the women, matching them limb for limb.

All the gods and their wives came with their retinues on golden chariots, curious to watch, and themselves struck by the arrows of Kāma, shivered all over their bodies.

*Sanskrit texts mainly describing the varieties of sexual pleasure.

In thirty-three well-loved forests Kṛṣṇa made passionate play with the thirty-three women for thirty-three days, and yet their desires were not satisfied. Rather did their passion blaze more fiercely, like fires that are fed with clarified butter.

# The Departure of Kṛṣṇa

Brahmā said: "Victory, victory, lord of the universe! Blessed are your feet, unqualified One! Formless, you take on form at will to show your grace to your devotees. A master of illusion, you wear by illusion the guise of a cowherd, well-disguised One. Upright, serene, beloved of all, restrained, profound in wisdom and bliss, more exalted than the highest, beyond Prakṛti, inner soul of all creatures, untainted, essential witness, manifest and unmanifest, pure, alleviating burdens, ocean of mercy, dispelling grief and sorrow, old age, death, fear and like evils, cage of refuge, rain of grace on your devotees, lover of your followers and a treasury of riches for them—*OṂ*! Homage to you!

"Arise, lord god of gods, giver of perfect bliss! Beatific son of Nanda, eternally blissful, homage to you! Go to Nanda's dwelling and leave Vṛndāvana. Remember the curse of Sudāman, which is to last for a hundred years. To comply with that curse of your devotee, you must leave your lover for a hundred years, after which you shall regain her and go to Goloka. Now go to your father's house, O god, and meet with Akrūra, your Vaiṣṇava uncle and fortunate and respected guest, O lord. Go with him to Madhupurī, blessed Hari, and break Śambhu's bow and the troop of your enemies.

"Slay the wicked Kaṃsa, enlighten your father and mother, build Dvārakā, and lighten the load of earth. Burn the Vārāṇasī of Śambhu, and Indra's stronghold, lord; tame Śiva's yawning might; cut off Bāṇa's arms; abduct Rukmiṇī; destroy Naraka; and marry 16,000 women. Leave your beloved, who is dearer than your life; go to Vraja, lord of Vraja. Arise! Arise before Rādhā wakes up, and good luck to you!"

Having thus spoken Brahmā withdrew to Brahmaloka with Indra and the gods, and Śeṣa and Śankara also went home. The gods showered flowers and sandal upon Kṛṣṇa out of love and devotion, and a disembodied voice spoke, "Slay Kaṃsa, who deserves death; set free your parents, and take away the burden of earth." Hearing these words, the lord who nurtures creatures very quietly stood up and left the blessed Rādhā sleeping where she lay.

# KAṂSA

## The Plotting of Kaṃsa

After Kṛṣṇa had killed the bull Ariṣṭa, felled Dhenuka, sent Pralamba to his death and held aloft Mt. Govardhana, and after he had tamed the snake Kāliya, broken the two lofty trees, destroyed Pūtanā and overturned the wagon, Nārada told Kaṃsa everything that had happened, step by step, beginning with the exchange of embryos between Devakī and Yaśodā. When he had heard the whole story from Nārada of divine sight, the wicked-minded Kaṃsa grew angry at Vāsudeva. Enraged, he reviled him in the assembly of all the Yādavas and considered what to do next, thinking, "Since the young boys Rāma and Kṛṣṇa will be invincible when they reach maturity, I must kill them before they gain their full strength. Here are the manly Cāṇūra and the mighty Muṣṭika; I shall destroy the two weak-minded children by means of a wrestling match against these two men. After inducing the two boys to come here from Vraja under the pretense of a great bow festival, I will make them join the contest. I shall send Akrūra, the heroic son of Śvāphalka, chief of the Yadus, to Gokula to fetch the two of them. Then I will command the ferocious and powerful Keśin who prowls around Vṛndāvana to kill the two in the woods. Or, if they come here into my presence, those two cowherd sons of Vāsudeva will be trampled by Kuvalayapīḍa the elephant!"

Plotting in this manner, the evil-souled Kaṃsa whose mind was set on killing the two heroes, Rāma and Kṛṣṇa, said to Akrūra, *"Bhoḥ! Bhoḥ!* lord of gifts! Do me a favor and follow my instructions. Mount your chariot and go from here to Nanda's city Gokula. There two wicked boys are growing up, the two sons of Vasudeva who were born from a portion of Viṣṇu—reportedly for my destruction. Bring the two boys here for a wrestling match that will be held on the occasion of my bow festival, fourteen days hence. My wrestlers Cāṇūra and Muṣṭika are skilled in combat; let the whole world witness the contest between them and the two boys! Or else the elephant Kuvalayapīḍa, urged on by his driver, will kill the two little children, the offspring of Vasudeva, when they arrive.

"When Vasudeva and the wicked cowherd Nanda are dead, I will kill my own father, the vile-minded Ugrasena. And then I shall carry off all the wealth in cows of those guilty cowherds who want my death. All the Yādavas are my enemies except you, lord of gifts, and I will proceed to their destruction one after the other. Than I shall rid this entire kingdom of my enemies and of the Yādavas. Therefore, hero, go as a favor to me, and persuade the cowherds to assemble at once after offering buffalo *ghī* and curds!"

So ordered, Akrūra, who was a great devotee of the blessed lord, grew happy at once, O brahmin, thinking, "Tomorrow I shall see Kṛṣṇa!" After saying to the king "So be it!" Akrūra, beloved of Madhu, mounted his elegant chariot and left the city of Mathurā.

# The Invitation to Rāma and Kṛṣṇa

Concentrating thus on Viṣṇu, his mind on the Self, bowing in devotion, Akrūra arrived in Gokula while some daylight still remained. He first saw Kṛṣṇa among the calves at milking time, his hue dark like a full-blown blue lotus, his eyes like the petals of a lotus just blooming, his breast marked with the *śrīvatsa* whorl, with long arms, a tall, broad chest and straight nose. Wearing a smile on his lotus-like face, he stood with his feet planted firmly on the earth, his toenails long and reddened, garbed in two yellow robes, adorned with forest flowers. With a white lotus for his earring, Kṛṣṇa looked like a blue mountain attended by the moon. And Akrūra also saw Balabhadra, the scion of Yadu, O twice-born one, dressed in blue, his skin white as a goose, jasmine or a moonbean, with long arms and lofty shoulders, his face a blossoming lotus, like another Mt. Kailāsa ringed with clouds.

When the great-minded Akrūra saw these two, his own face blossomed like a lotus and his body hair stood erect with delight, O seer. "This is the highest abode! This is the supreme goal—this portion of the blessed lord Viṣṇu that stands here in double form!" . . .*

So thinking, the Yādava approached Govinda. Bowing his head at Hari's feet, he said, "I am Akrūra." Govinda touched him with his hand that was marked with the flag, thunderbolt and lotus, and pulling him close embraced him tightly with affection. Greeted in this manner by Akrūra, Bala† and Keśava delightedly led him into their own home, where they received him properly. After eating a meal with the two of them, Akrūra told them how the evil-souled Dānava Kaṃsa had threatened Anakadundubhi and the goddess Devakī,

*Both Rāma and Kṛṣṇa are incarnations of Viṣṇu.
†Rāma.

how the wicked-hearted Kaṃsa had dealt with Ugrasena, and ended with the reason why he himself had been sent by Kaṃsa. When he had heard it all in full detail, Devakī's son, the lord, said, "I know all this, lord of gifts. I shall do what appears expedient in this matter, O lord, no more. Know that I shall kill Kaṃsa! Tomorrow Rāma and I will go with you to Mathurā, along with the cowherd elders who will bring abundant gifts. Don't worry, hero, for within three nights I will destroy Kaṃsa and his followers."

After thus commanding the cowherds accordingly, Keśava slept in Nanda's house along with Balabhadra* and Akrūra too. Then at daybreak the splendid Kṛṣṇa and Rāma arose to go with Akrūra to the city of Mathurā.

# The Hunchbacked Girl

On the king's road Kṛṣṇa saw a hunchbacked girl in the prime of youth going along carrying a jar of oil. "Whose oil are you carrying, lotus-eyed girl? Tell me the truth," said Kṛṣṇa in a playful manner. Addressed as though by a lover, Kubjā, the hunchbacked girl, filled herself with yearning for Hari, coyly replied, smitten by the power of his look, "Don't you recognize me, beloved? I am the one who is called Naikavakrā (crooked), employed by Kaṃsa as his masseuse. Kaṃsa is not happy with oil that is ground by anyone else. I receive most bountifully the benefit of his generosity."

"O sweet-faced girl," said Kṛṣṇa, "this shining fragrant oil fit for a king is worthy of our two bodies; give some to us!" When she heard this, the crooked girl answered pleasantly, "Please take it." And she gave them oil fit for their bodies, after which those two bulls of men, their limbs oiled in patterns, shone forth like white and black clouds flanking Indra's rainbow.

Then Śauri, who knew the cure that would make her straight, lifted her up by the chin with the two forefingers of his hands, suspending her vertically like a scale. And then he pulled her down by the feet and made her body straight. Now erect, she became the most beautiful of women. Filled with love, she spoke playfully and amorously, plucking at Govinda's garments, "Won't you come now to my house!"

At her words Śauri began to laugh, glancing at Rāma's face, and re-

*Rāma.

plied to Naikavakrā, that irreproachable hunchbacked girl, "Yes, I'll come to your house!" Chuckling at her and observing Rāma's face, Hari sent her away and roared with laughter.

# The Death of Kaṃsa

Their limbs oiled in patterns, wearing garments of blue and yellow and adorned with colorful garlands, Rāma and Kṛṣṇa entered the enclosure of the bow festival. After questioning the guards about the jewel of a bow, a votive gift, Kṛṣṇa gripped the bow and stretched it taut. Due to his strength, when he pulled the bow it broke with a loud crack that filled Mathurā. Arrested by the guards for breaking the bow, the two heroes struck down the army of guards and left the festival enclosure.

Learning of Akrūra's return and hearing that the great bow had been snapped, Kaṃsa said to Cāṇūra and Muṣṭika, "The two little cowherd boys have arrived. You must kill the two of them before my eyes in a wrestling match, for they threaten my life! If I am satisfied with their death in the contest I will give you what you desire, but not otherwise. Kill those two strong ones who are my enemies, by fair means or foul! If you do so, you will share equally in my kingdom."

After commanding the two wrestlers in this manner, Kaṃsa sent for the elephant driver to whom he announced loudly, "Station the elephant Kuvalayapīḍa at the gate of the wrestlers' arena. He must trample the two cowherd boys when they come through the gate for the contest!" After ordering this and after seeing to the construction of all the platforms, Kaṃsa, whose death was at hand, watched the sun rise.

As the townspeople mounted the many platforms, the kings and their wives ascended the royal dais. After sending a group of referees for the wrestling match into the middle of the arena, Kaṃsa himself mounted to his own high seat. Other structures were erected for the royal harem, some for the royal courtesans and others for the townswomen. Cowherd Nanda and the rest of the cowherds sat on other platforms while Akrūra and Vasudeva sat on the edge of theirs. Devakī sat among the townswomen, eager for her son, thinking, "I shall see the face of my son even if it be in his last moment!"

As the musical instruments were played, Cāṇūra bounded out; while the crowd shouted aloud Muṣṭika slapped his arm in challenge. Smiling slightly, the two young heroes, Balabhadra and Janārdana, dressed as cowherds, approached the gateway of the arena. Then

Kuvalayapīḍa, prompted by his driver, thundered towards the two cowherds to kill them, amid great gasps from the crowd in the arena, excellent brahmin.

Glancing at his younger brother, Balabhadra spoke up, "This elephant has been sent by our enemy, eminent lord. Let us kill him!" At his brother's words, O twice-born one, Mādhava, destroyer of enemy heroes, let loose a lion's roar. Grabbing the elephant's trunk with his hand, Śauri, slayer of Keśin, spun him around, that beast which was as strong as Airāvata.* And Kṛṣṇa too, lord of all creation, amused himself for a while between the elephant's feet and tusks, as if in childish play. Then breaking off the left tusk with his right hand, he pounded the elephant driver's head into a hundred pieces. Pulling out the right tusk, the furious Balabhadra beat the elephant's side-guards with it. Then jumping quickly on top of him, the mighty Rauhiṇeya† kicked the elephant in the head with his left foot, in rage. The beast, pummeled in fun by Balabhadra, fell down like a mountain struck by Indra with his thunderbolt. After killing Kuvalayapīḍā, who had been incited by his driver, the two boys whose weapons were the fine tusks of the elephant, their bodies covered with ichor and blood, entered the vast arena. Like two lions among deer, Balabhadra and Janārdana looked around with the playful pretense of arrogance.

A mighty shout arose at once in the great arena. "There is Kṛṣṇa! That is Balabhadra!" roared the astonished crowd. "Kṛṣṇa is the one who slew the dreadful child-killer Pūtanā, who overthrew the cart and broke the Yamala and Arjuna trees! This is the little child who mounted the snake Kāliya and trod him down, who carried aloft mighty Mt. Govardhana for seven nights! This is the great-souled one who killed in play the villains Ariṣṭa, Dhenuka and Keṣin. Look at this Acyuta!

"And the one in front is his elder brother, the first-born Balabhadra, mighty-armed, who gladdens the eyes and hearts of women. This is the boy described by those wise ones who are skilled in the meaning of the old stories when they foretold that a cowherd would rescue the drowning Yādava clan! This is a portion of Viṣṇu, origin of the whole world, which has now descended on earth to remove her burden!"

When Rāma and Kṛṣṇa were praised in this way by the townspeople, Devakī's chest suddenly began to burn and her breasts overflowed with maternal love. And Vāsudeva, having come as though to a great festival, appeared to have shed his old age and to have

*The god Indra's elephant.
†Rāma.

regained his youth when he beheld his sons. Both the townswomen and those of the royal harem stared wide-eyed at Kṛṣṇa, saying, "O friends, look at Kṛṣṇa's ruddy eyes and his face wet with drops of sweat from the effort of his battle with the elephant! He overwhelms us, looking as he does like a blooming lotus sprinkled with drops of autumn dew. Let us feast our eyes on him! O lovely woman, see the mighty body of this little boy, the destroyer of his foes, with the *śrīvatsa* whorl adorning his chest and his fine pair of arms. And don't you see that Balabhadra has also arrived, dressed in dark blue, his skin white as milk, the moon or a lotus? O friend, notice how Hari and Balabhadra are laughing as they play with the cavorting Muṣṭika and Cāṇūra!

"O friends, take a look at this Cāṇūra whom Hari has come to fight. Are there no impartial elders here? What a difference there is between Hari, whose tender body is not yet full grown, and this great demon whose bulging body is hard as diamond! Violent, demonic wrestlers led by Cāṇūra stand facing these fresh youths with delicate limbs, yet the referees are ignoring this contest between mere children and strong men! This must surely be a violation of the rules by the contest officials!"

While the townswomen were talking in this manner, lord Hari, tightening his belt, sprang into the midst of the crowd, shaking the earth. And Balabhadra, too, gracefully bounded forth, clapping his arm in defiance. It is a wonder that the earth was not shattered by their every step!

Then Kṛṣṇa of boundless stride battled with Cāṇūra while the Daitya Muṣṭika, fit for battle, fought with Balabhadra. Clutching and lifting each other, hurling themselves forward and throwing their fists, striking blows with the elbows, kicking and mauling each other, Hari and Cāṇūra fought a great fight. This violent and horrible battle between the two unarmed heroes requiring both strength and endurance took place before the eyes of the festival crowd. As the contest with Hari proceeded, bit by bit Cāṇūra began to lose his breath. He shook his hair from exhaustion and anger while Kṛṣṇa, in whom the world resides, contended playfully with him. When Kaṃsa saw that Cāṇūra's strength was fading while Kṛṣṇa was growing stronger, he became filled with anger and stopped the music. But at the moment when the drums and other instruments ceased, an orchestra of celestial musicians in great numbers sounded in the sky. The unseen gods, thrilled and delighted, cried out, "Victory to Govinda! Kill the demon Cāṇūra, O Keśava!"

After toying with Cāṇūra for a long time, Madhusūdana picked him up and whirled him around in an attempt to kill him. Twirling the demon wrestler around a hundred times, the enemy-killer burst him open on the ground, sending his spirit to heaven. Smashed onto the earth by Kṛṣṇa, Cāṇūra's body was shattered into a hundred pieces and the earth became a quagmire made by the rivers of his blood.

As Hari fought with Cāṇūra, the powerful Balabhadra battled with the demon wrestler Muṣṭika. He mauled him to death by pounding him on the head with his fists, on the chest with his knees and flattening him on the back of the earth. Then Kṛṣṇa knocked Kosalaka, the mighty king of the wrestlers, to the ground with a blow of his left fist. After the wrestler Cāṇūra had been killed, Muṣṭika slain and Kosalaka felled, all the other wrestlers ran away. And Kṛṣṇa and Saṃkarṣaṇa both pranced joyfully around the arena, compelling the cowherds of their same age to join them.

Kaṃsa, his eyes red with rage, shouted to the fleeing men, "These two cowherds must be forced out of the arena! Tie up the wicked Nanda with iron chains and beat Vāsudeva with a stick without regard for his old age! And those cowherds who are dancing before us with Kṛṣṇa—seize their cows and whatever other property they have!"

When he heard this, Madhusūdana began to laugh. He jumped onto the platform and quickly grabbed Kaṃsa as he was shouting these orders. Pulling him up by the hair, he knocked down the king, whose crown tumbled off as Kṛṣṇa fell on top of him. Ugrasena's son* lost his life under the weight of Kṛṣṇa, heavy as he was with the burden of the whole world. Gripping the dead body by the hair, Madhusūdana dragged Kaṃsa's corpse to the center of the arena, carving out a moat with the heavy weight of his dead body as if by the force of a mighty flood.

While Kṛṣṇa killed Kaṃsa, so Balabhadra in sport killed his brother Sumālin, who had approached in fury. Then everyone in the arena shouted aloud when they saw the lord of Mathurā killed so contemptuously by Kṛṣṇa. So the strong-armed Kṛṣṇa immediately clasped the feet of Vāsudeva and Devakī, followed by Baladeva; whereupon the two of them made Janārdana stand up. Recollecting the words that had been pronounced at his birth, they both stood with their heads bowed before him and said, "We have seen your feats, impossible to perform for Rudras, Maruts, Aśvins and Indra, the god of a hundred sacrifices. O lord, you are Viṣṇu himself who has come to rescue the world! We recognize you now and our delusion is dispelled!"

*Kaṃsa.

# ADULTHOOD

## The Building of Dvārakā

Once Śyāla called the brahmin Gārgya a eunuch in front of the Yādavas in Gokula, O twice-born one, and they all laughed. Furious at this, he went to the south and practised *tapas*, wishing for a son who would strike fear into the Yadu tribe. There he ate iron filings to propitiate Mahādeva; pleased with him, Hara granted him his wish after twelve years. Because the childless Yāvana had gratified the god, there was born to him through intercourse with his wife a son black as a bee, whose chest was as hard as a diamond point. The lord of the Yāvanas named him Kālayāvana, the Black Greek, consecrated him to his own kingship, and retired to the forest.

When Kālayāvana, drunk with lust for power, inquired about earth's powerful kings, Nārada told him of the Yādavas. Undertaking a mighty effort, he assembled thousands upon thousands of *koṭis* of foreigners equipped with elephants, horses and chariots. Day after day he marched, until his vehicles broke down, toward the city of Mathurā, O Maitreya, against the Yādavas. Kṛṣṇa then reflected that the Yādava army, defeated by the Yāvanas in battle, would be vulnerable to Magadha.* "A double disaster has struck the Yadus—the reduction of our army by Magadha, and the powerful Kālayāvana! Therefore I shall build a fortress that will be impregnable to the Yadu's enemies, which even women can defend, let alone the Vṛṣṇi heroes, whether I be distracted, drunk, asleep or absent, lest the wicked enemy in greater numbers overwhelm the Yādavas."

Intending this, Govinda asked the ocean for twelve leagues for his city, and in this he built Dvārakā. With vast parks and lofty ramparts, adorned with ponds by the hundreds and filled with mansions and palaces, it resembled Amarāvatī, the city of Indra. Janārdana led all the inhabitants of Mathurā into his new city, and then he himself returned to Mathurā because Kālayāvana was close by.

After his army was positioned outside Mathurā, the Yāvana saw Govinda leave the city unarmed. Recognizing Vāsudeva, whose own arms were his only weapons, who is not grasped even when pursued by the minds of great *yogins*, the king followed Kṛṣṇa until he entered the secret hiding place where the heroic Mucukunda, lord of men, was lying.

When the evil-souled Yāvana entered too, he saw the king lying on his bed, and thinking him to be Kṛṣṇa, he kicked him with his foot.

*A country east of Mathurā which invaded Kṛṣṇa's land.

Aroused, king Mucukunda saw the Yāvana. No sooner did he lay eyes on him than he scorched the Yāvana with fire born from his anger, Maitreya, and in an instant the creature was reduced to ashes. When Mucukunda had fought against the great Asuras in a bygone battle between the gods and demons, he suffered from lack of sleep for a long, long time; because of this, he had chosen from the gods the boon of sleep. And the gods had told him, "Whoever awakens you from your deep sleep will be turned to ashes at once by fire from your body!"

After he had burned up the evil Kālayāvana, Mucukunda looked at Madhusūdana and said, "Who are you?" The lord replied, "I was born in the lunar dynasty, in the tribe of Yadu, the son of Vasudeva." Recalling the words of old Gārgya, Mucukunda prostrated himself before Hari, lord of the universe, and said, "I recognize you as the supreme lord, a portion of Viṣṇu! Gārgya foretold long ago that, at the end of the twenty-eighth Dvāpara Age, Hari would be born in the lineage of Yadu. You are he, without a doubt, who has come for the benefit of mortals. I cannot endure your magnificent splendor!"

Thus praised by the wise Mucukunda, Hari, lord of all creatures who is without beginning or end, spoke, "O king of men, go to whatever heavenly realm you desire with your supremacy unimpaired, supported by my grace. When you have enjoyed an abundance of heavenly pleasures, you will be born into a noble family and, through my favor, you will remember your previous birth. Afterwards you will attain release."

Thus addressed, the king prostrated himself before the imperishable lord of the worlds. When he came out of the mouth of his cave, he saw people who were very short. Thinking because of this that the Kali Age had arrived, King Mucukunda went to Mt. Gandhamādana, the abode of Naranārāyaṇa, to do *tapas*.

After thus destroying his enemy by skillful means, Kṛṣṇa returned to Mathurā and seized Kālayāvana's army, which was rich in elephants, horses and chariots. Taking them to Dvārakā, he handed them over to Ugrasena. And the Yadu tribe lost their fear because of their enemy's defeat.

# The Longing of the Cowherd Women for Kṛṣṇa

Baladeva, who had pacified all the strife, O Maitreya, longing for the sight of his kinsmen, returned to Nanda's Gokula. There the foe-killer greeted the cowherd men and women as of old, with respect and affection. By some of them he was closely embraced, others he hugged as he spoke banteringly with the cowherd folk. The men had many kind words to say to Halāyudha,* while some of the women, piqued by their own affection, spoke impatiently with him. Others asked, "Can Kṛṣṇa, so dear to the people of the town, be happy—he who is somewhat fickle in his love? Does he speak mockingly of our behavior to the townswomen? Is he proud that he is lucky in love, he whose own affection lasts but a moment? Does Kṛṣṇa remember our melodious accompaniment to his song? Won't he return even once to see his mother? But why go on and on about him? Let us talk about something else, behaving without him as he does without us! Why have we left our fathers, mothers, brothers, and husbands and kinfolk for his sake, when he is so markedly ungrateful to us?"

"Nevertheless, does Kṛṣṇa ever say anything about coming here? O Rāma, don't deceive us! This Govinda, Dāmodara, has lost his love for us! His heart is given to the women of the town, and we will see him no more!" Invoking him with cries of "O Kṛṣṇa!" and "O Dāmodara!" the cowherd women laughed shrilly, their hearts stolen away by Hari.

Rāma comforted the women with sweet and gentle messages of love from Kṛṣṇa, which enchanted them. And Rāma made delightful conversation filled with laughter with the cowherd women as he had before, enjoying himself with them in the fields of Vraja.

# The Abduction of Rukmiṇī

Bhīṣmaka was king of Kuṇḍina in the region of Vidarbha. His son was Rukmin and his lovely-faced daughter was Rukmiṇī. Kṛṣṇa desired Rukmiṇī, and she smiled sweetly at him, but Rukmin, out of enmity, refused to give her to the discus-bearer when he asked for her hand. In fact, the powerful Bhīṣmaka of far-ranging bravery gave Rukmiṇī to Śiśupāla, urged on by Jarāsandha and Rukmin. And all the kings who were kindly disposed towards Śiśupāla, led by Jarāsandha, went to Bhīṣmaka's city for the wedding.

Kṛṣṇa too, accompanied by Balabhadra and the rest of the Yadus, went to Kuṇḍina to witness the marriage of the king of Cedi. The day before the wedding, Hari abducted the bride while Rāma and his other relatives bore the brunt of the opposition. At this the furious kings, the noble Pauṇḍraka, Dantavakra, Vidūratha, Śiśupāla, Jarāsandha, Śālva and the others undertook to kill Hari. But they were defeated by Rāma and the other Yadu leaders who had come.

*Lit. "plough-armed," nickname of Rāma.

Rukmin vowed, "I will not return to Kuṇḍina without having killed Keśava in battle!" and he pursued Kṛṣṇa in order to destroy him. But instead, the discus-bearer smashed his army with its elephants, horses, infantry and chariots, and threw Rukmin to the ground in play. After defeating Rukmin, Madhusūdana properly seized Rukmiṇī, who was thus taken by the *rākṣasa* form of marriage.

Rukmiṇī bore these sons to the heroic Kṛṣṇa: Cārudeṣṇa, Sudeṣṇa, Cārudeha, Susena, Cārugupta and Bhadracāru, and also a daughter Cārumatī. Kṛṣṇa took seven other beautiful wives: Kālindī, Mitravindā, Satyā, daughter of Nagnajit, queen Rohiṇī, of comely appearance, the daughter of the king of Madra, Suśīlā, whose ornament was her virtue, as well as Satyabhāmā, daughter of Satrajit, and the sweetly smiling Lakṣmaṇā. And besides these, the discus-bearer had 16,000 other women.

# Pradyumna and the Fish

On the sixth day after his birth, O seer, Śambara stole Pradyumna from the lying-in chamber of his mother Rukmiṇī, thinking, "He is destined to be my murderer!" After the kidnapping, he threw the baby into the dreadful salty ocean full of sharks, into a whirpool that arose among the waves, into the terrible abode of the sea monsters.

One of those fish swallowed the child that fell into the sea, but Pradyumna did not die, even when he was digested in the belly of the fish. Later, this fish was killed in the nets of fishermen, O brahmin, and given to Śambara, that best of the demons. His virtuous wife Māyāvatī, mistress of the whole household, while supervising the cooking, saw in the cut-open belly of the fish a glorious young boy, a superb shoot of the burned tree that had been Manmatha, the god of love.

As she grew curious, wondering, "Who is this? How did he get into the belly of a fish?" Nārada spoke to her, saying, "This is the son of Viṣṇu, who preserves and destroys the whole world. Śambara stole this child from the lying-in chamber and threw him into the ocean, where he was swallowed by this fish. And now he has come into your house. O woman of the lovely brow, protect him without reservation, this jewel of a boy!" Thus advised by Nārada, she took care of that boy from infancy, captivated by his surpassing beauty.

As Pradyumna grew to acquire the virtues of young manhood, O great-minded one, Māyāvatī, who walked like an elephant, became enamored of him. Blinded by love, great seer, her eyes and heart fixed only on him, she gave him all her magic tricks. Then Kṛṣṇa's son spoke to that lotus-eyed woman who was so attached to him, "Now why are you behaving in such an indecent manner toward me? You must have renounced your motherhood!"

So she told him the story. "You are not my own son. You are the son of Viṣṇu! You were stolen by Śambara and thrown into the ocean. I rescued you from the belly of a fish. Your own mother Rukmiṇī, most tender and loving, still weeps for you!" On hearing this, Pradyumna challenged Śambara to a fight, and that mighty hero accepted the challenge, his mind filled with fury.

This Yādava youth wiped out the entire army of the Daitya, and skipping seven magic tricks, used the eighth to kill the demon Śambara. Then flying into the air by magical means, he returned to his father's city. When the women saw him dropping from the sky into the women's quarters, along with Māyāvatī, Kṛṣṇa's wives mistook him for Kṛṣṇa. The virtuous Rukmiṇī, eyes brimming with tears of love, said, "This is the son of some fortunate woman, indeed, who has appeared among us in the bloom of youth! My son Pradyumna would be the same age if he were alive. What lucky woman is your mother, dear one, whom you adorn? Such is my love, and such is your beauty, my son, that you must be Hari's child!"

Meanwhile Nārada had arrived, together with Kṛṣṇa. He spoke to Rukmiṇī in the women's quarters, making her happy, "This is your son, woman of the lovely brow. He has returned after killing Śambara who stole him from your lying-in chamber as an infant. And this is Māyāvatī, the virtuous wife of your son, not the wife of Śambara. Hear why. After Śiva annihilated Manmatha, the god of love, Rūpiṇī, his wife, was determined that he be reborn. So, in a magical body, she seduced Śambara, exhibiting her lovely illusory form in the pleasures of love to the Daitya who was bewitched by her appearance. Your son is Kāma, reborn. And this is Rati, his wife, your daughter-in-law, who disguised herself as Māyāvatī, O lovely woman. There is no doubt about this at all!"

When the people of Dvārakā saw Rukmiṇī with her lost son by her side they were astonished. And as the whole town cried out "*Sādhu! Sādhu!*" both Rukmiṇī and Keśava were overcome with joy.

# The End of the Yādavas

Thus did Kṛṣṇa together with Baladeva put an end to the Daityas and the wicked lords of the earth for the good of the world. The lord descended to lift earth's burden by destroying all the armies with

Phālguna. After he had descended for the task of killing all the wicked kings on earth, he annihilated his own tribe through the pretext of a brahmin's curse. Leaving Dvārakā, Kṛṣṇa then abandoned his human form and, along with that divine portion, resumed his own position as Viṣṇu, O seer.

How did Kṛṣṇa destroy his own tribe, O brahmin, under the pretext of a curse, and how did Janārdana cast off his human body?

Viśvāmitra, Kaṇva and the mighty seer Nārada were observed at the great shrine of Piṇḍaraka by some young men of the Yadu tribe. Addled by their youth and impelled by fate, they dressed up Sāmba, the son of Mambāvatī, as a woman. First prostrating themselves, they said humbly to those seers, "This woman wants a son. Tell us what she will produce!"

Those seers, who were endowed with divine knowledge, were provoked at being so deceived by the youths and replied, "She will give birth to a club, superior to the whole world, that will crush the Yādavas. It will be the occasion of the destruction of the entire Yādava clan!"

Thus addressed, the boys told the whole story to Ugrasena. And just so, a club was born from Sāmba's belly. Ugrasena had that club ground into iron powder and thrown into the ocean where it became reed pollen. One spear-shaped chip that remained from the club which had been pulverized by the Yādavas and thrown into the sea was devoured by a fish. A foolish old fisherman, Jaras, killed the fish and took the spear out of its belly.

Lord Madhusūdana, although he knew the highest truth, did not want to undo what was ordained by fate. Wind, sent by the gods, prostrated himself before Keśava and announced, "I am a messenger sent in secret by the gods, O lord. Hear, lord, what Śakra tells you, along with the Vasus, Aśvins, Maruts, Ādityas, Rudras, Sādhyas and the rest. You, lord, who have descended here, were sent over a hundred years ago by the thirty gods for the purpose of lifting earth's burden. The wicked Daityas have been killed and earth's burden has been removed; now let the thirty gods in the triple heaven receive your continual protection! More than a hundred years have passed, Jagannātha, since your descent; now return to heaven if it please you! This is the message conveyed by the gods, O god. But if you prefer, stay here as long as your dependents require your presence."

"I am aware of all that you have said, messenger. I have already undertaken the overthrow of the Yādavas, for as long as the Yādavas are undestroyed, earth's burden remains. To alleviate this burden, I will accomplish their destruction soon, seven nights from now. When I have restored the land of Dvārakā to the waters from which it was taken, and when I have annihilated the Yādavas, then I shall go to the abode of the thirty gods. After I have shed my human body, the chief of the gods and the immortals should think of me as already there, accompanied by Saṃkarṣaṇa. I will have slain Jārasandha and the other kings who are the source of the earth's oppression without even a child of the Yadus being injured by them. After I lift earth's great burden, I shall come to protect the world of the immortals. Tell them this!" Thus addressed by Vāsudeva, the gods' messenger bowed to him, Maitreya, and by a divine course, appeared before the king of the gods.

Subsequently, the lord saw omens arising in the heavens, earth, and atmosphere both day and night presaging the destruction of the city of Dvārakā. When he saw them, he said to the Yādavas, "Look at these frightful portents! Let us go at once to Prabhāsa in order to appease them." At Kṛṣṇa's words, the great devotee Uddhava, a Yādava elder, prostrated himself before Hari and said, "O lord, tell me the right thing to do. I fear the lord will destroy the entire clan! O Acyuta, I perceive the signs of the annihilation of this tribe!"

"Go by the divine course, which will appear by my grace, to the meritorious place of Badaryāśrama, the purifier on the surface of the earth, on Mt. Gandhamādana, at the shrine of Naranārāyaṇa, where, by my favor, with your mind on me, you will achieve success. After destroying the clan, I myself will go to heaven. When I abandon Dvārakā, it will be flooded by the sea; only my house will remain in the ocean, from awe of me. There I will continue to be present out of desire for the welfare of my devotees."

Thus addressed, the elder prostrated himself before the god and went immediately to the sacred grove, the shrine of Naranārāyaṇa, encouraged by Keśava. And then, brahmin, all the Yādavas ascended their swift chariots and went at once to Prabhāsa with Kṛṣṇa, Rāma and the others.

After the Kukuras, Andhakas and Vṛṣṇis arrived in Prabhāsa, prompted by Vāsudeva, they engaged in a great drinking bout. A hot quarrel flared among the drinkers, kindled by insults, that portended their destruction through mutual friction.

What was the cause of that quarrel and friction among the men who were enjoying themselves? Tell me that, excellent brahmin.

The quarrel and friction arose out of talk about what was clean and what was unclean. While some were muttering, "This food is clean; that is not," their eyes grew red with anger, and overpowered by fate, they began to attack each other with their weapons. When their weapons were exhausted, they picked up reeds growing near at hand which looked like thunderbolts. And they slew each other in a dreadful fray with the reeds they had picked. Led by Sāmba, Pradyumna,

Kṛtavarman, Sātyaki, Aniruddha and others, by Pṛthu, Vipṛthu, Cāruvarman, Cāruka, Akrūra and the rest, O brahmin, the Yādavas battled each other with those reeds.

Hari attempted to restrain the Yādavas, but they thought Keśava had come as an ally of the enemy and so they kept on killing each other. Then Kṛṣṇa himself, furious with them, took up a handful of those reeds which turned into an iron club for slaughter. With this he felled the Yādava murderers; attacking with violence they all killed each other. Then, brahmin, the discus-bearer's horse-drawn chariot Jaitra arrived in the middle of the sea, while Dāruka* looked on. And the discus, club, bow, quiver, conch and sword circled Hari and departed by the path of the sun.

In an instant no one remained alive among the Yādavas except the great-souled Kṛṣṇa and Dāruka, O great seer. These two, angrily approaching Rāma, who was sitting at the foot of a tree, saw a huge snake come out of his mouth. Having crawled out of Rāma's mouth, the great hooded serpent demon, lauded by the snakes and Siddhas, went to the sea. After Ocean appeared before him bringing a hospitality gift, and after he had been worshiped by the excellent snakes, the serpent entered the water.

When he saw Bala's† departure, Keśava said to Dāruka, "Tell all this to Vāsudeva and Ugrasena; tell them all about the departure of Balabhadra‡ and the destruction of the Yādavas, and that I myself will abandon my body after performing Yoga. And tell all the people who inhabit Dvārakā, as well as Āhuka, that the ocean will flood the whole city. Therefore all of you must await the arrival of Arjuna; don't stay in Dvārakā after the Pāṇḍava§ leaves, but go where the Kaurava goes. And tell Kuntī's son Arjuna that according to my word you are my people, my family who are to be protected by his power. Take the people of Dvāravatī and go with Arjuna! Vajra will become king of the Yadus."

Thus addressed, Dāruka prostrated himself over and over again before Kṛṣṇa, and after circumambulating him repeatedly, he went to do as he had been told. That sagacious one then went to Dvārakā, spoke to Arjuna and presented the reign to King Vajra.

Then the blessed lord Govinda raised the supreme Brahman, identical with Vāsudeva, into himself and diffused it throughout all creatures. O noble one, the supreme person yoked himself, the fourth state of consciousness, to the undifferentiated Self and lay

*Kṛṣṇa's charioteer.
†Rāma.
‡Rāma.
§Arjuna.

there at ease. Honoring the word of the brahmin Durvāsas, O venerable one, he sat concentrated in Yoga, his foot resting on his knee.

Then Jaras the fisherman arrived carrying the spear made of that chip of iron left over from the club. Standing some distance away from the meditating god, he mistook his foot for the body of a deer and pierced his sole with the spear, excellent brahmin. When he saw that four-armed one, Jaras prostrated himself before him and said over and over again, "Have mercy on me! I did this unawares, thinking you were a deer. Please forgive me! I am consumed with remorse."

"Have not the slightest fear," replied the lord, "but go to heaven, fisherman, to the abode of the gods, with my blessing," whereupon a celestial chariot at once appeared. Mounting this chariot, the fisherman went to heaven by the grace of the lord.

When he had gone, the lord, yoking himself to the Self which is Brahman, imperishable, beyond thought, identical with Vāsudeva, without imperfection, unborn, immortal, the measureless Viṣṇu, the Self of all, having gone beyond the three *guṇas*, abandoned his human body.

# 4 Śiva

## To Śiva

*Praise be to you, Mahādeva!*
*Praise be to you, supreme lord!*
*Praise be to you, Śiva, auspicious god!*
*Praise be to you, embodiment of Brahman!*

*Praise be to you, great lord!*
*Praise be to you, the tranquil source,*
*the lord of Pradhāna and Puruṣa.*
*Praise be to you, master of yogins!*

*Praise be to Time, to Rudra,*
*to the great devourer, to the trident-bearer!*
*Praise be to you who bear the Pināka bow in hand!*
*Praise, praise to the three-eyed god!*

*Praise be to you, clad in the sky!*
*Praise be to you, with shaven head, who bears a staff!*
*Praise be to you, accessible by Dharma!*
*To you attainable through Yoga, praise!*

*You are Īśvara, Mahādeva, supreme Brahman and Maheśvara!*
*You are Parameṣṭhin, auspicious Śiva,*
*Puruṣa indivisible, and Hara!*

*You are eternal light supreme,*
*and you are Time, the supreme lord!*
*You are Puruṣa, the infinite,*
*and you are Pradhāna, which is Prakṛti.*

*I bow to you whose form is earth, water, fire,*
*wind and air, and also* ahaṃkāra, *egotism,*
*to you who are called Brahman!*

*I am prostrate before Virāj, the one whose head becomes the sky,*
*his feet the earth, his arms the directions,*
*and his belly space!*

*Praise be to him whose self is Rudra,*
*with majesty eternal,*
*Dancing before the eyes of those who dwell in heaven,*
*who imbibes supreme bliss at the end of time!*

*I praise the body of him who abides as lord within all creatures,*
*the god who is witness to all.*

*Praise be to him who is the self of Yoga,*
*whom the alert, breath-conquered silent* yogins,
*who look on everything indifferently,*
*behold as light!*

*Praise be to him whose self is the knowledge by which the* yogin,
*stains erased,*
*overcomes Illusion of limits infinite!*

*I throw myself at the feet of the supreme lord whose form is the universe,*
*whose radiance illuminates this world,*
*non-dual, and surpassing darkness!*

*I go for refuge to you, ultimate lord,*
*supreme and ever-blissful soul,*
*who rests on nothing but yourself,*
*without division,*
*supernal Śiva!*

# Introduction

Śiva is the deity of contrasts. The supreme divine *yogin*, self-controlled and celibate, he is at the same time the lover of his spouse who is often called his *śakti*, the divine energy without which the world would cease to move. By tradition, it is Śiva who always effects the periodic destruction of the universe, with his frenzied dance, but like the rhythms of a throbbing drum, this dance is also a creative act: the whole world dances to its beat. It is likely that Śiva, in the course of time, has gathered into his personality the often conflicting attributes of a variety of gods. His career, like that of Viṣṇu, is a long one largely lost to Hindu memory. Consistent with his mature form, however, is a series of unified polarities within his nature, and it is this unifying feature that characterizes the fearsome and auspicious Śiva most distinctly.

Śiva means "auspicious," as does Śankara, which is the name most frequently employed in the Purāṇas. But a predecessor of this deity, who has terrifying attributes, is found in the *Ṛg Veda* under the name of Rudra, the "howler," also a popular Purāṇic appellation. The name is accounted for in the Purāṇas in a curious way:

> Rudra, made from Brahmā's dying breath, leaped out of his mouth shining like a thousand suns, blazing like the Fire at the end of the Age. It was the god of gods, Rudra himself, howling most horribly. "Stop your roaring!" said Brahmā to the bellowing god. "Because of your howling you will be known in the world as Rudra, the Howler!"
> (*Kūrma* 1.10.23, 24)

In the traditional Hindu trinity of gods in which Brahmā is called the creator, and Viṣṇu the preserver, Śiva is known as the destroyer of the universe at the end of time, emphasizing his ferocious aspect as the deliverer of universal death. But just as Viṣṇu plays all three divine roles for his devotees, Śiva is also regarded by his loyal followers as creator and protector.

Śiva, in fact, is the only deity who generates being at the time of original creation by sexual coupling with his spouse, who is often described as the female half of the god himself. (See below, "The Origin of Women.") And it is Śiva and his *sákti*, or his "power," who are identified in the Purāṇas with the two impersonal principles (Prakṛti and Puruṣa) of the dualistic Sāṃkhya evolutionary theory, in which the universe springs from the union of these male and female entities. (See Ch. 1, "Prakṛti and Puruṣa.") Similarly, these originally impersonal principles have come to be identified in some of the Purāṇas with the sexual deity Śiva and his partner, and their creative activity is modeled on human sexual generation.

The various Purāṇic epithets for Śiva denote either aspects of his complex nature or divine deeds for which he has won notoriety. Bhairava, or "terrible," and Mahākāla, "mighty time," represent the fierce aspect of the god, while his beneficent side is signaled by the names Śiva, Śankara, and Śaṃbhu, which mean "auspicious," and Mahādeva, the "Great God." His Yogic skill is evoked in Mahāyogin, the "great Yogin," and Trilocana, "three-eyes." And Tripurāri, "foe of Tripura," and Kāmaghna, meaning "slayer of Kāma," refer to some of his famous feats.

The iconographic accoutrements of Śiva are many. Some of the stories of their origins are to be found in the Purāṇas; some are not. Most commonly he dresses as a mendicant *yogin,* his body smeared with ashes, wearing a tiger-skin and adorned with a snake, the crescent moon in his hair and the Ganges river flowing from his matted top-knot. To defeat his enemies he carries a trident and a skull-topped club, sometimes also his bow Pināka or Ājagava. And as a dancing beggar he holds aloft a beggar's drum, or a human skull. He dwells on Mt. Kailāsa, famous as the place where his faithful followers hope to go after death. He is surrounded by hosts of ghosts, goblins and ghouls called *gaṇas, bhūtas* and *pramāthas.* And his mount is Nandin, a gigantic bull.

The wife of Śiva has many names, and she too has a double personality, both benevolent and fierce. In both these forms she has a distinct personality of her own. As a loyal wife she is known as Pārvatī, the "mountain girl," daughter of the Himālaya mountain, also as Umā, "mother," Gaurī, "white," and Satī, "virtuous." As a maiden, Pārvatī seduces the great *yogin* Śiva by becoming an ascetic herself, wins him to marriage, then tries to persuade him to have children. Their relationship seems quite human: the wife cajoling her reluctant spouse, the husband busy at his task, ignoring her.

Śiva's wife also appears in ferocious form, as Durgā, the "inaccessible," and Kālī, the "black one." This is the goddess who refuses to marry unless defeated in battle by her spouse, and who threatens in anger to devour the world. Like Śiva, she is both generative and destructive in the same divine form; whereas Śiva annihilates the universe only at the end of time, however, the depradations of the goddess are unpredictable and uncontrollable, as in famine or pestilence. As Devī, which simply means the "goddess," the spouse of Śiva unites both personalities, ferocious and sublime. And as *śákti,* she is regarded as the motivating energy of the universe without which even Śiva is powerless to act.

The great god Śiva possesses a multiple personality, the various facets of which interrelate in different ways in different stories; no facet, however, stands out entirely alone. If it can be said that Viṣṇu has absorbed a variety of earlier deities into himself by the device of *avatāras,* and that Kṛṣṇa has done something similar in the successive stages of his life as child, youth and mature man, then Śiva has also accomplished a synthesis of different deities—while remaining a single personality himself. His character always includes complementary or opposing facets within a complex single self.

Dominant in Śiva's personality is the *yogin.* Śiva is above all the consummate celibate who has mastered control of all his senses and desires, who with the power won by this *tapas*, or self-discipline, controls the world. Closely related to the *yogin*, however, is Śiva's aspect as the *linga*, or phallus, in which form he is commonly worshiped today: the ever-erect but never expended *linga*, never exhausted and therefore always potent with both physical and spiritual benefits.

Curiously related to these aspects of his nature is Śiva as a reluctant family man, wed to Pārvatī in a traditional wedding ceremony. From the start, the marriage is a difficult one, for much as Pārvatī adores her husband, he is always an "outsider" who never quite conforms to happy domesticity and family life. Arriving in his father-in-law's courtyard as a begger, he performs a lewd and entertaining dance, then asks for Pārvatī's hand in marriage. As a god, he refuses to behave respectfully towards his in-laws, and his behavior incurs Pārvatī's father's wrath. Ostracized by another potentate, Dakṣa, Śiva sends his minions to destroy his sacrifice. And even with his own wife, Śiva continues to act in a pecular manner, refusing her importunities to have children. Offspring, in fact, are born to Pārvatī, but by odd means indeed. Gaṇeśa arises from the dirt washed off her body in the bath. And Kārttikeya is restored to Śiva after being born in a reed thicket from his father's spilt seed, and raised by six of the seer's seven wives. Śiva is most clearly a reluctant spouse and parent, his marriage bringing to a focus again and again the tension inherent in his double nature, both erotic and ascetic.

As annihilator of the universe, Śiva is called Mahākāla, or "mighty time," implying what is explicit in the Purāṇic mythology of time, that periodically the universe collapses into itself to become pure potential, after which all phenomena reemerge once again as before. (See Ch. 1, "The Origin and Nature of Time.") Śiva is regarded as the agent of this inevitable universal dissolution, whenever it occurs, just as Brahmā is the agent of each new creation. These gods act as agents of the cosmic process, however, and so does Viṣṇu, the preserver, as well. The gods do not act by will or whim in their creative and destructive acts, but according to the inevitable pulsations of a dynamic universe. For the devotees of each deity, however, their chosen god alone is believed to be motivator, cause and source of it all; he, or she, is regarded as identical with the entire process itself. In such a way is Śiva seen by one who celebrates him thus:

> Praise be to you, great god!
> Praise be to you, supreme master!
> Praise be to lord Śiva, the
> embodiment of Brahmā!

The entire universe is created by you;
The entire universe rests in you;
And the entire universe beginning with
Prakṛti is withdrawn into you,
O pervader of the universe!
(*Kūrma* I.10 43, 53)

Where Brahmā is generative by personality and Viṣṇu is beneficent and protective, Śiva is characteristically impatient, given to quick anger, unpredictable and enormously destructive when the energy controlled by his *tapas* is suddenly released, as it periodically is, in rage. He sears off the head of his own son Gaṇeśa with the fire of his third eye in an impatient fury, without taking time to find out that the boy is his son. He disembodies Kāma, the god of love, for distracting him from his meditations. In a thunderous and gruesome battle he utterly annihilates Tripura, city of the demons, and burns it to the ground, flooding the remains. Śiva's anger, when aroused, appears to know no bounds. He is the ultimate destroyer and his weapon is most usually fire.

Śiva is also famous as a dancer, but this facet of his personality is developed in only a rudimentary way in the Purāṇas. He dances at his betrothal to Pārvatī in a comic manner to the delight of the crowd. Nude and painted red and black he dances lewdly in the Pine Forest, distracting the wives of the seven famous seers, and incurring the wrath of their husbands. He dances on the cremation ground in order to dissuade the goddess from her destructive rage. And he dances divinely in the sky, his cosmic rhythms impelling the activity of the worlds. Yet nowhere in the Purāṇas do all these several dances coalesce into a single image, as they have done in subsequent Hindu tradition around the classic figures of the king of dancers, Śiva Naṭarāja, so magnificently portrayed in the bronze statues of south India. In the Purāṇas Śiva is known to be a dancer, but his dances—comic, lewd, destructive and creative in turn—seem to lack coherence, their purpose and the origin of their imagery still obscure.

A final theme recurs in the Purāṇas, that of Śiva as Kapālin, or "skull-bearer." And in this role, as naked beggar whose skull is his begging bowl, he also often dances. In a variety of ways, Śiva is closely associated with the attributes of death. Sometimes he is adorned with skulls, sometimes smeared with ashes from cremation grounds, and usually he is accompanied by the denizens of such funereal places: ghosts, ghouls and goblins. In this gruesome guise Śiva appears to be lord of the dead. As such, he roams the earth, begging with a bowl made of a human skull, unkempt, undressed, dirty, an outsider from society at large. One Purāṇic story calls him guilty of the murder of a brahmin, of which awful crime only Viṣṇu can release him. Yet it seems that this is only a fragment of Śiva's skull-bearer role. As is often the case throughout the Purāṇas, the stories told of Śiva as Kapālin seem to be but fragments of a richer mythology, or perhaps an active cult of the dead of which only a few tantalizing remnants survive. By far the most prominent aspect of Śiva in the Purāṇas is that of the ascetic family man. Both his roles as dancer and skull-bearer are vestigial, giving only faint clues to what might have been.

The complex character of Śiva that so frequently unites apparent opposites can be seen in two descriptions of iconographic significance which suggest designs for artisans to execute in form: Hari-Hara and Ardhanarīnara. Hari-Hara is half Viṣṇu, half Śiva, asserting the identity of these two principal male deities of Hindu tradition. This image presents a monistic view of the origin of the universe by identifying both generative gods as a single divine being, and calling this combined entity by both their names at once: Hari is Viṣṇu, and Hara is Śiva. This also may be a device by which Śiva claims the identity and prerequisites of his rival, Viṣṇu, through adoption rather than through contest. (This is in fact a recurring motif in the Purāṇas, often used to resolve potential competition between the gods for the position of supreme deity.)

Ardhanarīnara has a similar meaning, and perhaps a similar purpose, only in this case it is the Goddess whom Śiva adopts. The name signifies a being that is half female and half male, half goddess and half god. (See below, "The Origin of Women.") In some Purāṇic passages, sexual creation literally means generation by the cooperation of two originally independent and separate deities; for example, Prakṛti and Puruṣa in the impersonal evolutionary system of Sāṃkhya, or Śiva and Pārvatī, in its later and more personalized theology. The image of Ardhanarīnara represents an attempt to trace the male and female polarity itself to a single unitary source; hence the sometimes confusing language and imagery involved in insisting that two are in reality only one.

To identify the goddess as half of the generative god is to posit a single source for the universe while asserting a dualistic procreation at the same time. The great god Śiva is recognized to be the sole source of the universe, but he also reproduces in a dualist manner by copulating with the goddess who is in truth half of himself. This image can best be understood as a symbolic conciliation of the monistic and dualistic views of the origin of the world. Although all major Purāṇic deities have some generative functions, it is only Śiva who plays a dualistic, or sexual role in creation. And paradoxically, it is only Śiva's consort, the goddess, whether beneficent or cruel, who among the goddesses has an independent personality of her own.

In conclusion, Śiva is a deity with a complex and polarized personality. An outsider to society by nature, he unites ascetic and erotic, creative and destructive, male and female aspects of existence into a single divine character. Two metaphors might be identified to summarize Śiva's career: the unity of all polarities, so clearly symbolized in the sexual act itself; and sacrifice, implying that the birth or growth of any physical or spiritual reality comes only from the death or destruction of another. For example, each time the universe is annihilated, it emerges new and perfect in a fresh creation. Or, as the eternally erect *linga* refuses to expend its semen in physical release, it becomes the always potent generator of spiritual bliss. And conversely, the spilling of seed sacrifices the wisdom and self-control of the ascetic to the birth of progeny and the fertility of the physical world. Thus, in Śiva, the denial or death of one virtue permits the generation of another. All opposites are really complements, each requiring the other's sacrifice for its own existence and growth. In death lies new life, and in denial, renewal. This is what is abundantly asserted through the complex personality of the great god Śiva.

# Texts

## The Origin of Rudra, the Howler

When the god Maheśvara had left, the Grandfather resumed his seat on the broad, fragrant, navel-born lotus. After a long time there came out of the ears of the Archer,* the god of gods, two mighty heroic demon brothers, Madhu and Kaiṭabha. When the unborn lord Brahmā saw these two Asuras appear filled with fury, their bodies resembling monstrous mountains, he said to Nārāyaṇa, "You must destroy these two demons! They are thorns that threaten the three worlds!" At these words, lord Hari Nārāyaṇa ordered two men to kill the two demons. As he had commanded, a great battle ensued between these two pairs, O brahmins, in which Viṣṇu eliminated Kaiṭabha and Jiṣṇu† destroyed Madhu.

Then Hari Jagannātha, his mind filled with love, spoke these sweet words to the Grandfather who sat on the lotus; "O lord, please come down from your lotus as I ask for I cannot support you, splendid *guru!*" So the universal soul descended from the lotus and entered the body of Viṣṇu, the discus-bearer, where he merged with him and fell into the sleep of Viṣṇu. With a thousand heads and a thousand eyes, bearing conch, discus and mace, Brahmā, called Nārāyaṇa, slept then in the sea. There for a long time he experienced the bliss of the supreme soul that is without beginning, without end, without duality, itself the Self called Brahman. The next morning he resorted to his Yoga and assumed four faces. Then, adopting the nature of Viṣṇu, he poured forth creation in that form.

First, O gods, he emitted Sananda, Sanaka, Ṛbhu, Sanatkumāra

*Viṣṇu. †Arjuna.

and the first-born Sanātana. Utterly free from the delusion of opposites, abiding in supreme indifference, knowing ultimate truth, these seers did not deign to consider further creation. Because they were so unconcerned about the creation of the world, the Grandfather became distraught, due to the deception of Parameṣṭhin.* Then Janārdana, the ancient person who consists of the world, himself addressed his son, the lotus-born god, in order to dispel the illusion. "Remember the eternal trident-bearing god to whom you yourself once said, 'O Śankara, be my son!'"

At this, the Grandfather whose womb is the lotus, understood Govinda and began to perform the most difficult *tapas,* putting his mind on the creation of beings. At first, nothing whatsoever came forth from him as he did *tapas,* but after a long while, anger was born from his suffering. So filled with anger was he that teardrops sprang to his eyes and from these the Bhūtas and Pretas† were born. When lord Brahmā Prajāpati saw the dreadful creatures that sprang from his tears, he became furious and, despising himself, he departed this life. At this, Rudra, made from his dying breath, leaped out of his mouth shining like a thousand suns, blazing like the Fire of the end of the Age. It was the god of gods, Rudra himself, howling most horribly.

"Stop your roaring!" said Brahmā to the bellowing god, "Because of your howling you will be known in the world as Rudra, the Howler!" And the Grandfather of the world gave him seven other names, along with eight wives, eight immortal sons and eight forms.

Bhava, Śarva, Īśāna, Paśupati, Bhīma, Ugra and Mahādeva are his seven names. His eight forms are sun, water, earth, fire, wind, space, the consecrated brahmin and the moon. To those who contemplate and worship the god in these eight forms, Rudra grants the supreme goal. Suvarcasā, Umā, Vikeśī, Śivā, Svāhā, Diśā, Dīkṣā and Rohiṇī are the lord's wives, and these are his eight sons: Śanaiścara, Śukra, Lohitānga, Manojava, Skanda, Sarga, Santāna and Budha.

Lord Maheśvara, the god of gods, being so constituted, abandoned the Dharma of love and procreation and resorted to dispassion. Putting himself in the Self, he drank the eternal nectar known as *OṂ* which is Brahman and entered his supernal nature.

As directed by Brahmā, the blue and red god poured forth beings. With his mind, lord Śiva emitted three-eyed Rudras fearless and gleeful like himself, with matted hair, blue throats, holding Pinākas, bearing tridents and killing with spears. Vast numbers of omniscient Rudras, free from old age and death and untrammeled by passions appeared mounted on bulls.

*Supreme being; here, Viṣṇu.
†Surviving ghosts of people not properly cremated.

When the *guru* saw these hordes of resplendent blue and red Rudras who were immune to old age and death, he said to Hara, "You should not create such awful beings who are exempt from death, O god! Pour forth other creatures that are possessed of birth and death!"

But the blessed lord with matted hair, the chastiser of Kāma, replied instead, "Such a dreadful creation is not to my liking. Continue this creation yourself!" And since then, this god has remained inactive in the midst of of these Rudras. This explains the immobile form of the trident-bearing god of gods called Sthāṇu.

## The Birth of Pārvatī

Three little daughters endowed with beauty and virtue were born to Menā,* and she also had a fourth child, a son called Sunābha. Ruddy-limbed, red-eyed and dressed in red, the eldest daughter of Menā was named Rāgiṇi, O seer. Fair of limb, with eyes like lotus-leaves, the next was called Kuṭilā. Her hair was black and curly and she wore clothes and garlands of white. Menakā's youngest daughter was the incomparably beautiful Kālī, black as a lump of collyrium, with eyes as blue as a lotus blossom.

Six years after their birth, these three little girls began to practice *tapas*, O seer. And the gods observed these beautiful girls. The ascetic Kuṭilā, whose luster radiated like the rays of the moon, was taken up to Brahmaloka by all the celestials and the Vasus, where all those divinities said, "O Brahmā, tell us if this girl will give birth to a son who will be the killer of Mahiṣa!"

The lord of the gods answered, "This ascetic girl is not capable of supporting Śarva's semen. Let the poor girl go." Then, O Nārada, the angry Kuṭilā said to Brahmā, "I will do my best to bear the seed of Śarva that is so difficult to hold. Hear me now! I shall win over Janārdana with well-done *tapas*, O Grandfather, and thus shall I make Hara bow his head. This is the truth I speak!"

Vexed by this, the Grandfather, lord Brahmā, the original creator and the lord of the universe, said to the fierce Kuṭilā, great seer, "Because you pay no attention to my words, vile Kuṭilā, you will be burned by my curse to dissolve into water!"

Cursed in this manner by Brahmā, O seer, Himavat's daughter became water, a river in spate that inundated Brahmaloka. When he saw her waters overflowing, the Grandfather bound her firmly with

*The wife of the Himālaya personified.

fetters made of words, namely the Ṛg, Sāma, Atharva and Yajur Vedas. Thus contained the little daughter of the mountain remained in Brahmaloka, O brahmin. Changed entirely into water, she flooded even the white hair of Brahmā.

Then the girl named Rāgavatī was taken to heaven by the gods. When she too was offered to Brahmā, and Prajāpati spoke to her in the same manner, she also became furious and answered, "I shall perform such mighty *tapas* indeed that the slayer of Mahiṣa will be linked with my name!" But Brahmā cursed her too, saying, "Wicked girl, you have overstepped my word which even the gods themselves cannot transgress! You shall become the Twilight!" And so Rāgavatī,* daughter of the mountain, became the twilight, excellent seer, and received a body firmly conjoined with the Pleiades.

Realizing that she had lost two of her daughters, the unhappy Menā said to the third, "O don't!" to prevent her from doing *tapas*. Thus Menā, lovely daughter of the Fathers, named her third little girl Umā ("O don't!") when she went to the forest for *tapas*. There with her mind fixed on the god who holds the trident, whose banner bears the bull, having united with Rudra in her heart, she continued to practise intense *tapas*.

Then Brahmā said to the gods, "Go to Kālī, daughter of Himavat, and bring her here, she who is doing *tapas* in the Himālaya mountains." When the gods gathered to see the mountain daughter, they were so overcome by her brilliance that they could not approach her. Indra, along with the hosts of immortals, was overwhelmed by her glory. He told Brahmā of her superior splendor and simply stood there.

"This is surely the beloved of Śankara," said Brahmā, "who now disturbs you with her aura, outshining even your own luster. Don't be concerned, but go to your homes, knowing that Mahiṣa is already slain by this goddess in battle, and the demon Tāraka too." When they had been thus addressed by the god Brahmā, all the gods together with Indra went home, their trouble instantly dispelled by his words. And Himavat, the mountain lord, accompanied by his wife, dissuaded Umā from her *tapas* and took her home.

Now the great-minded god was roaming around those lofty mountains, high as Meru, engaged in the difficult vow of homelessness called Nirāśraya. One day Hara arrived at the great Himavat where he spent the night, after being reverently honored by the mountain. On the second day the lord of the mountain invited Mahādeva to remain there, saying, "Stay here, O lord, for the practice of the dis-

*Lit. "having a red hue."

cipline of *tapas*!" Thus invited by the mountain, Hara made up his mind to abandon the vow of homelessness. Settling into the hermitage, he remained there.

While the trident-bearing god of gods was living at the hermitage, Kālī, the lovely daughter of the mountain king, visited the spot. When Hara saw her approach, his beloved Satī born again, he honored her with a welcome and resumed his Yoga. And when the beautiful fair-hipped woman arrived, she folded her hands and worshiped Śiva's feet, in the company of her friends. After watching the little daughter of the mountain for some length of time, Śarva said, "This is not seemly!" and disappeared with his *gaṇas*.

When Pārvatī, full of wisdom, heard Śarva's cruel words, she was consumed with inner pain and said to her father, "O father, I shall go into the forest to practice severe *tapas* in order to win Śankara, the god who bears the Pināka." Her father pronounced, "So be it!" so she went to practice *tapas* at the broad mountain's foot.

There the friends of the princess Pārvatī did services for her, fetching kindling wood, grass, fruit and roots. She made for her amusement a splendid clay image of Hara holding a spear, and then blessed it herself. She did *pūjā* to him and gazed at him over and over again. Because of this the slayer of Tripura grew pleased with her worship.

He assumed the body of a young man carrying an *āṣāḍha** staff, girdled with *muñja* grass, wearing a sacred thread,† carrying an umbrella and wearing a deer-skin. With a water jar in his hand, his body reddened with ashes, he traveled from hermitage to hermitage until at last he reached the refuge of Kālī. She arose, along with her companions, O Nārada, honored him ceremoniously and asked him, "O mendicant, where do you come from? Where is your own hermitage? Where are you going? Tell me at once!"

"O maiden whose vows are pure," he replied, "my hermitage is in Vārāṇasī. I shall travel from here to the shrine at Pṛthūdaka." "What merit will you acquire at Pṛthūdaka, O chief of brahmins, and what fruit will you acquire at the places where you bathe along the way?"

"First I took a ritual bath at Prayāga, next at the sacred ford of Kubjāmra, then at Jayanta, Caṇḍikeśvara, Bandhuvṛnda and Karkandha, at the sacred ford of Kanakhala, at Sarasvatī, Agnikuṇḍa, Bhadrā and Triviṣṭapa. I also visited Konaṭa, Koṭitīrtha and Kubjaka, O flat-bellied one. At each of these I bathed dispassionately. And now I have come here to your hermitage.

*A staff of a special kind of wood carried by ascetics during the month of the same name.

†A three-stranded thread bestowed by a teacher on his pupil at the latter's initiation; it runs in a loop from the left shoulder to the right hip.

"After conversing with you here, I shall go on to Pṛthūdaka. Please do not be angry with what I am about to ask you. Brahmins respect the fact that I wither myself through *tapas*, O flat-bellied one, since I have disciplined my body since my youth. But why are you practicing this difficult *tapas*, a woman in the prime of life? I am doubtful and concerned about this. O radiant woman, the sweet pleasures enjoyed by young women in the bloom of youth diminish at full maturity. Furthermore, creatures on earth, moving and unmoving, aspire to gain by *tapas* either beauty, status or power, O mountain-born one, yet you possess an abundance of all these. Why then have you set aside your ornaments for matted hair? And why have you discarded silken clothes for tree bark?"

Then Somaprabha, an elder wizened by *tapas*, a companion of the princess, told the beggar how the matter lay, O Nārada. "Hear, excellent brahmin, the reason why Pārvatī practices *tapas*: she wants Hara for her husband."

When he heard Somaprabha's words, the mendicant shook his head and burst out laughing. "I say this to you, Pārvatī," he said, "who gave you such an idea? How can your soft creeper-like hand join the hand of Śarva that holds a snake? You dress in fine cloth while Rudra wears a tiger skin! You adorn yourself with sandal paste while he is smeared with ashes. None of this seems right to me!"

After he had said these things, chief of Brahmins, Pārvatī answered the mendicant, "Don't speak like this to me, beggar! Hara transcends all virtues! Whether the lord of the gods be auspicious or terrifying, rich or poor, with or without ornaments, whatever he is, he shall be my husband! Restrain this talkative beggar with quivering lips, moon-lustered Somaprabha, for worse than a slanderer is the one who stays to listen!"

After he had said these things, chief of brahmins, Pārvatī answered Śiva abandoned the body of a mendicant and took on his own form. So doing, he said, "Go, beloved, to your father's house. I shall send the great sages to the house of Himavat for your sake. The clay image you fashioned as the devotee of Rudra will be known in the world as Bhadreśvara. It will be worshiped by gods, Dānavas, Gandharvas, Yakṣas, Kimpurusas and Snakes, and also by men who seek their own welfare."

Thus addressed by the god, O seer, the daughter of the mountain king sped through the sky to her father's house. After leaving the little mountain princess, Śankara of great splendor went on to Pṛthūdaka and bathed there according to the rules. Then the eminent god Maheśvara, his taints removed after his bath, went on to mighty Mt. Mandara together with Nandin, his *gaṇas* and his mounts. When the destroyer of Tripura arrived with his *gaṇas* and the seven brahmin seers, the eminent mountain was thrilled, his hair bristling with delight. His heart rejoicing, that mountain performed a *pūjā* to the three-eyed god, together with all his fine *gaṇas*, with divine fruits, roots, tubers and the purest water.

# The Test of Pārvatī's *Tapas*

Hear with pleasure, O Sanatkumāra, the story of the most purifying *avatāra* of the great-souled lord Śiva called Jaṭila. Long ago Satī, Dakṣa's daughter, abandoned her body at her father's feast after he insulted her and she was reborn as Śivā, daughter of Menā and the snowy mountain Himavat. Desiring Śankara for her husband, she went to the deep forest with two companions and practised pure *tapas;* Śiva, skilled in various sports, sent the Seven Seers to the site of Pārvatī's *tapas* to examine her asceticism in person. Arriving there, these sages performed their inspection scrupulously, but even with their utmost efforts they were unable to distract her. They returned to Śiva, bowed, and told him what had happened. Thus having accomplished their task, they returned respectfully to Svarloka.

After the seers had gone home, lord Śankara, the begetter, decided to investigate Śivā's behavior himself. The mighty lord, who had himself become a serene ascetic through the appeasement of desire took the form of a *brahmacārin,* this our most wondrous lord. In the body of an ancient brahmin, glowing with his own luster, the luminous one who carried a staff and umbrella was happy at heart. Thus bearing the body of a matted-haired ascetic, Śambhu Śankara who is kind to his devotees went at once with great joy to the forest of the mountain daughter.

There he saw the goddess standing at a fire altar surrounded by her companions, pure like an auspicious digit of the moon. When Śambhu, who is loyal to his devotees, saw the goddess, he approached her eagerly in a friendly manner. When she saw him coming, this marvelous and splendid brahmin, his body covered with fine hair, his aspect serene, with a staff and animal skin, in the person of an aged *brahmacārin* with matted hair carrying a water jar, she worshiped him most graciously with all the offerings of *pūjā*. After joyfully honoring the *brahmacārin,* the goddess Pārvatī inquired respectfully about his health, "Who are you who have come here in the form of a *brahmacārin?* Where have you come from to brighten this forest? Speak, O choicest of those who know the Veda!"

Thus questioned by Pārvatī, the twice-born *brahmacārin* graciously replied at once in order to test Śivā's intentions, "Be assured that I am a twice-born *brahmacārin*. I am an ascetic, going where I please, a benefactor who gives help to others."

As he said this, Śankara the *brahmacārin* who is kind to his devotees stood at her side concealing his true nature. "What can I say, great goddess? There is nothing more to be said. A great perversion is going on here, I see, conduct that will bring disaster. For in your early youth when you should be enjoying fine pleasures and the attentions of others, you are doing *tapas* to no purpose at all! Who are you? Whose daughter are you? Why are you practising *tapas* in this lonely forest, *tapas* that is hard to master even for self-controlled seers?"

At these words, the supreme goddess began to laugh and replied politely to the excellent *brahmacārin*, "Hear my whole story, O wise brahmin *brahmacārin*. I was born in the land of Bharata, in the house of Himavat. Before that I was born in the House of Dakṣa as the maiden Satī, beloved of Śankara. When my father insulted me about my husband, I abandoned by body through Yoga. In this birth, O twice-born one, I won Śiva again by my great merit, but after reducing Manmatha to ashes, he abandoned me and went away. When Śankara left my father's house to do *tapas*, I was ashamed. So I came here for *tapas* myself, following the word of my *guru*. With mind, speech and action I have chosen Śankara as my lord.

"All this is the truth I speak and not a lie. Yet I realize my purpose is most difficult to obtain. How am I to succeed? In any case, it is because of my heart's desire that I am now practising *tapas*. Disregarding all the other gods who are headed by Indra, leaving aside even Viṣṇu and Brahmā, I want in truth to win for my husband only the one who holds the Pināka!"

When he heard these determined words of Pārvatī, O seer, the matted-haired Rudra said this with a smile, "What an idea you have in your head, goddess, daughter of Himācala!* Abandoning the gods for Rudra, you practise *tapas!* I am well acquainted with this Rudra, so listen to what I say. He has a bull on his banner. He is not a normal man. His hair is unkempt. He is always alone by himself. Above all, he is indifferent to the world. Therefore do not yoke your mind to this Rudra! Your lovely form, goddess, is wholly opposite to that of Hara. What you propose offends me; but you are free to do as you choose."

After saying this, Rudra in his *brahmacārin* form continued to ridicule himself in various ways before her in order to test her. When she heard the brahmin's untoward words, the goddess Pārvatī,

*Himālaya.

greatly provoked, answered him who was reviling Śiva, "This much I am sure of, that there is someone here who deserves to be killed, even though he appears at the moment to be inviolable. You must be some imposter who has come here in the guise of a *brahmacārin* in order to insult Śiva! Now I am angry with you, fool! You cannot possibly know Śiva, for your face is turned away from him. It infuriates me that I have honored you! On earth, one who insults Śiva has all the merit he has accumulated since birth reduced to ashes. And one who so much as touches a despiser of Śiva must perform expiation. Fie on you, dirty thief! Vile man, I know this Śiva whom you have described. He is the supreme lord! He adopts various forms through illusion so that you cannot know him definitively. Yet Rudra, granter of my wishes, beloved of the virtuous, is utterly without alteration!"

After Śivā, the goddess, had said this, she recited the truth about Śiva, describing Rudra as the unmanifest Brahman who is without characteristics. After listening to the goddess' words, the twice-born *brahmacārin* started once again to speak, but the mountain-born Śivā, turning her face away from any further abuse of Śiva, her mind's fancy fixed on him, spoke quickly to her companion:

"Stop this horrid brahmin from speaking out as he wishes, friend, or he will once again insult Śiva! The sin of one who reviles Śiva is not his alone, but those who listen to the insult also share in the guilt. Anyone, without exception, who reviles Śiva is to be killed by his servants. A brahmin who does so is to be shunned; one should leave his company at once. This wicked man is again going to speak ill of Śiva, but because he is a brahmin, he is not to be killed. He is, however, to be ignored and avoided at all costs. Let us leave this place at once and go somewhere else immediately so we will not have to converse further with this idiot!"

After Umā had said this, seer, and just as she was lifting one foot to go, Śiva appeared before her and caught hold of her garment. Assuming his divine form as it appears to those who meditate on him, Śiva made himself visible to Śivā and spoke to her while her face was still turned away from him.

"If you leave me, where will you go? O Śivā, I will not leave you alone. I have tested you, blameless woman, and find you firmly devoted to me. I came to you in the form of a *brahmacārin* and said to you many things, all out of desire for your own welfare. I am profoundly pleased with your special devotion. Tell me what your heart desires! There is nothing you do not deserve! Because of your *tapas*, I shall be your servant from this moment on. Due to your loveliness, each instant without you lasts an Age. Cast off your modesty! Become my wife forevermore! Come, beloved. I shall go to my mountain at once, together with you."

Śivā became overjoyed at hearing these words of the lord of the gods and abandoned immediately all the hardships of *tapas*. Trembling at the sight of Śiva's celestial form, Śivā kept her face modestly turned down and replied respectfully to the lord, "If you are pleased with me and if you have compassion for me, then be my husband, O lord of the gods."

Thus addressed by Śivā, Śiva took her hand according to custom and went to Mt. Kailāsa with her. Having won her husband, the mountain-born girl performed the divine offices for the gods.

# The Betrothal of Śiva and Pārvatī

Rudra, pleased to be so honored by the mountain, called to mind the great seers and Arundhatī.* Upon this call of the great-souled Śankara, these seers gathered on mighty Mt. Mandara with its lovely caverns. When the god who destroyed Tripura saw them coming, he rose to greet them, and honoring them, said this, "This fine mountain, worthy of honor and praise by the gods, is most fortunate to be released from evil by the touch of your lotus feet! Please stay here on the mountain, on the wide and beautiful flat plateau whose lotus-colored rocks are soft and smooth!" Thus addressed by the god Śankara, the great sages, along with Arundhatī, sat down on the tableland.

When the sages were seated, Nandin, leader of the *gaṇas* of the god, greeted them with *arghya* and other offerings and stood before them with his mind intent on devotion. Then the lord of the gods, for the increase of his own glory, spoke righteous and beneficent words to the gods and to the seven seers who were full of self-control.

"Listen, Kaśyapa, Atri and Vasiṣṭha, son of Varuṇa; Viśvāmitra, Gādhi's son, and Gautama, mark my words; listen, Bharadvāja, and you, Añgiras, hear what I say! My beloved Satī, Dakṣa's daughter, who (so they say) out of anger with Dakṣa gave up her life long ago through the insight of Yoga, has now been reborn as Umā, daughter of the king of the mountains. Go, excellent brahmins, and ask the mountain for her hand on my behalf!" When they were asked to do this, the seven seers replied, "by all means!" And saying, "*OṂ!* Praise be to Śankara!" they went to the Himālaya.

*The wife of one of the great seers, Vasiṣṭha.

Śarva spoke also to Arundhatī, saying, "You go too, lovely woman, for married women know the way of women's duty." When she had been reminded of this inviolable worldly custom, she said, "Praise be to you, O Rudra!" and departed with her husband.

When they reached the plain of herbs on the highest peak of Mt. Hima,* they saw the city of the mountain king that looked like the city of the gods. There after being ardently and respectfully worshiped by the mountain women, and by Sunābha and the other mountains, by Gandharvas, Kinnaras, Yakṣas and others in attendance, they approached the delightful palace of Mt. Hima, which was ablaze with gold. All those great-souled seers, their taints purified by *tapas*, gathered in front of the great gate and stood there waiting for the gate-keeper.

Mt. Gandhamādana, the door-keeper, came at once holding in his hand a great staff studded with rubies. The assembled seers said to him, "We are here to see the great lord of the mountains. We have come with a weighty purpose. Announce our arrival!" Thus addressed by the sages, the chief mountain Gandhamādana went to where the mountain king was sitting surrounded by his fellow mountains. The door-keeper fell to his knees on the ground, tucked his staff under his arm and put his hands up to his forehead. Then he said, "O mountain king, some sages have come to you with a purpose. They are standing at the gate eager to see you on business."

When he heard the door-keeper's words, the lord of the mountain arose and went to the gate himself, carrying the finest *arghya*. After leading them to the assembly hall with *arcya*† and *arghya* and other offerings, and they had taken their seats, the mountain spoke to them eloquently. "What is this rain that has fallen from a cloudless sky? This fruit that has ripened without a flower? This visit of yours is so unexpected as to be unbelievable! Today I am rich! Today I am truly the king of the mountains, excellent ones! My body is cleansed now that you have come to court! O best of brahmins, I am made pure by contact with all of you, just as one is purified by the sight of the Sarasvatī when one goes there on foot. I am your servant, O brahmins, who gains merit by your very presence! Tell me why you have come! I stand before you as your servant, O immortals, along with my wife, grandsons and attendants. Tell me what I can do for you!"

When they heard the words of the mountain king, the vow-keeping sages said to Aṅgiras, the elder, "Tell the mountain why we are here!" Thus directed, by Kaśyapa and the other seers, Aṅgiras ad-

*Himālaya.

†*Arcya* and *arghya* are synonyms for "guest gift."

dressed the king of the mountain with this fine speech: "Hear, excellent mountain, the purpose which has brought us to your place, along with Arundhatī, O mountain. We have been sent by the great-souled Śankara, the universal soul, the destroyer of Dakṣa's sacrifice, Śarva the trident-bearer, the three-eyed god who rides the bull, Jīmūtaketu, enemy-slayer, enjoyer of sacrifices, the lord called Śiva, Sthāṇu, Bhava, Hara, the terrible and violent great lord Mahādeva, the master of animals. By him have we been sent into your presence, O lord of the mountain.

"The lord of the gods wants to marry your daughter Kālī, the loveliest woman in all the world. Please give her to him! It is a fortunate father indeed whose daughter wins a handsome husband fully endowed with beauty and good family, excellent mountain. This goddess will be the mother of the four kinds of moving and unmoving beings, O mountain, since Hara is called their father. Let the gods who bow down to Śankara also worship your daughter! And so put your ash-covered foot on the head of your enemy!

"We are the suitors, Śarva the groom; your daughter Umā, mother of the whole world, is the bride. Do this for your own benefit!"

When she heard Aṅgiras words, Kālī hung her head, alternating between hope and despair. And the lord of the mountains said to Gandhamādana, "Go and summon all the mountains, then return." That swift mountain then went rapidly from house to house inviting Meru and the other excellent mountains on all sides. They came in a hurry, realizing this was a task of great importance. Filled with wonder they entered the hall and sat on golden seats: Udaya and Hemakūṭa, Ramyaka and Mandara, Uddālaka and Varuṇa, Varāha, Garuḍāśana, Śuktimat and Vegasānu, Dṛḍhaśṛnga and Śṛngavat, Citrakūṭa and Trikūṭa, and Mt. Mandaraka, Vindhya and Malaya, Pāriyātra and Durdara, Mt. Kailāsa and Mahendra, Niṣadha and Mt. Añjana. These major mountains and other lesser hills prostrated themselves before the seers and took their seats in the assembly hall.

Then the lord of the mountains summoned his wife Menā, and that beautiful, auspicious woman came, along with her child. Saluting the feet of the sages with respect, that ascetic woman greeted all her kin and entered the hall with her daughter. Then when the mountains were seated, O Nārada, the eloquent mountain addressed them all mellifluously, "I must tell you that these seven virtuous seers have requested my little daughter for Maheśvara. Speak to me out of your wisdom. You are my relatives and I shall not give her away against your wishes. Tell me what I should do."

When they had heard the words of Himavat, Meru and the other mighty mountains spoke as follows as they sat there in their seats, "The seers are the suitors and Hara, slayer of Tripura, the groom.

Give little Kālī to him, O mountain, for we find him to be a suitable son-in-law!"

Menā, too, spoke to her husband, saying, "Hear my word, chief mountain. It was for this very purpose that the gods worshiped the Fathers and gave her to us. The son she will bear to the lord of creatures will kill Mahiṣa, the Daitya chief, and the demon Tāraka as well!"

Thus addressed by Menā, the mountain lord, accompanied by the mountains, said to his daughter, "O girl, I now give you to Śarva!" And he said to the sages, "My little daughter Kālī, O seers rich in *tapas,* the bride of Śankara, bows in devotion to do you honor!" And Arundhatī took Kālī on her lap and encouraged her with words made auspicious by the frequent mention of Hara's name.

And the seven seers announced, "O mountain king, hear this. On the meritorious and lucky lunar day Jāmitra, whose qualities produce a good son-in-law, the third day after the moon's conjunction with Uttara-phālgunī, in the *muhūrta* called Maitra, Hara will take your daughter's hand in marriage with *mantras*. Now with your permission, we shall leave."

The mountain king worshiped those bulls among seers with fine fruits, roots and other offerings, according to the rules, and bade them each farewell. They sped through the domain of the Maruts to reach Mt. Mandara once again where they greeted Śankara. Bowing before him, they said to the mighty lord, "You shall be the husband and the mountain girl the bride! The triple world and Brahmā will be witness to the one who rides the clouds!"

The great lord Hara was delighted at this and honored the seers one by one, according to the rules, and Arundhatī as well. Thus worshiped, they went around to invite the gods. Brahmā, Viṣṇu and the Sun then came to see Hara. When they arrived, great seer, they made obeisance to Maheśvara. Then they entered his house, led by Nandin, where he received them all. Praising Hara in his presence, they sat down. Surrounded there by the hosts of gods, the lord of the mountain, with his unkept hair loose, shone forth like a mighty tree with sprouting shoots among the *arja* and *kadamba* trees in the forest.

## The Wedding of Śiva and Pārvatī

When he saw that the gods had assembled, Nandin told his master Śiva, who arose to give Hari a warm and affectionate embrace. Śankara graciously received all the gods, bowing his head to Brahmā, greeting Indra of a hundred sacrifices and paying due attention to the hosts of gods. Crying "Victory, O god!" the *gaṇas* led by Vīrabhadra, Śiva's followers, the Pāśupatas and others, ascended Mt. Mandara. And lord Śarva went to mighty Mt. Kailāsa with the gods to prepare for the marriage festival, where the blessed Aditi, mother of the gods, Surabhi, Surasā and other women were already busy with the decorations.

Hara was radiant, crowned with skulls, wearing a handsome saffron-colored *tilaka*, clothed in a lion-skin, decked out in earrings made of snakes that were black as bees, his bracelets bejeweled with cobras, adorned with necklaces, armlets and anklets, his matted hair piled high, riding on a bull. Before him went his *gaṇas* astride their own mounts, while the gods, led by Fire, came behind. Mounted on Garuḍa, Janārdana went forth together with Lakṣmī, while the Grandfather rode alongside the god on his goose.

The thousand-eyed god Indra, together with Śacī, rode on his elephant, carrying an open parasol of white cloth. The lovely river Yamunā sat on a tortoise, holding a beautiful white yak-tail fan in her hand. Mounted on an elephant, holding a fine chowrie fan white as a goose, jasmine or the moon was the beautiful river Sarasvatī. The six seasons, roaming the world at will, came too, bringing fragrant flowers of five colors for the great lord. Riding an elephant in rut that thundered along like Airāvata, Pṛthūdaka went there carrying unguents. Led by Tumbaru, Gandharvas followed after Mahādeva singing sweet songs, while Kinnaras made music, Apsarases danced, and seers praised the three-eyed lord of the gods with a trident in his hand.

There passed in the procession eleven crores* of Rudras, twelve crores of Ādityas, sixty-seven crores of *gaṇas* and forty crores of superior celibate seers. Countless numbers of hurrying hosts of Yakṣas, Kinnaras and Rākṣasas followed the great lord to the wedding festival.

The lord of the gods soon reached the foot of the lord of the mountains where other mountains riding elephants were converging on all sides. Then the blessed three-eyed lord bowed down to the mountain king who bowed in turn to the lord, gratifying him greatly. In this way did the bull-marked god, along with the gods and his retinue, enter the great city of the mountain king on the path shown by Nandin.

"Jīmūtaketu, the cloud-crested god, has arrived!" cried the townswomen, abandoning their housework in their eagerness for a glimpse of the lord. One lovely woman approached Śankara holding half a

*Like *koṭi* a word for a very high number, usually ten million.

garland in one hand and her hair in the other. Another one, her eyes distraught, hurried to see Hara with one foot reddened by lac, the other plain. Still another, having heard of the dread one's arrival, ran in his direction carrying a pigment pencil, only one eye darkened with collyrium. Another lovely woman, longing eagerly for the sight of Hara, went out naked like a fool, holding her robe and belt in her hand. Another young thin-waisted girl, slowed by the burden of her bosom, heard that the lord had already passed by and angrily cursed her youth. Causing confusion among the women of the town in this manner, Hara, mounted on a bull, went toward the heavenly palace of his father-in-law.

When they saw Śambhu enter the house of the mountain king, the women said, "Ambikā must have practiced difficult *tapas* indeed to win this mighty god Śambhu! It is he who rendered invisible the body of Kandarpa, whose weapon is flowers, who destroyed Dakṣa's sacrifice and the eye of Bhaga, who bears the trident and the bow Pināka. Glory, glory be to Śankara, trident in hand, robed in tiger-skin, Time's destroyer! Praise, praise be to the beloved of Pārvatī, adorned with earrings, wearing a cobra necklace!"

Thus honored, Śambhu mounted the wedding altar which was covered with designs and enjoyed by Fire, under a parasol held by the king of the gods, praised by Siddhas and Yakṣas, wearing a bracelet made of a snake, his body smeared with fine ashes, preceded by Brahmā, the first-born of creation, who went before him with a happy heart, and followed by Viṣṇu in the rear.

During the arrival of the slayer of Tripura with his retinue, accompanied by the seven seers, the people in the house of the mountain king were occupied with the adornment of Kālī, while the mountain divinities who had arrived busied themselves with their own offerings. Friends who await the wedding ceremony of a daughter are usually in a state of confusion!

When the women had finished preparing the mountain-born goddess, the pillar of her body was dressed in fine white cloth. Her brother Sunābha, who had arranged the celebration, brought her into Śankara's presence. While the gods who stood on the beautiful golden terrace witnessed the actions of Śankara and Kālī, the god and the slender-waisted woman began the ceremony to the delight of the crowd. There were all kinds of entertainments amid flowering trees and fountains, while on the ground richly fragrant powders were heaped here and there. For the delight and amusement of the mountain daughter and Hara, others struck them freely with ropes of pearls while the two of them reddened the earth with copious clouds of vermilion.

After these sports, Hara and the little mountain maid went together to the massive southern altar that is revered by the sages. Then the holy Himavat approached dressed in white cloth, holding in his hand the *pavitra** of sacred grass and the *madhuparka*† offering of milk and honey. The three-eyed god sat down facing the eastern region, which is presided over by Indra, while the king of the mountains was comfortably seated facing the north, the direction of the constellation of the seven seers.

The mountain, hands folded in greeting, spoke these fine words, obedient to his Dharma, to Śarva who was seated on his fine seat, "Accept the offering of my daughter Kālī, blessed one, the granddaughter of Pulaha's elder brother, the daughter's daughter of the Fathers!" So speaking, the lord of the mountain joined their hands together and presented his daughter to Śiva, saying aloud, "Take her, O lord!"

"I have no mother and no father, no kin and no relations by marriage. I dwell on the mountain peaks without a home. I accept your daughter, O king of the mountains!" So saying, the groom pressed the hand of the little mountain girl with his own. When she felt Śambhu's touch, she became ecstatically happy, divine sage. Then the groom mounted the altar with the daughter of the mountain, where together they offered white parched grain and ate the offering of milk and honey.

After this, Viriñca‡ said to the mountain-born girl, "Look at your husband's face that shines like the moon, O Kālī! Look fixedly in the same direction and walk around the fire." When she saw Hara's face, a shudder went through Ambikā just as the ground heated by the sun's rays shimmers in the rain. When the Grandfather repeated once again, "Look at your husband's face!" she replied shyly and softly to Brahmā, "I have seen." And then the bride and groom circumambulated the fire three times, after which they threw into it the parched grain together with the oblation.

Then the bridesmaid Mālinī seized Hara's feet and asked for a nuptial gift, to which he replied, "I shall give you what you desire. Release me!" So Mālinī said to Śankara, "Give to my friend the good fortune in love that runs in your family, Śankara, and then I will let you go!" To this Mahādeva answered, "Release me, Mālinī! And listen while I tell you about my fabled way with women. Madhusūdana, who wears a yellow garment and carries a conch, derives

*Lit. "purifier," a stalk of grass to pick out impurities from oblations.
†A honey and milk dish offered to participants at a sacrifice.
‡Brahmā.

his luck in love from me; it comes from my family." When he said this, Mālinī, garlanded by the good conduct of her own family, let go of the bull-bannered god.

While Mālinī was clasping Hara's lustrous feet, Brahmā had been watching Kālī's face, which shone brighter than the moon. As he looked at her, he began to shake until he spilled his semen. In consternation, he rendered it powerless in the earth, whereupon Hara spoke out, "O Brahmā, you are not to kill brahmins! There are great sages in your semen, Grandfather, the blessed Vālakhilyas!" After the great lord said this, 88,000 ascetics, known as the Vālakhilyas, were born from Brahmā's seed.

At the close of the wedding ceremony, Hara himself entered into the festivities. All night he made love with Umā, and he arose again at dawn. Śambhu was happy after he married the daughter of the mountain, and so were the gods, the Bhūtas and his *gaṇas*. After being honored by the mountain king, he returned at once to Mt. Mandara. Bowing to the gods, who were led by Brahmā, Hari and Indra, and worshiping each according to his rank, the god of eight forms took his leave and, along with his Bhūtas, settled down to live on Mt. Mandara.

## Dakṣa's Insult

Hear as I relate how Dakṣa offended all the immortals with his wickedness and deliberate negligence. Once long ago all the gods, demons, Siddhas and supreme sages went to Mt. Himavat to see the lord. Both the god and goddess sat on their celestial thrones and gave audience to these gods and other beings, O excellent brahmins. Dakṣa too went there with the immortals at the same time to see his son-in-law Hara and Satī, who was his own daughter. The god and goddess were so exalted that, upon his arrival, no special privilege was accorded to Dakṣa over the other gods.

Ignorant of the divine nature of his host and hostess, and erroneously thinking Satī to be just his daughter and no more, Dakṣa became hostile. He was impelled by fate as well as by this enmity. At a later time, when Dakṣa was consecrated for a sacrifice in his own domain, he refused to invite Bhava, whom he regarded as an enemy, and he began to despise his own daughter as well. He entertained all his other sons-in-law in turn and paid his respects to them a hundred-fold, but not to Śiva.

When Rudrāṇī* heard from Nārada's mouth that they were all assembled at her father's house, she informed Rudra and went there herself. The great goddess ascended her celestial chariot, which was ready nearby. Open on all sides and easy to mount, it was endowed with auspicious marks and was beautiful beyond measure. Resembling refined gold, it was covered with glittering gems, the top canopy made of pearls and wreathed with garlands. It was encircled by hundreds of jeweled posts with steps fashioned of diamond and gate-posts of coral. Blanketed with flowers it bore a large, sparkling gem-encrusted throne, a window of diamond-studded lattice-work and a flawless mosaic of precious stones. The forepart of the chariot was decorated with a cloud-white standard bearing the sign of a mighty bull and adorned with a jeweled staff. Its great portal was guarded by invincible Gaṇeśvaras with colorful staffs in their hands, their bodies protected by mail inlaid with precious gems. The chariot abounded with women skilled in drum, rhythm, song, flute and lute, who were smartly dressed and clever in speech. The great goddess mounted this heavenly chariot along with her beloved companions.

Two of Rudra's lovely handmaidens took up a pair of beautiful yak-tail fans with diamond-studded handles and wafted them back and forth. Between the two chowrie plumes the face of the goddess appeared like a lotus in the middle of two fighting geese. Over her crown-jewel, her servant Sumālinī, full of love, held a moon-like parasol strewn with pearls. That shimmering parasol shone above the face of the goddess like the orb of the moon over a jar of nectar. The smiling Śubhāvatī sat in front of Satī and delighted her by playing dice with her. And Suyaśā waited on the goddess after putting the lovely jeweled sandals of her mistress between her own breasts. One woman with limbs as gorgeous as gold held up a shining mirror, another a palm-leaf fan and still another a betel-box. One comely woman held in her hand a fine pet parrot, another carried beautiful fragrant flowers, while another lotus-eyed woman bore a jewel box. And again, one carried finely strained oil and the best collyrium, while others in similar positions did their own appointed tasks. Surrounding their mistress, the women attended her on all sides. The great goddess shone forth in their midst like a digit of the autumn moon in the center of a circle of stars.

Immediately following the sounding of conches, the great kettle-drum was beaten announcing departure. Melodious instruments sang aloud without being played, accompanied by the beat of clap-

*Śiva's wife.

ping hands and the sound of hundreds of drums. At the same time 800,000 Gaṇeśas marched in front, their splendor equalling Maheśa's. In their midst astride a bull, like a *guru* on an elephant, proceeded the illustrious lord of the *gaṇas,* worshiped by the moon and by Nandin the bull. Divine drums resounded in the heavens and beautiful clouds rumbled in the sky while all the seers danced and the Yogins and Siddhas rejoiced.

Rainclouds massed on all sides poured forth a shower of flowers on the canopy as the great goddess, accompanied everywhere by the hosts of other gods, entered her father's house as though in a flash. When Dakṣa saw her, infuriated because of his own loss of face, he ignored her, and paid scant attention even to her younger sisters. Then the moon-faced goddess Ambikā spoke strong words in a cool and collected manner to her father who was sitting in the *sadas.**

"Dear father, you are not worshiping properly according to the rules the god who commands all beings from Brahmā to the Piśācas! As if this weren't enough, you have made a pitiful, disgraceful *pūjā* to me, your eldest daughter. How could you?" Thus addressed, Dakṣa, truculent from rancor, said to her, "My other daughters are finer, more distinguished and more worthy of honor than you! Moreover I gladly hold in high esteem their husbands who are in all virtues superior to your spouse, the three-eyed one! That dark *tamasic* Śarva is arrogant in his soul, yet you revere him. Bhava offends me. For this I repudiate you!"

At this, the goddess furiously replied to her father Dakṣa, "Let all those who sit in the sacrificial *sadas* give ear to the mistress of the universe! Dakṣa, you have insulted my husband before me for no good reason, the great lord of the world in whom no faults exist. *Śruti* says that those who steal knowledge, those who betray a teacher, those who defile the lord of the Vedas are all great sinners who should be punished. Because of this, as your fate you will immediately suffer cruel and severe punishment befitting your egregious sin. Because you have failed to worship Tryambaka, the god of gods, be assured that your wicked family is ruined!"

After saying this to her father, the offended Satī, her wrath spent, abandoned her body and went to Mt. Himavat. That excellent mountain had been practising severe *tapas* for a long time and now attained the fruit of his merit. To grant a favor to the lord of the mountain, the goddess made him her own father by Yogic illusion. After Satī, afflicted with distress, had reproached Dakṣa and left him, the *mantras*

*The area of the site of sacrifice where the main priests sit.

too disappeared, and so the sacrifice was prevented from taking place.

When he heard of the goddess' departure, the destroyer of Tripura became enraged at Dakṣa and the seers and cursed them. "O Dakṣa," he said, "you despise Satī because of me while you honor all your other daughters and their husbands. Because of this, all your daughters will originate together at the sacrifice of Brahmā in the Vaivasvata Manvantara without benefit of a womb. In the Cākṣusa Manvantara, you will be a human king, the grandson of Pracīṇabarhis and son of Pracetas. At that time, too, I shall obstruct you again and again, hard-souled one, even in actions that conform to Duty, Success and Love."

Thus addressed by Rudra of infinite splendor, the miserable Dakṣa abandoned the body that had been born from Svāyambhuva and fell to the ground.

## The Destruction of Dakṣa's Sacrifice

King Dakṣa, Pracetas' son, who had been cursed long ago by Śaṃbhu for having insulted Bhava due to an old feud, was offering a sacrifice at the gate of the Ganges, Gangādvāra. All the gods were invited for their shares, along with Viṣṇu, and the chief sages came along with all the other seers. When the learned sage Dadhīci saw the entire family of the gods gathered there without Śankara, he spoke to the son of Pracetas, "Lord Rudra is followed by all beings from Brahmā down to the Piśācas. Why is he not being properly worshiped here as is his due?" To this Dakṣa replied, "In all the sacrifices there is no share assigned to him, nor are there any *mantras* to be offered to Śankara and his wife!"

The angry seer, a paragon of wisdom, spoke with a scowl to Dakṣa while the gods listened in, "Śankara is the source of all beings, the supreme lord of the universe! Surely when you realize this, you will worship him in every sacrifice."

"Hara is not beneficent *(śankara);* he is the terrifying Rudra, a devastator full of *tamas*!" replied Dakṣa. "He is naked and deformed, and he carries a skull. He cannot be the soul of the universe! Lord Nārāyaṇa is the king, the creator of the world. I worship this blessed god who consists of *sattva,* in all my actions."

Then Dadhīca said, "Don't you see the blessed lord of a thousand rays, the destroyer of all worlds, Parameśvara who consists of time? The keen-rayed Sun whom the learned reciters of the Veda extol, is himself an embodiment of Sankara. This fiery Rudra, the great god who carries a skull, whose neck is blue, the ruddy Hara, is the blessed Āditya the Sun, that god of a thousand rays who is to be praised by the *sāman, adhvaryu* and *hotar* priests! Witness this god who has fashioned the universe, whose form is Rudra, purpose of the three Vedas!"

Dakṣa answered, "These twelve Ādityas who have come for their shares of the sacrifice are the only known suns. There is no other sun." At his words, the assistant seers who had assembled to observe the sacrifice agreed, "Surely, this is so." Their minds pervaded by darkness, they failed to see the bull-bannered god whom they reviled hundreds of thousands of times more. The sages insulted both Hara, master of all creatures, and the Vedic *mantras* which, deluded by Viṣṇu's *māyā,* continued to honor Dakṣa's word. And all the gods who had come for their shares, led by Vāsava, failed to see lord Śiva, all except lord Hari Nārāyaṇa. The Golden Embryo, lord Brahmā, choicest among the knowers of Brahman, vanished in a flash before the eyes of all. When the lord had disappeared, Dakṣa himself went for refuge to Hari Nārāyaṇa, the god who protects the world. And Dakṣa fearlessly commenced the sacrifice while lord Viṣṇu, guardian of those who seek refuge in him, watched over it.

But the noble seer Dadhīca spoke up once again, seeing the hosts of seers and all the gods inimical to the Brahman of the Vedas. "There is not the slightest doubt that a man who neglects those worthy of honor and honors the unworthy acquires great evil. Wherever evil is embraced while good is ignored the gods send down harsh punishment at once!"

So speaking, the learned seer cursed the enemies of the lord who had gathered there, the brahmins, Dakṣa and his retinue. "Because you have ignored the Vedas and because you have reviled the supreme lord Mahādeva Śankara, whom the world adores, all of you whose minds follow despicable scriptures that insult the way of the lord, you who are hostile to the lord, will be deprived of the three Vedas. You whose learning and conduct have come to naught, who chatter with false knowledge, you shall all be crushed when the Kali Age comes, along with those born properly in that Age. The power born of *tapas* will utterly desert you and you will go to Hell. Hṛṣīkeśa will turn his face away from you even if you beseech him!" After saying this, the wise sage, treasure-house of *tapas,* stopped talking and turned his mind to Rudra, the annihilator of all sins.

Meanwhile, the all-seeing goddess, knowing of this, spoke to her husband Mahādeva, the great lord, the god who is master of creatures: "Dakṣa, who was my father in a previous birth, is holding a sacrifice without inviting you, Śankara. He is insulting both you and myself. The gods and the sages are accomplices in this deed. I want one boon from you. Destroy this sacrifice immediately!"

At her request, the lord god, supreme among the gods, suddenly emitted Rudra out of the desire to destroy Dakṣa's sacrifice. He had a thousand heads, a thousand feet, a thousand eyes, long arms, with a thousand hands. He was invincible like the Fire at the end of the Age, with fangs terrible to behold, bearing conch, discus and mace, cudgel in hand, roaring horribly, armed with the Śārnga bow and smeared with ashes. He was called Vīrabhadra, brimming over with the god of gods himself; just born, he attended the lord of gods with folded hands.

"Blessings upon you!" Śiva said to him. "Dakṣa is holding a sacrifice at Gangādvāra where he has insulted me. O lord of the *gaṇas,* destroy his celebration!" So Vīrabhadra, sent by his friend, took the form of a lion and devastated Dakṣa's sacrifice for fun. And the great goddess Bhadrakālī,* emitted by the furious Umā, went forth together with the *gaṇa* who rode a bull. Thousands more Rudras poured out of the blessed lord. Known as the Romajas (Hair-Born) because they were born from his hairs, they were his helpers. With spears, swords and maces in their hands, carrying spades and rocks, blazing like Rudra, the Fire of Time, they made the ten directions reverberate with their roars. They all proceeded towards Dakṣa's feast, surrounding the *gaṇa* leader, mounted on bulls and accompanied by their wives; they were a terrifying sight to see.

When they arrived at the place called Gangādvāra, they saw there the sacrifice of Dakṣa of infinite splendor. It abounded with thousands of celestial women and resounded with the songs of Apsarases, with the music of lutes and flutes and with the chanting of Vedas. When he saw Prajāpati† seated near the gods and sages, Vīrabhadra, accompanied by Bhadrakālī and the Rudras, said with the ghost of a smile, "We are all the servants of Śarva of infinite splendor. We have come out of desire for our shares of the sacrifice. Give us the portions we want! Or else tell us who gave the order that you are to receive the shares and not we, so that we may know who he is!"

Thus addressed by the *gaṇa* chief, the gods led by Prajāpati said to the lord, "There are no *mantras* prescribing your share of the sacrifice!"

When they heard this, those gods whose minds were obscured by illusion still ignored the lord, so the *mantras* deserted the gods and

*The goddess Kālī.

†Dakṣa.

went to their own home. Then lord Rudra touched the divine sage Dadhīca with his hand, and in the company of his wife and the *gaṇa* lords, addressed the deities: "You are arrogant with power, refusing as you do the authority of the *mantras*. Because of this I shall humble you and destroy your conceit!"

After announcing this, the leader of the *gaṇas* set fire to the sacrificial enclosure while the furious *gaṇa* lords tore up the sacrificial posts and threw them away. Seizing the *prastotṛ** priest, the *hotṛ* priest and the sacrificial horse, the terrifying *gaṇa* chiefs hurled them into the Ganges river.

Vīrabhadra too, his soul afire, gleefully paralyzed the outstretched hand of Śakra and those of the other deities as well; playfully plucking out Bhaga's eyes with his fingernail, he struck Pūṣan with his fist and knocked his teeth out. Then the mighty *gaṇa* with a smile boldly attacked the god Candramās with his big toe, in play. He ripped off both hands of Fire and pulled out his tongue for fun. Then, O lords of seers, he pounded the seers with blows in the head with his feet.

Next this huge and powerful being immobilized Sudarśana, Viṣṇu's discus which had arrived with Garuḍa, and pierced the god with sharpened arrows. When he saw this happen, the large-winged Garuḍa went for the *gaṇa* and beat at him rapidly with his wings, roaring like the ocean. But Bhadra himself poured out Garuḍas by the thousands. Greater than Vinatā's son,† they began to pursue Garuḍa. When he saw them, the clever bird who was most fleet, quickly threw off Mādhava, marvelous though he was, and fled.

At the disappearance of Vainateya,‡ Brahmā, the lotus-born god, arrived to stop Vīrabhadra and Keśava. He sang the praises of Parameṣṭhin and reverently appeased him. The blessed lord Viṣṇu himself appeared along with Ambā. When he saw the lord who had arrived with Ambā, that overlord of the gods surrounded by all his hosts, lord Brahmā, Dakṣa and all the celestials praised him. Dakṣa bowed with folded hands and celebrated the goddess Pārvatī, whose body was half the lord's, with various sorts of hymns.

Then the blessed goddess, ocean of compassion, smiled at Maheśvara, her mind content, and said to Rudra, "You are the creator, ruler and protector of the world. Show favor to Dakṣa and the gods!" At this the blue and red lord Hara with matted hair spoke to the prostrate gods and to the son of Pracetas§ with a slight smile, "I

*Second ranking priest of the Sāma Veda at sacrifices.
†Garuḍa.
‡Garuḍa.
§Dakṣa.

am pleased with all you gods. I am not only not to be reviled, but I am to be shown particular honor in every sacrifice. You too, Dakṣa, heed my word that protects all things. Abandon your worldly cravings and become my zealous devotee. By my grace you will become the lord of the *gaṇas* at the end of the Eon. Until then you will continue to rule your domain under the constraint of my commands." So speaking, the blessed one, along with his wife, and attendants, vanished from the boundlessly august Dakṣa's sight.

After that great god Śankara had disappeared, the lotus-born Brahmā himself addressed to Dakṣa these words for the benefit of the whole world. "Now that you have gratified the bull-bannered god, is your illusion dispelled? You should observe assiduously what the god has told you. The lord dwells in the innermost heart of all creatures. It is he that is seen by the wise reciters of the Veda who are absorbed in Brahman. He is the Self of all creatures, the seed, the supreme goal. Maheśvara, the god of gods, is he who is praised with Vedic *mantras.* He who worships only the eternal Rudra within himself, his mind yoked with love, gains the supreme goal. Therefore know the supreme lord to be without beginning, middle or end. Propitiate him zealously in act, mind and speech. With all your might and main avoid giving offense to lord Hara, for insulting acts destroy the self and lead inevitably to sin. The great Yogin who is your lord is the immortal Viṣṇu, the protector. Assuredly he is Mahādeva, the blessed god of gods. Those who believe that Viṣṇu, womb of the universe, is separate from lord Śiva will go to Hell because they are deluded, not grounded in the Veda. Those who follow the Veda see Rudra and Nārāyaṇa as a single god; they will enjoy release. He who knows Viṣṇu to be Rudra himself and Rudra to be Janārdana truly worships god and gains the supreme goal. Viṣṇu has poured forth this entire creation and Īśvara looks over it; thus this whole world has sprung from Rudra and Nārāyaṇa. Therefore cease your insult of Hara, but in your devotion to Viṣṇu also seek refuge in Mahādeva, who shelters the reciters of the Veda."

When he heard this speech of Viriñca, the Prajāpati Dakṣa sought shelter with the god who is master of the cows, garbed in a lion-skin. The rest of the great sages who had been scorched by the fire of Dadhīca's curse remained deluded and hostile to the god and were born henceforth in the Kali Ages. They were born into the families of brahmins on the strength of their earlier perfections, according to Brahmā's word, but they lost completely the power they had won through *tapas.* All of those who have fallen into Raurava and the other hells will be released from the curse at the end of the Eon, attaining in due time the sun-hued Brahmā, lord of the worlds. After being sent away by Svayambhū, they will propitiate Indra, the lord who rules the thirty gods, by the practice of *tapas,* and they will become as they were before through the favor of Śankara. Thus you have heard the whole story of the destruction of Dakṣa's sacrifice.

# Gaṇeśa

Once upon a time while Pārvatī was taking a bath, the always auspicious Śiva threatened Nandin, who was guarding her door, and went into the house. When that lovely woman, the mother of the world, saw Śankara arrive so unexpectedly, she stood up, embarrassed. After this happened, the auspicious Pārvatī, supreme Māyā, the supernal goddess, became eager to follow the good advice given earlier by a friend, thinking to herself, "I should have a servant of my very own! He should be favorable to me, a man of accomplishment who will obey my command and no other, one who will not stray even a hair's breadth from my side!"

Thinking these thoughts, the goddess fashioned from the dirt of her body a young man who possessed all these good characteristics. He was handsome, flawless of limb, sturdy, well-adorned, and most valorous and strong. She gave to him various garments, abundant ornaments and an incomparable blessing. "You are my very own son!" she said, "I have no one else here who is mine alone."

At her words, the youth bowed and said to Śivā,* "What task have you found for me? I shall do as you tell me." Thus addressed, Śivā answered her son, "Dear son, hear my words. From now on you shall be my doorkeeper. You are my very own child; I have no one whatsoever here but you who belongs to me. Let no one into my house without my permission, my son, no matter who, no matter where. Use force if necessary, dear son. I mean this truly!" And so speaking, she gave him a hard stick, O seer. Gazing at his handsome body, she was thrilled with delight.

Then she kissed his face lovingly, embraced him with affection and stationed him, staff in hand, at her door as chief of her *gaṇas.* And the beloved son of the goddess, the great heroic *gaṇa,* stood at the door of her house, holding the staff in his hand, out of desire to please Pārvatī. After she had put her son Gaṇeśa, lord of the *gaṇas,* in front of her door, Śivā herself stayed inside to bathe with her companions.

At that moment Śiva, skilled in various sports, arrived eagerly at

*Śiva's consort. Note spelling: Śivā is the goddess, Śiva the god.

the door, O lion among seers. Not knowing he was lord Śiva, Gaṇeśa said, "You may not enter here, O god, without permission of my mother who is inside bathing. Where do you think you're going? Get out at once!" Saying this, Gaṇeśa brandished his staff to stop Śiva.

Looking at him, Śiva said, "You silly fool, who are you to keep me out? Don't you recognize me, stupid? I am none other than Śiva himself!" But Gaṇeśa struck the great lord of many sports with his stick. This infuriated Śiva who said once again to his son, "You are an imbecile not to know me! I am Śiva, the husband of Pārvatī, daughter of the mountain! I shall go into my own house, idiot. Why are you standing in my way?"

After the god had spoken Gaṇeśa grew angry with Maheśa, who was going into the house, O brahmin, so he hit him again with his staff. At this Śiva became enraged. Mustering his own *gaṇas,* he asked them, "Who is this person? What is he up to? What is going on here, *ganas,* while you just stand there and watch?" . . .

The *gaṇas,* filled with fury, went to the guardian of the door at Śiva's behest and questioned the son of the mountain daughter. "Who are you? Where have you come from? What are you going to do? Get out now if you want to live! Now listen to us. We are Śiva's best *gaṇas* and doorkeepers. We have come to stop you, by order of lord Śankara. We can see that you are a *gaṇa* too, so we will spare your life, but otherwise you would be killed! For your own sake, stay far away from us. Why risk death by staying here?"

Even after this speech, Pārvatī's son Gaṇeśa showed no fear. Rebuking Śankara's *gaṇas,* he refused to budge from the doorway. When they had heard all he had to say, the *gaṇas* of Śiva who had gone there returned to the lord and told him what had happened. . . .

After hearing their words, Śiva said, "Listen, all you *gaṇas.* It is not right to go to battle over this, for you are my very own *gaṇas* and that other *gaṇa* belongs to my wife Gaurī. On the other hand, if I back down, O *gaṇas,* people might say, 'Śambhu is always cowed by his wife!' It is a weighty matter to know the right thing to do. That *gaṇa* by himself is only a mere child. What power can he have? Moreover, *gaṇas,* in the world you are experts in battle, and you belong to me. Why should you avoid a fight and thereby become useless to me? How can a woman be so obstinate, especially to her husband? It is she who is responsible for this! Now the mountain daughter will reap the fruit of her act! Listen carefully to what I say, all my heroes: wage all-out war! Let it come out as it will!" After making this speech, O brahmin, Śankara who is skilled in various sports stopped talking, excellent seer, according to the way of the world.

Thus addressed by their lord, the *gaṇas* made a supreme resolve to do his bidding. United, they went to Śivā's house. When Gaṇeśa saw the eminent *gaṇas* approach, armed for battle, he said to them, "Come if you will, all you lords of the *gaṇas* following Śiva's command! I am only one boy who obeys the order of Śivā. Nevertheless, the goddess Pārvatī shall witness the strength of her son, while Śiva shall see the power of his own *gaṇas!* The fight that is about to take place between a child and mighty men is a contest between Bhavānī* and Śiva. You are skilled in warfare, since you have fought before; I am a boy who has never been to battle. Nevertheless, I shall put you to shame in this conflict between the mountain-born woman and Śiva! For my part, I have nothing against you, but I shall humble you before Pārvatī and Śiva! Now that you know this, O *gaṇa* lords, let the battle be joined! Look to your master and I shall look to my mother. Let the outcome be as it will be, for no one in the three worlds can stop it now!"

Thus challenged, the *gaṇas* grabbed up all kinds of weapons and assaulted him, their arms bristling with sticks. They ground their teeth, cried "*Hūṃ!*" over and over again and attacked him shouting, "Look at him! There he is!" Nandin approached first, seized Gaṇeśa's foot and tugged at it while Bhṛgin grabbed the other foot. As they pulled at his feet, the *gaṇa* beat back their hands which clung to his sandals.

Then Gaṇapati, the heroic son of the goddess, seized a huge iron-stubbed club and stood at the door, bashing them all with it. Some had their hands severed, the backs of others were shattered, while still others had their heads and skulls cut off. The knees of some were smashed, the shoulders of others. All those who faced Gaṇeśa were hit in the chest. Some fell to the ground, while others fled in all directions. Some had their feet cut off while others retreated towards Śarva. There was not a one among them who faced up to Gaṇeśa in battle. Like deer who see a lion, they fled in all the ten directions. When all the *gaṇas* by the thousands had run away, Gaṇeśa returned to stand at the beautiful door. That destroyer of them all was a terrifying sight, looking like Time at the end of the Eon. . . .

After waging war with his army for a long time, O seer, even Śiva grew dismayed at the sight of his formidable foe. He stood in the middle of his troops thinking, "Gaṇeśa can only be killed by a trick! For surely there is no other way." Then all the gods and Maheśa's *gaṇas* were delighted to see both Śiva, embodied with qualities, and Viṣṇu come to the battle. Greeting each other with affection, they all

*Śivā.

celebrated. And Gaṇeśa, the heroic son of *śakti*, with his staff, following the way of heroes, was the first to worship Viṣṇu who brings happiness to all.

Then Viṣṇu said to Śiva, "You shall kill your enemy, O lord, but not without trickery, for he is hard to reach and full of *tamas*. I shall create a delusion." He conferred with Śaṃbhu, and after receiving Śiva's command, Viṣṇu began to prepare his trick. . . .

The heroic son of Śivā, endowed with great strength, saw the great lord Śaṃbhu arrive, trident in hand, eager for the kill. Recalling his mother's lotus feet, and emboldened by the *śakti* of Śivā, the mighty hero Gaṇeśa struck him in the hand with his spear. When Śiva whose protection is good saw the trident fall from his hand, he took up the Pināka bow, but the lord of the *gaṇas* made that too fall to the ground with a blow of his iron-studded staff. Since five of his hands had been clubbed, Śiva took up the trident with five others. "Aho!" he cried in the way of the world, "a great calamity has befallen me! Surely nothing worse than this can happen to the *gaṇas!*"

Meanwhile, the heroic Gaṇeśa, full of the power bestowed by *śakti*, attacked all the gods and *gaṇas* with his cudgel. Set upon by his club, they dispersed into the ten directions. None remained in combat with that wondrous fighter. When Viṣṇu saw that *gaṇa*, he exclaimed, "This is a lucky one! He is most powerful, most manly, a great hero fond of battle! I have seen many deities, Daityas, Dānavas, Yakṣas, Gandharvas and Rākṣasas, but there is none to equal this guardian in brilliance, beauty, valor and other fine qualities in any of the three worlds!"

As he was speaking in this manner, the *gaṇa* lord, son of *śakti*, brandished his club and hurled it at Viṣṇu. Recollecting the lotus-like feet of Śiva, Hari took up his discus and swiftly shattered that iron-studded club. The *gaṇa* then hurled a chip of the club at Hari, but the bird Garuḍa caught it and rendered it powerless. Thus did the time pass as the two mighty heroes, Viṣṇu and Gaṇeśa, fought with each other.

Once again, the choicest hero, the mighty son of *śakti*, recalling Śivā, took up his matchless staff and struck Viṣṇu with it. Unable to withstand the blow, Viṣṇu fell to the ground. But he sprang up at once and battled again with that son of Śivā. Seizing his opportunity at last, the trident-wielding Śiva took his stand in the north and cut off the head of Gaṇeśa with his trident. When Gaṇeśa lost his head, both the army of the *gaṇas* and the army of the gods stood stock still, rooted to the earth.

After Gaṇeśa was killed, the *gaṇas* held a great festival to the sound of hand drums and kettle drums. Śiva was sorry that he had cut off

Gaṇeśa's head, O lord of seers, but the mountain-born goddess Pārvatī was furious: "What will I do? Where will I go? Alas, alas, misery engulfs me. How will I ever lose this grief and sorrow that now are mine? All the gods and *gaṇas* have killed my son. I shall wreak utter havoc! I shall bring about the dissolution of the world!"

Grieving in this manner, the great goddess of the universe, enraged, fashioned in an instant hundreds of thousands of *śaktis*, or powers. Once created, they bowed to the mother of the world, blazed forth and said, "O Mother, tell us what to do!" At their words, O lord of seers, Mahāmāyā, Śaṃbhu's *śakti*, she who is Prakṛti, full of fury, answered them all. "O *śaktis*, O goddesses, you are to annihilate the world without a moment's pause. O my companions, devour with a vengeance the gods, sages, Yakṣas, Rākṣasas, my very own followers and all the rest as well!"

At her command, all the *śaktis*, consumed with rage, prepared to destroy all the gods and other creatures. They went forth to spread devastation, as fire licks up grass. The leaders of the *gaṇas*—Viṣṇu, Brahmā, Śankara and Indra, Kubera, king of the Yakṣas, Skanda and Sūrya—all these they sought to obliterate without ceasing. No matter where one looked, there were the *śaktis!* There were multitudes of them—Karālī (Gape-Mouth), Kubjakā (Hunch-Back), Khaṃjā (Cripple), Lambaśīrsā (Droop-Head)—and they all snatched up the gods in their hands and hurled them into their open mouths.

Witnessing this devastation, Hara, Brahmā, Hari, Indra and all the rest of the gods, *gaṇas* and seers said to themselves, "What is this goddess doing, this untimely annihilation of the world?" Thus they were uncertain and lost hope for their own lives. Gathering together, they conferred with each other, saying, "We must consider what to do!" Thus deliberating, they talked rapidly among themselves. "Only when the mountain goddess is satisfied will peace return to the world, and not otherwise, not even with a myriad efforts! Even Śiva, skilled in all sports, the deluder of the world, is filled with sorrow like the rest of us!"

A million gods were annihilated while Śivā was enraged; none could prevail. There was no one whatsoever to withstand the mountain-born goddess, O seer, whether her own devotee or that of another, whether god or Dānava, *gaṇa* or guardian of the quarters, whether Yakṣa, Kinnara or seer, not even Viṣṇu, Brahmā or lord Śankara himself! When they beheld her dazzling splendor flashing in all directions, all the gods were terrified and retreated to some distance away.

Meanwhile Nārada of divine sight arrived—you, O seer—to benefit the gods and *gaṇas*. After bowing to Brahmá, Viṣṇu, Śankara and myself, he met with them and spoke, reflecting on what was to be done. All the gods conferred with the great-souled Nārada, saying in unison, "How can our suffering be ended?" To this he replied, "As long as the mountain-born goddess is without compassion, you will be miserable. Make no mistake about this!"

And then the seers headed by Nārada went to Śivā and all propitiated her in order to appease her fury. Over and over again they bowed, singing hymns by the numbers. Placating her with devotion, they said to her, at the command of the gods and *gaṇas:*

"O Mother of the world, praise be to you! To you, Śivā! Glory be to you, Caṇḍikā, to Kalyāṇī, praise! O Mother, you are the primordial *śakti,* creatress of everything. You are the power that protects, the power that destroys! O goddess, be content! Be serene! Glory be to you, O goddess! The triple world is destitute because of your rage!"

Thus hymned by the seers led by Nārada, the supreme goddess continued to look furious and spoke not a word to them. So all the seers bowed again to her lotus feet and spoke diplomatically once more to Śivā with devotion, their hands folded in reverence:

"Forgive us, O goddess! Devastation is upon us! Your master stands before you, Ambikā, look at him! We are the gods Viṣṇu, Brahmā and the others, O goddess. We are your very own creatures who stand before you with our hands folded in worship. Forgive our fault, supreme goddess! All of us are utterly miserable. O Śivā, grant us peace!"

So speaking, all the seers, wretched and confused, stood together in front of Caṇḍikā with their hands folded in obeisance. When she heard what they said, Caṇḍikā grew pleased. And she answered those seers with a mind filled with compassion: "If you can revive my son, I shall stop my devastation. If you honor him and make him overseer of everything, then there will be peace in the world. In no other way will you be happy again."

Thus addressed, all the seers led by Nārada went to tell the gods what had happened. After they heard the story, all the miserable gods led by Śakra bowed, folded their hands, and related it all to Śankara. At their words, Śiva said, "Do whatever is necessary to benefit the worlds. Go the north and cut off the head of whomever you first encounter. After doing this, join that head to Gaṇeśa's body."

All this was done by the gods according to Śiva's order. They brought the body, washed it by the rules and worshiped it. Then turning their faces to the north, they went out. The first thing they met was an elephant with a single tusk. Taking its head, all the deities fastened it firmly to the body of Gaṇeśa. Worshiping Śiva, Viṣṇu and Brahmā, they bowed and said, "We have done as you told us. Now you must finish the task." And the gods and attendants beamed with happiness at these words, having obeyed the command of Śiva.

Again Brahmā, Viṣṇu and the gods bowed to their master, the lord who is without characteristics, god Śiva himself, and said, "Since all of us were born from your *tejas*, or energy, now let your *tejas* enter this body by means of the recitation of Vedic *mantras!*" And calling Śiva to mind, they all sprinkled blessed holy water on the corpse while reciting *mantras*. At the mere touch of the drops of water, Gaṇeśa regained both consciousness and life. The boy arose, by Śiva's wish, as though from sleep. He was handsome, noble and resplendent, with a pleasing shape, a jolly manner and a ruddy elephant head.

Everyone rejoiced, their sorrows banished, O lord of seers, at the sight of Śivā's son restored to life. Filled with happiness, they showed him to the goddess. When she saw her son alive, she too was overcome with joy.

# Kārttikeya

Hear, O Nārada, as I relate the holy story of old about the glorification of the fame of the child Kumāra Kārtika. Once Fire drank the spilled semen of the Pināka-bearing god,* O brahmin, and was overcome by it. Deprived of his strength, that infinitely shining god then went for help to the gods, who sent him at once to Brahmaloka. On his way, Fire met the goddess Kuṭilā. When he saw her, he said, "O Kuṭilā, this seed is most difficult to bear! Since it was spilled by Maheśvara, it would burn up the three worlds if uncontained. Therefore you take it! The offspring you bear from it will be auspicious."

When she learned this from Fire, Kuṭilā, the mighty river, remembered her ultimate goal and said to him, "Throw it into my waters." And so the goddess carried Śarva's semen and nourished it, while the blessed Fire was able to move around freely. Because Fire had held the seed for five thousand years, his flesh, bones, blood, fat, entrails, semen, skin and the hair of his body, his beard, eyes and head were all golden. Thus in the world, Fire is called Hiraṇyagarbha, the Golden Embryo.

After Kuṭilā had borne that fire-like embryo for five thousand years herself, she went to the abode of Brahmā. When he saw the great river in such distress, the lotus-born god asked her, "Who was it that

*Śiva.

placed this embryo in you?" And she replied, "O excellent one, it is the seed of Śankara that was drunk by Fire. When he could bear it no longer, he put it into me. I have carried this embryo for five thousand years, yet it will not be born!"

At her words, the lord answered, "On Sunrise Mountain there grows a vast fearsome thicket of reeds a hundred leagues wide. Go there, O beautiful woman of lovely hips, and cast the embryo onto the broad mountain plain. After ten thousand years a child will be born from it."

The beautiful woman heeded Brahmā's words and went to that mountain where the mountain girl, happy at last, released that embryo through her mouth. After abandoning the child, she returned in haste to Brahmā, where by the power of *mantras* the good Kuṭilā turned entirely into water. The vast thicket then grew golden with Śarva's seed—its trees, beasts, birds and other inhabitants as well.

In the fulness of ten thousand autumns a lotus-eyed child was born, shining like the morning sun. This blessed one lay on his back in the divine thicket with his thumb in his mouth and cried with the thunder of the king of clouds. Meanwhile six goddesses, the brilliant Kṛtikkās,* going about as they pleased, glimpsed the child lying in the reeds. Filled with compassion, they went to where Skanda lay. "Me first! Me first!" they cried aloud, eager to nurse the baby boy. When he saw them quarreling over him, he produced six faces, and so each of the Kṛtikkās lovingly cared for the infant. Thus the boy grew up, reared by the goddesses, O seer. Called Kārttikeya, he was supreme among the mighty.

Meanwhile, brahmin, the lotus-born god spoke to Fire, "How tall is your son Guha by now?" When he heard this, the ignorant Fire answered the god who was born from Hara, "I don't know who Guha is, O lord of gods." The lord replied, "Tryambaka's† semen that you drank long ago has been born as an infant in a reed thicket, O lord of the three worlds."

At the Grandfather's words, Fire sped there riding a swift ram. He encountered Kuṭilā who asked him, "Where are you going in such a hurry, O sage?" And he answered, "To see the infant child born in the reed thicket," whereupon she announced, "That child is mine!" And Fire retorted, "No, he belongs to me!"

Janārdana, roaming at will, happened upon the two of them in the middle of this dispute. He asked them both, "Why are you quarreling here?" And they replied, "We are arguing over the son that has been

*The Pleiades personified.
†Śiva.

born from Rudra's seed." The god Hari addressed the two of them, "Go to the slayer of Tripura* and do explicitly what the lord of the gods tells you to do."

At Vāsudeva's command, O Nārada, Kuṭilā and Fire went to Hara and asked him, "Whose son is he, in truth?" When he heard their words, his heart grew joyful and he said to the mountain woman, his hair erect with delight, "Good fortune! Good fortune!" At this Ambikā said to Hara, "O god, let us go and ask the child to choose. He shall be the son of the one with whom he seeks refuge."

"By all means!" said the lord whose banner bears the bull. He arose, along with Umā, Kuṭilā and the clever Fire. When they arrived at the reed thicket, Hara, Fire, Kuṭilā and Ambikā saw the little baby lying in the lap of the Kṛttikās. The six-faced infant child regarded the four of them thoughtfully and then became a *yogin* with four bodies. Kumāra went to Śankara, Viśākha to Gaurī, Śākha chose Kuṭilā and Mahāsena adopted Fire. At this, Rudra, filled with love, Umā, Kuṭilā and the lord god Fire were all overcome with utmost joy.

The Kṛtikkās then inquired, "Is this boy with six faces the son of Hara?" And Hara spoke to them affectionately with these wise words, O seer, "By the name of Kārttikeya he will be your little boy; as Kumāra he will be the immortal son of Kuṭilā; as Gaurī's son he will be called Skanda, and as Guha he will be mine. As Fire's little boy, he will be known as Mahāsena, and as the son of the reed thicket, Śāradvata. Because of his six faces, the long-armed one will be called Ṣaṇmukha, or Six-Face. So will the lord, the great Yogin, be known on the earth."

Having spoken, the trident-bearing lord recalled the Grandfather and the celestials who appeared at once. Prostrating themselves before that enemy of Kāma, and before Umā, the daughter of the mountain, looking graciously on Fire, Kuṭilā and the Kṛttikās, the divinities observed that magnificent six-faced child with six faces who resembled the sun, dazzling their sight with his brilliance. All the eminent deities who witnessed this spectacle said, "You, O god, along with the goddess and Fire, have done the task of the gods! Let us arise now and go to Kurukṣetra at the Sarasvatī river, where we will consecrate the six-faced god at an immortal golden shrine! He shall be the master of your army, O gods, Gandharvas and Kinnaras. He shall destroy Mahiṣa and the terrifying Tāraka."

Śarva said, "So be it!" and so the gods arose and went with Kumāra to bounteous Kurukṣetra where the celestials, Rudra, Brahmā and Janārdana along with Indra and the hosts of seers made

*Śiva.

thorough-going preparations for his consecration. Acyuta and the other gods anointed Guha with abundant water from the rivers that flow into the seven seas, and with choice herbs of a thousand different kinds. And while Kumāra of the heavenly form was being consecrated as commander-in-chief of the army, the lords of Gandharvas sang and troops of Apsarases danced.

## Śukra

The gods led by the Grandfather saw the chief of the *gaṇas* oppressed by the mighty powerful demons. Seeing this, lord Brahmā addressed the gods led by Śakra;* "Now is your chance. Go and help Śaṃbhu!" When the gods and Vasus heard the Grandfather's words, they flew in a hurry from the sky to Śiva's army. Their speed as they raced toward the Pramātha army seemed like the impetuous course of rivers flowing into the sea. And a horrible sound arose as the two armies, the gods and Pramāthas, clashed together.

Nandin found an opening and violently dragged Śukra, the Bhārgava, from his chariot like a lion attacking a little deer. That commander of the *gaṇas* felled all the guards and then led Śukra to Hara and handed him over. Lord Śarva threw that sage who had been brought before him into his mouth and made the disappearing Bhārgava enter his belly. That seer, the best of sages, after being swallowed by Śaṃbhu, remained in his belly, diligently praising the lord with these words:

"Glory be to you, O granter of boons, to Hara, possessing all virtues, to Śankara, to Maheśa, to Tryambaka! Praise be to you! Glory be to the giver of life, to the protector of the world, to the Man-Ape, to the fire that burned Kāma, to the enemy of Time, to Vāmadeva! Praise be to you! To Sthāṇu, to Viśvarūpa, to Vāmana, O all-mover, to Mahādeva, to Śarva, to Īśvara, let there be praise!

"O three-eyed Hara, O Bhava, O Śankara, O husband of Umā, O cloud-rider, O cave-dweller, O lover of the cremation grounds, smeared with ashes, trident in hand, O lord of animals, master of cows, Supreme Person, praise be to you!"

Thus praised with devotion by the best of sages, Hara was pleased, and said, "Choose a boon and I shall give it to you." And Śukra replied, "O best of gods, now give me this: show me a way out of your belly!" So Hara closed his eyes and said, "Chief brahmin, you may leave now!" And as soon as the lord had spoken, that bull of the Bhārgavas began to move around inside the belly of the god.

*Indra.

Wandering around inside Śaṃbhu's belly, the sage saw the worlds, the oceans, and the netherworlds covered with standing and moving beings. He saw the Ādityas, Vasus, Rudras, Viśvedevas and *gaṇas*, the Yakṣas, Kiṃpuruṣas and so forth and so on. He saw hosts of Gandharvas and Apsarases, seers, men, Sādhyas, cattle, worms, large black ants, trees, bushes, mountains, forest creepers, fruits, roots and herbs. He saw creatures that live on dry land and those that live in water, those that blink their eyes and those that do not, animals with four feet and those with two—all the standing and moving creatures. He saw those that are hidden as well as those that are visible, those with characteristics and those without. As he witnessed all this, the Bhārgava roamed around filled with curiosity. A divine year passed while the Bhārgava was inside the lord's belly.

Failing to discover any end to this, O brahmin, the seer grew weary. When he saw that he was worn out without finding an exit, the self-controlled sage bowed reverently to Mahādeva and turned to him for refuge: "O you who possess all forms, who are of vast proportion, owning prayer-beads of all shapes, O Mahādeva of a thousand eyes, I have come to you for refuge! Praise be to you, O Śankara, Śarva, Śaṃbhu with a thousand eyes, adorned with serpents at your feet! I am exhausted just by witnessing all the worlds inside your belly, so I have turned to you for refuge!"

At his words, the great-souled Śaṃbhu laughed and began to speak, "You are now my own son! O moon of the Bhārgava dynasty, you may leave through my penis! Moving and unmoving creatures alike will praise you by the name of Śukra,* have no doubt about this!" And so speaking, the lord released Śukra through his penis, and the sage went out.

When that moon of the Bhārgava dynasty of mighty majesty had emerged in the form of Śukra, he bowed to Śambhu and left at once to rejoin the army of the great demons. The Dānavas, delighted at his return, put their minds once more on doing battle with the *gaṇa* lords. Intent on victory, all the lords of the *gaṇas*, along with the hosts of the immortals, fought with the Asuras an all-out war.

# The Burning of Tripura

Hear how lord Bhava destroyed Tripura. Once there was a demon called Maya, of great magical power, who produced Māyā, Illusion. Defeated in battle, he began to practice severe *tapas*. When they saw

**Śukra* is also a word for semen.

what he was doing, O brahmins, two other Daityas, the mighty Vidyunmālin and the heroic Tāraka began to do supreme *tapas* too, in sympathy. Approaching Maya in brilliance as they performed *tapas* at his side, they resembled the three fires incarnate in little flames.

These Dānavas continued their *tapas,* and it consumed the triple world. Sitting in cold water in winter, amid the five fires* in summer, and staying outside during the rains, they mortified their precious bodies by eating only fruits, roots, flowers and water. Not observing regular meal-times, their bark garments caked with mud, immersed in duckweed and slime, both pure and impure, they became emaciated, fleshless, held together only by sinews. Because of the power of their *tapas,* the whole world was deprived of energy, glowing feebly without its luster.

While the three fires, those Dānavas, were burning up the three worlds, there appeared before them the Grandfather, friend of the world. And those Daityas, creators of havoc, greeted the Grandfather as he arrived. Then Brahmā, face and eyes filled with joy, spoke to those Dānavas who shone like the sun due to their *tapas,* "*Bhoḥ!* I am the giver of boons! I have come, my children, because I am pleased with your *tapas.* Choose what you desire! Tell me what you want!"

Maya, the master builder, eyes wide with happiness, answered the Grandfather who had made this promise, "O god, long ago in the battle over Tāraka the Daityas were defeated, beaten and killed by the gods with their weapons. Because of the continued hostility of the gods, the demons fled in fear and trembling. We found no haven or refuge to shelter us. Now, by my devotion to you, and through the power of *tapas,* I want to build a fortress that will be impregnable to the gods. This fort called Tripura which I shall build, O supreme successful one, by your grace, let it be invulnerable to creatures of both land and sea, to curses, to the power of the seers, to the weapons of the gods and to the gods themselves!"

Thus addressed by the all-maker Maya, the all-creator replied to that lord of the hosts of Daityas with a smile, "O Dānava, such total immortality does not exist for one who does not have good conduct. So you should build your fort of straw."

At the Grandfather's words, the demon Maya joined his palms and spoke once again to the lotus-born Brahmā, "Then let this fortress be destroyed by only one means: a single arrow shot once by Śaṃbhu. Otherwise it should be immune to attack."

"So be it," said the lord Grandfather to Maya. And he vanished like wealth won in a dream.

*I.e., four fires around and the sun above.

After the Grandfather had gone, those powerful demon Daityas radiated brilliantly with their *tapas* and with the gift of that boon. And the excellent, wise bull of the Dānavas, Maya, resolved to build his fortress, thinking, "How should I construct this fort? I shall build a triple city!"

Thinking this, the Daitya Maya built the city of Tripura with the power of his heavenly skill, following a plan in his mind. Here there was a wall running along the roadway, and there a gate-tower, watchtowers and lofty gateways. Here ran the broad king's highway with its main roads, by-roads, squares and market-places. And there stood the women's quarters and the sanctuary of Rudra, as well as tanks, pools, banyan trees, rest-houses, and public halls in the distance, with gardens and beautiful royal roads for the demons. Thus did Maya, who knew about city construction, build the fortress of Tripura according to the design in his mind. So we have heard.

Maya built one city of black iron. Tāraka was its king and he lived in the royal palace. He built a second city of silver, which shone like the full moon. Vidyunmālin was its lord, resembling a cloud garlanded with lightning. Maya built a third city of gold, in which he himself was lord and master. Tāraka's city was a hundred leagues wide, and so was the city of Vidyunmālin. Maya's vast city was as brilliant as Mt. Meru. The three cities came together during the time of the conjunction of the constellation Puṣya, a long time ago.

The Daitya Maya built Tripura just as the three-eyed god Śiva had built Puṣpaka. Along whatever road Maya took as he went resolutely from city to city, he ordered inns to be built of gold, silver and iron by the hundreds and thousands. These cities of the foes of the gods, studded with precious stones, shone radiantly with their hundreds of palaces and towering turrets as they traversed and surpassed all the worlds.

They had gardens, pools, wells, and ponds full of lotuses. They were filled with groves of Aśoka trees and the sounds of cuckoos, and abounded in broad picture galleries and four-chambered mansions. Maya had palaces built that were seventeen and eighteen stories high with banners and flags, decorated with garlands and wreaths and tiny tinkling bells. These palaces were huge, well-constructed and covered with stucco, perfumed and adorned with flowers. Obscured by the smoke of sacrifices in which many jars were filled, they looked like clouds or flocks of geese. The houses of Tripura, standing in rows, shone with ornaments of ropes of pearl as if mocking the beauty of the moon.

When the demon artist Maya built that fortress, he made it impregnable to his enemies, both gods and demons alike. The delighted demons, looking like death, entered the houses Maya had assigned them with their wives, sons and weapons. Like a pride of lions entering a forest, or sea monsters in the sea, or virulent diseases concentrated in a human body, those mighty enemies of the gods overran that city. Tripura teemed with a billion Daityas!

Like clouds they massed, flying up from Sutala and Pātāla, the netherworld domains of the Dānavas, and also flying from the mountains where they lived. As each arrived in Tripura he asked for his wish which Maya granted by his magic. In the evening full of moonlight, among the lotus ponds, in the parks, amid woods of mango trees and through groves inhabited by ascetics, those demons roamed like rutting elephants, their huge bodies anointed with sandal and oil, and dressed in fine new clothes. The happy Dānavas sported with their beloved amorous women and made all kinds of offerings. In the city that Maya built the mighty demons were happy, and set their minds on Success, Love and Duty. And so time passed pleasurably for those enemies of the gods who lived in Tripura, just as it did for the inhabitants of heaven.

Sons obeyed their fathers and wives their husbands. All the people forgot their quarrels and were content. Even the strong among the citizens of Tripura were filled with virtue, and the sons of Diti worshiped Hara at his sanctuary there. The sound of the recitation of the Blessing of the Day and the chanting of Vedic hymns mingled with the tinkling of anklets and the harmonies of flute and lute. The chief Dānavas dallying in Tripura heard the laughter of their choicest women and it captivated their hearts. A long time passed while the demons worshiped the gods, revered the brahmins and followed Success, Love and Duty.

But then Misfortune, Envy, Thirst, Hunger, Discord and Quarrel entered Tripura. At twilight those fearful evils stole into the city and settled in Tripura like diseases infiltrating a body. And Maya witnessed in a dream all those evils that had penetrated Tripura to possess the Dānavas. . . .

So the demons who lived in Tripura were ruined by fate. They deserted truth and virtue and did instead what was forbidden. They despised the holy brahmins, failed to revere the gods, ignored their teachers and even began to hate each other. They quarreled, mocked their own duty, ridiculed each other, and cried, "Me first!" They shouted at their teachers, refused to greet those who were worthy of respect, and they grew anxious for no reason, their eyes filling with tears. Lying around, they ate curds and barley with sour milk and *kapittha* fruit at night, and thus became impure. They urinated and touched water without washing their feet, and then went to bed without purifying themselves. They shrank from danger like rats from cats. And shameless in the practice of intercourse, they did not wash themselves after going to their women.

Those inhabitants of Tripura had previously practiced good habits, but they fell into wicked ways and began to harass the gods and sages rich in *tapas*. Even though restrained by Maya, they became bent upon self-destruction. Those disagreeable demons contended with the brahmins, thus following their own will like the elder gods before them. Those mad demons proceeded to ruin the abode of the celestials in heaven, and also the groves of seers rich in *tapas:* Vaibhrāja, Nandana, and the forest of Citraratha, Aśoka, Varaśāka and Sarvartuka. The dwelling place of the gods was wrecked, and the sacrifices to gods and brahmins were destroyed. The whole world was devastated by those evil enemies of the immortals, like crops overrun by a swarm of locusts.

When the Dānavas had become wicked and corrupt, and the groves of the *tapas*-rich sages had been devastated, all the creatures were terrorized by the lion roars of the demons as they stormed heaven. The triple world was stupefied with fear and grew dark with despair. The frightened Ādityas, Vasus, Sādhyas, Fathers and hosts of Maruts went for refuge to Brahmā, the great-grandfather. They gathered together before Brahmā who was seated on a golden lotus, and praised that god with five mouths and four faces, saying, "The Dānavas who live in Tripura are oppressing us, O faultless one. They are protected by your boon, so reprimand them as you would your servants! From fear of the Dānavas, O Grandfather, we scurry around like geese at the start of the rains, or deer in fear of a lion. So deranged are we because of the Dānavas, O sinless one, that we have even forgotten the names of our wives and sons! The god's houses are smashed, and the hermitages of the seers laid waste by the deluded and greedy demons, and now they are roaming around the world at will. If you do not rescue the earth at once, it will become devoid of men, sages and gods as they grind it to dust."

After this speech by the thirty gods, the lotus-born Grandfather spoke to them, and to Indra, his face lustrous as the moon, "The boon that I gave to Maya has now come to an end, O gods, just as I foretold. And Tripura, their city, shall be destroyed, O bulls of the thirty, not by a rain of arrows, but by a single shot. I do not see any one among you, bulls of the gods, who with a single arrow could put an end to the Dānavas' city, for Tripura cannot be annihilated by one of little valor, but only by the one great god, the Prajāpati Mahādeva.*

*Śiva.

If all you gods together request this of Hara, the destroyer of sacrifices, he will destroy Tripura. Each city is 10,000 leagues wide, so they can only be destroyed by a single mighty arrow if it is shot at that one moment when they are all three in conjunction with the constellation Puṣya."

At this, the Grandfather said, "Let us go!" to all the unhappy gods, and went to Bhava's seat. There they saw the mountain lord, trident in hand, the lord of past and future, in the company of Umā and the great-souled Nandin.

After all the gods entitled to their shares of the sacrifice and Brahmā were warmly welcomed by the god Śiva Rudra, they said to him, "The demons of fierce valor have performed awesome *tapas,* and oppress us. We have come to you for refuge! Maya, son of Diti, who built the fortress of Tripura with its shining gates, loves war, O three-eyed one. Fearless because of the boon which Brahmā gave them, the Dānavas have retreated into their fortified city, O chief of the gods, and they torment us, Mahādeva, as if we were servants with no master!

"The sons of Dānu have wrecked the gardens of Nandana and the rest, and they have captured Rambhā and the other lovely Apsarases. And they have stolen Indra's elephants, Kumuda, Añjana, Vāmana, Airāvata and the others too, Maheśvara. The demons have seized the horses which used to draw Indra's chariot, and now they are the chariot horses of the Dānavas. Our chariots, elephants, women and wealth have all been stolen from us by the Dānavas, and now our lives are in peril!"

Thus addressed by the gods led by Śakra, the three-eyed, boon-granting lord of the gods whose mount is the bull, said to the gods, "Fear the Dānavas no more, O gods. I shall burn up Tripura! Now do as I say. If you want me to set that Dānava city afire, then build me a proper chariot, and wait."

At the words of the naked Mahādeva, the gods said "So be it!" along with the Grandfather, and began to construct a marvelous chariot. The earth was its support, Rudra's two attendants its yoke-pole, Mt. Meru's peak the seat, and Mt. Mandara the axle. The lords of the gods made the sun and the moon the gold and silver wheels, the dark and light fortnights their two rims, and the gods Brahmā and all the other celestials the other moving parts. The encircling ropes were the two snakes Kambala and Aśvatara, while the planets Budha (Mercury), Aṅgāraka (Mars), Śanaiścara (Saturn), all the supreme deities and the sky itself formed the beautifully built bumper ring of that chariot. The golden *triveṇu* on the front was fashioned from the eyes of fork-tongued snakes, studded with gems, pearls, and sapphires by the joyous gods. . . .

Proud hosts of Pramāthas, massed like elephants, mountains or clouds, and roaring like thunder, surrounded the chariot, which was guarded by the gods and the immortals. Like the ocean filled with sharks, whales and fabulous fish tossing about at the end of the world, that choice chariot sped onwards full of light, rumbling like a thunderhead filled with lightning.

As the battle between the gods and Dānavas began, women and children were killed in that embattled city, while the furious great demon lords with their attendants rolled forward like the sea. The dreadful battle raged on with battle axes, boulders, tridents, thunderbolts and *kampanas,* fed by relentless hatred, until the battlefield was littered with bodies. As they attacked and bruised and killed each other, the bellowing of the immortals and the Dānavas was like the roaring of the ocean at the end of the Age. The streets of the city that had been bright with chips of gold and crystal ran red with blood. In an instant those streets were reduced to rubble and littered with severed heads, feet and hands.

Then the demon Tāraka, eyes wide with rage, appeared in the fray holding aloft trees and mountains, whereupon the wondrous hero Bhava closed the city gate. After mowing down the enemy on the ramparts, that great, marvelous, brave and potent hero, arrogant and proud of his powers, left the city howling horribly.

Then the mountainous Tāraka, acting like a crazed elephant, tried to seize Rudra's chariot, but was checked like an ocean creeping beyond its shores when Śiva, the three-eyed mountain lord with his mighty bow, and the four-faced Brahmā together challenged the Daitya, who was shaken like the ocean tossed about by the power of the wind. . . . The horrible Tāraka, eyes red with rage, was halted near Rudra by Nandin, who brings joy to his family. Nandin chopped down that lord of the Dānavas with his sharp axe like a perfume-selling wood-cutter fells a sandal tree. Struck down by that axe like a deer, the brave Tāraka drew his sword and attacked the lord of the *gaṇas.* But Nandin stripped him of his sacred thread and cut him down, bellowing raucously.

At Tāraka's death, a ghastly lion's roar rose up from the *gaṇa* lords along with the awful screech of conches. When Maya, standing nearby, heard the delighted shouts of the Pramāthas and the sound of their instruments, he said to Vidyunmālin who stood at his side, "What is this great noise I hear coming from many mouths, sounding like the ocean's roar? Tell me Vidyunmālin, what is the reason for these drums? The *gaṇa* lords attack, and the bulls of elephants flee!"

Snared by the hook of Maya's words, that foe-conqueror Vidyunmālin, blazing like the sun, went to the front of the battle with the gods and reported excitedly, "A hero as great as Yama, Varuṇa,

Mahendra and Rudra, the brave Tāraka who was the storehouse of your glory, the chief mainstay of every battle, has fallen to the *gaṇas* in the fight!" When the Pramāthas saw Tāraka crushed, his terrified eyes wide open and blazing with fire like the sun, their hair bristled with delight, and they began to roar like the clouds.

When Maya, in his colored robe, looking like a mountain of antimony in the midst of the battle, had heard the truth from his friend Vidyunmālin, he said, "We should waste no time, Vidyunmālin. By my own power I shall rid this city of its troubles!" Then the furious Vidyunmālin, together with the mighty demons, and Maya, the lord of Tripura, went forth immediately to dispatch the *gaṇas*. Wherever the two of them went, the city was emptied at once of Pramāthas. . . .

When they saw the thousand-rayed sun shining on Mt. Meru, the entire company of the gods roared like the oceans at the end of the Age. And then Hara set off again for Tripura accompanied by the thousand-eyed Śakra, sacker of cities, Kubera and Varuṇa. Impetuous Pramāthas of various kinds went too, with monstrous lion's roars and the sound of music. That divine army was like a moving forest while it proceeded along, with musical instruments as its sounds and raised umbrellas as its lofty trees.

When the Dānavas saw that huge and terrifying army marching on them, they began to shiver like the trembling seas. Gripping their swords, three-pointed spears, pikes, tridents, sticks and battle-axes, their thunderbolts and heavy clubs, their eyes red with rage and looking like winged mountains, they rushed to attack, like clouds assaulting the mountains in the rainy season. Happy at heart, those sons of Diti, the foes of the gods, along with Vidyunmālin and Maya, confronted the god of gods.

The army of the gods, whose minds were ready for death, grew doubtful of victory at the sight, their limbs suddenly weak. Roaring like thunderclouds, their fury like the thunder itself, the demons, ready to fight, attacked, and the two armies did awful things to each other. Pouring forth smoke from flaming weapons like the sun, those warriors, loving the fight, pulverized each other in rage.

Some fell when they were struck down by thunderbolts; others were torn apart by arrows. Some were split in two by discuses and fell into the watery deep. Their garlands, belts and necklaces broken, their clothes and ornaments torn off, gods and Pramāthas fell into the ocean full of sharks and crocodiles. And a mighty flood of weapons, of maces, clubs, lances, axes, thunderbolts, spears, swords and three-pronged arrows on all sides, a great flood of mountain tops hurled by the enraged enemy, and the Dānavas themselves with their swift horses, flaming like the sun and smoking, fell into the ocean's flood.

Even the stars in the skies shook, terrified by the awful carnage caused by the swift weapons thrown by the gods and demons. As small creatures are trampled when two elephants fight, so were the sharks and crocodiles crushed by the hosts of gods and demons that fell into the sea. . . .

Then, when the city of the Daityas came into conjunction with the constellation Puṣya, the three cities were joined together in a row. And Hara, the three-eyed master of the three strides, immediately shot his three-pronged arrow made of the three deities at Tripura. As he released his arrow, the sky which had been the color of the blue *bāṇa* tree, glowed golden, reddened as if by the sun. After he had shot that arrow made of the three gods at Tripura, Hara cried out, "Shame, shame!" When he saw Maheśvara so miserable, the elephant-gaited Nandin asked the trident-bearer, "What is the matter?" And the skull-bearer, marked with the moon, spoke piteously to Nandin, "Now Maya, my devotee, will die!"

At this, the powerful Nandīśvara sped quickly to Tripura, swift as the wind, or thought, and entered the city while the arrow was still travelling through the sky. That fierce *gaṇa* lord who glowed like gold spotted Maya and said, "O Maya, Tripura is about to be destroyed! I am telling you to escape, with your household!"

At Nandin's words, that demon who was steadfastly loyal to Maheśvara, stole out of Tripura with the principal members of his household. And Fire, in three forms, namely Hutāśa, Soma and Nārāyaṇa, burned up that city like a pile of straw. The three cities were destroyed by that flaming arrow just as prominent families are ruined by the wickedness of an evil son.

Elegant mansions with doorways, windows and balconies, lofty as Mt. Meru, Kailāsa or the peak of Mt. Mandara, and lovely palaces with numerous upper rooms and towering turrets, fountains and enchanting vistas, flying flags and banners of silver and gold, all these houses of Tripura were burned down in that Dānava calamity as they themselves turned into tongues of flame.

Some of the women of the chiefs of the Dānavas who had gone to the palace roofs, to the pleasure groves and gardens, to the windows and in the open air to embrace their lovers were consumed by the fire. . . . And some of those beautiful Dānava women, oppressed by the fire and abandoned by their lovers fell into the waters of the sea, their ornaments jangling. The women of Tripura cried out, "Oh my son!", "Oh my mother!" and "Oh my uncle!" as they trembled, harassed by the flames of the fire. Just as fire in the mountains consumes the lotuses in the ponds, so did the fire in Tripura devour the lotus-faced women. As snow in winter singes a mass of lotus flowers, so did this fire scorch the lotus eyes and faces of the beautiful women of Tripura. A confused jangling of belts with bells and tinkling anklets arose from the lovely, gentle women of the city as they were thus assailed by the blow from the fiery arrow of Śiva. When they fell into the waters of the sea as though for protection, the ocean began to blaze from the heat of the fallen houses that were licked by flames, just as the family of a wealthy man goes to perdition when stricken by the faults of a wicked son. The seething waters of that ocean began to boil due to the flaming houses, terrifying the whales, crocodiles, sharks, and other sea creatures that were being stewed.

Looking like Mt. Mandara, the lord of the mountains with a thousand peaks, that excellent city of Tripura with its towers and thousands of turreted mansions, decorated with necklaces of fire, fell into the sea with a monstrous roar, leaving only its name behind. . . .

Whoever recites this victory-winning story of Rudra's exploits will receive victory in his own undertakings from the bull-bannered lord. Whoever has this story recited at the *śrāddha* of his Fathers shall win that eternal merit which bestows the fruits of all sacrifices. This story is a blessed benediction; it is the means of getting a son. Whoever hears or recites this story goes to Rudra's heaven.

# Sunartaka the Dancer

O all-knowing Sanatkumāra, hear now about the *avatāra* of the great-souled lord Śiva called Sunartaka, the dancer. When the dark goddess Pārvatī, Himavat's daughter, went to the forest and did pure *tapas* in order to win Śiva, he was pleased with her severe *tapas,* O seer, and went to test her conduct and give her a boon. Joyous of heart, Śankara showed Śivā his own true nature and said to her, "Tell me what you desire!"

When she heard Śaṃbhu's words and beheld his magnificent form, Śivā was thrilled. She spoke to him with a bow, "If you are pleased with me, O lord of gods, and if you have compassion for me, then, O lord, be my husband! With your consent I shall go to my father's house, O lord. And you too should go to my father's side, protector. First ask him for my hand in the guise of a beggar and then make known your shining glory! Deign to make fruitful the householder's life to my father! Then according to the customary ceremony, lord, you can marry me, great god, in order to carry out the task of the gods. O lord, satisfy my desire! To you who are immutable and loving to your devotees, I have always been loyal."

At her words, the great lord Śaṃbhu who is loving to his devotees declared, "Let it be so!" Then he disappeared and returned to his own mountain. The youthful Pārvatī too, making herself beautiful for the occasion, departed for her father's house along with her two companions.

When Himācala* heard of Pārvatī's arrival, accompanied by his wife and his retinue, he went happily to see his daughter. When they saw her with face so serene, they ushered her into the house and, overjoyed, had a great festival held in her honor, out of affection. Menā distributed largesse to the brahmins while the fine lord of the mountain arranged to have an auspicious ceremony performed, complete with Vedic recitations, out of respect for his daughter. While Menā was content to remain in the courtyard with her daughter, Mt. Himavat went to the Ganges to bathe.

Meanwhile, Śaṃbhu who is loving to his devotees had become Sunartaka the dancer for fun. As he approached Menakā he carried a horn in his left hand, a drum in his right. He was clothed in red, wearing rags on his back like one skilled in dance and song. In this form as a dancer he pranced gleefully around Menakā's courtyard, singing an enchanting melody. He sounded his horn and drum and struck a variety of fetching poses. All the people of the town—men, women, children and elders—gathered there at once to see him dance. When they heard his sweet song and beheld his enchanting dance, they all became infatuated with him, O seer, even Menā. Her mind delighted with his performance, she went immediately to present him with golden vessels brimful of precious stones in order to show her appreciation.

But the dancer refused the jewels and asked for Śivā, her daughter, as alms instead. And he began once more to sing and dance with zeal. Stunned by his request, Menā grew furious. She berated the beggar and sought to turn him out.

Meanwhile, the mountain king returned from the Ganges to see a beggar-man standing before him in the courtyard. When he heard from Menā's mouth all that had happened, he too was enraged and he ordered the servants to throw the beggar out. But no one could force him to go, that one who shone with splendor like a blazing fire impossible to touch, excellent seer.

Then that beggar who was skilled in many sorts of sports showed to Śaila, the mountain, his infinite power. Śaila watched as he adopted the form of Viṣṇu, the shape of Brahmā, and the appearance of the Sun all in rapid succession. Then, O friend, the mountain saw

*Himālaya.

him assume the wondrous form of Rudra, together with Pārvatī, smiling brilliantly and delightful to behold. Amazed to see in this way the many forms of the lord, he was flooded at once with supreme bliss.

That choice beggar, player of games, asked the two of them for Durgā as alms; nothing else did he take. Then, prompted by Durgā's words, the supreme lord vanished and swiftly went to his own abode. A clear recognition of the lord arose in Menā and Śaila. They exclaimed, "He has tricked us! Lord Śiva has gone home! We must give to him our own daughter, the fine ascetic Pārvatī!" As they were thinking this, the supreme devotion to Śiva was born in them both. And Rudra, having had his jest, graciously performed the marriage ceremony with Pārvatī, according to the rules, which delighted his devotees.

# The Tāṇḍava Dance of Śiva

Dāruka, born of the demons, had achieved his prowess through *tapas* and was butchering both gods and eminent brahmins like the Fire of Time. Severely oppressed and beaten by Dāruka, the gods approached Brahmā, Īśāna, Kumāra, Viṣṇu, Yama and Indra. Knowing that the demon could only be killed by a woman, Brahmā and the other gods disguised themselves as women and went to do battle with him. But he overcame them, too, O brahmins, so they all went to Brahmā and told him what had happened. In his company they went to Śiva, Umā's lord, and led by the Grandfather they bowed before the lord of the gods in manifold ways. Then Brahmā spoke up, "O lord, Dāru is a cruel demon! Protect us by killing this Daitya Dāruka, who is to be slain by a woman!"

When he had heard Brahmā's report, the lord of the gods, smiter of Bhaga's eyes, said to the mountain-born goddess with a hint of laughter, "I ask your help, my beauty, for the sake of the world. Go and destroy Dāruka who can only be slain by a woman, O fair-faced one!" At his words the lord's mistress, who is the fire-drilling block* of the world, entered the body of the god, intending to be born for Dāruka's destruction. Meanwhile, Brahmā and the gods, who were led by Indra, were unaware that she had entered that supreme deity, the lord of the gods, with a portion of herself.

When the omniscient four-faced god Brahmā saw the lustrous

*Fire was drilled by twirling a stick (a male symbol) into a block (a female symbol); thus the fire-drilling block can represent a "womb."

daughter of the mountain standing at Śaṃbhu's side as before, even he was fooled by her tricks. For as Pārvatī entered the body of the god of gods, she made for herself another body from the poison that stood in his throat. Knowing with his third eye that she had done this, Śiva, Kāma's foe, emitted the black-throated goddess from his own throat. When this goddess, Kālī, with the pitch-black throat, was born, there arose at the same time ample, abundant, auspicious Victory. And Parameṣṭhin was pleased with Bhavānī because she would accomplish the defeat of the demons.

When the hosts of the gods and the Siddhas, led by Śakra, Upendra* and the lotus-born Brahmā, witnessed the birth of this luminous goddess with the inky-black poison-filled throat, they fled in terror. Also terrifying were the eye that appeared in her forehead, the crescent moon on the crown of her head, the sharp fangs in her mouth, the spiky trident in her hand and the ornaments adorning her body. Along with the goddess were born the chief Siddhas and the ghoulish Piśācas, all of them adorned with ornaments and robed in celestial garb.

At Pārvatī's command, the supreme goddess with the black throat slew the Dānava Dāruka, who had been tormenting the overlords of the gods. Her violence, however, knew no bounds, O brahmins, so the whole world became sick with the fever of her rage. Then Bhava, the lord, took the form of a boy by illusion, and began to howl aloud at a ghost-filled cremation ground in order to quell the fire of her rage.

When she saw the lord in the form of a child, she was fooled by his Māyā and offered him milk from her breasts, O brahmins. This clever boy drank up her wrath along with the breast milk; with this anger he became the guardian of the fields, adopting eight different forms for the protection of the fields. Thus was the goddess weaned of her anger by this boy.

Then at twilight the joyous trident-wielding god of gods performed a frenzied dance to gain her favor, accompanied by all his ghosts and goblins. Drinking the nectar of Śaṃbhu's dance only as far as her throat, the supreme goddess herself danced with glee in that place of ghosts and witches. All the gods, together with Brahmā, Indra and Upendra, bowed before Kālī and the goddess Pārvatī and sang their praises.

Thus you have heard in brief the story of the Tāṇḍava dance of the trident-bearing god. There are others, however, who hold that the dance of the lord is really the bliss of Yoga.

*Lit. "younger brother of Indra," a pejorative name for Viṣṇu in some Śiva-oriented texts.

# The Dance of Śiva in the Sky

After speaking to the *yogins,* the blessed supreme lord began to dance, revealing his supernal divine nature. The *yogins* witnessed the lord Mahādeva, the ultimate abode of splendor, dancing with Viṣṇu in the cloudless sky. They saw that lord of creatures who is really known only by those *yogins* who have mastered the principles of Yoga. The brahmins watched the dance of the universal soul himself, the god who impels the world and who is the source of the universal illusion. It was indeed the lord of creatures whom they saw dancing, at the recollection of whose lotus feet one loses all fear born of ignorance. They witnessed that Yogin whom *yogins* behold as light, those meditators who are always alert and serene, who have mastered their breath and are filled with devotion.

The brahmins saw Rudra dancing in the sky, that supreme liberator who instantly releases people from their ignorance, who is kind and benevolent to his devotees, the god with a thousand heads, a thousand feet, a thousand arms and forms, with matted hair, the crown of his head adorned with the crescent moon, clothed in a tiger-skin, holding a trident in his huge hand, bearing a staff, with the sun, moon and fire as his splendor. He was terrible to behold, with gaping mouth, projecting fangs, blazing forth like ten million suns, standing at the same time both inside and outside the egg, emitting the incandescent fire that burns the whole world at the end of time. Thus the *yogins* beheld the dance of the lord god who fashioned the universe. . . .

"We all worship you, sole lord, primordial person, lord of breath, Rudra whose Yoga is eternal, who resides in our hearts, Pracetas, the purifier, who consists of Brahmā. Sages who are calm and serene, who have meditated on the immovable Self within their bodies, see you to be the immaculate womb of Brahman, golden in hue, the supreme seer, higher than the most high and that which is beyond it. From you has come forth the progenetrix of the world. You are the Self of all. You are the atom, smaller than the small and greater than the great. Thus do the wise say that you are everything.

"Hiraṇyagarbha, the Golden Embryo that is the inner Self of the world, has been born from you. At birth the primordial person emanated from you. The creator of the universe fashions the universe according to your ordinance. You have originated all the Vedas and they will lodge in you at the end. We behold you dancing, source of the world, lodged in our own hearts! By you does this wheel of Brahmā turn. You, sole guardian of the world, are filled with Māyā.

We take refuge in you! We adore you! You are the soul of Yoga, the master of consciousness who dances the divine dance! . . .

"When we recall your lotus feet, the seeds of our rebirth are utterly destroyed. With minds restrained and bodies prostrate, we seek your favor, sole lord. Hail to Bhava, the source of existence, to Time, to All, to Hara, to you! Praise be to Rudra, to Kapardin, to you! Glory be to Fire, O god! Praise be to Śiva!"

After this hymn, the lord god Kapardin, Bhava, who rides the bull, returned to his normal state.

# The Sages of the Pine Forest

There is a beautiful Pine Forest where certain virtuous sages, always loyal to Śiva, used to occupy themselves continually with meditation on him. Those lords of seers performed worship to Śiva three times a day and praised him continuously with all kinds of divine hymns.

Once upon a time all those chief brahmins, devotees of Śiva, intent upon meditation on Śiva, went into the forest to gather fuel. Meanwhile Śankara adopted a misshapen body in order to test them and appeared there colored blue and red. Utterly resplendent in appearance, he was naked and decked out in ornamental ashes. Holding his penis in his hand he made lewd gestures. Thus Hara himself went to the forest in an affectionate mood, thinking to do a favor to his devotees who lived there, and with whom he was well pleased.

When they saw him, some of the wives of the sages were terrified. But others, amazed and excited, sought to approach him. While some of the women embraced him and others grasped his hand, they lost themselves in rivalry with one another. At this moment the eminent seers returned. When they beheld this revolting person, they were upset and overcome with anger. Much aggrieved, all the sages, fooled by Śiva's trick, cried out, "Who is this? Who is this?"

When that pure, naked man said nothing at all, the noble seers spoke to that terrible apparition, "Your behavior is disgusting! You are ruining the way of the Veda! Therefore that penis of yours shall fall to the ground!"

When they said this, the *linga* of the pure Śiva's supernatural body fell off at once. Blazing like fire, that penis, or *linga*, burned up everything in its way. Wherever it went it burned things down. Śiva's fiery *linga* went to the netherworld and to heaven. It traveled throughout the world but nowhere did it come to rest. The worlds grew troubled and the sages unhappy. No one could find shelter, neither gods nor seers.

All the gods and seers, not recognizing Śiva, were miserable. They assembled and quickly went together to Brahmā for refuge. When they arrived the brahmins honored and hymned Brahmā the creator and told him all that happened. When he heard what they said, he recognized that they had been deluded by Śiva's illusion. Worshipping Śankara, he said to the excellent seers:

"O brahmins, you are wise but you have done a contemptible thing, you who are so critical when the ignorant act this way! Who can hope for his own well-being after obstructing the god Śiva? One who does not welcome a guest in the middle of the day has his good *karman* taken away, and after leaving to that man his own evil *karman,* the guest departs. How much worse, then, is it to deny hospitality to Śiva!

"As long as Śiva's *linga* roams the three worlds there will be no prosperity. This is the truth I speak. You should do whatever is necessary to pacify Śiva's penis. O sages, consider carefully what is to be done."

Thus addressed, the seers bowed to Brahmā and said, "What shall we do, lord? Show us our duty!" After these lords of seers had spoken, Brahmā, grandfather of all the worlds, himself addressed the seers: "Go and worship the mountain-born goddess. You must placate Śiva! When she assumes the form of a vulva the penis will become calm. Listen to the rule I tell you now. If you treat her with affection, she will be agreeable.

"Put a jar filled with water from a sacred ford, *durva* grass and barley in the center of a splendid eight-petalled diagram. Cast a spell on the jar with Vedic *mantras,* doing worship according to the rules of *śruti,* and while recollecting Śiva. Anoint the *linga* with that water, O supreme seers. When it is consecrated with Śatarudrīya *mantras,* it will come at last to rest. After putting in place the mountain-girl in the form of a *yoni,* place the blessed shaft on top of it and once more cast a spell on it. Propitiate the supreme lord with perfumes, sandal wood, flowers and incense and with the *pūjā* of food and other goods. Placate him with prostrations, hymns, holy songs and instruments. Then perform the *svastyayana* ceremony for godspeed and cry out:

"'Victory! Be gracious, lord of gods who brings happiness to the world! You are the creator, protector, and destroyer who is beyond *OṂ*. You are the beginning of the world, the womb of the world, the interior of the world. Be at peace, great lord! Protect all the worlds!'"

"When you follow this procedure, well-being will return to the world, without a doubt. The three worlds will not decay and felicity will prevail. . . . After gratifying the daughter of the mountain and also the one whose banner bears the bull by the preceding rule, the supreme *linga* will be brought to rest."

After this the gods and sages propitiated the mountain-born girl and Śiva according to the injunction dictated by the *mantras* for the sake of Dharma. . . .

When the penis was pacified, prosperity returned to the world, O brahmins, and that *linga* became famous in the three worlds as Hatakṣema, or Śivā-Śiva. Because the *linga* is worshiped, happiness abounds in the triple world in every way.

# Brahmā, Viṣṇu and the Linga of Śiva

Lord Viṣṇu spoke:

Long ago, when everything animate and inanimate was lost in that one awful ocean, Śiva himself appeared in order to awaken Brahmā and myself. There was only this dreadful undifferentiated ocean made up of darkness in the midst of which I myself, with one thousand heads, one thousand eyes, one thousand feet and one thousand arms, lay sleeping, self-controlled, bearing conch, discus and mace. Meanwhile I saw at a distance a god of boundless light, shining like ten million suns, circled by luster, the four-faced god whose Yoga is great, the person of golden color, wearing a black antelope skin, the god who is hymned with Ṛg, Yajur and Sāma Vedas.

In the twinkling of an eye, glorious Brahmā himself, choicest of those who know Yoga, came to me and smiled as he spoke. "Who are you? Why are you here? For what reason are you staying here? Tell me, O lord! For I am the creator of the worlds, the self-existent, the great-grandfather." Thus addressed by Brahmā I replied, "It is I who am creator and destroyer of these worlds time and time again!"

While the argument was going on like this there appeared by the illusion of the supreme god a matchless *linga* whose self was Śiva displayed for awakening. It was bright as the fire of Doomsday, wreathed with garlands of flame, free from growth and decay, without beginning, middle or end. Then the unborn one, the lord, said to me, "Go quickly downwards; I will go upwards. Let us discover the limits of this."

Having made this agreement, the two of us—myself and the Grandfather—went quickly upwards and downwards, but for a hundred years could find no end to it. Amazed and frightened, confused by the illusion of the god who carries a trident, we called to mind the perfect lord. Pronouncing the great sound *OṂ*, the transcendent syllable, bowing with our hands folded we praised the matchless Śaṃbhu. Being so praised the supreme lord became manifest; the great Yogin shone forth brilliant as ten million suns. Appearing to devour the sky with his hundred million mouths, he displayed a thousand hands and feet; sun, moon and fire were his eyes. He stood there with bow in hand, carrying a trident, wearing a tiger-skin garment, his sacred thread a snake, making a sound like a kettledrum of clouds.

Thus spoke the great god, "I am pleased with you both, O best of the gods. Now see that I am the greatest god and fear no more! Ages ago the two of you eternal ones were produced from my limbs. Brahmā, Grandfather of the worlds, lies in my right side. Viṣṇu, the protector, dwells in my left. And Hara is born in my heart. I am entirely satisfied. I will give to you both whatever you desire."

Having said this, the god Śiva, Mahādeva himself, inclined towards benevolence, embraced Brahmā and me. Then Nārāyaṇa and the Grandfather were very pleased of heart. They prostrated themselves before the great lord when they saw his face. "If you are pleased with us, and if a boon is to be granted, then let us be constantly devoted to you, O god, the greatest lord!"

## The Skull-Bearer

Long ago the whole world with its stationary and mobile creatures was one vast ocean. Sunk in that utter darkness, awful to behold, were the mountains and trees. Sun, moon and stars were lost in it, as were fire and wind. It was undifferentiated, unfathomable, void of being and non-being alike.

The lord lay sleeping in this sea for a thousand years. At the end of his night, he assumed a form made of *rajas* and poured forth the worlds. This form had five faces and was wonderful to see, wise in the Vedas and Vedāngas, the creator of the world with its moving and unmoving beings. Another form also appeared, made of *tamas*. It had three eyes, carried a trident, wore matted hair and displayed prayer beads. Then the great-souled one emitted the dreadful *ahaṃkāra*, or egotism, which overcame the two gods Brahmā and Śankara.

Rudra, wrapped in egotism, said to the Grandfather, "Who are you who have come here? Tell me who sent you!" And the Grandfather replied, also out of egotism, "Who are you? Who are your father and mother? Tell me this!" In such a way did Brahmā and Īśa argue long ago. And from this quarrel were you born, Nārada, beloved of the Kali Age. And as soon as you were born you rose up into the sky carrying a peerless lute and making joyful music.

Śaṃbhu stood full of disdain before the lotus-born Brahmā, whose downcast face next to Śaṃbhu's looked like the moon eclipsed by the planet. When the master of the worlds had thus been surpassed by the lord god Parameṣṭhin, his fifth face, dark with rage, said to Rudra, "I assert, O three-eyed one, that you consist of *tamas,* that you are naked, clad in space, that you ride a bull and that you are the destroyer of the worlds!"

Thus addressed, the angry Śankara, the unborn lord, fixed that face with an evil eye, longing to burn it up with fire. Then the three-eyed god displayed five faces of his own. They were white, red, shiny gold, dark blue and bright yellow. When the fifth head of the Grandfather beheld these faces, each equal to the sun, it spoke up, "When water is stirred up it produces bubbles. So what?"

The great-souled Śankara was infuriated at this, so he cut off that coarse-mouthed head of Brahmā with the tip of his fingernail. When it was severed, that skull fell onto the palm of Śankara's left hand, where it stuck fast.

Then the blessed blue and red lord with knotted hair emitted from himself Kālabhairava to hold the skull of Brahmā. "You will perform penance," he said, "in order to destroy evil and benefit creation. As my agent, you shall go begging throughout the world, skull in hand."

So speaking, he also sent out a young maiden, wreathed in flame, called Brahmahatyā or Brahmin-Murder, with gaping mouth and projecting fangs. "Horrible woman," he said, "follow the three-eyed god until he reaches the divine city of Vārāṇasī to expiate this crime." So speaking, the god Maheśvara also addressed Bhairava, the Fire of Time, "Roam the whole world for alms as I command. Seek out Nārāyaṇa, the lord of the gods, free from flaws, who will make plain to you the means of removing your guilt."

After lord Hara, the universal soul, had heard the words of the deity of deities, he traveled around the three worlds with the skull on his hand. Assuming a misshapen body, radiant with splendor, wise and matchless in purity, crowned with a pile of twisted hair, surrounded by arrogant Pramāthas, shining like ten million of suns, Mahādeva blazed forth with his eye that is the Fire of Time. After drinking the blissful heavenly nectar of Parameṣṭhin, the lord of many games and sports went abroad in the three worlds.

When they saw that black-faced Śankara Kālabhairava, the race of women, endowed with elegance, pursued him. They sang all sorts of songs and danced before the lord. When they observed his smiling face, they coyly wrinkled up their brows.

After visiting the quarters of the gods, Dānavas and others, the trident-bearer went to the abode of Viṣṇu, where Madhusūdana sat. When he beheld that divine place, Śankara, benefactor to the world, together with his select Bhūtas, started to go inside. But the mighty guardian of the gate obstructed the supreme lord who bears the trident, ignorant of his divine nature. That great-armed doorkeeper was called Viṣvaksena. Robed in yellow, with conch, discus and mace in hand, he had been born from a portion of Viṣṇu.

Then one of Śankara's ghastly *gaṇas* named Kālavega did battle by Bhairava's order with the one who sprang from Viṣṇu, so we have heard. Viṣvaksena, eyes red with rage, overpowered Kālavega, and turning towards Rudra, hurled the dreadful discus Sudarśana. The god Mahādeva, destroyer of his foes, enemy of Tripura, the trident-bearer, watched Viṣvaksena with contempt as he flew at him all of a sudden. That mighty marvel resembled the Fire at the end of the Age, but Mahādeva pierced him with the point of his trident and threw him to the ground. Mortally wounded, Viṣvaksena glimpsed death like one struck down by disease, lost his great strength and gave up his life. After killing Viṣṇu's minion, Śiva entered the house with the bulls of Pramāthas, carrying the corpse of Viṣvaksena.

When lord Hari saw Īśvara, source of the world, he split open his head and made a stream of blood gush forth, saying, "O lord of infinite splendor, accept this as my alms! It seems most fitting for you, destroyer of Tripura!" Although that river of blood flowed from the god's forehead for a thousand divine years, the skull of Brahmā Parameṣṭhin was never filled.

After praising Kālarudra* with Vedic *mantras* preceded by great reverence, lord Hari Nārāyaṇa said to him, "Why are you carrying around the head of Brahmā?" So the blessed supreme lord told him all that had happened. And the imperishable Hṛṣīkeśa, lord of the gods, summoned Brahmahatyā and directed, "Release the trident-bearer from this skull!"

Even when addressed in this manner by the foe of Mura, she refused to quit his side. Pondering this, Viṣṇu, the all-knowing womb of the world, said to Śankara, "You must go at once to the

*Śiva in his destructive aspect.

divine shining city of Vārāṇasī, where the lord swiftly destroys the guilt of everyone in the world."

So out of a desire for the welfare of the world, lord Śiva went for sport to all the secret sanctuaries and sacred fords. Everywhere he went the mighty Yogin was hymned by the Pramāthas, whose own Yoga was great, while he cavorted with the corpse of Viṣvaksena in his hand. Even Hari Nārāyaṇa himself assumed another form and pursued the lord, eager for a glimpse of the dance. When he saw Govinda, the eternal lord of Yoga whose banner is marked with a bull pranced around and around.

Then Rudra, whose mount is Dharma, along with his retinue and Hari, repaired to the city of Mahādeva called Vārāṇasī. At the mere entry of the lord into that city, Brahmahatyā with the matted hair went down to the netherworld in dismay, crying *"Hā, hā."* and bellowing loudly.

The god Hara Śankara then entered the supreme sanctuary and put down the skull of Brahmā before the *gaṇas.* Lord Mahādeva, ocean of compassion, laid down the corpse of Viṣvaksena and gave it to Viṣṇu, saying, "Let him come to life again! Those who continually reflect upon my marvelous guise as a skull-bearer will have their guilt erased instantly in this world and the next. Whoever comes to this best of sacred fords, takes a ritual bath by the rules, and satisfies the Fathers and the gods, shall be freed from the guilt of brahmin-murder. Whoever dwells in this place recognizing that the world is not eternal, to him I grant at death supreme wisdom, the ultimate goal."

So speaking, the lord embraced Janārdana and vanished in an instant along with his Pramātha lords. And after receiving Viṣvaksena from the trident-bearer, lord Kṛṣṇa himself assumed his supernal form and went at once to his own abode.

# Kāmadeva, the God of Love

Why did Śaṃbhu, the god of gods, burn Kāmadeva, the god of love? Tell me this, said Narada. And Pulastya replied, When Satī, the daughter of Dakṣa, had gone to the realm of Yama, the three-eyed god smashed Dakṣa's sacrifice and went away. Then Kandarpa,* whose weapon is flowers, saw the bull-bannered god alone, without a wife, and struck him with the arrow of madness. Hit by the maddening shaft, the crazed Hara wandered around forest groves and

*Name of the god of love.

ponds. Stricken with madness and remembering Satī, Mahādeva found no rest, divine seer. He was like an elephant pierced by an arrow.

Then the lord of the gods fell into the Kālindī river,* O seer, whose waters turned black, burned by Śankara's immersion. Since then, the Kālindī's water has flowed black as bees or collyrium. That river with its sacred fords looks like a lock of earth's hair. Then Mahādeva roamed by holy rivers, ponds and streams, by lovely river banks, tanks and lotus ponds, through beautiful mountains, forest groves and mountain ridges. Wandering at will, nowhere did Mahādeva find repose.

One moment he sang aloud, divine seer, and the next he roared. For a while Śankara mused about Dakṣa's lovely daughter with her tender body, and then he fell asleep. At times when Hara slept he would see the little daughter of Dakṣa in a dream and cry out, "O cruel one, stay with me! O foolish woman, why have you deserted me, O blameless one? Abandoned by you, innocent woman, I am consumed by the fire of love. O Satī, you must be angry with me. Don't be mad, beautiful woman, but speak to me who lies prostrate at your feet! Without ceasing I hear you, I see you, I touch you, I celebrate you, beloved, and constantly embrace you. Why don't you say something to me?

"Who can fail to feel compassion at the sight of another in tears, especially when that one is her own husband? You are most merciless indeed! Once you said to me, thin-waisted woman, 'I cannot live without you,' but it was a lie! Come near, come near! O sweet-eyed one, I am burning with love! Embrace me or this fire will not abate. I swear this is the truth, beloved!" Crying aloud in this manner, Śiva awoke suddenly at the end of his dream. Then he groaned over and over again in the forest, his throat open wide.

Then from a distance Kāma spied him whose sign is the bull, moaning and groaning. He drew his bow again and straightaway pierced him with another arrow named Saṃtāpa, or Remorse. Stricken with remorse, Śiva grew even more aflame; burning in this way, he roamed around the world hissing and snorting. . . .

Followed by Madana, Hara entered the dreadful Pine Forest where the seers and their wives were living. When the seers saw him, they bowed their heads to the lord who said, "Give me alms!" But all the sages stood there in silence, O Nārada, so he wandered around from hermitage to hermitage. When the wives of the Bhārgavas and Ātreyas† saw him appear, they became agitated. All their resolve completely deserted them, except for Arundhatī and the comely

*The river Yamunā.
†Brahmin families.

Anasūyā, whose minds remained concentrated on honor and concern for their husbands. All the other women, utterly in disarray, pursued Maheśvara, lost in love, their senses burning with desire. Those wives of the seers left their own homes empty and followed him wherever he went, as elephant cows pursue a bull in rut.

At this spectacle, O seer, the Bhārgavas and Āngirases and all the other sages became filled with rage and proclaimed, "Let his penis fall to the ground!" So the god's *linga* fell off, rending apart the earth, and the blue and red trident-bearer disappeared.

That fallen *linga* split open the surface of the wealth-giving earth, and descended to the netherworld, rending the cosmic egg. The earth quaked, with its mountains, lakes and snakes, and all the realms of the netherworld trembled with their moving and unmoving beings. When he saw earth and the other worlds shaking, the Grandfather went to the milk ocean called Kṣīroda to see Mādhava.* Finding Hṛṣīkeśa there, he bowed reverently and said, "O god, why are the worlds shaking?" And Hari replied, "Brahmā, Śiva's *linga* has been made to fall off by the great seers and earth is suffering under its weight!"

When the Grandfather heard this most marvelous tale, he repeated over and over again, "Let us go there, O lord of gods!" So the Grandfather god and Keśava, master of the world, went to that secluded spot where Bhava's *linga* lay. At the sight of that immortal *linga*, Hari mounted Garuḍa, chief of the birds, and flew aloft, while lord Brahmā, lost in wonder, entered the netherworlds. When Brahmā on his lotus chariot had mounted upwards all the way, he did not find its top, O brahmin, and returned, astonished. Viṣṇu, refuge of the world, went to the seven netherworlds, discus in hand, but when he emerged, great seer, he had found no bottom. Both Viṣṇu and the Grandfather then approached the *linga* of Hara, and with folded hands they both began to praise Śiva. . . .

Then Kāmadeva, armed with his bow and flower arrows, appeared once more before the wandering Maheśa, some distance away. When Hara saw Smara in front of him again, he glared at him from head to toe, his third eye puffed up with rage. Ignited by the stare of the three-eyed god, the resplendent Madana began to go up in flames, O brahmin, starting from his feet upwards, just like a dead tree. When he saw his feet on fire, the one whose weapons are flowers dropped his wondrous bow and it broke into five pieces. . . . which turned at once into trees: *campaka, bakula, pātala,* jasmine and coral trees. With his body in flames, Smara dropped his arrows on the earth where they became fruit-bearing trees by the thousands. By the grace of

*Viṣṇu-Kṛṣṇa.

Hara, sweet trees of all kinds, mangos and others, sprang up, to be savored even by the excellent deities.

After the noble and eternal Rudra had burned Smara to ashes, he controlled his own body and went to the frosty mountains to practice continual *tapas* in order to gain merit. Thus was Kāma with his bow and arrow incinerated by Śaṃbhu, best of the gods, long ago. Since then that great bowman who was worshiped of old by the gods has been celebrated as Ananga, the bodiless god.

# The Illusions of Śiva

All beings, past, present and future, evolve from Śiva, mature in Śiva and dissolve in Śiva. He is thought to be the kinsman, friend, preceptor, protector, guide, truthful teacher, wish-granting tree, brother, father and mother of Brahmā, Indra, Upendra and the moon, of gods, Dānavas, Snakes, and Gandharvas, of human beings and all other creatures. Śiva consists of everything. He himself is that which is to be known by mankind, and he is both beyond the ultimate and the ultimate itself. His supreme divine *māyā* is all-pervasive, O seer. The whole world with its gods, demons and people, is situated in him.

Everyone alike, whether he be a hero, a Viṣṇu, another deity, or a valiant man, is smitten by the powerful mind-born Kāma, his special attendant. Hari was deluded by desire, by the majesty of Śiva's illusion, O lordly seer, when he molested the wives of others. Indra, lord of the thirty gods, was fascinated by Gautama's wife; wicked of soul he committed evil with her and incurred the curse of that seer. Even Fire, most excellent in the world, was tricked by Śiva's *māyā;* because of his pride he was overcome by lust, but Śiva extricated him from it.

Wind, the breath of the world, was also fooled by Śiva's *māyā*. Long ago Vyāsa was smitten by desire and lusted after the wives of another man.* The hot-rayed Sun, ensnared by Śiva's *māyā,* became filled with desire at the sight of a mare and took the form of a stallion. And Moon, beguiled by Śiva's *māyā* became lustful and abducted his *guru's* wife; but Śiva came to his rescue.

Long ago even the two seers Mitra and Varuṇa who stood erect in *tapas* were deluded by Śiva's *māyā*. When they saw the youthful Urvaśī, they became filled with lust. Mitra shed his semen into a pot, while Varuṇa spilled his in the water. Born of Mitra, Vasiṣṭha arose from the pot while Agastya, as radiant as the submarine fire, was born of Varuṇa.

*When he begot sons for the childless Vicitravīrya by the injunction of levirate.

Dakṣa, too, son of Brahmā, waylaid by Śaṃbhu's *māyā* along with his brothers, grew eager for intercourse with his sister Aditi. And many times Brahmā, duped by Śiva's *māyā*, desired intercourse with his own daughter, and with other women as well. The great *yogin* Cyavana, fooled by Śiva's *māyā*, sported with Sukanyā and became love-struck. Kaśyapa, beguiled by Śiva's *māyā*, became lustful; out of delusion long ago he sued for King Dhanvan's daughter. Deceived by desire, Garuḍa, wishing to abduct the maiden Śāṇḍilī, had his wings scorched by her the moment she found him out.

The seer Vibhāṇḍaka became lustful when he saw a female; by Śiva's order, his son Ṛśyaśṛnga was born from a doe. Gautama, the seer, his mind deluded by Śaṃbhu's *māyā*, was shaken to see Śāradvatī naked and made love with her. That ascetic kept his spilled seed in a trough from which was born Droṇa, choicest among those who bear arms. Parāśara, the great *yogin*, duped by Śiva's *māyā*, sported Satyavatī, the virgin daughter of a fisherman, who herself had been born from the belly of a fish. And Viśvāmitra, fooled by Śiva's *māyā* and overcome by desire, dallied with Menakā in the forest. Losing his wits, he quarreled with Vasiṣṭha, but through the grace of Śiva he became a brahmin.

The evil-minded Rāvaṇa, son of Viśravas, grew lustful through Śiva's *māyā* and kidnaped Sītā, incurring thereby even his own death. And the eminent, self-controlled seer Bṛhaspati, deluded by Śiva's *māyā*, sported with his brother's wife; from this union Bharadvāja was born.

Thus, O Vyāsa, I have described the power of the great-souled Śankara's illusion. What more do you want to hear?

# The Weapons of Śiva

Hear, O Kṛṣṇa, mighty Śaivite, the great and excellent glory of the supreme lord Śaṃbhu, increasing devotion, which I, Upamanyu, have witnessed! While practicing *tapas*, I saw Śankara with his weapons and retinue, together with Viṣṇu, the other gods and the immortals. Of three parts,* he stood on one foot, his felicity unhindered, eternal, with huge fangs, monstrous teeth and mouths filled with flames. Blazing with the light of two thousand points of fire, he had many eyes, a thousand feet and all kinds of threatening weapons.

I witnessed him who continually annihilates the universe at the

*I.e., bent in neck and hips according to the canon of iconography.

end of an Eon, Maheśvara himself, who burns up everything in the triple world with its moving and unmoving creatures in half the wink of an eye. Erect in *tapas*, I saw at Rudra's side the immortal, ultimate secret weapon, which no other weapon whatsoever can equal or surpass: that which is called Vijaya* in the three worlds, the trident of the trident-bearer. It is a horrendous death-dealer, a striking and throwing weapon that has the power to rend the entire earth, dry up the vast ocean and fell the whole wheel of celestial lights without the slightest hesitation.

It was this weapon that long ago slew Māndhātar and all his troops; he was the son of Yuvanāśva, that Cakravartin of mighty splendor, who conquered the triple world. And in the hand of the enemy-destroying king Śatrughna, this great, sharp, savage, terror-begetting trident also felled that conceited Haihaya, the demon Lavaṇa after he challenged all contenders in battle. After annihilating this Daitya, it returned to Rudra's hand.

Three-pointed, the trident stood there with its brows knitted in a frown, threatening in appearance like a smokeless fire, resembling the newly risen sun. I saw this incomparable weapon stand there in the form of a man holding a sharpened axe, carrying the sun in its hand as well as a noose like that of death; it was adorned with snakes and other decorations, having the form of Fire at the end of the Eon. This same trident, which was the bane of the kṣatriyas when the Bhārgava Rāma relied on its strength in battle, was bestowed on Rāma by Śiva long ago when that infuriated seer devastated the kṣatriyas by destroying them twenty-one times.

Then I saw the incandescent discus Sudarśana with a thousand faces and two thousand arms, a deity in human form. Shining with two thousand eyes and a thousand feet, blazing like ten million suns, it consumed the triple world with fire. And I saw the sharp, glittering thunderbolt, utterly magnificent with a hundred spikes. I saw, too, the great refulgent bow Pināka with its quiver, and a spear, sword and noose together with a monstrous fiery hook, the massive divine mace and all sorts of other weapons, as well as the weapons of the world guardians. All these I saw by the side of the blessed Rudra!

Brahmā, the Grandfather of the world, was sitting to the right of the god, in his celestial chariot, swift as thought, along with his goose.† And Nārāyaṇa, bearing conch, discus and mace, was at his left side, seated on Garuḍa, Vinatā's son. Svāyambhuva and the other Manus, Bhṛgu and the rest of the seers, the celestial Śakra and the other gods all accompanied him. With his spear, peacock and bell,

*Lit. "victory."
†Brahmā's riding animal.

Skanda stood next to the goddess, radiant like fire. Nandin stood in front of Bhava carrying a trident, while all kinds of creatures, *gaṇas* and Mothers were in attendance. These deities surrounding Mahādeva on all sides reverently saluted the great lord and sang to him a variety of hymns.

Everything there is to see or hear in this world I beheld with amazement at the side of the lord! Summoning up great fortitude at that spectacle, O Kṛṣṇa, I folded my hands and offered many praises, lost in utmost rapture! When I saw Śankara face to face, I worshiped him according to the rules in a voice choked with tears, overcome with devotion.

# The Origin of Women

Hear, friend of great wisdom, about the matchless form of Śiva called Ardhanarīnara, half woman, half man, who grants wishes and fulfills the desire of the creator. When all the creatures poured forth by Brahmā failed to reproduce, he grew disturbed in his mind and suffered greatly on account of this misfortune. Then Brahmā heard an unearthly voice speak out, "Make a creation born from coupling!" and he decided to do so. But since no race of women had yet arisen from the lord, the lotus-born god was not able to produce a copulative creation.

When it occurred to him that such creatures could not be born without the power of Śaṃbhu, Brahmā began to practice great *tapas* while concentrating, with love in his heart, on the supreme lord conjoined with Śiva, the supreme *śakti.* Soon Śiva grew pleased with Svāyambhuva, the self-existent, who was yoked in intense *tapas,* so he assumed the wish-granting form of the lord whose consciousness is complete, and came before Brahmā as half woman, half man.

When he saw the god Śankara united with delightful *śakti,* Brahmā bowed formally and praised him with folded hands. Then the lord Mahādeva, creator of the universe, spoke most graciously to Svāyambhuva with a voice like rumbling clouds, "My dear Grandfather, blessed son, truly I know the whole of your heart's desire. You are now doing *tapas* so that your creatures will multiply. I am pleased with your *tapas* and I shall grant your wish!" And as he spoke these sweet words—they were both noble and naturally gentle—Śiva separated the goddess Śivā from a part of his body.

When he saw this supreme *śakti* detached from Śiva, the creator prostrated himself before her, his soul humbled, and asked, "In the beginning I was emitted first by your master, the god of gods, O Śivā, after which all creatures were charged with their duties by the great-souled Śaṃbhu. Out of my mind I fashioned the gods and all the other creatures, O Śivā, but they do not reproduce themselves. I must create them over and over again. I want to make all my creatures multiply by producing henceforth a creation that proceeds from copulation. But the immortal race of women has not yet emerged from you, and I have no power to produce them myself. Indeed, all the *śaktis* originate from you. Therefore I am asking you for the supreme *śakti*, which is the mistress of the universe!

"Glory be to you, O Śivā, mother, beloved of Śiva! Give me the power to pour forth the race of women! O mother, know that the world with its moving and unmoving beings is hallowed by having its source in you. And I ask from you another favor, O goddess of boons. Have compassion on me and grant my desire! Praise be to you, mother of the world! For the increase of moving and unmoving beings, with the lord as your spouse, O omnipresent woman, become the daughter of my son Dakṣa, O mother of welfare!"

Thus implored by Brahmā, the goddess, supreme mistress, gave that power to Brahmā, the creator, saying, "Let it be so." Whereupon Śivā, the goddess who is Śiva's *śakti*, consisting of the world, emitted from between her eyebrows a single *śakti* whose brilliance equaled her own. When Hara, best of the gods, the great lord who is a flood of compassion, player of games, saw that *śakti*, he addressed the mother of welfare with a smile, "O goddess who has been propitiated by the *tapas* of Brahmā Parameṣṭhin, be gracious! Out of your great affection, grant his entire desire!"

The goddess accepted the command of the supreme lord with a nod of her head and became Dakṣa's daughter, as Brahmā had requested. Having lent her incomparable power to Brahmā, O seer, Śivā entered lord Śaṃbhu's body and lord Śaṃbhu disappeared.

From that time onward, the female sex has been established in this world. Brahmā gained bliss and creation by copulation was born. Now you have heard the story of that great supreme form of Śiva, half woman, half man, dear one, who brings abundant wellbeing to the virtuous. Whoever recites or hears this holy story enjoys complete happiness and attains the ultimate goal.

# Hari-Hara

The gods went to the dwelling place of Viṣṇu, enemy of Mura, made obeisance to the god and asked him why the world was so disturbed. When he heard their words, the blessed lord said, "Let us go to the abode of Hara. He is very wise; he will know why the world is shaking, with its moving and unmoving beings." Thus addressed by Vāsudeva, the gods, led by Indra, set out for Mt. Mandara with Janārdana in front. Enveloped in darkest ignorance, they thought the mountain was empty, for they saw there neither god nor goddess, nor even Nandin the bull.

When the glorious Viṣṇu perceived that the eyes of the gods were clouded, he began to speak, "Don't you see the great lord who stands before you?" And they replied, "No, we do not see the lord of the gods, the husband of the mountain-born goddess! And we do not know what has deprived us of our sight!"

Then he who consists of the world said to them, "You yourselves have offended the god! Intent on your own self-interest, you have most wickedly destroyed the embryo of Śiva's wife Mṛḍāṇī. Because of this, knowledge and discrimination have been taken away by the god who bears a trident. It is for this reason that you do not see him even though he is standing right in front of you!

"Therefore, for the purification of your bodies and in order to see the god, most diligently expiate yourselves by the *taptakṛcchra* vow and take a ritual bath at the place of the lord, using 150 jars of milk, O gods." . . . And so the gods performed the *taptakṛcchra* vow by reciting the Śatarudrīya hymn and subsisting successively on hot water, hot milk, hot *ghī* and air for three days each.

After they had observed this vow, the gods were released from evil. Their stains removed, they addressed Vāsudeva, lord of the gods, "O Jagannātha, tell us where to find Śaṃbhu! Keśava, we are going to bathe him with ablutions of milk and other substances, according to the rules." At this, lord Viṣṇu told the gods, "Śankara resides in my body. Don't you see him here? This is the established Yoga!"

"No, we don't see in you the slayer of Tripura!" they replied. "Tell us the truth, O lord of gods, where is Maheśa?" Then the immortal-souled Hari, enemy of Mura, exhibited to them the divine *linga* of the lord Hara which was lying on the lotus of his heart. Whereupon the gods one by one bathed that endless, eternal, firm, immortal *linga* with milk and other offerings. They smeared it with yellow ointment and with fragrant sandal paste and then zealously worshiped the god with *bilva* leaves and lotus flowers. Perfuming the air with aloes, they devotedly proffered the best herbs. Reciting his 1,008 names, they bowed before the lord, pondering in their hearts how the two gods, Hari and Īśvara, could have entered into union since they had sprung from *sattva* and *tamas*, respectively.

The immortal lord knew what they were thinking, and so he assumed a universal form that bore all the auspicious marks and possessed every kind of weapon. The gods saw him at last with his three eyes, wearing earrings made of snakes and lotuses, sporting a topknot of matted hair, with a banner bearing bird and bull, along with Mādhava, whose chest bore a serpent necklace, and whose loins were draped with a yellow garment and an antelope skin; he was holding a discus and a sword in his hands, carrying a plough and a bow, and possessed the Pināka, the trident and the Ajagava weapon, with knotted hair, a skull-topped staff, a skull and a bell, and was making the skies echo with the call of his conch, O great seer.

When the gods, led by the one who sits on a lotus, saw Hari-Śankara, they bowed before him and cried aloud, "Praise be to you, immortal all-pervader!" And they considered the two to be wholly one.

# 5 The Goddess

## To the Goddess

*O Goddess who removes the suffering of your supplicants, have mercy!*
*O mother of the whole world, be gracious!*
*O mistress of the universe, protect the world!*
*Have mercy!*
*You are the mistress of all that moves and moves not!*

*You alone are the foundation of the world,*
*residing in the form of earth.*
*O you whose prowess is unsurpassed,*
*you nourish the world in the form of the waters.*

*You are the power of Viṣṇu, endless energy.*
*You are the supreme seed of the universe.*
*O Goddess, this world is deluded by your illusion!*
*When gracious, you are the cause of release on earth.*

*O Goddess, all the sciences reside in you.*
*You are all women, and you are the world.*
*By you alone, as mother, is this world filled.*
*How can we praise you, who are yourself the praiseworthy expression of the high and low?*

*Praise be to you, Nārāyaṇī, whose hands and feet are everywhere,*
*With heads, faces and eyes in all directions,*
*Who watches and listens on all sides!*

*O Mistress of the universe, whose nature is the world,*
*filled with all powers,*
*Save us from danger!*
*O goddess Durgā, praise be to you!*

*Praise be to you, Kātyāyanī, with kindly face!*
*O three-eyed Goddess, protect us from our fears!*

*Praise be to you, Bhadrakālī!*
*May your horrendous trident, with points of flame,*
*Destroyer of all demons, guard us from danger!*

*May your bell that annihilates the glory of the Daityas when it fills the world with sound,*
*Protect us from evil, as your sons!*

*Smeared with the mire of demon blood and fat,*
*ablaze with rays,*
*May your sword be auspicious!*
*O Caṇḍikā, we bow to you!*

*Be gracious to those who are prostrate before you,*
*O Goddess who removes the suffering of the world!*
*Worthy of worship from those who inhabit the triple world,*
*Bestow boons upon these worlds!*

# Introduction

A number of goddesses are named in the Purāṇas and their personalities are varied. The principal roles they play include wife, lover and destroyer. The wives of Brahmā and Viṣṇu appear to be mere appendages of their divine spouses, having neither stories nor personalities of their own to speak of. But Śiva's wife, often called simply Devī, or "the Goddess," appears to be a collection of different personalities, both beneficent and fierce, like Śiva himself. It is not clear whether her different names signify what were originally different deities, or whether the welter of epithets the goddess bears simply describe the varied attributes of what has always been a single deity.

It seems necessary to question the origins of goddesses in Indian tradition, since the earliest literature of this tradition, the Vedas, makes scarce mention of female deities of any kind. But the problem is even larger than this. Both Viṣṇu and Śiva, for instance although their origins are in part traceable to Vedic gods, display complex personalities in the epics and Purāṇas that come virtually out of nowhere, with divine feats and attributes unknown to Vedic tradition. And so do the goddesses. An explanation for this may lie in the undocumented religious practices of the indigenous, agricultural peoples of India who inhabited the Indus Valley long before the proto-Sanskrit speaking nomadic Āryans invaded northwest India, *ca.* 1500 B.C. The Āryans succeeded in dominating the composite society that ensued for over a millennium. The Vedas, their oral literature, reveal a sacrificial cult that honored heavenly deities, such as Varuṇa of the sky, Indra of the thunderstorm and Sūrya, the sun, to the virtual exclusion of both goddesses and divinities of earth. On the other hand, the archaeological remains of Indus Valley culture abound in female figurines and phallic objects, probably used in some religious practice, and almost certainly directed toward the fertility of people, animals and the earth. It may be the case, therefore, that the Purāṇic goddesses are remnants of the fertility worship of non-Āryan indigenous people of the Indian sub-continent. In the course of time their Āryan conquerors slowly absorbed the native religious traditions until, in Epic and Purāṇic literature, the older stories were at last retold in the official language of the Āryans themselves, Sanskrit. (By the same process the religious practices and beliefs of the lower classes became part of the upper-class or dominant tradition of the land.)

Almost every goddess in the Purāṇas is married to a god, with the exception of the fierce and war-like Durgā and Kālī. Perhaps the marriage of gods and goddesses in Hindu mythology reflects a synthesis that in fact occurred between two different races and cultures in the early history of Indian culture. Certainly the goddesses as wives are utterly dependent upon their gods, much as the indigenous race was subdued and rendered subject by the conquering Āryans. In any case, it seems that only fragments of the careers of the goddesses in Indian tradition remain in the stories found in the Purāṇas.

In present-day rural India, the goddess brings fertility or pestilential death, depending on her mood. She is both the giver of life, as mother, and the terrifying force that takes it away, prematurely, by famine or disease. In the Purāṇas, however, other roles predominate for female deities. The goddess is a wife, lover or war-like destroyer, but never simply a mother. An amorphous group called the Mothers, created by Śiva, do appear briefly, and threaten to devour the world. (See Ch. 6, "The Mothers.") But no goddess physically gives birth or manifests so-called maternal or nurturent qualities. Epithets describing the goddess as the source of the universe are the same as those applied to the gods Viṣṇu and Śiva.

> In such a way then, does the divine goddess, although eternal, take birth again and again to protect creation. This world is deluded by her; it is begotten by her; it is she who gives knowledge when prayed to and prosperity when pleased. By Mahākālī is this

> entire Egg of Brahmā pervaded, O lord of men. At the awful time of dissolution she takes on the form of Mahāmārī, the great destructress of the world. She is also its unborn source; eternal, she sustains creatures in time. . . .
> (*Mārk.* 89.33-35)

This language reveals a monistic view of world origins, but is by no means unique to the goddess. It includes what appear to have become generalized formulae of creation applied without discrimination to any originating deity, male or female. The only exceptions are the epithet Ambikā, "Mother," and Mahāmāyā, "Great Illusion," which only the goddess bears, implying that hers is the power that originates not through biological motherhood, but by casting a magic spell, the insubstantial dream that is the world.

Each of the principal male deities, Brahmā, Viṣṇu and Śiva, has a loyal and devoted spouse as his appropriate companion. Brahmā's wife, Sarasvatī, is occasionally mentioned, but in the briefest of terms. As a goddess, she has no story of her own. The Sarasvatī, however, as the famous holy river that springs from the Himālaya mountains and runs underground at Kurukṣetra, is often eulogized in glowing terms. (See Ch. 6.) All rivers in the Purāṇas are female and every one of them is holy and pure, conferring blessings and benefits on those who bathe in them. They are the sites of hermitages and sacred fords, where the faithful devotees of every god are repeatedly urged to worship. In fact, a substantial portion of the material of the Purāṇas is devoted to the glorification of these hermitages and shrines, almost always located on or near a river bank. Numerous feminine rivers are celebrated in this manner, especially the Ganges and the Yamunā, and many places of pilgrimage sites are given, the most prominent of which are Prayāga and Vārāṇasī, modern Banaras. But it is relatively seldom that a full personality is accorded to the rivers, so that even Sarasvatī remains virtually characterless as Brahmā's official wife. One delightful exception is the petulant Yamunā, whom Balarāma drags around with his plow, forcing her to flood the Kurukṣetra plain because she has refused to cater to his drunken whim and present herself near his side so he might bathe. (See Ch. 6, "The River Yamunā.")

Viṣṇu's devoted wife is called Lakṣmī or Śrī, the goddess of good fortune. It is occasionally implied that she who blesses people with prosperity may also curse them with its lack. (See "The Birth of Kālī and the Final Battle," below.) But for the most part Lakṣmī abides at Viṣṇu's side as an adornment of the lord. She, too, has little personality of her own. Even in the story of the Churning of the Ocean (Ch. 2), which prominently features her birth, she has little to do. She leaps from the ocean's foam onto the chest of Viṣṇu, which is her proper place, and there she stays.

Only Pārvatī, Śiva's spouse, has a distinct personality, her own family background, and a group of interesting stories. (See Ch. 4.) She is called by several names, for instance Umā, "mother," Gaurī, "white," and Satī, "virtuous." Determined to marry Śiva, she herself renounces the world to practice *tapas* as he does, an unheard of effort for a girl. She succeeds in gaining power over the god by this means, and they are duly wed. In another birth, also married to Śiva, she is so outraged when her father insults her divine spouse that she immolates herself in fire, thus becoming the original divine *satī*, or supremely virtuous woman. Elsewhere, desiring children, she engages in a variety of subterfuges to seduce her reluctant, meditating husband; the most disastrous of these efforts results in the disembodiment of Kāma, god of love, who is burned to ashes by Śiva's rage.

In all these stories, Pārvatī shows a determined character: she wishes to be the perfect wife and to bear children. As Satī she is the daughter of Dakṣa, primal progenitor, one of the sage sons of Brahmā the creator. (See Ch. 1, "The Origin of the Seers and the Manus.") As Pārvatī she is the daughter of the Himālaya mountain, the "little mountain maiden." (See Ch. 4, "The Birth of Pārvatī.") This mountain legacy is characteristic of both the goddess and of Śiva, her spouse, whose sacred abode is Mt. Kailāsa and who, as an ascetic mendicant, roams homeless in the mountain fastnesses without a family or clan.

All three of these goddesses, Sarasvatī, Lakṣmī and Pārvatī, whether vestigial or fully active, are devoted, loyal wives. Like Sītā in the epic *Rāmāyaṇa,* who is identified with Lakṣmī as Rāma is with Viṣṇu, their role is to support their better half; in every case, the god, their spouse, comes first in importance. Even for plucky Pārvatī, the purpose of her difficult role appears to be to persuade the ascetic god to cease the austerities that rob the world of fertility in order to marry and have progeny himself.

Most of the stories of Śiva and Pārvatī are entertaining because they resemble mundane domestic life. But there is very little sexual imagery involved; they are a respectable married pair. The union implied in Pārvatī's attempts to seduce her spouse is made more explicit elsewhere in the Purāṇas, where god and goddess are viewed as lovers for whom either sexual union or the imagery associated with it are of utmost importance. But there the goddess plays the role of lover rather than of wife.

Śiva and *śakti* are consorts, but *śakti* is not exactly a personal goddess. *Śakti* means energy or power, and as a feminine term, is regarded as the motivating and creative force of an otherwise inactive, passive male deity. Without this motivating force no creative act is possible for him. Pārvatī, for example, is frequently called Śiva's *śakti*. Implied here is that creativity—whether physical or spiritual—results from the union of opposing forces. This is symbolized in sexual terms of somewhat abstract and impersonal nature in the union of Śiva, male principle, and his *śakti*, or female principle.

> There is only one *śakti* and one possessor of *śakti* called Śiva. All other powers and possessors of power arise from Śarva and *śakti*. . . . This whole world has arisen from *śakti* and the possessor of *śakti*.
> (*Kūrma* 1.11.42,47)

Much more intimate and personal is the mythology of Rādhā and Kṛṣṇa, the romantic lovers among the cowherd folk in the forest of Vṛndāvana. (See Ch. 3.) Rādhā, who never becomes Kṛṣṇa's wife, is always depicted as the lover who longs for him when he departs. This separation from the beloved comes to represent the longing of man's soul for god, or spiritual wholeness. While the Goddess in her role as wife strongly supports the Indian social order, Rādhā's love for Kṛṣṇa violates this order, putting the love of the devotee for god above all other claims in life. When Kṛṣṇa plays his flute in the woods at midnight, even the otherwise respectable cowherds' wives rise from their beds to go and dance with him. And Rādhā, the luckiest of them all, wins his love in return.

As was the case with Śiva's *śakti*, Rādhā has little independent personality of her own. It is the loving couple together that symbolizes the union of all mundane opposites in the unity of divine reality; this unity is one of the recurring themes of Hindu religious thought, and it runs throughout the Purāṇas. Just as Śiva embodies opposing forces within a single personality, so in a different way does the goddess as lover united with her god symbolize the same unity in sexual terms.

Most rare in the Purāṇas is the one goddess who is independent of a god—without husband, consort or lover. Called Durgā, the "inaccessible," or Kālī, the "black one," she is war-like, bloodthirsty, insatiable and cruel. She crushes and devours her enemies without pause. She has one story, and it is of a war. When Mahiṣa, a demon who takes shape as a buffalo, is oppressing the gods and defeating them in a battle, Durgā comes to life to lead and win the fight. Where does she come from? She springs out of the many and various powers of the gods who individually and collectively have lacked the strength to defeat the demon on their own. Once born, however, she is unstoppable, paying homage to no one nor heeding anyone's orders but her own. Her mount is a lion and her names are many, including Caṇḍī, Cāmuṇḍa and Bhadrakālī, all of them denoting her ferocious nature.

This goddess has no husband or consort; nor will she bow to one. In the course of the contest against her, Mahiṣa, who is losing, tries to trick her into defeat by offering her marriage, suggesting that a woman like herself should not be on the battlefield at all. Her reply:

> I may be stubborn, but there is a desire in my heart, great demon. Only he who conquers me in battle shall be my husband!
> (*Vāmana* 29.36)

And then her lion mauls his buffalo to death, as prelude to her final annihilation of the demon himself.

Kālī, the "black one," springs from Durgā's forehead when her brow grows inky black with rage. She has the same terrifying personality as her source, the same independence, and like Durgā, her fury knows no bounds. The characteristics of these destroying goddesses are found also in the "Mothers," whose professed desire is to devour all the worlds out of hunger. (See Ch. 6, "The Mothers.") The reason for their rage is nowhere clearly explained, but the nature of the goddess as a devastating predator who thrives on human blood and shattered bones is made abundantly and gruesomely clear.

Sometimes this fierce goddess is called the spouse of Śiva. Matching his two-sided personality, she is said to have two aspects also. As Pārvatī she is benign, and as Durgā she is destructive. That these are aspects of a single goddess, however, is sometimes clearly stated:

> As good fortune, the goddess bestows wealth on men's homes in times of prosperity. In times of disaster she appears as misfortune for their annihilation.
> (*Mārk.* 89.36)

In conclusion, most of the goddesses in the Purāṇas appear as the wives or lovers of gods. The single exception is the fierce and unpredictable destroyer called Durgā or Kālī. The goddess as consort symbolizes unity in duality; the polarities of existence, symbolized in male and female deities, are united through marriage or through sexual embrace. As in the mythology of Śiva, monistic and dualistic views of the nature of divinity are harmonized through the imagery of sex. For the most part, however, the destroying goddess has no such two-sided character. In her the universal powers of destruction run riot, utterly without control. Whereas Śiva annihilates the universe whenever the inevitable time of dissolution rolls around, the goddess' destructive force may erupt at any time. The world is imperiled by her threat, for unlike the Mothers, who are eventually subdued by the gods, there is no one who can dominate her power.

Although the testimony offered about the nature of the goddess in the Purāṇas is complex and often confusing, as is the case with other deities, it would seem that a critical feature of the ferocious goddess is her lack of control. She is raw power, energy untamed by discipline or direction. The pairing off of male and female deities in Purāṇic mythology appears to provide a check to this excess, the other side of which is found in the intense asceticism of the meditating *yogin*. Coupling these two extremes, a balance is achieved between the opposing forces of the universe that is unknown to the solitary ascetic whose self-control inhibits growth, and unknown as well to the ferocious goddess whose excesses threaten to destroy all life. Whether as wife, lover, or other half of the male deity's body, the goddess represents the energy of the universe, which, unchecked, wreaks havoc, but without which nothing is born, moves or lives. Controlled by its opposite force, this energy is channeled into the natural creativity of the world, and poured forth by a generative deity. As Śiva and *śakti* together demonstrate, neither one can stand entirely alone, for either pure asceticism or untamed fury by itself would annihilate the world. In balance together, they assure its fruitful continuity.

# Texts

## The Blazing Tower of Splendor

Tell, O bard, you who are wise in all matters, of the *avatāra* of Umā, mistress of the world, from whom Sarasvatī was born, the goddess who is celebrated as the original Prakṛti of the supreme Brahman, formless yet possessing form; tell of Satī who is eternal, consisting of bliss! The bard replied: O ascetics, now hear with love the great supreme story by the mere knowledge of which a man gains the highest goal.

Once there was a battle between the gods and Dānavas. The immortals were victorious through the power of the goddess Mahāmāyā. Vainglorious, the immortals sang their own praises, "We are great! We are wonderful! What can those demons do to us now? Terrified at seeing our utterly irresistible might, they have gone to the place of the Snakes, crying 'Run! Flee!'" And the Gods all cried out, "How splendid is our mighty power that has wrought havoc on the Daitya race! How great is our good fortune! How happy are we!" In this vein did they describe their success.

At this, a blazing tower of splendor appeared. Witnessing this hitherto unseen apparition, the gods were greatly surprised. "What is this? What is this?" they asked each other in strangled voices, unaware that the supreme power of the dark goddess was about to destroy their pride. Then the overlord of the gods ordered them, "Go and find out what this is!" Sent by the chief of the gods, Vāyu approached the mighty mass. Alerted, the ponderous power said to him, "*Bhoḥ!* Who are you?" The wind replied with bravado, "I am Vāyu, the breath of the world. This entire creation with its moving and unmoving creatures is woven lengthwise and crosswise upon me. I am the support of the universe. I set the whole world in motion!" At which the towering splendor said, "If you are able to move this straw that I hold, O wind, then do so at will." With diligent effort the ever-mobile wind tried to blow away the straw. When it did not budge, he became ashamed.

Silenced, Vāyu returned to Indra's assembly and related the circumstances of his defeat, "All of us gods think we are omnipotent. This is a lie! In fact there is nothing that we really master, however small." And then, attended by the Maruts, he called on all the gods to find out for themselves. When they failed to learn anything, Indra himself went forth. When she saw Maghavan approaching, the unendurable splendor immediately disappeared. Amazed, the thousand-eyed Vāsava thought over and over again, "I shall take refuge in this one whose behavior is so marvellous!"

Meanwhile, in order to take away their pride and to do them a favor, the female Śiva, whose body is pure compassion, became visible as the goddess Umā, consisting of existence, consciousness and bliss—at noon on the ninth day of the white half of the month Caitra. Shining in the center of that mighty tower of splendor, illuminating space with her glory, she exclaimed, "I am truly Brahman!" thus enlightening all the gods. Holding in three of her hands a boon, a noose, and a hook, and making the 'fear not' gesture with the fourth, adored by the scriptures, she was lovely in the pride of her blooming youth. Wrapped in a red robe, garlanded and anointed in red, resembling a *koṭi* of love gods, shining like a *koṭi* of moons, Mahāmāyā spoke, she whose form is the inner guide of all, the witness in every creature, whose nature is the supreme Brahman.

"Neither Brahmā, nor Viṣṇu, who is the gods' delight, nor lord Śiva, enemy of Pura, are entitled to pride before me in any way. Why speak of other gods? The supreme Brahman, the sun on high, the syllable *OṂ* encompassing the pairs of opposites—all this am I. There is no one higher than I. Formless yet possessing form, consisting of all the reals, with undefinable attributes, eternal, consisting of both causes and effects, sometimes taking the form of a lovely woman, sometimes of a man, sometimes both, I am the goddess who assumes all forms. . . . Ignorant of my true nature, all you gods glory in your omnipotence to no avail. It is by my power alone that you have defeated all the sons of Diti. As a magician makes a wooden puppet dance, so do I, the goddess, make all creatures act. Wind blows, fire burns and the world-protectors continually do their duty wholly out of awe of me. . . . So recognize who I am, O gods, and renounce your pride! Worship me, the eternal Prakṛti, with love!"

When they heard this compassion-filled speech of the goddess, all the gods praised the supreme mistress, their heads bowed in devotion, "O goddess of the world, forgive us! O supreme goddess, be gracious! May our pride be gone forevermore! O mother, take pity on us!" Abandoning arrogance from that moment on, the assembled gods worshiped Umā as before and as was fitting.

# Śiva and *Śakti;* the Great Goddess

After emitting Marīci and the other seers, the Grandfather, god of gods, began to practise severe *tapas* along with his mind-born sons. While he was doing *tapas* there emerged from his mouth the three-eyed lord Rudra, resembling the Fire of Time, trident in hand. His body was half woman, half man, fearsome and dreadful to behold. Brahmā said, "Divide yourself in two!" and disappeared in fright.

Thus ordered, Rudra split himself into two parts, one female and the other male. Once again, he divided the male half into eleven parts, the Rudras. These eleven Rudras, called Kapālin, Īśa and so on, O brahmins, were charged with the work of the three worlds. The lord then divided the female half in various ways: gentle and fierce, beautiful and ugly, with complexions dark and light. These, O powerful brahmins, are known on earth as the *śaktis,* or energies. They are Lakṣmī and the other goddesses by whom the goddess Śānkarī pervades the universe.

Once again separating herself from the mighty Śankara by the command of Mahādeva, the goddess approached the Grandfather, lord Brahmā, who said to her, "You shall be the daughter of Dakṣa!" Following his order, she appeared before Prajāpati. On Brahmā's order, he gave the goddess Satī in marriage to Rudra the trident-bearer, who accepted her from Dakṣa as his wife. After reproaching Prajāpati, this supreme goddess Satī was in the course of time reborn as Pārvatī, the daughter of Menā by her husband Himavat.

This eminent mountain presented Pārvatī to Rudra for the benefit of all the gods, the three worlds and himself. That goddess Maheśvarī, also called Śivā, Satī and Haimavatī, whose body is half Śankara's, was worshiped by the gods and demons. All the gods, with Indra and the seers, recognize her matchless glory. Śankara knows of it and also Hari himself.

When the seers had heard the story told by Viṣṇu in the form of a tortoise, they bowed to Hari and once again asked, "Who is this blessed goddess whose body is half Śankara's, called Śivā, Satī, and Haimavatī? Tell us at our bidding exactly who she is!" When he heard the seers' query, the great Yogin Puruṣottama, concentrated on his exalted position and replied:

This particular knowledge, a glorious mystery, was first imparted by the Grandfather on the top of Mt. Meru. It is the ultimate Sāṃkhya* of the followers of Sāṃkhya, the highest knowledge of Brahman, the sole means of release for beings drowning in the ocean of existence. Haimavatī is considered to be Maheśvara's *śakti,* his power or energy, consisting of knowledge, always eagerly active, called the vault of heaven, the final goal. Śivā is ubiquitous, infinite, beyond the *guṇas,* all encompassing. Though single, yet she is multiply dispersed; having the form of knowledge, she is always eagerly active. Incomparable, abiding in complete reality through the lord's splendor, she is by her nature rooted in him, like the pure radiance of the sun. This single *śakti* of Maheśvara sports in his presence in higher and lower forms by taking on a multitude of disguises. It is she who produces the universe. The world is her product; it is not a product of the lord, nor his doing, so say the seers. . . . This goddess is the mistress of the universe who sets all thing in motion.

Lord Maheśvara is called Kāla (Time), Prāṇa and Hari. On him is this whole world woven. He is hymned as Kāla, Agni, Hara and Rudra by those who know the Veda. Kāla pours forth beings; Kāla destroys creatures; everything is subject to Kāla, but Kāla is subject to no one. Pradhāna, Puruṣa, the principle, the large *ātman* and the *ahaṃkāra,* and all the other principles are pervaded by the Yogin, Kāla. His *śakti,* or energy, progenitrix of the entire universe, is known as Māyā (Illusion). By her the lord Puruṣottama causes the whole world to err. *Śakti,* namely Māyā, who takes on all forms, is eternal and illuminates everywhere the omniform nature of Maheśa. And there are three other principal forms that have been fashioned by the god: the powers of knowledge, action and vitality. The eternal Māyā has established possessors of *śakti* for all the *śaktis,* O chief brahmins, but she herself has no beginning. Māyā, embodying all the powers, is irresistible and unconquerable. The master of all powers, the magician Kāla is the lord who fabricates time. Time produces everything and destroys it as well; Time supports the universe; this whole world depends on Time.

Because of the proximity of Parameṣṭhin, who is the eternal overlord of the gods, the lord of the universe, Śaṃbhu, and the lord who consists of Time, Māyā becomes Pradhāna and Puruṣa. So Māyā proceeds: single, omnipresent, eternal, alone, undivided, Śivā. There is only one *śakti* and one possessor of *śakti* called Śiva. All other

*In the sense of "wisdom."

powers and possessors of power arise from Śarva and *śakti*. Some hold that there is a difference between power and the possessor of power, but *yogins* who know the truth see no difference between them. The mountain-born goddess Pārvatī is the *śakti* and Śankara is the possessor of *śakti;* this distinction is described in the Purāṇa by the reciters of the Veda. The goddess Viśveśvarī, devoted to her lord Maheśvara, is said to be the object of experience, and the red and blue lord with matted hair is said to be the experiencer. Śankara, the god Viśveśvara who killed Manmatha, is said by the wise to be the thinker, and the goddess is said to be the thought. So is it said, brahmins, by the seers of all the Vedas who see the truth: this whole world has arisen from *śakti* and the possessor of *śakti*." . . .

When the goddess is born as Himavat's daughter, she manifests her divine form, saying: "Know me to be the supreme power vested in the highest lord, without rival, eternal, the only one who is beheld by those who seek release. I am Śivā, source of the universe, the Self inside all things, embodied in eternal sovereignty and wisdom, the everlasting motivator, whose abundance is without limit, ferry across the ocean of existence. I shall give you divine sight. Now see my supernal form!"

So speaking and granting insight to her father Himavat, the goddess showed him her divine form as the supreme deity. She blazed forth like a *koṭi* of suns, a self-contained ball of fire, wreathed with thousands of flames, like a hundred fires of time. With gaping mouth and projecting fangs, unassailable, adorned with a braided top-knot and carrying a trident in her hand, she was a ghastly, terrifying sight. Then she was composed, her countenance serene, filled with endless marvels, marked with a digit of the moon and shining like a *koṭi* of moons. Again she appeared wearing a crown, holding a mace, adorned with anklets, heavenly garlands and celestial clothing, anointed with divine perfume, carrying conch and discus. She was a beautiful sight, three-eyed, clothed in a tiger-skin, standing supreme both inside and outside the cosmic egg. The eternal goddess who consists of all *śaktis*, whose body is the universe, whose lotus feet are worshiped by Brahmā, Indra, Upendra and the chief *yogins*, stood before Himavat, who witnessed this supreme deity covering the universe, with hands and feet on all sides, heads and faces turned in all directions.

Seeing such a magnificent sight, the supernal form of the supreme goddess, the king, enraptured, was overcome with fear. Putting himself in the Self, recalling the syllable *OṂ*, he praised the supreme goddess with her 1,008 names. . . .

Still frightened after worshipping her in this manner, Mt. Himavat bowed to the goddess once more with folded hands and said, "I am terrified to see your horrible divine form, O goddess. Show me another one!"

Thus prayed to by the mountain, the goddess Pārvatī withdrew and manifested herself once again in another shape. She became bright and sweet-smelling like the petal of a blue lotus, now with only two charming eyes and arms, crowned with dark locks. Her lotus-like feet were red, her shoot-like hands incarnadine. Standing tall, curvaceous and beautiful, luminous with a *tilaka* on her forehead, utterly lovely, with beautiful limbs, most delicate in appearance, she bore on her breast a generous garland made of gold. Smiling slightly, her lower lip red as the *bimba* fruit, wearing tinkling anklets, she stood there with a tranquil face, heavenly, the abode of infinite power.

When he saw her appearance in such a beautiful form, the excellent mountain lost his fear and spoke to the goddess with a happy heart, "At this moment my birth is fulfilled! My *tapas* has borne fruit, now that you, unmanifest and serene, have appeared in person before my eyes! You have poured forth this whole world. Pradhāna and the rest of creation abide in you and will be dissolved in you. O goddess, you are the ultimate goal!" . . .

Whoever recites this glorification of the goddess with attentive mind in the presence of brahmins is released from all evil.

# The Demons Madhu and Kaiṭabha

King Suratha asked Mārkaṇḍeya, "Who is this goddess whom you call Mahāmāyā, lord? How did she arise and what are her feats, twice-born one? Her grandeur, her nature, her origin—all this I want to hear from you, best of those who know the Veda!"

"She is eternal and embodies creation," said the sage. "The whole world is pervaded by her, but manifold are her origins nevertheless. It is said that when she becomes manifest to accomplish the task of the gods, she is born in the world. She is also considered to be eternal. Hear now from me her various manifestations.

"At the end of the Eon, when Viṣṇu had fallen into Yogic sleep stretched out on Śeṣa, and the world was nothing but one vast ocean, two dreadful demons called Madhu and Kaiṭabha arose from his ear wax, bent on killing Brahmā. Sitting on the lotus that had grown from Viṣṇu's navel, Brahmā Prajāpati saw the two fierce Asuras appear while Janārdana lay fast asleep. Single-minded in concentration and with a steadfast heart he praised the meditative sleep that lay upon Hari's eyes in order to awaken him.

"I exalt you, blessed Sleep of Viṣṇu of matchless spendor, mistress of the universe, mother of the world who both preserves and destroys. . . . Armed with sword, spear, mace and discus, carrying conch, bow and arrows, bludgeon and *bhuśundi*, you are kind, gentler than all the gentle, utterly beautiful, supreme among both high and low; you are the goddess supernal! You are the energy of every substance, no matter what, no matter where, existent or non-existent. Who am I to praise you—you who poured forth the world? If the god who sustains and consumes the world has been mastered by Sleep, who is left here to praise you? Since Viṣṇu, Īśāna and I myself have been made by you to take bodily form, how can I offer you praise? In truth, you are celebrated for your exalted glory! Now bring the lord of creation Acyuta quickly back to consciousness, so he may destroy those two dangerous demons, Madhu and Kaiṭabha!"

The dark goddess, thus praised by the creator, in order to arouse Viṣṇu so that he might kill the two demons, came forth from his eyes, mouth, nostrils, arms, heart and chest, and stood before Brahmā, whose origin is hidden. Released by Sleep, Janārdana Jagannātha rose from his resting place on the ocean and saw the two evil-natured demons Madhu and Kaiṭabha, heroic and valorous, eyes red with rage, filled with eagerness to kill Brahmā. Springing up, lord Hari battled against the two of them for 5,000 years with only his bare arms for weapons. . . .

The lord, bearing conch, discus and mace, killed those two demons by splitting open their heads with his discus. And in this manner was born the goddess, praised by Brahmā himself. Listen now while I relate the majesty of this goddess.

# The Origin of the Goddess from the Gods

Once long ago there was a battle between the gods and demons that lasted a hundred years, in which Mahiṣa was the leader of the Asuras, and Indra, sacker of cities, was the chief of the gods. In this contest the army of the gods was defeated by the more powerful demons. When Mahiṣa had conquered all the gods, he became their leader. So the gods, utterly defeated, put the lotus-born Prajāpati before them and went to Īśa and Viṣṇu, the god whose banner bears Garuḍa. In the dwelling place of these two deities, the thirty gods related at length the exploits of Mahiṣa and their own defeat.

"Mahiṣa himself has taken charge of the offices of Sūrya, Indra, Agni, Vāyu, Yama, Varuṇa and the other gods. All the hosts of gods have been expelled from heaven by this evil-souled demon and have spread all over the earth like mortals. You have been told all about this struggle against the enemy of the gods. Now we have come to you for protection. Let us plot his destruction!"

When they heard this speech of the gods, Madhusūdana and Śaṃbhu grew angry, their brows knitted in frowns. Pure energy blazed forth from the discus-bearer's mouth as he filled with rage, and from Brahmā and Śankara as well. From the bodies of Indra and the other gods too emerged great *tejas* and all their energies united into one. As the gods witnessed this fiery crest of energy pervading all the directions and blazing forth like a mountain peak aflame with the sun, this matchless energy that sprang from the bodies of all the gods, its light illuminating the three worlds, became concentrated in one spot and took form as the goddess. Her mouth was born from the energy that arose from Śaṃbhu; from Yama's energy came the hairs of her head, and from Viṣṇu's her arms. From the energy of the moon were born her two breasts; from Indra's her waist. From Varuṇa's energy came her calves and thighs, and from energy itself, her genitals. From the energy of Brahmā arose her feet, her toes from the Sun's; from the Vasus' came her fingers and hands, and her nostrils from Kubera's. Her teeth sprang from the energy of Prajāpati and her three eyes from that of Fire. From the energy of the two twilights came her eyebrows, and her ears from the wind's. In this manner was the goddess Śivā born from the *tejas* of the other gods.

When the immortals, who were tormented by Mahiṣa, saw this goddess emerging from the energy of all the gods combined, they all rejoiced and all gave her their own weapons, crying aloud, "Victory! Victory! Our leaders will be victorious by *tejas!*"

The Pināka-bearer gave her a trident which was drawn out of his own weapon, while Kṛṣṇa gave her a discus severed from his own. Varuṇa gave the conch to her; the oblation-eating Fire, his spear. The Wind gave her a bow and two quivers full of arrows. Producing a thunderbolt from his own thunderbolt, Indra, lord of the gods, gave it to her; this thousand-eyed god also gave her the bell from his elephant Airāvata. Yama gave her a staff from his staff of time; Varuṇa, lord of the waters, gave her a noose; Prajāpati a necklace of beads; and Brahmā a water-jar. Sun put his own rays into the pores of her skin and Time gave her his sword and shining shield. The milk ocean bestowed on her a shining necklace, two never-fading garments, a celestial crown jewel with a pair of earrings and upper-arm bracelets, a lustrous half-moon, bangles for all her arms, a pair of bright anklets, and jeweled rings for all her fingers and toes. Viśvakarman gave her an immaculate axe, impenetrable armor and all manner of weapons. The ocean placed on her head and breast an incomparable wreath of undecaying lotuses and put in her hand a beautiful lotus flower. Himavat gave her the lion for her mount and an abundance of jewels. Kubera, lord of wealth, gave her a goblet full of wine. And Śeṣa, lord of the Snakes, who supports this earth, gave her a necklace of Snakes studded with large gems.

The goddess, thus honored by the other gods with ornaments and weapons, roared aloud ebulliently, cackling again and again with demoniac laughter. The whole sky was filled with her hideous cries; as her monstrous bellow reverberated forth, all the worlds shook, the oceans trembled and the mountains quaked, while the joyful gods cried out, "Victory!" to the goddess who rides a lion; and the seers praised her too, their heads bowed low in devotion.

When they saw the three worlds shaking, the foes of the gods who had readied their armies sprang up, their weapons raised aloft. "*Aho,* what is this?" cried the demon Mahiṣa, accompanied by all the Asuras as he rushed in fury toward the sound. Then he saw the goddess pervading the three worlds with her splendor, while the earth sank under her feet and her crown towered above the sky, shaking the whole netherworld with the hiss of her bow-string, filling the universe in all directions with her thousand arms.

Between this goddess and the enemies of the gods a battle was joined spanning the blazing directions, with all manner of striking and throwing weapons. The great demon called Cikṣus, leader of Mahiṣa's army did battle with the gods, as did Cāmara, accompanied by a four-fold army. The mighty demon Udagra (Ferocious) fought with 60,000 chariots and Mahāhanu (Big-Jaw) battled with a million; Asiloma (Sword-Hair) fought with fifty million and Bāṣkala entered the fray with six million. With vast multitudes of elephants and horses, Ugradarśana (Terrible Sight) fought in that conflict accompanied by a million chariots. And the mighty Daitya called Biḍāla (The Cat) battled in that war surrounded by a half a million chariots, while the demon Kāla (Time) was accompanied by as many as five million. Then myriads of other great Asuras with their chariots, elephants and horses fought in that battle with the goddess. And Mahiṣāsura was encircled in the conflict by thousands of millions of chariots, elephants and horses. They fought against the goddess with lances, slings, mighty clubs, swords, axes and three-bladed pikes.

Some flung spears, other nooses; with blows of the sword the demons went forth to kill the goddess.

But this goddess Caṇḍikā, raining down her own striking and throwing weapons, cut down those of her enemy as if in play. Her face serene and praised by the seers, the goddess thrust her striking and throwing weapons into the bodies of the demons. The lion mount of the goddess, her mane shaking with fury, moved through the Asura army like fire through a wood. And Ambikā's snorts as she struggled on the battlefield became troops in the battle by the hundreds of thousands. They fought with axes, with slings, with three-bladed pikes; sustained by the power of the goddess, they annihilated the demons. Some of her troops sounded war drums and others blew conches, while still others beat the small drums in that grand celebration of war.

Then the goddess with her trident, club and showers of spears, with swords and other weapons, destroyed the demons by the hundreds. Some, confused by the ringing of her bell, were felled by the goddess with her trident, club and showers of arrows. Others she lassoed with her noose and dragged along the ground. Some were split in two by blows of her sharp swords, while others were pulverized by her attack, and still others lay felled by her club on the earth. Some of that enemy horde vomited blood after being hammered by her club. Others fell to the ground pierced in the chest by her trident. The mountain-like tormentors of the thirty gods, huddled together on the battlefield, overcome by a shower of arrows, gave up their lives. Some of those mighty demons—some whose arms were cut off, others whose necks were severed, some who were decapitated, others cut in two at the waist, and still others with legs dismembered—fell to the ground. But some who had been cloven in two by the goddess, each half bearing one arm, one eye and one foot, and others who had lost their heads rose up again. These headless trunks, still grasping their fine weapons, battled against the goddess. Other dead bodies were also dancing on the battlefield, keeping time to the rhythm of the musical instruments. Headless corpses holding swords, spears and lances in their hands shouted out, "Stand still! Stand still!" to the goddess. Other demons with limbs torn off made a shudder go through the host.

The earth became unfit to walk on where the ferocious battle raged because of the vast rivers of blood from the felled elephants, horses and demons that flowed through the middle of the Asura forces. Ambikā sent that mighty demon army to perdition in a flash, just as fire consumes a heap of grass and wood. And the lion, roaring aloud, shaking his mane, plucked the life-breath from the bodies of those enemies of the gods. After that battle between the great demons and the goddess with her troops, the gods in heaven praised her, raining down showers of flowers.

# The Death of Mahiṣa, the Buffalo Demon

When his army was being destroyed in this manner, the demon Mahiṣa himself, in the form of a buffalo, terrorized the troops of the goddess. Some of them he beat with his snout, others he trampled with his hooves, still others he lashed with his tail, while some were ripped to shreds by his horns. Some were thrown to the ground by his bellowing and the speed of his charge while others were felled by the gusts of his panting breath. After felling her troops, the demon rushed to attack the lion that was with the great goddess. At this Ambikā became enraged. The mighty, virile buffalo, whose hooves pounded the earth, also grew furious, smashing the lofty mountains with his horns and bellowing aloud. Trampled by his violent sallies, the earth was shattered, and the ocean, lashed by his hairy tail, overflowed on all sides. Shaken by his slashing horns, the troops were utterly dispersed. Mountains tumbled by the hundreds from the sky, struck down by the wind of his snorting breath.

When she saw this great demon attacking, swelling with rage, Caṇḍikā then became furious enough to destroy him. She threw her noose and lassoed the great Asura. Thus trapped in that mighty battle, he abandoned his buffalo shape and became a lion. At the moment Ambikā cut off its head, a man appeared, sword in hand. As soon as Ambikā cut down that man along with his sword and shield, the demon became a huge elephant. With a roar he dragged the goddess's lion along with his trunk, but while he was pulling the lion, she cut off his trunk with her sword. Then the great demon resumed his wondrous buffalo shape, causing all three worlds with their moving and unmoving creatures to tremble.

Provoked by this, Caṇḍikā, mother of the world, guzzled her supreme liquor, laughing and red-eyed. And the Asura, puffed up with pride in his own strength and bravery, bellowed aloud and tossed mountains at Caṇḍikā with his horns. Pulverizing those mountains that were hurled at her with arrows sent aloft, the goddess, excited by anger, her mouth red with liquor, cried out to him and his invincible troop, "Roar and bellow, but only as long as I drink the mead, you fool! In a moment the gods will be howling at you when you die by my hand!" So speaking, the goddess flew up and trod on his throat with her foot, piercing him with her spear. Crushed by her foot, overcome by the power of that goddess, the demon came half-way out of his own mouth. Still battling in this way, he was felled by the goddess who cut off his head with her mighty sword. So that demon Mahiṣa, his army and his allies, who had so distressed the three worlds, were all annihilated by the goddess.

At Mahiṣa's death, all the gods and demons, mankind and all creatures living in the three worlds cried "Victory!" And when the entire army of the lamenting Daityas was annihilated, the whole host of the gods went into exultant rapture. The gods and the great celestial seers praised that goddess, while Gandharva lords sang aloud and hosts of Apsarases danced.

## The Birth of Kālī and the Final Battle

As they had been commanded, the Daityas, led by Caṇḍa and Muṇḍa, formed a four-fold army and sallied forth, their weapons raised aloft. They saw the goddess, smiling slightly, positioned on her lion atop the great golden peak of a mighty mountain. When they saw her, they made zealous efforts to seize her, while other demons from the battle approached her with bows and swords drawn. Then Ambikā became violently angry with her enemies, her face growing black as ink with rage. Suddenly there issued forth from between her eyebrows Kālī, with protruding fangs, carrying a sword and a noose, with a mottled, skull-topped staff, adorned with a necklace of human skulls, covered with a tiger-skin, gruesome with shriveled flesh. Her mouth gaping wide, her lolling tongue terrifying, her eyes red and sunken, she filled the whole of space with her howling. Attacking and killing the mighty demons, she devoured the armed force of the enemies of the gods. Seizing with one hand the elephants with their back-riders, drivers, warriors and bells, she hurled them into her maw. In the same way she chewed up warriors with their horses, chariots and charioteers, grinding them up most horribly with her teeth. One she grabbed by the hair of the head, another by the nape of the neck, another she trod underfoot while another she crushed against her chest. The mighty striking and throwing weapons loosed by those demons she caught in her mouth and pulverised in fury. She ravaged the entire army of powerful evil-souled Asuras; some she devoured while others she trampled; some were slain by the sword, others bashed by her skull-topped club, while other demons went to perdition crushed by the sharp points of her teeth.

Seeing the sudden demise of the whole Daitya army, Caṇḍa rushed to attack that most horrendous goddess Kālī. The great demon covered the terrible-eyed goddess with a shower of arrows while Muṇḍa hurled discuses by the thousands. Caught in her mouth, those weapons shone like myriad orbs of the sun entering the belly of the clouds. Then howling horribly, Kālī laughed aloud malevolently, her maw gaping wide, her fangs glittering, awful to behold. Astride her huge lion, the goddess rushed against Caṇḍa; grabbing his head by the hair, she decapitated him with her sword. When he saw Caṇḍa dead, Muṇḍa attacked, but she threw him too to the ground, stabbing him with her sword in rage. Seeing both Caṇḍa and the mighty Muṇḍa felled, the remains of the army fled in all directions, overcome with fear.

Grabbing the heads of the two demons, Kālī approached Caṇḍikā and shrieked, cackling with fierce, demoniac laughter, "I offer you Caṇḍa and Muṇḍa as the grand victims in the sacrifice of battle. Now you yourself will kill Śumbha and Niśumbha!" Witnessing this presentation of the two great Asuras, the eminent Caṇḍikā spoke graciously to Kālī, "Since you have captured Caṇḍa and Muṇḍa and have brought them to me, O goddess, you will be known as Cāmuṇḍā!" . . .

So speaking, the honorable goddess Caṇḍikā of fierce mettle vanished on the spot before the eyes of the gods. And all the gods, their enemies felled, performed their tasks without harassment and enjoyed their shares of the sacrifices. When Śumbha, enemy of the gods, world-destroyer, of mighty power and valor, had been slain in battle and the most valiant Niśumbha had been crushed, the rest of the Daityas went to the netherworld.

In such a way, then, does the divine goddess, although eternal, take birth again and again to protect creation. This world is deluded by her; it is begotten by her; it is she who gives knowledge when prayed to and prosperity when pleased. By Mahākālī is this entire egg of Brahmā pervaded, lord of men. At the awful time of dissolution she takes on the form of Mahāmārī, the great destructress of the world. She is also its unborn source; eternal, she sustains creatures in time. As Lakṣmī, or Good Fortune, she bestows wealth on men's homes in times of prosperity. In times of disaster she appears as Misfortune for their annihilation. When the goddess is praised and worshiped with flowers, incense, perfume and other gifts, she gives wealth, sons, a mind set upon Dharma, and happiness to all mankind.

## Bhadrakālī and the Thieves

Once a certain Vṛṣala king who wanted children undertook a human sacrifice to Bhadrakālī. By chance the sacrificial victim escaped and his trail was followed by the king's attendants in the middle of a murky night. Not finding the victim in the dark, they happened by accident upon the son of an eminent Aṅgiras priest sitting in the "hero" posture, guarding the fields from deer, wild pigs and other animals. Noticing this blameless man and thinking they were fulfilling their master's desire, they bound him with a rope and led him to the sanctuary of the goddess Caṇḍikā, their faces blooming with joy.

According to their custom, the thieves fed him, anointed him, dressed him in unwashed garments and decorated him with ornaments, oils, garlands, *tilakas,* and other adornments. Equipped with offerings of perfume, lights, wreaths, parched grain, shoots, sprouts and fruit, they made the human victim sit amid the paraphernalia of bloodshed in front of Bhadrakālī to the noisy accompaniment of songs, hymns, drums and cymbals.

Then the king of the Vṛṣala thieves, preparing to make sacrifice to the goddess Bhadrakālī with the blood of a human victim, drew out a sharp, tooth-edged sword that had been charmed with magic spells. When the goddess Bhadrakālī saw what was happening before her eyes, the illicit immolation of the peaceable son of a brahmin seer who was a friend to all creatures, she judged this to be the most despicable act of men who glory in murder, who willfully follow the path of error while disdaining the family of the blessed Kālavīra, their minds puffed up with the greed of possession, with natures full of *rajas* and *tamas*.

When she saw these Vṛṣalas preparing the sacrifice, the goddess Bhadrakālī instantly jumped out of her image with a blazing body that was utterly unendurable with Brahmā's splendor. Ebulliently manifesting herself with her retinue, her dreadful swollen face flashing with indignation, wrath and ferocity, with knotted eyebrows, curving fangs and copper-red eyes, she sprang forth in fury, with murderous intent and hideous laughter. With the self-same sword of the king, the goddess severed the heads of those wicked thieves, and she and her troops drank greedily from their necks that were streaming with blood. Staggering from excessive drink, she and her retinue sang, cavorted and played ball with the rolling skulls.

Truly, the transgression of the spells of the great always produces such fruit as this. It is no great wonder, Viṣṇudatta, that, even with the loss of his own head imminent, this seer was unmoved. For there is nothing to fear from any quarter whatsoever for those supreme ascetics, for the devotees of the blessed lord Viṣṇu who approach his feet for protection with minds friendly to all beings. The knots of their hearts bound tight in recollection of the Self, they can endure even such calamities as the loss of life, yet remain free from enmity and ever vigilant. Such men are protected in all the various vicissitudes of their lives by the blessed lord himself, even by means of the choice weapons of the enemies of the gods themselves!

# Sarasvatī and King Navaratha

Navaratha was a king continually intent on righteousness and gift-giving and utterly devoted to virtue. Once while out hunting he saw a ferocious Rākṣasa. Filled with great fear, O bulls of seers, he fled. Enraged, that mighty demon Duryodhana, looking like fire, ran after him, a spear in his huge hand. Terrorized, King Navaratha spied not far ahead of him a fine refuge, the well-protected sanctuary of Sarasvatī. Reaching it at top speed, the wise king saw before his eyes the goddess Sarasvatī herself, and saluted her with bowed head and folded hands. This conqueror of enemies praised her with reverent words and fell like a log to the ground, saying, "I have come to you for help! I worship the great chaste goddess who is before me, the divinity of speech, who is without beginning or end. I praise the womb of the world, the excellent Yoginī, the supreme spouse of the Golden Embryo, the three-eyed, moon-topped goddess! I honor her who knows supreme bliss, a portion of the highest consciousness, the embodiment of Brahman. Protect me, supreme goddess, who has come to you for refuge!

Meanwhile, the furious lord of the demons had approached the sanctuary of the goddess Sarasvatī to kill the king. Arrogant with power, with spear raised aloft, he prepared to enter the retreat of the mother of the three worlds, which shone like the moon. At the same time, a mighty creature that blazed like the sun at the end of the Age appeared and split open the demon's breast with his pike, knocking him to the ground. "Leave quickly, great king; there is nothing more to fear in this place," said the creature, "the Rākṣasa is dead!" With a bow and a happy heart, O chief of brahmins, King Navaratha returned to his own city, which was like that of Indra, destroyer of strongholds. And there, full of devotion, he installed an image of the goddess Sarasvatī, worshipping that mistress of the god with a variety of sacrifices and oblations.

# 6 Seers, Kings and Supernaturals

## Introduction

Although the Purāṇas contain an encyclopedic variety of contents, their mythological material is not as diverse as it may first appear. Dealing primarily with the activities of the gods, the Purāṇas create a universe of images unique to their own world of thought. This universe includes not only a symmetrical map of space and time, as represented above in Chapter 1, but also a survey of sacred pilgrimage sites found in the land of Bharata, a cast of human semidivine characters other than the gods, and finally a typical dramatic scenario that forms the backdrop of many, if not most, of the Purāṇic stories of the gods: a battle between the gods and the demons.

This recurring contest is of Vedic origin, although its lineaments are never made entirely clear in the Purāṇas. The demons are known to be the elder brothers of the gods; they are the Daityas, sons of their mother Diti, as opposed to the Ādityas, sons of Aditi. The demons are also called Dānavas, meaning sons of Dānu, also a Vedic name; the original Dānava is Vṛtra, enemy of the heroic god Indra. And finally, the demons are called Asuras, the gods Suras or Devas, the "Shining Ones." Paired from their early origins, their sibling rivalry persists throughout the Purāṇas without ultimate resolution until the end of time.

The gods and demons are in constant contention as to who will receive the sacrifices offered by mankind, and, by implication, power over heaven and earth. In the Purāṇas, this theme of recurrent contest between the forces of good and the forces of evil—for the demons impede fertility while the gods promote it—continues with vigor, but the Vedic deities have yielded first place to the great Hindu triad of gods, Brahmā, Viṣṇu, Śiva, and to the goddess. It is most often Viṣṇu or Śiva in the Purāṇas who defeats the demons in the end, rather than Indra or another Vedic god. And even when the Vedic deities do appear, they usually do so in a group rather than individually. This group includes both the major and minor gods of Vedic mythology: Indra, Varuṇa, Vāyu, and the collective Aśvins, Maruts, Sādhyas and Viśvedevas. Appearing as a crowd and "led by Indra," who is their chief, they have no individuality of their own. And it is their inability to best the demons that repeatedly leads them to troop off in a body to request Brahmā, the "Grandfather," for aid, as if they were all one large family.

This, in fact, is the typical dramatic situation within which Viṣṇu and Śiva perform their salvational deeds. They rescue men occasionally, but usually they save the "host of gods" in heaven, i.e. the demoted Vedic gods who are no longer powerful enough to save themselves. The opening passages of "The Burning of Tripura" in Chapter 5 repeat the details of this typical Purāṇic frame story: the hosts of gods are threatened by the powers of the three most potent demons, Bali, Maya and Kālanemi, who have won their powers as a reward from Brahmā for practicing severe *tapas.* The gods then go to Brahmā for refuge, and he in turn calls on Śiva for help.

The contest is never finally resolved, moreover, for the vanquished party always rises again. In "The Battle of the Gods and Demons" the gods lose, but this merely provides the occasion for Viṣṇu to descend as Vāmana the Dwarf to restore the balance (see Ch. 2). It is as if forces in the universe, identified as good and evil, have been personified in the host of Vedic gods and the crowd of demons, respectively. Thus good and evil are chronically in contest in the universe as well as within the bosom of a man; yet their complementary nature is made evident by the fact of their brotherhood and also by the similarity of their names, which are constantly paired: Daitya and Āditya, Asura and Sura.

Furthermore, when the Vedic deities do appear individually in the Purāṇas, their stories have different emphases than in Vedic literature, showing again how a religious universe different from that which went before has been constellated in the Purāṇas. Indra, hero of the thunderstorm, who used to bring nourishing rain to his people and cows in the *Ṛg Veda,* becomes identified as the murderer of a brahmin in the Purāṇas for his slaughter of Vṛtra, guilty and hounded for his crime. He threatens Kṛṣṇa's cowherds with destruction through a rainstorm; no longer is he a friend to man. His famous thunderbolt is fashioned from the bones of Dadhīci, a seer, but only as the result of a boon from Śiva, whence comes its power. And he plays an almost comic role in "Indra and the Ants," where his excessive arrogance leads him astray until the greater deity Viṣṇu teaches him a lesson.

The lengthy tale of Prahlāda, a demon mentioned in Vedic literature, appears to have one purpose alone—to show the virtues and benefits of worshiping Viṣṇu without stint, even if a demon boy does so. And Soma, that fine substance pressed and imbibed by the Vedic priests as part of their elaborate Vedic sacrifice, said to confer insight, has become in the Purāṇas the moon whose liquid rays nourish all life on earth. Thus in a variety of ways are the Vedic gods superseded, replaced or controlled by the great Hindu triad of gods. There is no contest between them, for the Vedic gods inhabit the lower heavens while the domains of Viṣṇu and Śiva—Vaikuṇṭha and Kailāsa—are higher still. While the Vedic deities occupy the eight directions, the triad resides atop Mt. Meru in the center of the universe (see the Introduction to Chapter 1 for a diagram of this). The Vedic gods troop off to fight their brother demons for their shares of the sacrifice, but neither side prevails until Viṣṇu or Śiva appears to win the day. Yet it is only because of this chronic battle between good and evil in the world that Śiva sometimes interferes, as for example to level the wicked city of Tripura, and that Viṣṇu descends in *avatāras* for the benefit of the world. This ongoing battle provides the occasion time and again for the beneficent action of the great gods towards the lesser gods and men.

It may appear that most of the action in Purāṇic stories involves gods, both Vedic and Purāṇic. But there is also a cast of human and semi-divine characters that include the seers, kings and supernatural beings.

For the most part seers or sages are wise and holy brahmins who are deserving of respect; they are usually married, but still live austere lives, often in hermitages, practicing *tapas,* or self-restraint. This practice, for them as for the celibate *yogin,* gains for the doer enormous powers; hence the awe in which they tend to be held by their associates. In any Hindu story, the seer has his particular place, often as wise teacher or sacrificer, and a number of such sages appear in the Purāṇas.

According to tradition, Vyāsa is the compiler of the Purāṇas as well as of the Vedas and the epic. But he only occasionally appears as the narrator or auditor of a tale. More frequently appearing in these roles are Maitreya, Nārada and Mārkaṇḍeya. Maitreya, in fact, is the most common vocative, and yet there is no story revealing who he is. Nārada is somewhat better known as a seer who appears in the *Ṛg Veda,* patriarch of the celestial Gandharva musicians, and the inventor of the lute. Mārkaṇḍeya is known for his long life, his numerous rebirths, and his great knowledge that falls just short of wisdom—it grants him sight of Viṣṇu asleep on the cosmic ocean, but not supreme release.

In the creation stories of the Purāṇas a group of seers is identified as the "mind-born" sons of Brahmā because they spring to life from his thought before all other beings. These are Bhṛgu, Pulastya, Pulaha, Kratu, Aṅgiras, Marīci, Dakṣa, Atri and Vasiṣṭha. These nine recur in irregular ways throughout Purāṇic narratives: as the collective called "the Seven Seers," as patronymics for other seers, and, as in the case of Atri and Vasiṣṭha, in person. These may have been the names of ancient families of Veda-knowing seers who dominated the oral tradition influencing the Great Purāṇas. Yet no clear lineages can be traced. If they were originally historical personages or families belonging to the schools of Vedic recitation, they have become entirely legendary in the Purāṇas.

Purāṇic seers tend to display certain characteristic traits. They are austere due to their *tapas*, proud, aloof, resolute and full of virtue. Their signal flaw is a tendency to anger, as Viśvāmitra (whose lineage is in fact suspect since he was born a kṣatriya) so clearly demonstrates. In the story of Hariścandra and Viśvāmitra, however, the seer is a parody of virtue, demanding so much in the name of brahminhood that he destroys King Hariścandra's family and fortune. Thus seers in the Purāṇas are distinctly human, and represent themselves more or less as they could have appeared in their brahminic role in ancient Indian society. They are somewhat elaborated into legend, but not altogether without humanity.

Kings, as kṣatriya heroes, also appear in the Purāṇas, their stories generally embellished by imagination, but with their human nature clearly showing through. Some of these kings have clans and lineages recounted in the *Mahābhārata*, as do Parikṣit, Yayāti and Hariścandra, which suggests that they may have been historical persons. But like the seers, they have become entirely legendary figures in the Purāṇas.

These kings are honest, upright, virtuous upholders of Dharma, for the most part. As Hariścandra announces in his story:

> According to the laws of Dharma, a king who knows his duty is to give gifts, to protect, and to raise his bow to wage war.
> (*Mārk.* 7.18)

And when a king rules his people well, peace reigns in his kingdom, as under the protection of King Pṛthu:

> While Pṛthu ruled his kingdom, there was long life, prosperity and happiness for all. There was no poverty, sickness or evil . . . no

> misfortune and no fear. People were always happy, knowing neither pain nor sorrow. . . . In the reign of King Pṛthu, people lived entirely within the Dharma.
> (*Matsya* 10.29, 30, 33)

A king's occupation also requires hunting in the forest, and this pursuit often leads him to an interesting adventure, as it does Vidūratha, or Duṣyanta in the story of Śakuntalā. Furthermore, the interdependent relations between kings and brahmins are made abundantly clear in these stories. Brahmins and kṣatriyas, in fact, are the only two castes regularly depicted in the Purāṇas, and they are shown interrelating in a variety of mutually beneficent ways, despite occasional tension between them. Kings govern kingdoms, go to war, and pay brahmins fat fees for sacrifices. Priests perform sacrifices, give wise counsel, and use the power acquired by *tapas* to benefit their rulers, by enabling them to have children, for example.

Rarely are stories told of lower castes or of women, except in the Śiva Purāṇa, where a variety of outcastes and women become Śiva's devotees. One interesting exception to this is the Caṇḍāla grave-picker, in the story of "Hariścandra and Viśvāmitra," who, as Dharma in disguise, becomes a moral example of a sort, demonstrating one of the awful possibilities that may result from a bad rebirth. In any case, the stories in the Purāṇas deal largely with brahmin priests and kṣatriya kings, the two upper classes of ancient Indian society, and it is their values (described more systematically in the Hindu law codes) that prevail. What of the lower castes and women? Their stories we can never know.

The cast of supernatural characters in the Purāṇas is small, but consistent. Various creatures appear, as collectives, to support the dramatic action of the gods. For example, Gandharvas and Apsarases, the musicians and dancing girls of heaven, usually display their talents to celebrate some victory for the gods. And more rarely, the Cāraṇas, or celestial minstrels, are included too. Sometimes, as in the case of Urvaśī, the Apsaras, they have dealings with human beings. Or, as in the mountains near Atri's hermitage, they sport on earth in the most lovely natural spots. But usually they are thought to inhabit heaven as happy, beneficent and amorous creatures, with little individuality. Heaven is also inhabited by the Siddhas, an amorphous group of worthies. These are presumably human beings whose virtue has won them rebirth in the celestial realms, for the name Siddhas signifies "accomplished ones."

Yakṣas and Kinnaras are groups of more earthly beings, the latter only dimly depicted. Yakṣas are thought to inhabit holy places, such as Gayā and Vārāṇasī. Sometimes they are thought to be beneficent, like the group of Yakṣas who attend Kubera, god of wealth. But other times they are more threatening, like the Yakṣa of Vārāṇasī who describes his kind this way:

> We Yakṣas are by nature cruel of heart; we eat anything, including flesh; we are habitually violent!
> (*Matsya* 179.10)

Less well regarded are the Snakes, or Nāgas and Uragas, who inhabit the netherworlds and whose shrines appear on earth. Snake worship, or rather their propitiation, appears to have been an ancient practice in India, where even today thousands of people a year lose their lives to snake-bite. In the story of Kāliya, Kṛṣṇa pacifies a threatening poisonous snake; in the story of Prahlāda, his father orders snakes to attack him; and even the great lord Viṣṇu has adopted the snake as a form in which he resides, as Ananta or Śeṣa, on the cosmic ocean between creations. Ananta is regarded as foremost among a number of mighty snakes whose domain is the netherworlds. And whereas the Gandharvas, Apsarases and Yakṣas are heavenly and earthly spirits, born of imagination, the Snakes derive from human experience, deified and propitiated for their power to harm.

More clearly terrifying are the Rākṣasas, Gaṇas, Bhūtas, Pramāthas and Piśācas, the demons, ghosts, ghouls and goblins. The Rākṣasas are demons who may be found on earth, in frightening places like the woods, and also in the netherworlds. The others form the entourage of Śiva in his role as lord of destruction and the dead. They haunt cremation grounds and also fight on Śiva's side in all his battles. Among these, the Gaṇas have the most distinctive personality as his personal attendants, fierce in the protection of their master. Śiva's most famous son is Gaṇeśa, lord of the Gaṇas. The word means simply "troop," but it has taken on an ominous meaning due to the terrifying character of Śiva, their lord. Yet to become a Gaṇa, Śiva's servant, is one of the boons to which his devotees aspire.

The disposition of all of these supernatural beings recalls the spatial arrangement of the Purāṇic universe. The Gandharvas, Apsarases, Cāraṇas and Siddhas inhabit the heavens, along with the Immortals, the virtuous dead. Yakṣas and Snakes are found primarily on earth, while Rakṣasas, Gaṇas, Bhūtas and the rest dwell in the netherworlds, rising up to haunt the earth. There is a kind of symmetry between the good and evil creatures that recalls the symmetry between the gods and demons in their battles, a natural balance as it were among the throngs of supernatural beings.

These beings interact with the world of human beings to some degree, in both benevolent and malevolent ways, but the most important class of supernaturals in this regard is the host of the Fathers, or departed ancestors. Incumbent upon each living Hindu eldest son is a ritual for the dead called *śrāddha,* performed to assure the continuing contentment of the male kin that have gone before. And each man expects his son to do the same for him. Just as the Vedic gods were thought to be "fed" by their sacrificial offerings, so are the Fathers "satisfied" in similar fashion by these ceremonies. When pleased, they aid the living; when displeased, they hinder their kin.

> When they are satisfied, the Fathers will grant you your desire. . . . Indeed, is there anything your ancestors will not give to you when they are satisfied?
> (*Garuḍa* 89.11)

The tension that exists between family and ascetic life in Hindu society is made abundantly clear in the story of "The Fathers." Ascetic life is highly prized, but only for some. For if everyone renounced the world, society would cease and mendicant ascetics would have no means of support. So asceticism and the mendicant life, however highly respected in Indian culture, always depend on the existence of householders for their basic support. So do the gods, and so do the Fathers, and this is the claim the Fathers make on Ruci in our story, when they urge him first to marry, then to have offspring, to do sacrifices to his Fathers—and only then to renounce the world. Thus the four Hindu stages of life are reinforced here, just as the propriety of the four classes is in other stories. As is the case in so many of the Purāṇic stories about seers and kings, the traditional values of upper class Hindu tradition are bolstered by a moral tale.

If "The Fathers" has a masculine context, and if the funeral rites are performed by sons for their male ancestors alone, what of the women? In fact, women, as goddesses, supernaturals or as human heroines are few and far between in the Purāṇas. This is a masculine literature, recited by men to men, in which even stories of normal child-bearing are hard to find. Peculiar means of reproduction abound, as for example: the seer Kaca becomes Śukra's son by being swallowed and splitting open his belly to be born; the seers Agastya and Vasiṣṭha are born in water jars from their fathers' spilt seed; Kārttikeya too is born from his father Śiva's spilt seed in a reed thicket and nurtured by the wives of the Seven Seers; Gaṇeśa arises from the dirt on his mother's body; and several odd stories are told of the birth of the Maruts, in one of which Indra enters inside their mother's womb in order to split the embryo into many pieces in his rage.

What then is the meaning of the story of the Mothers, that ravenous horde of furious creatures determined to devour the world? More like witches than mothers, they are Śiva's brood, spawned to defeat the demon Andhakas, so the story goes, but even he cannot control them. Only a group of other goddesses in fact have that power, and they are rewarded for success in so doing by becoming Viṣṇu's lovers. If there is no social context evident from which these Mothers spring, as there is for the Fathers, then what human fear is captured in their gruesome tale? Perhaps a fear that the powers of destruction, personified as female, will annihilate the world. If the celibate ascetic represents one extreme ideal in Hindu imagination, the devouring Mothers would depict its opposite: the one, complete self-mastery; the other, utter abandonment to greed. It is a need to balance these two extremes that motivates Hindu mythology, and the balance is achieved in a variety of ways, most notably through the love and/or marriage of a divine pair of deities: Viṣṇu and Śrī, Kṛṣṇā and Rādhā, or Śiva and *śakti*.

Finally, the geography of the Purāṇas is essentially a religious one. Holy mountains are frequently cited, both mythical and real. Mt. Meru is the center pole of the Purāṇic universe, circled by the seven continents, and by the sun, moon, planets and stars. Mt. Mandara, Mt. Gandhamādana and Mt. Govardhana, as well as numerous others, have their roles in different stories, their location more in the imagination than in earthly geography. But Mt. Himavat, or Himālaya, the mountain range to the north of India, is not only a person, father of the wife of Śiva, Pārvatī, the "mountain maid," but also an important place of pilgrimage, and it is lovingly described in the story of Atri's hermitage.

The Purāṇas list and describe numerous other sites of pilgrimage within the land of Bharata, usually in a stylized manner. Of course sacrifices to the gods and meditation by ascetics are approved forms of religious devotion, but pilgrimage to a sacred spot is presented as the ideal way to achieve one's "highest goal." Interestingly enough, this goal is not unequivocally seen to be release from rebirth, as it is in other Hindu texts, but can be either such release or, more importantly, rebirth in the heaven of one's chosen god, either Viṣṇu or Śiva. This may be accomplished by a visit to the god's shrine in Vārāṇasī.

> Not by gifts, nor by *tapas,* nor even by sacrifice or knowledge is the marvelous goal attained which can be found in Vārāṇasī. . . . A wise man, even if beset by a hundred obstacles, gains that supreme goal which ends suffering, if he should live here, and goes to the supreme abode of Śiva where there is no birth, old age or death.
> (*Kūrma* 1.29.39.40, 42)

Where are these holy places to be found? There are two sorts of pilgrimage sites: the hermitages of seers, like that of Atri, found often in the mountains and by rivers, and the sacred fords, found on the banks of holy rivers. It is, in fact, the rivers that are the holiest of holy places in Purāṇic thought. To bathe in them provides spiritual purification of an unsurpassable sort, and to make a pilgrimage to a riverside shrine is the utmost act of faith a devotee can offer to his god.

Numerous rivers and a variety of sacred fords are mentioned in the Purāṇas, some sacred to a single god, and others including the shrines of several deities. In northern India, the Ganges and the Yamunā rivers are most frequently adored, and their sacred fords Prayāga, Gayā and Vārāṇasī—the modern Allahabad, Gayā and Banaras—most often eulogized. Rivers and places in southern India are occasionally mentioned too; a complete list of holy spots in the land of Bharata, both north and south, as given in the Purāṇas, might offer a clue as to the origins of this literature. For it seems plausible that the devotional stories told in the Purāṇas were preserved in oral form by the priests of these hermitages and shrines, that these were in fact the places where this oral tradition was preserved. Nothing else presents itself so repeatedly and so obviously within the stories themselves, not the courts of kings nor the occasion of great sacrifice, as is the case with the epic. Given the devotional nature of much of the contents of the Purāṇas, it well may be that the pilgrimage site serves not only as an interesting subject of Purāṇic stories, but as the place and means of their preservation as well.

In sum, the Great Purāṇas include a vast wealth of mythological and legendary material. While most of it is dedicated to the worship of the gods Viṣṇu and Śiva, and to a lesser extent, of Brahmā and the goddesses, and also to the places where these gods are to be worshiped, other characters of some importance also appear. First among these are the Vedic deities, relics of an earlier mythology, demoted to be sure, who form a host of gods that periodically battle with their demon brothers. Ostensibly fought over the shares of the sacrifices human beings offer them, their battles take on the aura of a contest between good and evil, thereby providing opportunity for the greater gods, Viṣṇu and Śiva, to intercede on behalf of the good. And this dramatic contest makes up the typical scenario in which the feats of the major gods of the Purāṇas take place.

Part of the continuing drama includes a cast of supernatural beings, from the celestial Gandharvas and Apsarases to the ghastly Bhūtas and Pramāthas, Śiva's funereal crew. They provide a heavenly and demonic chorus echoing the actions of the deities. Usually appearing in groups (they have, with few exceptions, little individuality of their own) they are distributed more or less equally among the heavens, earth and netherworlds. Thus the symmetry of space and time is echoed in the brotherhood of the rival gods and demons, and in the natures of the lesser supernaturals as well.

Hindu society is also represented in the Purāṇic stories, although to a lesser extent than the actions of the gods. Brahmin seers and kṣatriya kings dominate the legends and stories told of human beings, while the lower classes and women scarcely appear at all. Although full of imaginative elaborations, the stories of seers and kings do convey human personalities and social values—most notably in the nature of the virtuous sage, the duties of the noble king, and in the interdependence of the two. It is as if the battle between good and evil on the plane of deity becomes a contest between virtue and vice in the realm of humanity. And the overall purpose of many if not all of these Purāṇic stories about men is to reveal the problems human life presents to each, and to resolve them in the name of virtue with a moral lesson of some kind.

The story of "The Churning of the Ocean" in Chapter 2 sums up this over-arching motif of Hindu mythology. Couched in the form of gods and demons, it shows in a most entertaining way the struggle between good and evil, between creative and destructive forces in the universe. This struggle is depicted as a continuous one, forming the very foundation of this single, multi-layered universe inhabited by gods, supernaturals and mankind together. The polarities represented by gods and demons in this story are felt to be complementary, for just as the contenders for the nectar are in actuality brothers, so is the battle never fully won. And as "The Churning of the Ocean" so delightfully asserts, the contest is not so much a war as a cooperative effort which ultimately produces universal benefits. Without this tension between polarities, between apparently opposing sides, continuing creation would be impossible. So the contest goes on forever, its purpose to benefit the universe so that it may continue to bear fruit.

# Texts

## SEERS

### Mārkaṇḍeya and the Cosmic Ocean

At every dissolution, Nārāyaṇa, the Yogin, assumes the nature of *sattva* and becomes the sun. Then he dries up the ocean with his scorching rays. First he swallows all the seas, rivers and wells, and then his rays suck up the water in the mountains. Penetrating earth with his rays, he descends to Rasātala where he gulps the fine waters of the netherworlds. Finally the supreme lotus-eyed person sucks out all the urine, blood, and whatever other moisture lies in the bodies of living creatures.

Next, lord Hari becomes the world-shaking wind that inhales all the human airs—Prāṇa, Apāna, Samāna and the rest—along with all the hosts of gods and ghosts. Then the qualities of fragrance and smell are absorbed into the earth. Tongue, taste and viscidity merge into water, while the qualities of form, breath and motion merge into air; sound, hearing and empty space are absorbed into the atmosphere. All the world's illusions are instantly annihilated by the lord. The mind, the universal intelligence, and the one called the knower-of-the-field* are absorbed into the lovable supreme being Hṛṣīkeśa.

A blazing fire with a hundred flames is kindled in the branches of the trees blown by the wind as they rub against each other. This fire, called Saṃvartaka, ignites the world with its mountains, trees, thickets, creepers, reeds and grass, its celestial chariots, numerous cities, and every other place where people hide.

*Technical expression for the embodied soul.

Hari, *guru* of the world, reduces all the worlds to ashes and then puts out the fire by his own action, thus heralding the end of the Age. Then mighty Kṛṣṇa becomes a thousand rains, a hundred-fold, to gratify the earth with heavenly water as an oblation. Under this milky offering, the sweet waters of heaven, auspicious and holy, earth vanishes entirely. Covered by the flooding waters of the rains, earth becomes one vast watery ocean, empty of all life. All the great creatures are lost within that lord of limitless power, while earth, into which sun, air and space have already been absorbed, also dissolves. After drying up the oceans and embodied beings, and after burning them with fire and flooding them with water, the one eternal lord goes to sleep. Assuming his original form, that noble Yogin of infinite power sleeps, absorbed in Yoga, pervading the water of that immeasurable ocean for many thousands of Ages. And no one whatsoever knows him, whether manifest or unmanifest.

As Hari was sleeping in that vast ocean long ago, O brahmins, a miracle occurred. Hear now about the curiosity of Mārkaṇḍeya. The great seer had been swallowed by the magnificent god and was in the lord's belly for many thousand divine years. There he roamed around, making a pilgrimage to the sacred fords around the earth, the holy hermitages and the domains of the gods. He visited various countries, territories and many cities reciting prayers, doing sacrifices and performing intense *tapas* with serenity.

But then Mārkaṇḍeya slipped out the god's mouth, where because of the god's illusion, he did not recognize himself. There Mārkaṇḍeya saw the world and the ocean shrouded in darkness on all sides. He grew acutely afraid, doubting that he would survive. When he spied the sleeping god, he was thrilled and utterly amazed.

Surrounded on all sides by water, Mārkaṇḍeya looked around and thought, "What am I to think of this? Am I deranged, or am I dreaming? Surely I am imagining that the world has disappeared, for such a calamity could not really happen!" And he stood there thinking, "The moon, the sun and the wind are gone, the earth and the mountains too. Where can they be?"

But then he saw a Person as big as a mountain sleeping half-submerged in the sea like a cloud looming on the horizon. He shone radiantly in the darkness, like sunshine through a cloud, blazing with his own splendor, like the midnight sun. Mārkaṇḍeya went closer to see the god, and said in wonder, "Who are you?" at which point the seer was swallowed once again.

Back in the belly of the god, the bewildered Mārkaṇḍeya thought it all had been a dream. So as before, he roamed the earth, visiting the holy fords and various other hermitages. He saw sacrificers making sacrifice, receiving fine fees, and brahmins by the hundreds, in the belly of the god. He saw all the castes, headed by brahmins, observing proper conduct and the four stages of life, the same as I have previously described to you. Thus for more than a hundred years did the wise Mārkaṇḍeya wander over the entire earth without finding any end to the god's belly.

Then once again he slipped out of Hari's mouth. This time he saw a little boy hidden in the branches of a banyan tree, absorbed in play in the middle of the water of that vast ocean under a misty sky, in a world empty of all other life. Filled with wonder and curiosity, the seer was not able to look upon the boy who shone like the sun. Standing near him in the water, he thought to himself, "I think I have seen this once before. I think that I am being fooled by the illusion of a god!"

So that bewildered Mārkaṇḍeya began to swim away through that unfathomable ocean, his eyes blinking in fear. But the lord Viṣṇu, appearing as the little boy, addressed him, saying, "Welcome! Don't be afraid of me, my son. There is nothing to fear. Come over here." The seer Mārkaṇḍeya, overcome with fatigue, answered the little child, "Who dares to speak my name and thus insult my *tapas?* Who dares offend my holy and famous thousand-year *tapas?* I am not accustomed to such treatment, even from the gods! Why even Brahmā, lord of the gods, treats me with respect. Who now risks his life by greeting me, with my terrible *tapas,* with the words 'Hey, Mārkaṇḍeya!'"*

After these angry words of the great seer, lord Madhusūdana spoke again, "I am your begetter, my child. I am Hṛṣīkeśa, your father and teacher, the ancient one who grants long life. Why do you not come near to me? Long ago your father Aṅgiras wanted a son and worshiped me by doing severe *tapas.* Then he chose you, of boundless energy, as the boon earned by his fierce *tapas.* Now I am talking to you, the mighty seer of infinite power who abides in the Self. Who but the son of the Self of all creatures with his *yogic* power would be able to see me playing on the vast ocean—who but yourself?"

With joyful face and eyes wide with wonder, that Mārkaṇḍeya of great *tapas* folded his hands and touched his head. The long-lived seer, honored in the world, announced his name and family, and bowed with devotion to the lord, saying, "I want to understand the illusion, faultless one, by which you appear in the middle of the ocean in the form of a boy! What do people call you, lord? I think you

*The reason for the seer's indignation is that the child should have identified his own name and family first when addressing an elder.

must be the great-souled Viṣṇu, for who else but he could exist here?"

"I am Nārāyaṇa," replied the lord, "the beginning and end of everything. I am given names like 'the thousand-headed god.' I am Puruṣa, the sun-hued Person, the Vedic sacrifice among sacrifices, the fire that conveys the offering and the immortal chief of the sea creatures. I am Śakra who sits in Indra's seat; I am Parivatsara* among the years. I am the Yogin; I am called the Age, and I am the whirlpool at the end of time. I am all creatures, all gods, Śeṣa among the snakes and Garuḍa among the birds. I am the destiny of all creatures under the name of Time. I am Dharma and the *tapas* of ascetics.

"I am the heavenly river, the vast ocean of milk, the supreme truth and the sole progenitor. I am Sāṃkhya, Yoga, and the highest goal. I am sacrifice, and duty, and I am called the master of knowledge. I am the sun, the wind, the earth, the sky, the waters, the seas, the constellations and the ten directions. I am the rain, Soma, Parjanya and the sun. I am in the ocean of milk and I am the submarine mare's-head fire. When I become the fire Saṃvartaka I drink the water oblation. I am the Ancient One and the ultimate goal.

"I am the source of past, present and future, O brahmin. I am everything you see and everything you hear. Whatever you are aware of in the world, know that to be me. By me was the universe poured forth long ago, and even now I shall create again. Watch me! Age after age this universe comes forth from me, O Mārkaṇḍeya; I know this to be true!

"Roam happily inside my belly if you want to learn my Dharma. Brahmā resides in my body, as do the gods and seers. I am the foe of demons when I manifest my Yoga. I am the one-syllabled *mantra OṂ* of three meanings: Success, Love and Duty, prior to these three paths of life and revealing their true goal."

After saying all this, the great-minded primeval lord Viṣṇu swallowed the great seer Mārkaṇḍeya in a flash, and he found himself inside the lord's belly once again.

# Nārada

Nārada said: When the mendicants who had taught me what I knew had departed, I did the following in my childhood. I was my mother's only child. She was a naive woman, a servant. As I, her son, had no

*One year of a five-year cycle called an Age.

other recourse, she lavished her love on me. Being herself dependent, she was unable to provide for me, though she was eager to do so. People in the employ of a rich man are like wooden puppets. I lived with a brahmin family to which I devoted my attentions, a little boy five years old, innocent of any knowledge of direction, place or time.

One night my mother went out of the house to milk the cow, and on the way she stepped on a snake which, urged by Time, bit the poor woman. Thinking it was a favor of the lord who wishes his devotees well, I at once set out in a northerly direction. I passed through prosperous countrysides, cities, villages, pastures, mining camps, hamlets, mountain settlements, plantations, woods and parks, over mountains variegated with colorful minerals, where the tree limbs had been broken off by elephants, through pools with safe water, lotus ponds visited by the gods with warbling birds and whirring bees.

Then, still alone, I saw a large forest dense with reed, bamboo, and cane, fearful and dangerous, infested with snakes, owls and jackals. Exhausted in body and soul, hungry and thirsty, I bathed, drank and rinsed at a river pool, until I was rested. Then, sitting under a peepal tree in the deserted wilderness, I began to reflect on the Self which, as I had heard, dwells in oneself. While I was meditating on his lotus feet, my mind was overcome with emotion and my eyes filled with tears of yearning. Hari slowly became present in my heart. Filled with the fullness of love, my body thrilled. I was enraptured; merged in an inundation of bliss I saw no more duality. But when this dear vision of the form of the blessed lord faded, and I to my sorrow no longer beheld him, I rose quickly, disturbed and distressed. Straining to see him again, I collected my mind in my heart; but though seeing, I was blinded, frustrated as one diseased.

While I was thus striving in the wilderness, he spoke to me, invisible, in a deep and gentle voice, as though to assuage my sorrow, "Child, you cannot see me in this life, for I am invisible to sham *yogins* whose taints have not been removed by maturity. I showed you this form to inspire your longing; for the good man who longs for me slowly relinquishes all desires. When by long attendance on good people your mind has become steadfastly fixed on me and you have abandoned this unspeakable world, you shall become mine. A mind that is fastened on me will never stray: even when creation comes to an end, he will by my grace remember me."

With this he ceased speaking, that great being, the lord who showed no other mark than sky; and with a sense of grace I bowed my head to him who is greater than the great. Chanting the names of the eternal unabashedly, and recalling his mysteries and good deeds, I contentedly roamed the earth, biding my time, without passion or envy. While I was thus immersed in Kṛṣṇa, detached and pure of soul, my time came in due course like a flash of lightning. As I assumed this pure *bhāgavata* body, the old elemental one fell off, like *karman* extinguished. When at the end of the Eon the lord had taken back this universe and was lying on the waters of the ocean about to go to sleep, I entered inside him by the path of his breath. At the end of a thousand Ages, he rose and was about to create when Marīci, I and the other sages were reborn from his breath.

Now I wander through the three worlds, within and without, never failing in my vow, with free entrance everywhere by the grace of great Viṣṇu. I wander about while playing this god-given lute adorned with the music that is *brahman*, and sing the stories of Hari. And as I sing of his feats, the lord whose fame is so dear to me soon affords me a vision of himself in my heart, as though he had been called. The repetition of the works of Hari, by those who contemplate him, is time and again a boat on the river of existence, a refuge for those who are rendered mindless by their yearning for sensual pleasure. The self, battered by lust and greed, is not so calmed by *yogic* restraints as by the service of Mukunda.*

I have narrated to you everything you asked me—the secret of my birth and works—to gratify your soul.

Having thus spoken with Vyāsa, the blessed Nārada took his leave, and playing his *vīṇā* went wherever chance would take him. Aho! Blessed is the divine sage who, singing the glory of Kṛṣṇa in rapture, brings pleasure to this sick world with his lute.

# Kaṇḍu

On the lovely, deserted and sanctifying bank of the river Gomatī, full of bulbs, roots and fruits, of kindling, flowers and *kuśa* grass, covered with all kinds of trees and creepers, and adorned with many blossoms, resonant with many birds, enchanting and grazed by various herds of deer, there stood the hermitage of Kaṇḍu, O best of seers, rich at all seasons in fruits and flowers and adorned with a stand of plantain trees. There the seer did great and marvelous *tapas*, with vows, fasts, restraints and the observances of baths and silence:

*Viṣṇu.

in summer he sat surrounded by the five fires; in the rainy season he stayed outdoors; in winter he stayed immersed in the river up to his chin. Thus did he mortify himself.

The gods, Gandharvas, Siddhas and Vidyādharas became greatly amazed at the spectacle of the prowess of the hermit's *tapas*. With the force of his *tapas* Kaṇḍu heated up the three worlds of earth, atmosphere and heaven. "Aho, what fortitude! Aho, what extreme *tapas!*" exclaimed the gods.

They diligently took counsel with Śakra, upset from fear of Kaṇḍu, seeking to obstruct his *tapas*. Knowing their purpose, Śakra, the Slayer of Vala, spoke to the callipygous Apsaras Pramloca, who was proud of her beauty and youth. She was fine-waisted, with beautiful teeth, full hips and ample breasts, and endowed with all the fine marks of beauty. "Pramloca, go quickly where that hermit is doing *tapas* and seduce him, my pretty, to deplete his power of *tapas*." Said Pramloca, "I always obey your words, my lord, chief of the gods, but here I am afraid that I will risk my life. I am afraid of this great hermit who observes the vow of celibacy; he is awesome with the fire of his *tapas* and his glow is like fire and sun. Knowing that I have come to obstruct him, Kaṇḍu will be angry, and that extremely powerful man will lay an unendurable curse on me. There are many other Apsarases who take pride in their beauty and youth, who have fine waists and pretty faces and big uptilted bosoms, and who are adept at seduction—put them to the task!"

Śacī's consort replied to her words, "Let the others be; you are the most skilled, my lovely! I shall give you Love, Spring and Wind to help you. Go with them, fine-hipped girl, to that great hermit."

Hearing Śacī's command, that lovely-eyed nymph went off with the others by way of the sky. When she arrived there, she saw that charming wood and the fiercely practicing and taintless hermit in his hermitage. . . . Slowly she strolled with the others through the woods, and beholding its charms and marvels the beautiful woman opened her eyes wide in wonderment. Pramloca said to Wind, Love and Spring, "Help me out! Each of you be ready!" and confident of her powers of seduction she added, "I shall now go where that hermit is keeping himself. Today I shall change that driver of his body who has harnessed the horses of his senses into a poor charioteer whose reins are slipping, at the command of lust! Be he Brahmā, Viṣṇu or Śiva, today I shall lay him open to the wounds of the arrows of love!" With these words she proceeded to the hermit's hermitage, where the wild beasts were tamed by the power of his *tapas*.

She positioned herself on the river's bank and at a short distance from him the beautiful nymph began to sing as sweetly as the cuckoo. Thereupon Spring quickly displayed its power, and out of season the cuckoos began to sing enticingly. Wind blew the fragrance of the sandal woods of Mt. Malaya, every so slowly dropping all kinds of pure flowers. Love approached carrying his blossom arrows and disturbed the thoughts of the seer.

When he heard the music of her song, the hermit wonderingly ventured out, propelled by the arrows of Love, to where the fine-browed nymph was standing. Seeing her he said happily, his eyes wide with wonder, his robe drooping, staggering, his body covered with goose bumps, "Who are you and who do you belong to, you fine-hipped, lovable, sweet-smiling wench? You are stealing my heart, lovely-brows! Quick, tell me the truth, slim-waisted girl."

Said Pramloca, "I am your serving girl; I have come here for flowers. Give me your orders now: what are you telling me to do?" Scarcely had he heard her words before he lost his composure. Bewildered, he took the woman by the hand and entered the hermitage. Love, Wind and Spring went back to heaven, satisfied they had done their duty. They went to Śakra and told him what had happened between the two of them. Upon hearing this, Śakra and the gods were pleased and relieved.

Kaṇḍu meanwhile had entered his hermitage with Pramloca, and by the power of his *tapas* gave himself at once the handsome, lovable body of a sixteen-year-old, endowed with beauty and youth, most enticing, adorned with divine ornaments, wearing celestial robes, desirable, made up with divine garlands and perfumes, fit for all pleasures. When she saw his fine manhood, she was amazed and delighted, exclaiming, "Aho, the power of *tapas!*"

He gave up bathing, worshiping the dawn, praying, offering oblations, studying, adoring the gods, keeping vows, fasts and observances and meditating, and happily made love to her day and night. His heart smitten with love, he did not realize that he was losing *tapas*. So addicted did he become that he forgot dawn, night, day, fortnight, month, season, half-year and year, in fact all time, while the fine-hipped nymph, skilled in the moods of love as well as conversation, made love with him.

Hermit Kaṇḍu stayed with her at Mandaradroṇī for over a hundred years, indulging his lusts. Then she said to the great man, "I want to go back to heaven, brahmin." The hermit, who was still in love with her, replied, "Stay a few more days!" At his words the slender woman remained for another whole century, indulging in pleasure with the great-souled man.

"Give me leave, reverend, I am going to heaven," she pleaded.

"No, stay!" he replied, so the lovely-faced nymph stayed another century.

"I am going to heaven, brahmin!" she stated with a pretty, affectionate smile, but he replied to the long-eyed woman, "You remain with me here, fine-browed girl. You are not going for a long while." Fearful of his curse, the fine-buttocked nymph stayed on for a little under two hundred years. Time and again the slender woman prayed him for leave to return to Indra's heaven, but every time the lordly man said, "Stay!" Out of fear of his curse, but being also clever and aware of the grief from loss of affection, she did not leave the hermit. And when the great seer made love to her day and night, love was forever fresh to the lustful hermit.

Then, one day, the hermit left his hut in a great hurry and the lovely nymph asked, "Where are you going?"

"The day is ending and I have to worship the twilight; otherwise I am remiss in my rites."

She began to laugh cheerfully and said to the great hermit, "How is it that only now the day is ending for you, O sage in all Dharma? It is long gone! Who would not be astounded at what you say?" Said the hermit, "This morning you came to this lovely river bank, my dear. I saw you and you entered my hermitage. Now it is twilight and the day is drawing to a close. Why are you jesting? Tell me what you mean!"

Pramloca said, "True enough, I came in the morning, but centuries have passed since then!"

Disturbed, the hermit asked the long-eyed woman, "Tell me, timid thing, how much time have I spent dallying with you?"

Pramloca said, "Sixteen hundred years, six months and three days have gone by."

Said the seer, "Are you telling the truth, or is this a joke, my lovely? I thought I had not been with you for more than a day!"

Pramloca answered, "Why should I lie to you, especially since you are asking me as you leave?"

When the hermit heard her words, he cried, "Fie! Fie on me!" and berated himself for his misconduct. "All my *tapas* is lost! The wealth of the knowers of Brahman has been dissipated; my wits are robbed! Someone has created woman to befuddle! By my conquest of myself I had knowledge of the highest Brahman! A curse on this shark called lust which made me go this way! Vows, all the Vedas and all other means of salvation have been destroyed by desire, which is the road to all hells."

Thus blaming himself, the hermit, wise in Dharma, said to the sitting Apsaras, "Go where you want, slut! You have done what you had to do for Indra, shaking me up with the gestures of love. I won't reduce you to ashes in the fire of my wrath. I have lived with you in the friendship of the seven steps which the strict observe. But where are you to blame? What have I done for you? It is my fault entirely that I lost mastery over my senses. Still fie on you, disgusting seductress, for destroying my *tapas* as a favor to Śakra!"

While the brahmin seer was speaking in this vein to the fine-waisted nymph, she broke out in a sweat and trembled all over. And to the sweating and shivering woman that best of seers said irately, "Now go! Go!" Tongue-lashed, she hurried out of the hermitage and flew into the air, wiping away her sweat with tree blossoms.

## Śukra and Kaca

Long ago the gods and demons contested who should rule the triple world with its moving and unmoving beings. Eager to win, the gods asked Aṅgiras' son Bṛhaspati, the seer, to be their chief priest, while the demons chose Kāvya, who is also known as Uśanas and Śukra. These two brahmins had always been fierce rivals.

The gods defeated the Dānavas who were sent to fight them, but Kāvya restored them to life with the power of his magical knowledge. So they always sprang up and made war on the gods again. But when the demons killed the gods in the vanguard of the battle, the wise Bṛhaspati could not revive them. The sage did not possess the secret that the mighty Kāvya knew: how to restore the dead to life. And so the gods were utterly dismayed.

Trembling with fear because of Uśanas, the gods went to Kaca, eldest son of Bṛhaspati, and said "We love you! Please love us in return, and give us your utmost help. If you go and find out Śukra's secret, that brahmin of infinite splendor, we shall give you part of our shares of the sacrifice. He can be found in the company of Vṛṣaparvan, where he protects the Dānavas, and no one else. Only you can conciliate him! And Devayānī, the beloved daughter of this great-souled seer, only you can win her over! If you make her happy with your virtue, piety, sweetness, good conduct and self-control, you shall succeed in getting the secret knowledge for our side." Thus ordered by the gods, Bṛhaspati's son Kaca said, "So be it!" and set out to find Vṛṣaparvan.

After hastening there, O king, Kaca, honored by the gods, bowed to Śukra in the city of the demon-chief and said, "I am Kaca, the grandson of Aṅgiras the seer, the son of Bṛhaspati, who have appeared before you. Let me be your pupil! I shall be an excellent student for you, O *guru*, performing outstanding *brahmacārya* in your house. Let me do so, O brahmin, for a thousand years!"

"Welcome to you, Kaca!" answered Śukra. "I believe what you say. I shall honor you who are so worthy of honor, and through you, your father Bṛhaspati as well!"

"So be it!" said Kaca, faithfully accepting the vow assigned by Uśanas Śukra, the son of the seer.

Kaca observed the rules and the holy times, as he was taught, O Bhārata, honoring both his teacher and Devayānī. He gratified that virtuous Bhārgava maiden, who was in the bloom of her youth, by bringing her flowers and fruits and doing errands for her. And the wanton Devayānī followed him around, that self-controlled brahmin, doing services for him, too, in secret. Thus did Kaca observe his strict vow for five hundred years.

One day the Dānavas spied Kaca in the forest, herding cows. Angry to see him, they slew him in secret, out of enmity for Bṛhaspati and for their own protection. After killing him, they cut him into little pieces which they gave to the jackals, while the cows went home without their cowherd.

When Devayānī saw the cows coming out of the forest without Kaca, she said to her father, the Bhārgava, "O lord, you have offered the *agnihotra,* and the sun has set; but the cows have returned without their keeper, for Kaca is nowhere to be seen! Apparently he has either been captured or killed! Truly I cannot live without him!"

Śukra responded, "I shall restore him to life by saying 'come here!' " And so he pronounced the revivifying spell to summon Kaca. At the summons, Kaca, son of the wise Bṛhaspati, came running from some distance and bowed to Śukra, exclaiming, "I was killed by Rākṣasas!"

Once again, as it happened, the brahmin Kaca went to the forest, chanting the eternal Veda, this time to gather flowers at the request of Devayānī. When the Dānavas saw him picking flowers in the forest, they killed him again. This time they ground him into a powder which they gave to the brahmin Śukra in his wine.

Once more Devayānī said to her father, "I can't find Kaca whom I sent to gather flowers. Either he has died or he has been murdered! Truly, I cannot live without him!"

"Daughter," Śukra answered, "Bṛhaspati's son Kaca has indeed gone the way of the dead. Even after I revived him with my knowledge, he has been killed again. What am I to do now? Don't grieve for him, Devayānī! A woman like you should not weep for a mere mortal man when you are attended by brahmins, Brahmā and

Indra, the gods, demons, Vasus and Aśvins, and the whole world, because of the power of my *tapas!* Yet it is impossible for me to restore this brahmin to life after he has been killed a second time."

Devayānī said, "Why should I not lament this son and grandson of a seer, whose grandfather was the most venerable Aṅgiras, whose father is Bṛhaspati, and whose treasure is *tapas?* I love this handsome Kaca, the able *brahmacārin,* rich in *tapas,* always doing something worthy. I shall follow Kaca's path. I shall refuse to eat!"

Thus passionately addressed by Devayānī, the great seer Kāvya answered, "The demons must hate me indeed, for they keep killing my pupils! Those violent Dānavas want to put an end to brahmins, but this is a useless undertaking. Now their end will surely come, for they have killed Kaca. Who can escape punishment for murdering a brahmin? Not even Indra could do that!" Then Śukra called on Kaca for an answer, and he spoke up softly from inside his belly.

"You are in my belly!" cried Śukra, "Who put you there? Speak up, my child!"

"By your grace," replied Kaca, "I remember everything that happened to me, forgetting nothing. I still have my *tapas,* and I recall the terrible pain! O Kāvya, the demons beat me, burned me, and crushed me to powder, and then they gave me to you in your wine to drink. How can the magic of the demons overcome a brahmin's magic while you stand by doing nothing?"

Śukra said, "What can I do to help you now? Kaca can live only if I die. You can see Kaca again, Devayānī, only if my stomach is ripped open!"

So Devayānī answered, "I am consumed by two sorrows that burn like fire: your destruction and the death of Kaca. I shall find no solace if Kaca dies, but without you I cannot go on living either!"

"You are a clever one, son of Bṛhaspati, to whom my Devayānī is so devoted," Śukra said. "Now I shall teach you the knowledge that restores life to the dead, unless you are Indra in the guise of Kaca! For no one but a brahmin can escape from my belly with his life. So I shall teach you now my secret. When you emerge from my stomach, ripping me open, you shall thereby become my son. Then you shall revive me, my child. After you have learned this secret from your teacher, which will bring you wisdom, look to the care of the Dharma!"

Thus the brahmin Kaca learned from his teacher how to revive the dead and, splitting open Śukra's belly, he burst out like a full moon at dusk rising over the white horn of the snowy mountain. And when he saw that store of learning lying dead, Kaca restored his life with the secret knowledge. He then saluted his teacher and announced, "Those who fail to respect the venerable *guru*, who is a treasure among treasures and a beneficent bestower of boons, who is radiant with the brilliance of the snowy mountain, go to wicked worlds, having no refuge."

When Uśanas Kāvya himself saw once again the handsome form of Kaca, whom he had drunk when he was intoxicated with wine, he realized that he had been duped and rendered unconscious by the wine. Rising in anger, he made the following proclamation to the brahmins about drinking wine, "From this time forward, any slow-witted brahmin who commits the sin of drinking wine shall lose his Dharma. He shall be considered equivalent to a brahmin-murderer, to be punished in this world and the next."

After this announcement, that mighty lord, measureless storehouse of the treasure of *tapas*, summoned the stupid Dānavas and said, "You demons are fools! The clever Kaca shall live on as my pupil! He has learned the knowledge of restoring life, and now this brahmin is as powerful as I am, equal to Brahmā himself. Let all worthy brahmins, obedient to their teachers, and all the gods and demons alike obey this injunction against wine, whose limits I have promulgated in the law of brahmins for all the world!"

After living with his *guru* for a thousand years, Kaca gained permission to go to the abode of the gods, as he desired.

# Agastya and Vasiṣṭha

Once long ago Viṣṇu, the primal person, became the son of Dharma and practiced mighty *tapas* in the Gandhamādana mountains. Śakra grew alarmed at his *tapas* and sent Mādhava and Ananga, Spring and Love, along with a bevy of Apsarases, to stop him. But songs, words, and other inducements offered by Love and Spring failed to attract Hari to the objects of the senses, and so Kāma, Madhu and the crowd of women grew discouraged.

To amuse them, the first-born male produced a woman out of his thigh, as a magic trick for the inhabitants of the triple world. And in the presence of the gods, Hari spoke to those two, along with the Apsarases, saying, "This nymph shall be famous in the world as Urvaśī!"*

**Uru* means "thigh."

Mitra then desired Urvaśī and summoned her, saying, "Make love to me!" to which she answered, "Of course." But as that Apsaras with eyes like blue lotuses rose up into the sky, she was grabbed from behind by Varuṇa. She repulsed him, crying, "Mitra chose me for his wife before you did, my lord," to which Varuṇa answered, "Then at least think well of me!"

"All right," she said and fled. But Mitra cursed her, saying, "Since you have taken up the Dharma of a prostitute, go now to the world of men and make love to Purūravas, grandson of Soma!"

Because of this, Mitra and Varuṇa threw their ready semen into a jar of water, from which were born the two divine seers Agastya and Vasiṣṭha.

## Vasiṣṭha and Viśvāmitra

After Hariścandra had been toppled from his throne to go to the abode of the thirty gods, the brilliant priest Vasiṣṭha emerged from his home in the waters. After spending twelve years in the Ganges river, that seer heard all about the actions of Viśvāmitra, about the ruin of Hariścandra, whose deeds were noble, about his dealings with the Caṇḍāla, and how he sold his wife and son. When the blessed, illustrious Vasiṣṭha heard the story, because he was so fond of King Hariścandra he grew angry at the seer Viśvāmitra, saying, "When Viśvāmitra killed my hundred sons I was not so furious as I am now that I have heard how Hariścandra was forced to give up his kingdom, that illustrious, great-souled man, reverent towards gods and brahmins, truthful, tranquil, envying no one, not even his enemies, sinless, with virtue in his soul, that respectful king who relied on me! This king, with his wife, sons and dependents has been reduced to the lowest circumstances, expelled from his kingdom and ruined by Viśvāmitra in a variety of ways. Because of this, I curse that foolish, stubborn enemy of brahmins, that destroyer of sacrifices, to become a heron!"

When he heard that curse, splendid Viśvāmitra, Kauśika's son, cursed him back, saying, "Then you shall become a crane!"

After both of them, the high-born Vasiṣṭha and Viśvāmitra the Kauśika, had been turned into birds by each other's curses, these two of infinite splendor, mighty in strength and bravery, began to fight with each other in the bodies of another species. The crane was 2,000 leagues tall, while the heron was 3,096. As the two valiant birds beat at each other with blows of their wings, their battle terrorized the world.

The heron, shaking its wings, its eyes swollen red with blood, beat at the crane which, craning its neck, slashed at the heron with its talons. Cast loose by the wind that rose from their wings, the mountains tumbled to the ground, and the wealth-giving earth, struck by the falling mountains, began to quake. The trembling of the earth made the ocean's waters flood, and she tipped over to one side, about to plunge into the netherworld.

Living creatures were destroyed—some by the crashing mountains, some by the flooding ocean waters, and others by the earthquake. The whole world was terrified, mindlessly shrieking, "*Hā hā!*" utterly deranged, as the orb of earth overturned.

"O my dear!"

"O my beloved!"

"O my child, run away!"

"I'm standing over here!"

"Beloved!"

"Darling!"

"The mountains are falling; escape quickly!"

While people were confounded in this way, averting their faces in terror, the Grandfather arrived, accompanied by all the gods. That lord of the universe addressed those two furious birds, "Stop fighting! Let the worlds return to normal!" But even when the two birds heard the words of Brahmā, whose origin is unknown, they persisted in their rage and fought on.

When the Grandfather god observed the devastation of the world, he took away the bird natures from those seers for their own benefit. After they had regained their former bodies and their darker natures had been dispelled, the god Prajāpati spoke to Vasiṣṭha and Viśvāmitra, bull of the Kauśikas, "My beloved Vasiṣṭha and worthy Kauśika, stop this battle that you began in your ignorant forms as birds. Both your fighting and the results of King Hariścandra's Royal Consecration are destroying the earth! Indeed, the excellent Kauśika has done no harm to this king, O brahmin, for in helping him to attain heaven, he has been his benefactor. You are both creating obstacles to your *tapas* by your passionate anger, so give it up! And good luck, for brahmin power shall prevail."

At his words, the two of them grew ashamed, and embracing one another with affection, they forgave each other. Then, worshiped by the gods, they all went home, Brahmā to his place, Vasiṣṭha to his abode, and the Kauśika, Viśvāmitra, to his hermitage.

# KINGS

## Pṛthu and the Milking of the Earth

Long ago there was a Prajāpati in the lineage of Svāyambhuva, the Self-Existent, named Anga who married Sunīthā, the hideous daughter of Mṛtyu.* Their son was a mighty king, called Vena, who was prone to wicked and lawless behavior. Spreading his evil ways around the world, he even stole the wives of other men. When the great seers begged him to restore Dharma in the world, he refused. And so, fearing anarchy, they killed him with a curse.

Then those irreproachable brahmins churned his body with their power, and races of foreigners, black as collyrium, were produced from that part of him that had come from his ugly mother's body. And from the portion which came from Anga's body arose a righteous man, for Anga had practiced virtue. This man sprang from Vena's right hand, carrying a bow, arrows and mace, his body radiating a heavenly brilliance and sporting a jewelled armor and upper-arm bracelets. And so, due to wide-ranging effort, Pṛthu, the "wide-ranger", was born. Even after his consecration as king by the brahmins, he continued to practice intense *tapas*.

Through a boon of Viṣṇu, Pṛthu became the ruler of the world. When he saw that there was no Dharma, no study of the Veda and no sacrifice on earth, that infinitely powerful king angrily made ready to set it afire with his arrow. But the earth took the shape of a cow and began to run away.

When Pṛthu, his bow aflame, pursued her, she came to a stop and cried out, "What am I to do?" "O faithful one," he answered, "fulfill the needs of all the standing and moving creatures of the world, at once!" And earth said, "So be it."

The king then made Manu Svāyambhuva earth's calf† and milked her with his own hands, whereupon the pure food that nourishes all creatures was produced. When the cow was milked by the seers with Soma as the calf and Bṛhaspati as the milker, they produced the milk which was *tapas* in the bowl which was the Vedas. Then earth was milked by the Vedas with Mitra as the milker and Indra as the calf,

*Death.
†Devout Hindus milk cows only when the calves are present.

and invigorating power was the milk that was produced in the golden bowl of the gods. And in the silver vessel of the Fathers, Svadhā appeared when Antaka was the milker and Yama the calf. Dhṛtarāṣṭra milked earth, with Takṣaka as the calf, to produce poisonous milk in the bottle-gourd jar of the snakes. When earth was milked by the demons into an iron pot, the milk was Maya, the oppressor of Śakra, by whom illusion was set in motion, with Prahlāda Vairocana as the calf and Dvimukha as the milker.

When, of old, the Yakṣas milked the earth, seeking invisibility, with Vaiśravaṇa as the calf, they produced milk in a raw earthen pot, O king. And when Sumālī was the calf and Raupyanābha the milkman, earth was milked by the ghosts and goblins to yield a bloody membrane. Perfumes appeared in a vessel made of lotus leaves when the Gandharvas and hosts of Apsarases milked earth; Caitraratha was the calf, and Vararuci, learned in the knowledge of the dance, the milker. Earth was milked by the mountains to produce all kinds of precious stones and heavenly herbs in a stone bowl, with Mt. Meru as the milker and Mt. Himālaya the calf. The trees milked earth for new shoots, with the Śāla tree, full of blossoms and creepers, as the milker, in a bowl of Palaśa wood, and with the fig tree, most generous of all the trees, as the calf. And earth was milked by others, too, each for whatever he most desired.

While Pṛthu ruled his kingdom there was long life, prosperity and happiness for all. There was no poverty, sickness or evil in the reign of Pṛthu, no misfortune and no fear. People were always happy, knowing neither pain nor sorrow. The great king uprooted the mighty mountains with the tip of his bow in order to level the surface of the earth for the welfare of his people. There were no cities, villages or fortresses, no weapons and no wanton destruction. There was no unhappiness and no interest in the pursuit of success. In the reign of King Pṛthu people lived entirely within the Dharma.

These are the results of the milking of the earth which I have told you. And so at all sacrifices and *śrāddhas,* one who knows what I have just related should put in everybody's pots exactly what they want. Because earth thus became the daughter of the law-abiding Pṛthu, and because she won his affection, she is called Pṛthivī by the wise.

# Ilā and Sudyumna

Before Manu had children, his lordly priest Vasiṣṭha, it is told, performed an oblation to Mitra and Varuṇa in order to secure offspring for him. Manu's wife Śraddhā, who was keeping a milking vow, approached the *hotar,* prostrated herself and begged for a daughter. When summoned by the *adhvaryu* for the recitation, the *hotar* had her plea so heavily on his mind that he made a mistake in pronouncing the demand-for-the-oblation. Because of the *hotar's* mistake a girl by the name of Ilā was born.

When he saw the girl, Manu said to his guru, not too cheerfully, "Reverend, how has this ritual of you brahmins, who are supposed to know the Brahman, come to be perverted? Aho, woe! There should not have been any distortion of the rite. You know the *mantras,* you have *tapas,* your evil has been burnt away—how then could a falsifying perversion of the intention of the rite have occurred among you who are like gods?"

The blessed great-grandfather had been aware of the *hotar's* error, and upon hearing Manu's words he replied, "The distortion of the intention is due to an error by your *hotar.* Nevertheless I shall take measures, under my own power, to ensure that you have good offspring." Thus resolved, the famous priest gave praise to the Primordial Person, in order to change Ilā into a man. The blessed lord Hari was satisfied and gave a boon, and it was because of that boon that Ilā became the man Sudyumna.

One day Sudyumna roamed in the forest on a hunt. He was accompanied by a few ministers, mounted on a horse from Sindh, and held a bow and marvelous arrows. Thus armed, the hero rode northward in pursuit of deer. He entered the Sukumāra Forest at the foot of Mt. Meru, where Śiva was gallivanting with Umā. Scarcely had Sudyumna, that slayer of enemy hordes, entered the forest before he saw himself changed into a woman and his stallion into a mare. All the men in his party saw with consternation their own sex changed, and they stared at one another.

"How did this country come by this feature? Who gave it that?" asked the king to whom the story was being told, "Answer my question, for I am curious in the extreme!" And Śukra told the story.

Once the seers of good vows came there to visit Śiva, and they made space light up so that all darkness was dispelled. When Ambikā saw them she was greatly embarrassed, for she was naked, and she hurriedly rose from her husband's lap to put on her skirt. The seers, upon witnessing the self-indulgence of the fondling couple, turned away and went on to the hermitage of Nara and Nārāyaṇa. Lord Śiva wished to do his beloved a favor and said, "Whoever enters this spot henceforth shall become a woman!" Thenceforth men have avoided this forest.

Sudyumna, a woman now, roamed through that forest with her

followers. Then, when she came in the vicinity of his hermitage, Budha saw the lovely maiden surrounded by her women, and he fell in love with her. The fine-browed maiden returned his love, and Budha, the son of King Soma, became her husband and he begot on her a son, Purūravas.

King Sudyumna, who had been changed into a woman, thereupon remembered his family teacher Vasiṣṭha; so we have heard. When he saw the state Sudyumna was in he was overcome with pity, and he hastened to Śiva seeking to restore Sudyumna's manhood. Gratified, the blessed lord, who wished him well but also wanted to keep his own pledge true, spoke as follows, "Your relation shall be a man one month and a woman the other. Under this condition he shall govern the earth as he pleases."

Henceforward, having by the grace of his *guru* regained intermittent manhood, Sudyumna ruled the earth. But his subjects did not love him. He had three sons: Utkala, Gaya and Vimala, who became kings in the South and had a loving regard for the Dharma. When the time was ripe, the Lord King of Pratiṣṭhāna made over his realm to his son Purūravas and retired to the forest.

## Purūravas and Urvaśī

The nymph Urvaśī made up her mind to live in the world of men after she had been cursed by Mitra and Varuṇa. There she saw the splendid king Purūravas, who was most generous, virtuous, a mighty sacrificer, truthful, handsome and intelligent. At the mere sight of him she lost all pride, lost her interest in the delights of heaven, and thought only of him with devotion. And when he saw her who surpassed all women in loveliness with her delicacy and charm, her coquettish ways, her laughter and her other virtues, he could think only of her. Enraptured with each other, gazing only at one another, the two of them forgot every other purpose in life.

King Purūravas spoke boldly to Urvaśī, "I love you, woman of the beautiful brow! Be kind to me, and love me too!" Thus addressed, Urvaśī answered, overcome with modesty, "All right, if you will meet my conditions." At her words, he spoke again, "Tell me the conditions." And she replied, "These two lambs near my bedside are like by own children; do not take them away. Also, I must never see you naked. And I shall eat only *ghī*!" To these the king agreed, saying "So be it!"

And so the king, his joy increasing every day, made love with her for 60,000 years in Alakā, Kubera's abode, in the groves of Citraratha, amid clusters of pure lotuses, in beautiful lake Mānasa, and elsewhere. Urvaśī, too, her love increasing every day, lost her desire for heaven because of her happiness with him. But without Urvaśī the world of the gods had lost its charm for the Apsarases, Siddhas and Gandharvas.

Then one night Viśvāvasu, aware of the contract between Urvaśī and Purūravas, in the company of his Gandharvas, stole one of the lambs from their bedside. Urvaśī heard its bleating as it was carried away through the sky and cried out, Who has stolen my son? I am without a protector! To whom can I go for refuge!"

When the king heard this he did not get up, because he thought, "The goddess will see me naked!" So the Gandharvas stole the other lamb too, and sped away. When Urvaśī heard the bleating of the second lamb as it was carried away, she grew most upset and cried out again in anguish, "I have no protector! I have no husband! I am dependent on a coward!" So the king, seeing it was dark, indignantly grabbed up his sword and cried out, "Stop thief! You're dead!" And he attacked.

Just then the Gandharvas produced a brilliant flash of lightning so that Urvaśī saw the king undressed. Instantly she disappeared, her contract broken. And the Gandharvas returned to heaven, leaving the lambs behind.

The king, excited and most happy of heart, led the two lambs home, but he failed to find Urvaśī. Not seeing her there, he roamed around naked, looking like a madman, until he came to Kurukṣetra where he found her with four other Apsarases in a pond full of lotuses. Still crazed, he sang out this many-syllabled hymn, "O wife, stay with me! You who are so terrible to my heart, stay! You who have deceived me with words, stay!"

"Stop this unseemly behavior, mighty king!" replied Urvaśī. "I am pregnant. Return here at the end of a year when your child is to be born. Then I shall spend the night with you." And the king went home, happy at her words.

Urvaśī then told the story to the Apsarases, "This is the fine man with whom I lived for all this time, and whom I loved." When they heard this, the Apsarases exclaimed, "Well done! He has a beautiful body! We should like to live with him too, for all time!"

When a year had passed King Purūravas returned. And Urvaśī bore him a healthy son. After giving him the child, she spent one night with him, and she became pregnant again; this happened five times. Then she said to the king, "Out of love for me, all the Gandharvas wish to give you a boon, great king. So choose a boon!" The king replied, "All my enemies are conquered, my faculties are unimpaired, I have a fine family, and my army and treasury are limitless.

There is nothing further to win except the right to share Urvaśī's world. I want to spend all my time with Urvaśī!"

When he had finished speaking, the Gandharvas gave Purūravas a pan with fire in it, and said to him, "You are a man who observes sacred tradition. If you want to share the world of Urvaśī, then divide this fire into three parts and make sacrifices. By doing this you shall win your desire without fail." Thus admonished, he took the fire-pan and left.

In the middle of the forest he thought, "Alas! What have I done? I am a real fool! I have carried off the fire-pan instead of Urvaśī!" So he left the pan of fire in the woods and went back to his own city. But there, in the middle of the night, unable to sleep, he thought, "That fire-pan the Gandharvas gave me so that I might share Urvaśī's world—I left it in the woods! I had better return to where I left it and retrieve it!" But when he got there, it was nowhere to be seen.

On the spot where he had left the fire-pan there had grown up a *śamī* tree entwined with an *aśvattha* tree. When he saw this, he thought, "That pan of fire that I left here has turned into these trees! Since this is the form that fire has taken, I shall take them both and return to my city. I shall make their wood into fire-drills, and worship the fire that springs from them!"

So he returned home and fashioned fire-sticks. Counting with pieces of wood the size of a finger's width, he chanted the Gāyatrī *mantra*, marking each syllable that he recited with a piece of wood.

Having produced fire with the drilling sticks, he divided it into three fires and made a sacrifice according to Vedic custom, intending as the result to share Urvaśī's world. After offering numerous fire sacrifices by the rule, he attained the heaven of the Gandharvas and was united with Urvaśī at last.

# Hariścandra and His Son

Hariścandra, who was childless, dejectedly sought refuge with Varuṇa at the advice of Nārada, saying, "O lord, may a son be born to me. If he be a man child, great lord, I shall sacrifice him to you." "So be it," said Varuṇa, and a son Rohita was born to him.

"A son has been born to you, so sacrifice him to me!"

"A victim is not fit for sacrifice before it is over ten days old."

So when the child was past ten days old, Varuṇa returned and said, "Sacrifice!" He replied, "The victim is fit only when its teeth are grown."

"It's teeth are grown now, so sacrifice!"

He replied, "When its milk teeth have fallen out, it is fit for sacrifice."

"Its teeth have fallen out, so sacrifice!"

"The victim is pure when new teeth have come out."

"They have come out now, so sacrifice!"

"King, a kṣatriya is a pure victim only when he can bear armor."

Thus was the god beseeched by Hariścandra, who was stalling for time out of love for his son, for his heart was constrained by his affection. And the god looked at him.

Rohita, recognizing what his father was trying to do, and eager to save his life, took up his bow and repaired to the forest. Upon hearing that his father had been afflicted by Varuṇa with a swollen belly, Rohita returned to the village, but Indra stopped him. Śakra ordered Rohita to make a saintly tour of the earth with visits to places of pilgrimage, and he lived in the forest for a year. The slayer of Vṛtra returned to him likewise in the second, third, fourth and fifth year, disguised as an aged brahmin, with the same advice.

After spending the sixth year in the forest, Rohita came back to his town and bought from Ajigarta his second son, Śunaḥśepa, and presented him to his father, after saluting him, as the victim for his sacrifice. Hariścandra, well spoken of among the great and of wide renown, worshiped Varuṇa and other gods with a human sacrifice, and he lost his swollen belly. At the ritual Viśvāmitra was the *hotar*, the self-controlled Jamadagni the *adhvaryu*, Vasiṣṭha the *brahman*, and Āyāsya the *udgātar*.

Gratified, Indra gave him a chariot made of gold—Śunaḥśepa's story shall be related later on. Beholding the king's and the queen's steadfastness in keeping his word, Viśvāmitra was greatly pleased and bestowed on him an inimpeded course, and the power to dissolve his mind in earth, earth in water, water in fire, fire in wind, wind in ether, ether in the source of being, and that source in the Great Self. Within this he meditated upon a fraction of wisdom, burnt with that wisdom his ignorance; and having transcended that fraction through his consciousness of the bliss of *nirvāṇa*, he remained, unfettered, with his own being, ineffable and beyond thought.

# Hariścandra and Viśvāmitra

Long ago in the Tretā Age there lived the noble sage-king Hariścandra, virtuous of soul, who was an earth-protector of refulgent fame. Under the rule of that king there were neither famine nor disease, no untimely death among people, and no citizens with a taste for evil. No one became drunk with wealth, power, *tapas* or wine, and no females were born who failed to reach maturity.

Once when that long-armed king was hunting game in the forest he heard the sound of women's voices repeatedly crying, "Help!" Abandoning the deer, the king said, "Don't be afraid! What fool dares to perpetrate evil while I rule?"

Meanwhile, the dreadful Vighnarāj, who obstructs every undertaking, was following that outcry, thinking, "The valorous Viśvāmitra, who practices mighty *tapas*, maintaining his vows, has now successfully mastered the Sciences, something Bhava and the other gods have not ever been able to do. Being under the control of such a self-restrained seer who observes the disciplines of patience, silence and thought, the Sciences are crying out in fear. What can I do? 'The chief of the Kauśikas* is powerful and we are weak compared to him!' Thus the frightened females are lamenting. This problem seems to me most difficult to resolve! But on the other hand, King Hariścandra has appeared, repeating, 'Don't be afraid!' Let me enter into him at once; then I shall succeed as I desire."

After Vighnarāj had occupied the king's body, according to his plan, the king spoke out in anger, "Who is this wicked man who binds fire in the hem of his garment while I am present as the king, radiant with power, heat and glory? Now he shall endure the long sleep of death, for I shall pierce all his limbs with my arrows which obscure the heavens when loosed from my bow!"

Viśvāmitra was enraged to hear these words from the king, and at the anger of that great seer, the Sciences left him in a flash. But when the king, now deserted by Vighnarāj, saw Viśvāmitra, that treasury of *tapas*, he grew afraid, and began to tremble like the leaf of an *aśvattha* tree. The seer cried out, "Stand up, you wretch!" to which the king who had prostrated himself obsequiously, replied, "O blessed lord, this is not my fault. It is my Dharma. Do not be angry with me, seer, for being devoted to my duty! According to the laws of Dharma, a king who knows his duty is to give gifts, to protect, and to raise his bow to wage war."

"To whom are you supposed to give? Who is to be protected? And with whom must you wage war, O king?" replied Viśvāmitra, "Tell me at once if you respect Dharma!"

Hariścandra answered, "Gifts are to be given to the eminent brahmins, then to the poor. Those who are afraid are always to be protected. And war is to be fought against one's enemies."

*Viśvāmitra.

"If you, as king, fully observe the Dharma of kings, then give me my due reward, for I am a brahmin eager to retire."

With inner excitement, the king heard these words; he considered himself reborn, and made this reply to the Kauśika, "Tell me without hesitation what I am to give to you, O holy one! Know that it is already given, however difficult to acquire, whether it be gold, or money, my son, my daughter's dead body, my kingdom, my city, my fortune, or my life itself—whatever your heart desires!"

"O king," said Viśvāmitra, "What you have offered as a gift is more than acceptable. First, give me the fee for a Royal Consecration."

"O brahmin," answered the king, "I shall give you that fee. Now choose whatever else you want, lion among brahmins!"

"This earth with its oceans, mountains, villages and hamlets, O hero; all of your kingdom, complete with your chariots, horses and elephants! Also your granary, your treasury, and everything else you own, O faultless one, except your wife, your son, your own body, and your merit which always follows the doer. What more is there to say, knower of all Dharmas? Give all this to me!"

Happy of heart, his face serene, the king said "So be it!" folding his hands in reverence at the speech of that seer.

Then Viśvāmitra spoke again, "If you give everything to me—your kingdom, the earth, your army and your money—who shall be king, O royal seer, when I, an ascetic, sit on the throne?"

"At the moment when I give you the earth, O brahmin, you become its master, let alone the king!"

"If you have given me the entire earth, O king," said Viśvāmitra, "then you must leave this territory which is mine, abandoning your sword belt and all your ornaments, and donning tree-bark garments, along with your wife and son!"

Saying, "So be it!" and so doing, the king set out to leave with his wife Śaibyā and his own little son. But as he was leaving, Viśvāmitra barred his way, saying, "Where are you going without first giving me the Royal Consecration fee?"

"I have given you my kingdom free and clear!" answered the king, "All that is left, O brahmin, are these three bodies!"

"Nevertheless," said Viśvāmitra, "you still owe me the sacrificial fee, for a broken promise is fatal, especially a promise made to a brahmin. As long as brahmins take pleasure in performing the Royal Consecration, O king, then they should receive their fee. 'Promised gifts are to be given, assassins must be fought, and the miserable must be protected.' This you have already declared!"

So Hariścandra answered, "O lord, it is not possible at present, but I shall give you the fee in the course of time. Be kind to me, O brahmin-seer, and take into account my truthful nature!"

"How long shall I have to wait for you, O lord of men? Tell me at once, or else the fire of my curse shall consume you!"

"In a month," said Hariścandra, "I shall give you your fee, O brahmin-seer. Right now I have no money. Please grant me your indulgence."

"Go then, fine king," said Viśvāmitra, "observe your Dharma. May your path be auspicious and free from enemies!" And so the king departed, having been given leave, followed by his beloved wife who was not accustomed to going on foot.

When the townspeople saw their noble king leaving the city with his wife and son, they followed him and cried out, "Why are you leaving us, protector? We are burdened by constant troubles! You are a virtuous man, O king, the benefactor of the townspeople! Remain our leader, royal seer, if you observe Dharma! Stay for a little longer, O chief of kings! With the bees of our eyes we drink in your lotus face; when shall we see you again—you whom kings precede and follow on your way?

"It used to be that his wife followed behind him, carrying his little son, while his servants rode in front, mounted on their elephants. But now this same chief of kings, Hariścandra, goes on foot! What will become of your delicate face with its lovely brow, fine skin and noble nose when it is coarsened with dirt from the road? Stop, stop, O best of kings, and observe your Dharma!

"Compassion is the highest virtue, especially for a kṣatriya. What benefit are our wives, our children, our wealth or our grain, protector? We shall leave all this behind to follow you like a shadow. Alas, protector! Woe, mighty king! Alack, master! Why are you deserting us? Wherever you go, we shall follow. Wherever you are, there lies our happiness. Whatever city you live in, there is our heaven, O king!"

The king was overcome with sorrow at the townspeople's words, as he stood there on the road full of compassion for them. But Viśvāmitra saw him there, upset by the people's talk, and he approached him, eyes wide with anger and impatience, saying "Shame on you! Your behavior is wicked! You are a deceitful man of crooked speech. Having given me your kingdom, now you want it back!" At the seer's harsh words, the king shook and cried out, "I am going!" And so speaking, he left at once, dragging his wife by the hand.

As Hariścandra pulled his delicate wife along by the hand, the Kauśika beat her with a wooden stick. Suffering greatly to see his wife so abused, the king cried out, "I'm leaving!" and lapsed into silence. After Viśvāmitra's speech, the king left slowly, followed by his wife Śaibyā and his little son.

The king went to the heavenly city of Vārāṇasī, where the attendants of the trident-bearing lord Śiva announced, "This place is not to be enjoyed by mere men!" And when that miserable man who had been traveling on foot with his loyal wife entered the city, he saw Viśvāmitra standing there in front of him. Hariścandra bowed respectfully to that great seer, joined his palms and said to him, "Accept my life and the lives of my wife and son as your hospitality gift, O seer; they are at your disposal. Permit us to obey your wishes!"

But Viśvāmitra answered, "The month is up, O royal seer. Now give me the Royal Consecration fee, if you recall your promise!"

"O brahmin of undying *tapas,* the month is over only today, and half of the day still remains. Wait only this long!"

"All right, great king. I shall return later. But if you do not pay me today, I shall curse you!" And saying this, the brahmin left while the king worried, "How shall I give him the promised fee? Where are my rich friends? Where now is my own wealth? I do not have enough money; how can I escape further degradation? Shall I give up my life? But if I do, to which region shall I go, dying a worthless man who has not kept his promise? As a wicked thief of brahmin property, I shall become a louse, the lowest of the low. Or I shall become a servant; it is better to sell myself!"

Then his wife, in a tear-choked voice, spoke to the king who was upset and preoccupied, his face downcast, "Don't be unhappy, O great king, but observe your truth. For a man devoid of truth is to be avoided like a burning ground. There is no higher Dharma for a man, or so they say, than maintaining his truthfulness, O tiger among men! . . .

"I have borne a child, O king, fulfilling my purpose, for the wives of noble men exist to bear children. Sell me and give the money to the brahmin!"

The king fainted when he heard her words. When he regained his wits, he moaned in misery, "You have said a most dreadful thing to me, beloved. Have you forgotten your happy talks with me, wretch that I am? Alas, how can you say this, O sweet-smiling woman? How can I do the unspeakable thing that you have said?" And, saying this, the noble man cried out. "Woe! Alas!" over and over again, and then fell unconscious to the ground. . . .

Meanwhile the great ascetic Viśvāmitra had arrived, in fury like the End of Time, seeking his booty. When he saw the king lying senseless on the ground, he sprinkled him with water and said, "Get up, great king, and give me the money that I seek! The unhappiness of one who owes a debt increases every day!" Revived by the icy water, the king regained his wits, but seeing Viśvāmitra, he fell again into a faint. At this the seer flew into a rage. Reviving him again, the fine brahmin seer said this to the king, "Give me my fee, if you observe

Dharma! By truth the sun shines; earth is upheld by truth; truth is the ultimate Dharma; on truth is even heaven held aloft. If a thousand Horse Sacrifices are weighed against the truth, it will outweigh even them. But what is the use of talking nicely to a cruel man who is ignoble, whose intentions are base, and whose speech is lies? Righteousness prevailed when you were king, or so they say. If I do not receive my fee today, O king, then when the sun strikes the western mountain I shall most certainly pronounce a curse on you!" So speaking, the brahmin left. And the poor, dispossessed and fleeing king, afflicted by that brutal, rich man, was sick with fear.

His wife spoke up again, saying, "Do as I told you, lest, burned by his curse, you die!" And so, at her repeated urging, Hariścandra said, "Dear one, I shall be ruthless and sell you. That which even the cruelest of men cannot do, that shall I do, if I am able to pronounce the awful words!"

Thus speaking to his wife, the wretched man went to the city and announced, his eyes and throat streaming with tears, "*Bhoḥ! Bhoḥ!* people of the town! Hear what I have to say! Do you want to know who I am? I am inhuman, base, either a monster or a Rākṣasa, or even more wicked than that! For I have come to sell my wife, rather than give up my own life. If anyone among you has use for this woman, who is dearer to me than my own life, as a servant, then let him speak up at once, while I am still alive!"

A certain aged brahmin who was there said to the king, "Hand over that slave girl to me. I shall pay cash, for I am very wealthy. My own dear wife is delicate and cannot work. Therefore give this woman to me! Here is a fitting price appropriate to the skill, beauty and virtue of your wife. Give her to me as my servant!"

At this speech of the brahmin, King Hariścandra's heart was torn with grief, and he said nothing in reply. So the brahmin tied the money in the hem of the king's tree-bark garment, and dragged his wife away by the hair.

When their son Rohitāsya, in his crow's-wing haircut, saw his mother being taken away, he clutched at her garment with his hand and cried aloud. So the queen shrieked, "Let me go, O noble man! Oh let me loose to see my son, for it will be difficult indeed to catch sight of him later on, O friend! Come see me, my child, your mother sold into slavery! But do not touch me, prince, for now I am untouchable to you!" But at her words, and seeing his mother being dragged away, the child ran after her, crying, "Mother!" his eyes filled with tears.

Furious at this, the brahmin kicked the boy who followed. But weeping still, and still crying, "Mother!" he would not let her go.

"Master, be kind to me!" cried the queen, "and also buy my son!

For even though you have purchased me, without him I shall do for you poor work! Indeed, be gracious and kind to unfortunate me. Unite me with my son, like a milch-cow with her calf!"

And so the brahmin answered, "Take this money, and give me the boy. The wages fixed by those who know the Dharmaśāstra for a woman and a man are 100, 1,000, or 100,000, while others say ten million." And tying the money in the hem of the king's garment, he took the boy and tied him up with his mother.

When he saw the two of them being led away, his wife and son, King Hariścandra moaned miserably, sighing hotly over and over again. "Now has my wife become a slave, she who has never before been looked upon by wind, sun, moon or the populace! And my son, with his delicate hands and fingers, who was born into the Solar Dynasty, has been sold. Shame on me, wicked man that I am! Alas, beloved wife! Alas, dear son! My dishonorable conduct has made me a slave to fate, and still I do not die!" While the king was lamenting, the brahmin disappeared, swiftly conducting the two of them through the tall trees and lofty houses.

Then Viśvāmitra arrived, asking for the money. So Hariścandra turned it over to him. When he saw the trifling amount that had come from the sale of the queen, the Kauśika was furious, addressing the king who was overcome with grief, "You rotten kṣatriya, if you consider this to be an adequate payment for me, then you shall soon observe the mighty power of my accomplished *tapas*, my spotless brahmin-nature, my dreadful majesty and my flawless learning!"

"I shall give you more, my lord," pleaded the king, "Wait just a little longer, for now I have nothing, since I have just sold my wife and son."

"A quarter of the day remains, O king. I shall wait for this. Now say no more." And speaking these harsh and cruel words to the king, the angry Kauśika took the money and left at once.

When Viśvāmitra had gone, the king, submerged in fear and sorrow, resolved to sell himself, and cried aloud, his face turned down, "If anyone wants to buy me for his slave, let him speak up quickly, while the sun still shines!"

At this, Dharma suddenly appeared, wearing the body of Caṇḍāla.* He was stinking, ugly, coarse, hairy, and ruthless, with projecting teeth. He was black, potbellied, with haggard yellow eyes and rough speech. Carrying a bunch of birds, he was adorned with garlands taken from the bodies of the dead. In his hand he bore a skull, and he was long-faced, horrible and ghastly as he shouted raucously aloud.

*An outcaste.

Surrounded by a pack of dogs, he was hideous, and he held a club in his hand.

"I want you now!" the Caṇḍāla said. "State the price, whether a trifle or a fortune, for which you can be bought!" Staring at him, awful as he was, with his fierce aspect, crude speech and uncouth manner, the king asked him, "Who are you?"

"I am a Caṇḍāla," the Caṇḍāla replied, "known in this fine city as Pravīra. I am the notorious executioner of criminals, who gathers woolen blankets from the dead."

"I don't want to be the slave of a Caṇḍāla, for it is a disgusting thing to be! Better to be burned by the fire of a curse than to submit to the orders of a Caṇḍāla!"

During this speech Viśvāmitra arrived, that treasury of *tapas*. His eyes wide with anger and impatience, he addressed the king, "This Caṇḍāla is offering you a lot of money. Why do you not give all of it to me, for the sacrificial fee?"

"O blessed Kauśika," said Hariścandra, "I know that I was born into the Solar Dynasty. How can I, even in need of money, become a Caṇḍāla's slave?"

"If you do not give me the Caṇḍāla's money you earn from the sale of yourself, then in time I shall surely curse you. This I guarantee!"

King Hariścandra, fearing for his life, seized the seer's feet, and cried out in great distress, "Have mercy on me! I am a slave! I am in pain! And I am loyal to no one but you! O brahmin seer, be kind to me! It is evil for me to associate with a Caṇḍāla! I shall be your servant, for the remainder of the fee, O tiger among seers, following your will in all I do, obeying your command!"

"If you are my servant," Viśvāmitra answered, "then I shall sell you to the Caṇḍāla as a slave, for a large sum of money!"

"If the brahmin Kauśika can be satisfied, then take me now and I shall be your slave," the king replied.

And so the Caṇḍāla said, "You have protected the earth, dotted with many villages, for the extent of a hundred leagues. But now you are in bondage to the Kauśika." So speaking, the dog-cooker, happy at heart, gave the money to Viśvāmitra, and after tying up the king, who was bewildered by the blows of a stick, his faculties deranged, grieving as he was over the separation from his beloved kin, the Caṇḍāla led him to his hamlet.

King Hariścandra, living in the ghetto of the Caṇḍāla, sang this song, morning, noon and night: "I can picture my young wife, with her wretched face, and in front of her, our own unhappy son. Burdened with sorrow, she remembers me, thinking, 'Shall the king come to set us free? Having gotten enough money to pay the brahmin, surely there is some left!' But that doe-eyed woman doesn't know me; worse has been done! For I have lost my kingdom; I have been abandoned by my friends; I have sold my wife and son; and I have become a Caṇḍāla. Alas! This is the sum of my misfortunes!" Continually inhabiting this state of mind, he thought of his beloved son and the wife who filled his heart, bereft of everything and profoundly miserable.

After a while King Hariścandra became a robber of clothes from the dead, following the orders of his master on the burning-ground. He was thus commanded by that Caṇḍāla who was a thief of dead men's clothes, "Stay here day and night watching for the arrival of corpses. One-sixth per corpse is to be given to the king; three parts are mine; and two portions are your wages." Thus ordered, he went to the place of the dead, which was in the southern quarter of Vārāṇasī.

That burning ground was filled with ghastly sounds, covered with hundreds of jackals, strewn with the skulls of corpses and reeking with evil-smelling smoke. It was crowded with ghosts, goblins, ghouls, witches and Yakṣas, filled with the quarreling of great *gaṇas* and Bhūtas, thronged with vultures and jackals, circled by packs of dogs, strewn with piles of bones, and suffused with a nauseating stench. It was pervaded with the awful uproar of the cries from friends of the numerous dead: "Alas, my son; my friend; my relative; my brother; my child; my darling!" and "Woe, my husband; my sister; my mother! Alas, my maternal uncle; my grandfather; my maternal grandfather; my grandson, alas! Where have you gone, my kinsmen? Oh, come back to me!"

On this burning ground was heard the monstrous outcry of those who were wailing in this manner. And there the eyes of corpses stood open, unblinking, while their relatives stood, eyes closed, along the row of pyres. The place was filled with the crackling sound of burning flesh, marrow and fat—the blackened half-charred corpses, showing their rows of teeth in ghastly grins amid the fires, were cackling, "This is the body's final state!"

The crackling of the fires, the cawing of the crows, the wailing of relatives dismayed by the delight of the Pukkasa marauders, and the monstrous, horrible merry-making of the ghosts, goblins, ghouls, *gaṇas* and Rākṣasas sounded like the roaring at the end of the Eon. On that burning ground great heaps of buffalo and cow dung were piled up, along with mounds of ashes and heaps of bones. With crow droppings on the various offerings, wreaths and lamps, and the many dreadful sounds, that burning ground was like the depths of hell. Impenetrable due to terrifying shrieks, it resounded with unholy howls of jackals with their bellies set afire, frightening even to fear itself. Because of the dense crowds of the dead, that burning ground was ghastly with its clamor and lamentations.

There the miserable King Hariścandra arrived, trembling with fear and stricken with grief. "Alas, my servants, ministers and brahmins!" he cried, "Where has my kingdom gone, O creator? O Śaibyā! Alas, my son, my son! Having abandoned me to my misfortune, where have they gone?"

Then repeating over and over again to himself what the Caṇḍāla said, all his limbs rough and filthy, long-haired and smelly, and carrying a flag,* he rushed to and fro with a staff in his hand like death, thinking, "I shall get this price for this corpse. This much is for me; this much goes to the king and this much is for my boss, the Caṇḍāla!" And he raced around in all directions. Thus the king, while still alive, entered into another life.

Covered with rags made of worn-out garments patched together, his face, arms, belly and feet smeared with ashes and dust from the funeral pyres, his hands and fingers sticky with all kinds of fat, marrow and bone, he sighed deeply, intent upon the satisfaction of eating the porridge left for various corpses. His head adorned with trappings made from the wreaths of the dead, he rested neither night nor day, crying incessantly, "O woe is me!" Thus twelve months passed as if they were a hundred years. . . .

Then one day the wife of that king came wailing to the burning ground carrying her son who had been killed by a snake-bite. "Alas, my son!" she cried over and over, thin and wan, out of her mind, her hair hidden under the dust. "Alas, my king!" said the queen, "Now see your dead son lying on the ground, the son you used to watch at play. Now he is dead from the bite of a well-fed snake!"

When he heard the wails of the lamenting woman, the king went quickly over to her, thinking, "Will there be a blanket on the corpse?" He failed to recognize his weeping wife, who due to her suffering during their long separation had become like a woman born into another life. And when that princess looked at the king with his matted locks, at him whose hair used to be so well-groomed, she did not recognize him either, looking as he did like a withered tree.

Spotting that child who bore the marks of a noble person, now wrapped in a funeral cloth after being bitten by a poisonous snake, the king began to think, "This handsome face looks like the orb of the moon, with its noble brow, high-bridged nose and long, black, curly hair. His pair of eyes resembles lotus blossoms, and his lips are red like *bimba* berries. His canine teeth, his wrists and his long arms

*The flag is to identify his untouchable status, as a warning to others.

betoken a long life. His hand is marked with four lines, bearing the signs of barley and the fish. His fine-veined foot has a high arch, and his soft skin bears three navel wrinkles. Alas, how grievous! This boy must have been born into the family of a king! And now he has been brought to this dreadful state by hard-souled death! At the sight of this dead child cradled in his mother's lap, my son Rohitāsya comes to mind, with his lotus eyes. My child should be this same age by now, unless he has been brought under the power of death!"

"Alas, my son," said the queen, "What evil agency has come to envy us so as to cause this monumental sorrow whose end is not yet known? O my husband! O my king! How can you confidently remain somewhere else without coming to comfort sorrowful me? The royal seer Hariścandra has lost his kingdom; he has been abandoned by his friends; and he has sold his wife and son. What more can you do to us, Creator?"

And as she spoke, that king who had fallen from his station, recognized his wife and his dead son. "Could this be my own child, dead?", the king reflected, "How terrible! This is Śaibyā and my son!" So speaking, he wept, consumed with sorrow, and fell into a faint. And then she recognized him, even in his dreadful condition, whereupon she too fell unconscious to the ground, where she lay still. When king and queen regained consciousness, suffering enormously, they wept together, utterly confounded by the burden of their grief. . . .

"O king," then said the queen, "is this a dream or is it real? Tell me what you think, eminent one, for my mind is confused. If this is really happening, O Dharma-knower, then there is no virtue in Dharma, in the worship of brahmins, nor in protecting the earth. There is no Dharma, let alone truth or honesty or benevolence, if you, who have been totally devoted to Dharma, have been toppled from your kingdom!"

At her words, the king began to tell that slender-limbed woman, stammering with hot sighs, how he had come to be a dog-eating Caṇḍāla. And, weeping with hot sighs, that grief stricken woman told him timorously how their son had died. . . .

Then the king constructed a funeral pyre, put his son on top of it, and together with his wife, folded his hands and concentrated on the supreme lord Hari Nārāyaṇa who dwells in the secret hollow of the heart, the lord of gods Vāsudeva, who is without beginning and end, Brahmā, Kṛṣṇa, robed in yellow and holy. As he was meditating on him, all the gods and Vāsava,* who were led by Dharma, rapidly ar-

*Indra.

rived. Approaching the pyre, they all exclaimed, "*Bhoḥ! Bhoḥ*, king! Listen, O lord! This is the Grandfather who stands before you, and holy Dharma himself, as well as all the Sādhyas, Viśvedevas, Maruts, the guardians of the quarters, and the Cāraṇas, the Snakes, Siddhas, Gandharvas, Rudras and Aśvins—all these and many more, and Viśvāmitra, too, who has been until now unable to befriend the triple world. But now even Viśvāmitra wants to offer friendship and good will!" Then he ascended to reach Dharma, Śakra and Gādhi's son Viśvāmitra.

Then Dharma spoke, "Don't commit violence! For I am Dharma and I have come to you, pleased with your patience, your self-restraint, your truthfulness and all your other fine qualities."

And Indra said, "O eminent Hariścandra, I am Śakra who has come to your side. You have won the eternal realms, with your wife and son; heaven, so difficult to gain for other men, has been won by your actions!"

Then from the heavens Indra rained down a shower of flowers, annihilating sudden death, where Hariścandra was standing near the funeral pyre. And a great rain of blossoms, with the sound of celestial kettle-drums, fell on all sides around the gathering of assembled gods.

That son of the great-souled king came to life, with a delicate body and in good health, his mind and faculties clear. King Hariścandra, restored to his fortune, and robed in celestial garments and garlands, at once embraced his son, and so did his wife. His heart immediately flooded with contentment and filled with utmost joy.

Indra addressed him once again, "You shall attain the highest goal, illustrious one, along with your wife and son. Now mount to heaven, as a reward for your good deeds!" . . .

"Praise be to you, king of the gods!" cried Hariścandra, "Hear what I have to say, full of respect, to you who are benevolent and kind. My mind is plunged in sorrow, for the people of my city in Kosala are still there. How can I go to heaven now, while leaving them behind? Abandoning one's loyal followers is said to be a mighty sin equal only to the murder of a brahmin, the killing of a teacher, the slaughter of a cow and the taking of a woman's life. I cannot see happiness in this life or the next for one who deserts his loyal, devoted, innocent supporters, who must not be forsaken. Therefore, O Śakra, you go to heaven without me. Only if they go to heaven with me, lord of the gods, shall I go; if they cannot, I shall go to hell with them." . . .

"It shall be as you desire," said Śakra, lord of the three worlds, and Dharma, both of them with gracious hearts, and also Viśvāmitra, Gādhi's son. Then all of them sped quickly to Hariścandra's city, where the four castes were upheld. With the lord of the gods at his side, the king began to speak: "Heaven, so difficult to attain, has been won by all of you, through Dharma's kindness. Go there at once!" And having descended from heaven to earth with a myriad chariots, Indra said to the people of Ayodhyā, "Ascend to heaven!"

After listening with affection to the speech of Indra and the king, the great ascetic Viśvāmitra led out Rohitāsya, the prince, and consecrated him as king in the beautiful city called Ayodhyā, before the gods, seers and Siddhas. Then all the king's friends, happy and fortunate, together with the king, accompanied by their wives, sons and servants, mounted up to heaven; step by step, chariot to chariot they climbed aloft. And King Hariścandra was thrilled with utmost joy.

After attaining surpassing well-being through those chariots, the king sat in the structure of a heavenly city, surrounded by fine ramparts and walls, while Uśanas, illustrious teacher of the Daityas, witnessing his happiness, and wise in the elements and purposes of all knowledge, sang there a verse:

"There has never been,
nor shall there be,
a king like Hariścandra!"

# Parikṣit

At one time King Parikṣit, wandering about in the forest on a hunt with bow in hand, became very tired, hungry and thirsty while in pursuit of a stag. Finding no water he entered a hermitage, where he saw a hermit sitting tranquilly with his eyes closed. He had stopped the functioning of his senses, breath, mind and spirit, and was totally at rest; he had reached the stage beyond the three stages of consciousness, and so had become Brahman without qualification. From this hermit, crowned with a disheveled hair tuft and covered with a hide of *ruru* deer, the king now requested water for a parched palate. Not being offered so much as straw, or a place to sit, not shown welcome and hospitality, he felt himself slighted and became angry. Unprecedented fury and resentment toward that brahmin suddenly took hold of the king, who was afflicted with hunger and thirst. With the tip of his bow he irately put a dead snake on the seer's shoulders and left to return to his city, wondering, "Did he have his eyes closed because all his faculties were suspended, or did he fake his trance because he did not want to bother with a rotten king?"

That hermit's son, a highly irascible boy, was playing with other children when he heard about the insult the king had done his father, and he cried, "Fie on the lawlessness of kings, those puffed-up crows, those gods at the doorsill, slaves that insult their masters! That self-styled noble has been appointed doorkeeper by the brahmins: how dare a doorman eat from the same dish inside the house? Now that the blessed Kṛṣṇa has departed as the punisher of the wayward, I myself shall punish those who have broken the dam. Watch my power!"

With these words to his young companions, his eyes bloodshot with rage, he touched the water of the river Kauśikī and hurled the thunderbolt of his curse; "Seven days from now the snake Takṣaka shall at my command bite that transgressor, that burning coal to his family, who insulted my father!" Then the boy went to the hermitage, and when he saw his father with the snake's carcass around his neck, he broke into tears of grief.

Āṅgirasa, when he heard his son's lamentations, opened his eyes slowly and saw the dead snake on his shoulders. He discarded it and asked his son, "Calf, why are you weeping? Who has thwarted you?" His son told him. When the brahmin heard that the king had been cursed undeservedly, he did not approve of his son. "Aho!" he exclaimed, "alas, you have committed a grave offense! For a small slight you have imposed great punishment. Your mind is not ripe yet. A king who is called supreme cannot be measured by other men, for protected by his irresistible power, his subjects enjoy success with nothing to fear. When the title of a king is not heeded—a king whose palm displays the wheel*—all the world is prone to theft and is at once doomed to perish, as undefended as a chariot that has lost its bumper ring. Guilt will be upon us today if, because of the plundered wealth of our king (who expires without issue), the masses, who are mostly robbers, kill or curse one another, and loot cattle, women and properties. If the Āryan Dharma of men, which means behaving according to class and stage of life, and is based on the Veda, dissolves, what is left is miscegenation of the classes—as though they were dogs or monkeys—of people solely motivated by Success and Love. Our king is a famed sovereign who protects the Dharma, himself a great Bhāgavata, a royal seer who has offered up the Horse Sacrifice. He was hungry, thirsty and tired; he did not deserve a curse from us!

"O lord who art the soul of all, pray forgive the evil done by a child, still green of knowledge, to those innocents he ought to have supported! However, even though slighted, cursed, cast off, or even

*In Indian palmistry the outline of a wheel on the palm betokens kingship.

killed, the lord's devotees do not seek revenge, although they have the power!"

Thus the great hermit, who himself had been insulted by the king, did not consider it an outrage, outraged though he was at what his son had done. Truly good people in this world neither revel nor grieve when enemies afflict them with conflict, for their Self transcends the *guṇas*.

Meanwhile the king, reflecting upon the wrong he had done, was quite distressed: "Aho! I have acted ignobly and meanly to this innocent brahmin, whose power was suspended. Surely inescapable disaster shall soon be mine because of my mocking the deity of my *karman*. So be it, but be it upon me who perpetrated the evil, so that henceforth I cannot do it again. This very day may the fire of an irate brahmin family burn down my kingdom, army and ample treasury, lest my criminal mind do even more harm to brahmins, gods and cows!"

While he was thinking this, he heard about the words of the seer's son, and thus knew his doom would befall him through a snake by the name of Takṣaka. He thought it was well that the fierce bite of Takṣaka would soon precipitate the renunciation of one too self-indulgent. Casting off both this world and the next, after having first reflected that indeed they should be relinquished, he sat down by the immortal river, where he committed himself to the service of Kṛṣṇa's feet, intending to fast himself to death. For who about to die would not pay service to that river sanctified by the dust of Kṛṣṇa's feet and bestrewn with rippling *tulasī* leaves, which purifies the world and its kings? . . . And while this god among kings was sitting there starving himself to death, the hosts of gods in heaven gave praise to him and joyously showered him on earth with blossoms and sounded their kettle drums.

# Yayāti

Śuka related that Yati, Yayāti, Saṃyāti, Ayāti, Viyāti and Kṛti were the six sons of Nahuṣa, and they were like the six faculties of the soul. Yati did not want the kingdom which his father left him, because he knew that, when caught in the constraints of sovereignty, a man does not know the Self. When his father was toppled by the brahmins from his rank due to his dastardly designs on Indrāṇī, being thereby doomed to become a boa constrictor, Yayāti became king. He assigned to his younger brothers the four directions. Taking the daughters of Kāvya and Vṛṣaparvan as his wives, he ruled the earth.

The king asked, "The blessed Kāvya was a seer, and Nahuṣa just a kṣatriya. How did this marriage of a kṣatriya with a brahmin woman come about?" So Śuka told the story.

Once, long ago, the blooming daughter of the king of the Dānavas, Śarmiṣṭhā by name, strolled in a city park full of flowering trees and lotus ponds humming with bees. She was in the company of a thousand maidens, including Devayānī, the daughter of Kāvya. Coming to a pool, the lotus-eyed maidens left their fine raiment on the bank and played about splashing one another. Then they saw Śiva coming by with the Goddess on his bull, and the embarrassed girls rose quickly and put on their garments. Unwittingly Śarmiṣṭhā took Devayānī's, mistaking it for her own, and the other said angrily, "Aho! Look at that unbecoming conduct of this slave girl, grabbing what only I may wear, a bitch snatching the offering at the sacrifice! The brahmins have created this world with their *tapas;* they are the mouth of Puruṣa; they hold up the light; they show the safe path. The world protectors, the gods themselves, speak to them with deference; indeed they are the lord, the Universal Soul, the sanctifying abode of Śrī herself! And among such grand brahmins we are Bhṛgus to boot. Her Asura father is our student, and she holds my garment, the slut, like a śūdra the Veda!"

When the *guru*'s* daughter abused her this way, Śarmiṣṭhā, hissing furiously like a snake, replied to her, biting her lip in predicament, "You brag a lot, beggar girl, without knowing how to behave yourself. Isn't it true that you wait on our house like a crow?" While berating Devayānī with such scathing words, although she was her *guru*'s daughter, Śarmiṣṭhā angrily flung her into a well, took her clothes and went home.

It so happened that Yayāti, who was hunting, came by and, being thirsty, saw her in the well. The king gave the naked girl his own upper cloth and compassionately pulled her out by her right hand. In a loving voice Kāvya's daughter said to the hero, "King, conqueror of enemy cities, you have taken my hand! There shall be no more taking of my hand, for it has been taken by you. This marriage of ours has been made by the gods, not man, O hero, since you set eyes on me while I was trapped in this well. No brahmin shall take my hand, king, because of a curse of Bṛhaspati's son Kaca, whom I had cursed first." Yayāti realized that this was something he had not intended, but was offered him by fate. Knowing that his own heart had gone out to her, he accepted her proposal.

When the valiant king had gone, Devayānī tearfully recounted to

*Kāvya.

her father all that Śarmiṣṭhā had said and done. Distressed, the reverent Kāvya condemned his own servitude as priest, and praising the carefree life of pigeons, he left the city with his daughter. But Vṛṣaparvan, when he learned of his *guru*'s contrary mood, prostrated himself on the road with his head at the other's feet to placate him. The blessed Bhārgava, whose anger lasted half a second, told his pupil, "King, fulfill my daughter's wish, for I cannot desert her." When he agreed to that condition, Devayānī voiced her desire, "Wherever I go when my father marries me off, there she shall follow after me as my servant!" Seeing the danger to her people and the gravity of the matter, Śarmiṣṭhā waited on Devayānī as a slave with a thousand maidens.

Kāvya gave away his daughter to Yayāti, along with Śarmiṣṭhā, saying, "King, never put Śarmiṣṭha in your bed." But, sire, when Śarmiṣṭhā saw that Devayānī was blessed with children, she eventually, when her season came, secretly chose her friend's husband for herself. Propositioned by the princess for a child, the Dharma-wise king considered the Dharma, and, while mindful of Kāvya's words, in time gave in to destiny. Devayānī bore Yadu and Turvasu, and Vṛṣaparvan's daughter Śarmiṣṭhā gave birth to Druhyu, Anu and Pūru. Devayānī was insulted in her pride when she found out that sons had been born to the Asura woman, and, overcome with anger, went home to her father. Her loving husband followed his beloved, entreated her with words, clasped her feet, and so on, but he was unable to placate her. Irately her father told him, "Woman chaser, cheater, old age which debilitates men shall take hold of you!" Said Yayāti, "I am not sated of my lust for your daughter, brahmin. Let me transfer my old age to whomever will accept it."

Having won this respite, he spoke to his eldest son, "Give me your youth, son, if you will accept my old age, which was wished upon me by your mother's father, for I have not had my fill of pleasure, calf. Then, for several more years, I shall gratify my senses with your youth." Said Yadu, "I cannot abide your interfering senility! A man's thirst is not slaked before he has known the delights of copulation." Turvasu, solicited by his father, and Druhyu and Anu as well, refused, being ignorant of Dharma and mistaking the fleeting for permanent.

Yayāti then asked his son Pūru, younger of years but greater in virtue, "Pray do not refuse me, my calf, like your elder brothers!" Said Pūru, "King, what man in this world who is made of the self of his father, by whose grace he finds the supreme good, is able to thwart him? The best son carries out his father's unspoken thoughts;

the middling has first to be told; and the worst does it without faith. But he who refuses is his father's excrement!" Thus Pūru joyfully took over his father's old age, and with his son's vigor the king pursued his pleasures as he pleased. Like a father protecting the subjects of the seven continents, Pūru ruled, while Yayāti, with all faculties intact, pursued his pleasures and indulged himself fully. Each day Devayānī in private bore her lover the greatest love with heart, speech, body and possessions. He offered up richly recompensed sacrifices to Hari, the sacrificial Puruṣa, the god who is all Vedas and all gods, him in whom all this has been formed like a cloud in the sky, who appears manifold and then vanishes like a dream, an illusion, a desire; to him—to the subtle Lord Nārāyaṇa, Vāsudeva who dwells in the cave of the heart—Yayāti sacrificed without attachment, holding him in his heart. Thus for thousands of years the emperor pursued his heart's desire with his borrowed senses and heart, and yet was still not sated.

While he was thus living for the pleasure he found in his woman, he realized that he was denying his Self, and dejectedly he recited this chant to his beloved.

"Listen, Bhārgavī, to this chant describing the life of one like me, who lived in a village and whom the sages of the forest deplored. A certain he-goat, seeking his pleasure in the woods, saw a she-goat which by her own fault had fallen in a well. The lustful goat thought of a means to pull her out; by pawing the bank of the well with his hooves he made a ramp, and when the pretty she-goat emerged, she made love to that goat. When other she-goats saw that she had elected him, a fat, bearded, generous and expert stud, they lusted after him. The goat, singly showering pleasure on many, made love, as he was possessed by the demon of lust, and did not know himself.

"When the she-goat who had come to grief in the well saw him couple with another goat he liked better, she could not stand it. She deserted that lover, an enemy in the guise of a friend, whose passion lasted briefly and who freely indulged his senses, and aggrieved, she went to her owner. Unhappily the passionate he-goat went after her in a bleating voice, but failed to appease her on the way. The owner of the she-goat, a brahmin who knew magic, in anger cut off his well-hung testicles, but later restored them for some reason. His testicles restored, the he-goat mated for a long time with his well-retrieved she-goat, and until this very day remains unsatiated.

"In the same fashion, fine-browed woman, I too am constrained by my love for you and bewitched by magic. I do not know myself. All the rice, barley, gold, cattle and women on earth are not enough to satisfy the heart of a greedy man. Desire is never satiated by indulgence in objects of desire; fire only grows larger with every butter offering. When a man has no bad feelings for any creature and looks on all with equanimity, all of space is one great festival. He who hopes for shelter should quickly rid himself of that thirst which the wicked men find hard to slake, and which becomes a source of trouble that does not dry up with his old age. One should not share a seat in private with even one's mother, sister or daughter, for the powerful senses drag even a wise man along. A full thousand years have passed while I indulged myself, yet day after day the thirst renews itself.

"Therefore I forsake this thirst, and putting my mind on Brahman, I shall live with the deer of the forest and transcend duality and ego. He who realizes that all that is seen and heard is unreal, and does not think of it or involve himself with it, who knows that all creation is the destruction of self, is a sage who has beheld the Self."

Having thus spoken to his wife, he restored his vigor to Pūru and took back his old age, dispassionately. He made Druhyu king of the Southeast, Yadu of the South, Turvasu of the West, and Anu of the North; and he consecrated Pūru, the greatest of all his sons, to the entire orb of the earth, placed his brothers under him, and went to the forest himself. As a bird that has fledged leaves its nest, so he in an instant left behind the six senses which he had indulged for so many years. Rid of all attachment, freed from the three *guṇas* by the experience of Self, he confidently took the Bhāgavata road to the pure, supreme Brahman that is Vāsudeva.

# Vidūratha

Once there was a king named Vidūratha, whose fame was celebrated throughout the earth. He had two sons, Sunīti and Sumati. Once upon a time Vidūratha went to the forest on a hunt, where he saw a huge cave that looked like earth's mouth. At the sight, he thought, "What is this awful hole in the ground? It was never here before. I think it must lead to the netherworld!"

As he was pondering this in that deserted forest, he saw the brahmin ascetic named Suvrata approaching. Surprised, the king ashed him, "What is this crevasse that exposes the bowels of the earth?" To which the seer replied, "Don't you know, O lord of earth? I know you should be told, for a king should be aware of everything that happens in his territory.

"There is a mighty and ferocious Dānava, who lives in Rasātala, called Kujṛmbha, the Yawner, because he made earth yawn wide. He is the one who produces all the precious stones on earth and in the three heavens, O master of the monkeys. How can it be that you have never heard of him? That evil-souled demon stole the club named Sunanda that Tvaṣṭar fashioned long ago, and uses it to kill his enemies in battle. When he went to the netherworld, he split open the earth, making a passageway for all the demons. In this way was the wealth-giving earth cleft wide open by the club Sunanda. How can you enjoy the earth unless he is subdued?

"This fierce and mighty demon, whose weapon is that club, impedes the gods and destroys their sacrifices to make the Dānavas grow strong. Only when you have killed this enemy, who lives in the netherworld, shall you become the supreme lord who rules the entire earth!

"The wise tell of the strength and weakness of the club Sunanda. It loses its power when touched by a woman, only to regain its strength on the next day. The wicked demon does not know the mighty properties of this club; he does not know that it loses its force at a woman's touch. O lord of earth, now that I have told you about the power of this evil-souled Dānava, act accordingly! His monstrous hole lies near your city! Why do you wilfully ignore it?"

After the ascetic had spoken and gone, the king returned to his city and conferred with his wise counselors. He told his ministers everything he had heard, about the power of the club and how it loses that power, while his maiden daughter Mudāvatī, standing nearby, overheard the consultation between the king and his ministers.

Several days later, the Daitya Kujṛmbha kidnaped that girl, who was in the bloom of youth, while she was in a forest grove accompanied by her friends. When the king heard about it, his eyes filled with rage, and he addressed both his sons, "You two know the forest well. Go there at once! There is a cave on the bank of the Nirvindhyā river. Follow it to the netherworld, and kill that evil-minded demon who has captured Mudāvatī!"

The two boys found the cave, followed Kujṛmbha's footprints, and fought him furiously with their troops. A horrible battle ensued, without pause, with iron-studded clubs, spears, tridents, battle-axes and arrows. Then, by a magic trick, the Daitya captured the two sons of the king in the fray and slew all their soldiers. When the king heard this, excellent seer, he announced in dismay to his army, "Whoever kills this Daitya and sets my wide-eyed daughter free, to him I shall give her hand in marriage." Thus the king, abandoning hope, made a proclamation to his city, O seer, in order to gain the release of his daughter and sons.

When Vatsaprī, the heroic son of King Bhālandana, full of valor and armed with missiles, heard the announcement, he went before that noble king. Saluting him respectfully, he addressed that fine friend of his father, bowing modestly, and said, "Command me at once! By virtue of your power, I shall kill the Daitya and free your daughter and two sons!"

The king then joyfully embraced the son of his good friend and said, "Dear boy, may you succeed! Vatsaprī shall become king in my place if he can execute my order! Act quickly, my son, while your mind is resolute!"

Then without hesitation that hero with his sword and bow, girded with wrist and finger guards, went through the hole to the netherworld. There that king's son made a loud twang on his bowstring which filled the whole netherworld with its sound. When the Dānava lord Kujṛmbha heard the thrumming of the bowstring, he rushed forth in fury, surrounded by his troops. And the battle was joined between him and the prince, army against army, strength against strength.

After three days' fighting, the Dānava ran for his club, his soul afire. That club, fashioned by the illustrious Prajāpati Tvaṣṭar, stood in the women's quarters where it was worshiped with perfumes, garlands and incense. Knowing about the power of that fine club, Mudāvatī arched her neck and touched it. Under the pretense of worshiping it, that lovely girl caressed it many times before the mighty demon picked it up again.

The Asura lord went off to combat with the club, but its blows rained on his enemies without effect. When his ultimate weapon, the club Sunanda, proved powerless, O seer, the Daitya began to fight his foe in the fray with striking and flying weapons. But with these the demon was no match for the king's son, because his strength had been dissipated by the slender Mudāvatī.

When the son of that lord of earth had beaten the Dānava's striking and flying weapons, and had destroyed his chariot as well, the demon attacked with sword and shield. But the prince slew his attacker most violently, that insolent enemy of Indra and the thirty gods, with a flaming weapon that blazed like the fire of time. Struck in the heart by that fiery missile, the foe of the Thirty died at once. At the same time the great Snakes in Rasātala rejoiced, a shower of flowers fell on the king's son, the Gandharva lords sang, and celestial music sounded in the sky.

After killing Kujṛmbha, Vatsaprī set free the two sons of the king and his beautiful daughter Mudāvatī. At the death of the demon, the leader of the snakes called Ananta, or Śeṣa, took the club. He had surmised Mudāvatī's plan, that lord of snakes, and was delighted with her because that lovely girl, knowing the effect of the touch of a woman's hand on that club, had stroked Sunanda over and over again. So the snake king joyfully gave Mudāvatī the name Sunandā, from the club Sunanda, O twice-born one.

Vatsaprī then immediately led her and her two brothers before their father, prostrated himself, and said to him, "O father, your two sons have been returned, and Mudāvatī as well, as you commanded me. Now what shall I do?" The king, his heart filled with rapture, cried aloud, "Sādhu! Sādhu! My child, my child! How lucky am I! I am blessed by the gods in three ways, my child: that I have won you as a son-in-law, that my enemy has been defeated, and that my children have returned unhurt! Now, as I promised, take in joy the hand of my maiden daughter, the lovely-limbed Mudāvatī, on an approved day. Make my words come true, O prince!"

"I shall do as you command," replied Prince Vatsaprī, "Whatever you say, that I shall do. Know, father, that in this matter I am ruled by you." And so the chief of kings performed the wedding ceremony for his daughter Mudāvatī and Vatsaprī, the son of Bhālandana. The virile Vatsaprī made love with her in the most beautiful places, and on the roofs of palaces.

After some time, his father Bhālandana grew old and went to the forest, and Vatsaprī became king. He continued to make sacrifices to the Yakṣas and guarded his subjects with Dharma. The people were protected like children by that great-souled king, under whose rule they prospered. There was no mixing of castes, no fear whatsoever of robbers, scoundrels or wicked men, and no fear of misfortune of any kind during his reign.

# Saubhari

Once all the land, as far as the sun rises and as far as it sets, was the domain of Māndhātar Yauvanāśva. That king begot on Śaśabindu's daughter Bindumatī his sons Purukutsa, Ambarīṣa and Mucukunda; the latter became a *yogin*. He had fifty sisters who chose Saubhari for their husband.

Saubhari had been performing extreme *tapas* plunged in the water of the river Yamunā. There he witnessed the ecstasy of the king of fish when he indulged in copulation, and the brahmin was aroused. He asked the king for one of his daughters. The king replied, "Brahmin, obtain your maidens at a Bridegroom Choice!"* "He must have thought me displeasing to women," Saubhari mused, "thinking, 'this man is decrepit and ugly, wrinkled, gray and tremulous.' That is why he gave me that answer. Well, I shall make myself irresistible to celestial women, let alone mortal princesses!" This the lord decided, and did.

Eventually he was introduced by the steward into Saubhari's opulent maiden quarters, and he was chosen by the fifty girls as their sole husband. A great quarrel arose among them over him, in which all friendship went with the wind, each shouting, "He suits me better than you!" for they were all in love with him.

Saubhari, that Vedic brahmin who had performed unsurpassable *tapas,* lived with them in opulence among priceless luxuries, in palaces, by garden pools with pure water, in *saugandhika* groves, amidst costly couches, seats, garments, ornaments, baths, ointments, banquets and garlands. He was served by well-adorned men and women, and he enjoyed himself at all times, while birds, bees and bards sang to him.

When the king of seven continents saw that brahmin's householder life, he was astonished and relinquished all self-pride, although he enjoyed the splendor of a universal king. While the brahmin indulged himself in all manner of pleasures in his various mansions, he was no more sated than fire is with drippings of butter. Then one day that Vedic brahmin reflected upon the denial of his Self, and he saw that it was all caused by having watched fish copulate. "Aho!" he thought, "behold the degree of degradation of an ascetic of strict vows and conduct! Because of the passions of one fish in a river my long-held Brahman has been allowed to slip away. He who wants release should abandon the proclivities of the dissolute with all his soul. He should not let his senses out of control; rather, he should roam alone in secret places and yoke his spirit to the eternal Lord. If he has a proclivity, let it be toward good people avowed to God! Once a solitary ascetic, I have, because of a fish's copulation, become fifty lovers with five thousand ejaculations! I can see no end to desires in this world and the next, while my mind is pulled away by the ropes of illusion and finds profit solely in the senses."

Thus, after having lived for a while as a householder, Saubhari renounced the world. Dispassionately he went to the forest, and his faithful wives followed him. Performing severe, self-mortifying *tapas*

*A form of marriage in which the maiden freely chooses her husband.

there, the self-controlled man united himself with fire in the supreme Self. And witnessing his road to the Self, his wives followed him by virtue of his power, as flames that one by one die in a doused fire.

# Śakuntalā

I shall relate the dynasty of Pūru in which you have been born, Bharata, and in which both royal and brahmin descendants were born. . . . Raibhya had a son named Duṣyanta. This Duṣyanta once when hunting came to the hermitage of Kaṇva, where he saw a seated woman. She illumined the place with her splendor like a Lakṣmī, the Illusion of God herself, and he fell in love on the spot. In the company of several escorts he addressed the fine-hipped woman. Delighted by the sight of her, his fatigue immediately dispelled, he smilingly and lovingly asked her in a mellifluous voice, "Who are you, lotus-eyed one? Whose are you, ravishing woman? What do you seek to achieve here in this unpopulated forest? I am sure that you are a nobleman's daughter, slim-waisted maiden, for the mind of a Paurava does not delight in Adharma."*

Said Śakuntalā, "I am the daughter of Viśvāmitra and was abandoned in the forest by my mother Menakā. The reverend Kaṇva is aware of the facts. What can we do for you, hero? Be seated, lotus-eyed king, and accept our hospitality. Here is wild rice. Please eat it and stay if you wish." Duṣyanta said, "This is a fitting response for a maiden born in Kuśika's lineage, fair-browed damsel! Indeed the daughters of kings choose for themselves bridegrooms of the same stature." "*OṂ*," she replied, and the king, who knew the dispositions of time and place, married Śakuntalā legally with the Gāndharva rite.† The royal seer, whose virility was not fruitless, placed his manhood in his queen and on the morrow returned to his city.

In due time she gave birth to a son. Kaṇva happily performed the rites for the prince in the forest, and the child with his vigor tamed lions in play. Thereupon the beautiful woman took her son, whose bravery was unsurpassed—he was born from a fraction of a fraction of Hari himself—and went to the presence of her husband. When the king did not accept his wife and son, though both were without blame, a disembodied voice in the sky said within the hearing of all creatures, "The mother is the father's water bag; he is the father by whom the son has been begotten. Support your son, Duṣyanta; do

*Lawlessness. †I.e., for love.

not despise Śakuntalā. A son who bears semen rescues his father from Yama's domain, O king. You are the placer of his seed; Śakuntalā has spoken the truth!"

When his father passed away, Bharata became a famous Cakravartin; and the greatness of him who was born from a portion of Hari was sung on earth. He had the mark of the wheel on his right palm, that of a lotus chalice on the sole of his foot. When he was consecrated sovereign king in a grand ceremony, the lord offered up fifty-five sacrificial horses by the river Ganges, with Māmateya as his priest. And by the river Yamunā another seventy-eight. He gave away largesse, for Duṣyanta's son Bharata had laid his fire at Śacīguṇa, where a thousand brahmins received huge herds of cows. After sacrificing one hundred thirty-three horses to the amazement of the kings, Bharata transcended the magic of the gods and joined Bṛhaspati himself. At Māsināra he gave away at one rite fourteen million black, white-tusked, gold-caparisoned elephants. No kings before Bharata had performed such a grand ritual; nor will others ever attain it after him—as though they could clasp heaven with their two arms.

# VEDIC GODS AND DEMONS

## The Māndehas at Twilight

Night is called Uṣā; Day is called Vyuṣṭi, and Twilight is said to lie between day and night. When the terrifying and dreadful time of twilight comes, the ghastly Rākṣasas called Māndehas try to devour the sun. Prajāpati pronounced a curse on these Rākṣasas, O Maitreya, that they would die every day without losing their bodies. Because of this, a ferocious battle rages between them and the sun every morning, at which time wise brahmins sprinkle water, great seer, accompanied by the Brahman which is *OṂ*, and the spell of the Gāyatrī *mantra*. The wicked demons are burned up by that water, which turns into a thunderbolt.

When the first offering is made in the *agnihotra*, accompanied by *mantras*, the thousand-rayed light of the sun shines forth radiantly. The syllable *OṂ* is the lord Viṣṇu of the three realms, the master of speech. When it is pronounced, these Rākṣasas go to perdition. The sun is the supernal portion of Viṣṇu, the unobstructed inner light of the god. The syllable *OṂ* names the sun and is its supreme motivator. Propelled by the syllable *OṂ*, the bright light of the sun burns up all the evil demons called Māndehas.

Therefore this act of worship to the morning twilight must be performed, for he who fails to honor the twilight murders the sun! Protected by brahmins, Vālakhilyas, and other deities, the blessed sun bursts forth each day, ready to oversee the world.

# The Battle between the Gods and Demons

This is how the Daitya Bali was made king, O strife-lover, Prahlāda became counselor, and Śukra, his priest. All the demons including Maya came to watch when they heard that the demon Bali, Virocana's son, was to be consecrated king. Attending the arrival of his relatives, and honoring each one in turn, he asked them all this question, "How can I become prosperous?"

They all assured him, "O god-killer, listen to what you should do to assure your own good fortune and also benefit the rest of us! Your grandfather was the mighty demon-protecting hero Hiraṇyakaśipu, who became Śakra* in the three worlds. Viṣṇu, the supreme god, came to him in the form of a lion and shredded him to bits with his claws, before the eyes of the Dānava chiefs. Then, O great-armed one, the trident-bearing Śankara seized the kingdom of the great-souled Andhaka for the purposes of the gods. Your uncle Jambha was killed by Śakra, and Kujambha was butchered like an animal before your eyes by Viṣṇu. And Mahendra killed Śambhu, Pāka, and even your brother Sudarśana, as well as your own father Virocana, just as I'm telling you!"

After hearing about the annihilation of his family by Śakra, O brahmin, the Dānava Bali called up his army with all its mighty demons. Some demons came to battle with the gods in chariots, some on elephants, others on horses and still others on foot. The powerful, ferocious army-protector Maya went first, Bali marched in the middle and Kālanemi brought up the rear. Vāma, whose valor is well-known, took up the left flank, while the terrifying Tāraka marched at the awful right flank. O lover of battle, there were thousands, millions and billions of Dānavas that advanced to fight the gods!

*Indra.

When he heard about this demon army, Śakra, leader of the gods, said, "Let us go to war with these demons who have assembled their armies!" So speaking, the mighty lord, king of the gods, swiftly mounted his own vehicles, and sallied forth eager for battle. The Ādityas, Vasus, Rudras, Sādhyas, Viśvedevas, and the two Aśvins, the Vidyādharas, Guhyakas, the Yakṣas, Rākṣasas and Snakes, the royal seers and Siddhas, various Bhūtas—all together they mounted up, some on elephants, some on chariots and others on horses. Riding on their white chariots drawn by birds, O Nārada, they all attacked the army of the Daityas which was waiting there.

Meanwhile, the wise Garuḍa, son of Vinatā, arrived with the supreme god Viṣṇu on his back. With bowed head the thousand-eyed Indra, together with all the other fine gods, honored the immortal master of the triple world who had arrived. Then Kārttikeya, carrying a mace, marched in the vanguard of the army of the gods; Viṣṇu guarded the rear and Indra strode in the middle. Jayanta advanced in support of the left flank, O seer, while the powerful Varuṇa, supported the right. Then the magnificent army of the immortals protected by Skanda, Indra, Viṣṇu, Varuṇa, who is the lord of the waters, and Sūrya, their multitudinous arms raised high with striking and flying weapons, met the enemy forces in the field.

The battle between the gods and demons took place on the lovely slope of Sunrise Mountain, on a pure and treeless plain where there were no birds. The clash between those two armies on that mountain was horrible, O seer, like the ancient war between the monkeys and the elephants. Battle-dust churned up before the fray was ruddy like a cloud in the sky reddened by the sun at twilight, O divine ascetic.

The tumultuous battle began. Nothing could be made out in the gloom, but on all sides people cried out "Cut!" and "Slash!" without pause. A ghastly, deathly river of blood pouring from both demons and gods began to settle that cloud of dust. As the air cleared, the gods and their supporters, along with the clever Skanda, all together attacked the great demon army. Gods, protected by the arms of Kumāra, killed Dānavas, while the attacking Daityas, guarded by Maya, slew gods. And those supreme deities, without tasting the nectar of immortality, were beaten in that battle by the Daityas, as was Skanda, O Nārada!

At the sight of the defeated gods, the foe-killing Viṣṇu, whose banner bears Garuḍa, bent his bow and flooding the foe with arrows, killed them on all sides. The Daityas, who were being destroyed by Viṣṇu with his iron-beaked arrows, went for refuge to the great demon Kālanemi, who allayed their fears. Recognizing that

Mādhava* was invincible, that mighty demon swelled up like a neglected disease, seizing and throwing into his gaping mouth whomever he could reach with his hand—god, Yakṣa or Kinnara. The furious chief of the Dānavas, together with the sons of Diti, pounded away at the army of the gods, at Indra, the sun and the moon, even though he was armed only with the nails of his hands and feet. The battle was like the Fire at the end of Time, eager to burn up the whole world in all directions, to the breadth and height of earth and heaven.

When they saw their mighty opponent Kālanemi growing monstrous, the leaders of the gods and Gandharvas, the Siddhas and the chief Sādhyas and the Aśvins fled in all directions, their eyes rolling in terror. And the Daityas, jumping up and down with glee, swollen with arrogance, with their striking and flying weapons, rendered Hari powerless, him whose beloved crown is worshiped by the hosts of immortals.

At the sight of those Daityas led by Maya and Bali, whose chief was Kālanemi, Viṣṇu's eyes grew red with rage. Without a moment's pause he nocked his bow with his chest-splitting thunderbolt arrows called Nārācas and inundated those trembling heroes, together with their chariots, elephants and horses, with a flood of arrows like a water-bearing cloud covering the mountains. The demons, led by Bali and Maya, overwhelmed by those arrows shot from Hari's hand, those crescent-shaped Nārācas resembling death's crook, fled at once. Thereupon the hundred-faced demon chief Kālanemi was sent to the fore, and he advanced towards Keśava, the protector of the world, whose strength is infinite, the chief of that divine army.

At the sight of this hundred-headed monster who looked like a mountain peak, with his mace raised aloft, Viṣṇu quickly dropped his bow and took up his discus. When the demon had seen that highly respected god, who with a broad grin hewed down Daityas like tree branches, he said to him in a voice rumbling like the clouds, "This enemy who wreaks havoc on the army of the sons of Dānu, who destroyed Madhu in a towering rage, who killed Hiraṇyākṣa, who is pleased with an offering of flowers—where can this troublemaker go, now that he has come into my field of sight? If he confronts me now in battle, that lotus-eyed god will never go home again! The assembly of the gods will see him bite the dust, his limbs slack, crushed in my fist!"

After saying this to Madhusūdana,† Kālanemi, lips trembling, rage

*Viṣṇu.
†Viṣṇu.

rising, let fall his club on Garuḍa, chief of birds, like Indra's thunderbolt on the mountain. When Viṣṇu saw that dreadful club shot from the Dānava's hand speeding through the air, he split it in two with his discus, just as the *karman* of an unfortunate man severs him from the object of his desire due to his previous deeds. After mowing down the club, Viṣṇu attacked the Dānava and cut off both his swarthy arms. The limbless Kālanemi looked wholly different, like a blazing mountain. And then, in fury, Mādhava cut off his head, which rolled on the ground like a ripe coconut. Armless and headless, like a tree shorn of its branches, the demon stood there, a topless trunk, looking like Mt. Meru, the immobile king of the mountains. The supreme Garuḍa, son of Vinatā, felled him with his chest, O seer, as mighty Indra with his thunderbolt made that hero, shorn of arms and head, fall from the heavens to the earth. At the death of this protector of the Dānava army, the Daityas were overwhelmed by the gods, and dropping their weapons and shields, their hair loose, those demon chiefs all ran away, except for Bāṇa.

As Bāṇa turned to face the enemy, the Dānavas returned with their weapons, once more eager to fight the celestials. So Viṣṇu of infinite splendor, who knew that the son of Bali was invincible, addressed the gods, "Fight without a care!" Thus urged on by Viṣṇu, the gods led by Śakra, went forth to battle the Dānavas, while Viṣṇu himself vanished.

Knowing that Mādhava had gone away, Śukra* said to Bali, "Govinda has abandoned the gods! Now, Bali, you shall win the war!" Delighted to hear his priest announce that Janārdana had left, the splendid demon grabbed up his club and attacked the army of the gods again. Seizing weapons in his thousand arms, Bāṇa rushed at the divine army, killing gods by the thousands. And the mighty Maya, using his magic to assume many different forms, battled that army of the gods, O seer. And the demons Vidyujjihva (Lightning-Tongue), Pāribhadra, Vṛṣaparvan (Bull-Joints), Śatekṣaṇa (Hundred-Eyes), Vipāka (Calamity) and Vikṣara (Stream-Away) also attacked the army of the gods.

While Janārdana was gone, the gods led by Śakra were massacred by the sons of Diti until most of them retreated. Then all the demons led by Bāṇa and Bali, eager to conquer the triple world, attacked the broken and routed troops of gods from behind. When they were thus beaten by the Daityas, Indra and the gods, filled with terror, abandoned the triple heaven and fled to Brahmaloka, along with

*The priest of the demons.

Indra, after which Bali became the ruler of heaven with his sons, brothers and relatives.

Lord Bali became Śakra, O brahmin, Bāṇa became Yama, Maya became Varuṇa, Rāhu became Soma, and Prahlāda became Fire. Svarbhānu became Sūrya, and Śukra became Bṛhaspati. All the enemies of the gods took the places of the other official deities. This awful battle between the gods and the demons, in which Bali became Indra, took place at the beginning of the fifth Kali Age, at the end of Dvāpara.

# Indra and Vṛtra

We have heard that Viśvarūpa had three heads, O Bhārata, one to drink Soma, one to drink wine, and one to eat food. His male ancestors were gods, and he offered the gods their portions publicly at the sacrifice, and in a loud voice. But secretly he gave a portion to the Asuras when he sacrificed, out of love for his Asura mother. The king of the gods discovered this breach of Dharma, which mocked the gods, and fearfully and wrathfully he cut off all his heads at once. His Soma-drinking head became a heathcock, the wine-imbibing head a sparrow, the food-eating head a partridge. Although he was capable of averting it, Indra took the guilt of brahmin murder into his folded hands for the space of a year. Then, for the purification of the creatures, Hari* distributed it in four parts over earth, water, trees and women. Earth accepted a quarter of the brahmin murder on the strength of a boon that her holes would fill up, and the wind is earth's visible form of it. The trees accepted a quarter with the boon that cut-off limbs would grow again; its visible form is resin. The women accepted a quarter of the guilt with the boon of being always lustful; in them the guilt is manifest every month in their flux. The waters accepted a quarter with the boon of being present in all liquids; it is seen in their bubbles and foam, and water thus casts it off.

With his son killed, Tvaṣṭar offered up sacrifice for an enemy to kill Indra: "Grow into an Indraśatru," he said, "and kill my enemy at once." Thereupon there arose from the southern fire a gruesome creature which was like death for the worlds at the end of the Age. From day to day he grew in all directions with the speed of an arrow. He resembled a mountain on fire with the refulgence of the armies of

*Here Hari is Indra.

clouds at twilight; he had a beard like a point of molten copper and eyes like the sun at noon. He climbed the sky on a blisteringly blazing trident, dancing and bellowing and shaking the earth with his foot. His cavernous maw drank up the sky; his tongue licked the stars of the Bear and devoured the tree worlds. When the people saw him yawn again and again with his huge, terribly fanged mouth, they fled trembling into all ten directions.

Since he covered these worlds with darkness, this most grisly rogue got the name of Vṛtra.* The bull-like gods attacked him and struck him with masses of their various celestial missiles, but he devoured them all. . . . [By the grace of Viṣṇu, Indra obtained his thunderbolt from the bones of the seer Dadhīci, and the gods attacked Vṛtra and his army of Asuras.]

Indra raised aloft the thunderbolt crafted by Viśvakarman from the bones of the seer, and valiantly, filled with the power of the lord, surrounded by all the hosts of gods, he gloried on top of his elephant, hymned by throngs of seers, and brought joy to the three worlds. Just as an angry Rudra assailed Andhaka, O king, so Indra attacked mightily to smite Vṛtra amidst his leaders of Asura armies.

Then unfolded the gruesome war between gods and demons in the first part of the Tretā Age by the river Narmadā. Upon beholding the thunderbolt-brandishing Śakra, who glowed with his own luster, followed by the Rudras, Vasus, Ādityas, Aśvins, Ancestors, Fire, Maruts, Ṛbhus, Sādhyas and Viśvedevas, the Asuras were enraged; led by Vṛtra they joined the battle, O king. Namuci, Śambara, Anarvan, Dvimūrdhan, Ṛṣabha, Ambara, Hayagrīva, Śankhaśiras, Vipracitti, Ayomukha, Puloman, Vṛṣaparvan, Praheti, Heti, Utkala, the Daityas, Dānavas, Yakṣas and Rākṣasas by the thousands, led by Sumālin and Mālin, all decked in gold, counterattacked the vanguard of Indra's army, irresistible like death's minions, and routed it, unafraid, bellowing violently, with clubs, maces, arrows, missiles, hammers, spears, pikes, battle axes, swords, hundred-killers, catapults, and scattered on all sides with their striking and throwing weapons the bulls of the gods. They became invisible, covered as they were all around with showers of arrows flying nock to pile, as the lights of the sky are obscured by masses of clouds. But their floods of weapons never reached the soldiers of the gods, for they were shattered in mid-flight into thousands of pieces by the nimble-handed gods. Their arsenal of weapons exhausted, they pelted the celestial army with mountain peaks, trees and rocks, which too were shattered as before.

*The "encloser."

Discovering that the armies of the gods were unhurt and unscathed by their masses of weapons, with not a wound to show for all the trees, rocks and peaks, the Vṛtra-led demons trembled. All their projectiles hurled at the celestial host favored by Kṛṣṇa bounced off them as harmlessly as the insults of plebeians bounce off the great. Seeing their energy stretched to the breaking point, the demons, who were not devotees of Hari, became demoralized, and with their mettle expended decided to flee and desert their leader in the thick of battle.

When spirited Vṛtra saw his Asura followers running, his army broken by panic and in full flight, this gallant warrior, smiling heroically, said these apposite words pleasing to the brave, "Vipracitti, Namuci, Puloman, Maya, Anarvan, Śambara, listen to me! To all the living death is assured, and no remedy has yet been devised. If heaven and fame are gained by it, who would not choose death, and rightly so? Two sorts of deaths are deemed hard to attain: that of the *yogin* who abandons his carcass through meditation on Brahman, and that of the never-retreating hero upon a warrior's bed!"

Welcoming death on the battlefield and esteeming it higher than victory, Vṛtra seized hold of his pike and attacked Indra, as Kaiṭabha of yore attacked Nārāyaṇa in the waters. He hurled his pike with alacrity at Indra, and as that weapon flickered with tongues of the fire of Doomsday, the heroic prince of demons roared and cried, "Die, sinner!" Watching that pike fly through the sky, swooping like a meteor and as hard to face, the thunderbolt-wielder remained undisturbed. He cut through it with his hundred-jointed bolt and sheared off the serpent-like arm of Vṛtra. With one arm cut off, Vṛtra furiously assailed Indra, who still held his Vajra, with a club and hit him on the chin while Maghavan's divine elephant fell and the thunderbolt dropped from his hand.

Gods, Asuras and the hosts of Siddhas and Cāraṇas hailed the miraculous feat of Vṛtra. But then, realizing the danger Indra was in, they wailed. Indra was ashamed to pick up his thunderbolt, which had slipped from his hand, before his enemy's eyes, but Vṛtra said, "Hari, seize your thunderbolt; kill your enemy! This is not time to despair!"

Thereupon the mighty war leaders Indra and Vṛtra fell to fighting. Enemy-taming Vṛtra took hold of an iron club and hurled the dreadful weapon at Indra with his left hand, but Indra pierced both the club and the elephant trunk-like arm at the same time with his hundred-jointed bolt. The Asura, streaming with blood, with his arms cut off at their base, resembled a mountain shorn of its wings, which under Indra's blows was falling from the sky. The Daitya, resting his lower jaw on the earth and his upper jaw in heaven, with his flitting tongue deep in his mouth licking the sky, seemed to devour the three worlds with his deathlike tusks. The giant, mocking the mountains with his bulk, a walking king of mountains wearing out earth with his feet, swallowed up Indra and his elephant, like a mighty and powerful boa constrictor devours an elephant. On seeing him swallowed by Vṛtra, the gods, Prajāpati and the great seers cried out in woe. But, albeit swallowed by Vṛtra and dropped in his belly, Indra, who was girt with Viṣṇu and the power of his Yogic illusion, did not die. The lord, the slayer of Vala, split open Vṛtra's belly with his bolt, came out and forcibly severed his enemy's mountainlike head. But the thunderbolt cutting fast through his neck from all sides only caused his head to fall after as many days had passed as there are from solstice to solstice.

Then in the skies the drums burst into sound, and the Gandharvas, Siddhas, hosts of great seers praised him with the *mantras* of the Slaying of Vṛtra and showered him joyously with flowers. And as all the worlds were watching, O enemy-tamer, the inner light of Vṛtra escaped and joined the higher world.

## Dadhīci's Bones

Once upon a time, O lord of seers, all the immortals, the Vasus and the rest, were defeated by the Daityas who were assisted by the demon Vṛtra. After they had thrown down all their clashing weapons at Dadhīci's hermitage, the gods were violently overthrown. Then all the gods, along with Indra and the seers who were being killed, sped to Brahmaloka and began to tell about their troubles.

When Brahmā, Grandfather of the worlds, had heard what the gods said, he told them what Tvaṣṭar had in mind. "Tvaṣṭar has begotten a mighty lord of all the Daityas, filled with majesty, in order to destroy you, O gods, and his name is Vṛtra. So you must try to kill him! Hear how, O wise ones; I shall tell you for the sake of Dharma.

"Long ago the mighty seer Dadhīci, a sense-controlled ascetic, propitiated Śiva and won the boon of having thunder-bolts for bones. Ask him for his bones, which he will surely give to you. Then fashion a thunder-bolt out of those bones, and kill Vṛtra with it, without fear."

At Brahmā's words, Śakra, his teacher, and the mortals, went at once to the beautiful hermitage of Dadhīci. When Śakra saw the seer there, full of power, he bowed respectfully with folded hands and praised him, accompanied by his teacher and the immortals. That hermit, wisest of the sages, divined his purpose and sent his wife, Suvarcā, inside the hermitage.

Then the king of the gods, together with the immortals, in order to accomplish his purpose, bent upon the science of Success, said to the lord of seers, "All of us gods and seers have been thwarted by Tvaṣṭar, so we have come to you for refuge, O generous giver of shelter, O mighty follower of Śiva! O brahmin, give us your bones that are made of thunderbolts! I shall fashion my own thunderbolt out of your bones, and with it I shall kill Vṛtra who menaces the gods!"

At his words, that seer, who was devoted to helping others, concentrated on his guardian Śiva and relinquished his body. The fetters of life loosened, the seer Dadhīci went at once to Brahmaloka. A shower of flowers fell from the sky, and all the gods were astonished.

Then Śakra summoned the cow Surabhi to lick clean the bones so he could make them into weapons with which to challenge Vṛtra. At his command, Viśvakarman fashioned weapons of various kinds out of those diamond-hard bones made out of thunderbolts by Śiva's grace. He made a thunderbolt of cane, the arrow called Brahmaśiras, and many other weapons from other bones.

Then Indra took up his thunderbolt, and strengthened by the power of Śiva, attacked Vṛtra in fury, just as Rudra assaults death, O seer. The well-girt Śakra quickly and mightily cut off Vṛtra's head with his bolt, like a mountain-top. And the inhabitants of the three heavens rejoiced, the immortals celebrated Śakra, and showers of flowers fell from the sky.

# Diti and the Maruts

After Diti's sons were killed by Indra, she implored her husband Kaśyapa, "O lord, you are my protector! Give me a son who will destroy Śakra!" And Kaśyapa replied, "If you remain pure for a thousand divine years, dark-eyed woman, you shall give birth to a son who will destroy your enemies and rule over the triple world. There is no other way." At these words of her husband, Diti began to practise self-restraint. And after performing the rites of impregnation, the seer went off to Mt. Udaya.

When that fine seer had gone away, the thousand-eyed Indra sped rapidly to his hermitage and spoke to Diti, "Let me be your obedient servant!" And the goddess, impelled by fate, agreed. The sacker of cities gathered fuel and did other tasks for her, effacing himself and waiting for his chance, like a snake.

Then once, after that ascetic woman, yoked to *tapas,* had lived in purity for a thousand years, she washed her hair and fell asleep with her head on her knees, her hair loose so that the tips of her locks brushed her feet. The thousand-eyed Indra seized the opportunity of this impurity, O Nārada, and entered the belly of his mother through her nostril.

After penetrating the womb of that mother of the Daityas, the angry sacker of cities saw a large baby lying face up with his hands on his hips. The Vasu* saw on his face a piece of flesh that shone like pure crystal, so he picked it up in his two hands. Then, swollen with rage, the god of a hundred sacrifices squeezed that lump of flesh between his hands until it was hard. One half of it grew upwards and the other half grew downwards until that lump of crystal flesh had become a thunderbolt with a hundred jagged knots. Then, O brahmin, with that hundred-spiked thunderbolt, he sliced the embryo that had been conceived in Diti into seven parts, roaring raucously.

When Diti awoke, O Nārada, she saw what Śakra had done and heard the shrieking voice of her son. "Fool," cried Śakra, "stop your crying and gurgling!" And saying this, he cut each of the seven parts again into seven. This is how the attendants of the god of a hundred sacrifices, who are called the Maruts and go before Indra as vanguards, were born from the impurity of their mother.

Then Śakra with his thunderbolt left Diti's womb. Fearful of her curse, he said, "Don't be angry with me! For it is not my fault that your son was punished. It was due to your own misconduct." And Diti answered, "No, it is not your fault. I think it was destined long ago that I became impure, even though my time had come." So speaking, the lovely Diti herself comforted her sons, and sent them away with the king of the gods.

# The Seer's Wives and the Maruts

Pulastya said, Listen while I tell you the origin of the ancient Maruts, beginning with Svāyambhuva, up to the present Manvantara. The son of Svayambhū Manu was called Priyavrata. However, his son

*Indra.

Savana, honored in the three worlds, died childless, O divine seer, and his wife wept with grief and sorrow. She refused to give her husband over to the funeral fire, embracing him and lamenting like a woman without a guardian, "My husband, my protector!"

A disembodied voice spoke from the sky, "Don't cry, O queen. If you possess supreme truth, then this fire belongs to you as well as to your husband." When she heard that ethereal voice, Sudeva, the queen, said, "I mourn for this sonless king, but not for my miserable self, O sky-goer!"

The voice replied, "Weep no more, wide-eyed woman, for you shall have seven sons by this king. Ascend the fire at once. I have spoken the truth, now put your faith in it!" Thus addressed by the sky spirit, the young woman, loyal to her spouse, placed her worthy husband on the pyre, lit the fire, and concentrating on him, entered into the fire herself.

Then, in a flash, the radiant king rose aloft with his wife. Moving freely he flew through the sky with his queen, the daughter of Sunābha. And while the king was flying through the heavens, O Nārada, the queen's menstrual period arrived. By divine Yoga, he remained in the sky with his wife for five days. On the sixth day, the king thought, "Now her season shall not go fruitless!" And that sky-traveler had intercourse with his slender wife. But his semen fell out of the sky. After the semen had been emitted, the king and his wife went by the celestial pathway to Brahmaloka, O ascetic rich in *tapas*.

The wives of the seven seers—Sumānā, Mālinī, Vapuṣmatī, Citrā, Viśālā and Haritālinī—saw with delight that cloud-colored semen falling from the sky. When they saw it resting on a blue lotus, O ascetic, they thought it was the nectar of immortality, and sought it out, desiring eternal youth. They took a ritual bath, worshiped their husbands, and gaining their approval, they drank the semen of the chief of kings from the lotus blossoms, thinking it to be divine nectar. As soon as they had consumed that semen spilt by the chief of kings, those wives of the ascetics lost all their brahminical luster. And so the seers all abandoned their errant wives.

The wives gave birth to seven sons, O seer, who wailed most horribly, filling the whole world with their shrieks. Then lord Brahmā, Grandfather of the world, appeared. Approaching the babies, he said, "Don't cry, strong ones. You shall become sky-wanderers called the Maruts!" With these words Brahmā, lord of the gods, the Grandfather of the world, commanded them to become the sky-wandering Maruts. And these were the original Maruts, those of the Svāyambhuva Manvantara.

# Soma

The holy seer Atri, surpassing all the worlds with his majesty, became the father of Soma, O brahmins. That magnificent seer stood erect, with his arms raised, stiff as a pole, a rock or a brick wall. Virtuous in body, speech and mind, he practised that great *tapas* called Most-Difficult for three thousand divine years, so we have heard.

While he was standing there at attention, unblinking, retaining his semen, that learned brahmin's body turned into Soma. The Soma of that seer who cultivated the Self rose up and began to flow out of his eyes, illuminating the ten directions. At the command of Brahmā, those ten goddesses* were impregnated with that Soma; unable to bear it alone, they carried it all together. That embryo shone forth in all directions, illuminating the worlds like the cool-rayed moon.

But those women could not keep that embryo in the womb, and so it fell from them onto the wealth-giving earth in the form of moonlight. When Brahmā the Grandfather saw Soma descending from the sky, he made him ride on his chariot out of a desire to benefit the worlds. That chariot was made out of the gods, O learned ones. Its purpose was Dharma; it was true to its promise, and it was yoked with a thousand pure white horses, so we have heard.

When Soma, that supreme-souled offspring of Atri, fell to earth, the seven famous and holy mind-born sons of Brahmā, including Aṅgiras, the son of Bhṛgu, gave praise with numerous verses from the Ṛg, Yajur and Atharva Vedas. Being praised, the shining Soma began to swell, nourishing the three worlds. And Brahmā made twenty-one circuits of the ocean-bounded earth on his chariot.

Soma's power fell also to earth where plants spring from it, luminous with all its splendor. With these plants Soma feeds the world and the four kinds of creatures. Thus holy Soma is the sustainer of the world, excellent brahmins. After winning his power by *tapas*, through the praises of the gods, and by his own actions, the eminent Soma practised *tapas* for a thousand lotus-counts of years. The golden-hued goddesses of the ten directions support the world by themselves, and their master is Soma, famous for his work.

Then Brahmā, best among the knowers of Brahman, gave to Soma (as the moon) sovereignty over the seeds, the plants, the brahmins and the waters, O excellent brahmins. That best of ascetics, the splendid Soma, was consecrated as king of kings with great do-

*That is, the directions.

minion, and he nourished the worlds with his own substance. And the wise Pracetas Dakṣa gave his twenty-seven loyal daughters, called the Nakṣatras,* to Soma, as his wives.

After acquiring that mighty sovereignty, lord Soma, lord of all who possess Soma, ordered a royal consecration with enormous fees. Hiraṇyagarbha was the *udgātar* priest while Brahmā held the office of *brahman* priest and the blessed lord Nārāyaṇa was the *sadasya* accompanied by the original brahmin seers headed by Sanatkumāra. And the fee that Soma gave to those priests and *sadasyas* who were led by the brahmin seers was the three worlds, so we have heard, O twice-born ones!

Nine goddesses attended him: Śinī and Kūhu (New Moon Days), Vapus (Beauty), Puṣṭi (Prosperity), Prabhā (Splendor), Vasu (Wealth), Kīrti (Fame), Dhṛti (Resolution), and Lakṣmī (Good Fortune). At the end of the sacrifice, all the gods and seers worshiped that alert and singleminded Soma as the chief, supreme king of kings, creator and protector of the ten directions.

After he had won that sovereignty so hard to attain, to the acclaim of the seers, his attention to discipline began to wander, O brahmins, and he lost all his self-control. He kidnaped the beautiful wife of Bṛhaspati named Tārā, and behaved contemptuously to all Aṅgiras' sons. Even at the entreaty of the gods and holy seers, he refused to return Tārā to Aṅgiras. Uśanas, who had been the splendid pupil of his father Bṛhaspati, long before, attacked Aṅgiras from behind, O brahmins. And because of his affection for Bṛhaspati, the lord god Rudra took up his bow and attacked Uśanas in turn from the rear. That great-souled god took aim at the gods and loosed his best weapon at the brahmin seers, who thereby lost their glory. From these events, the mighty battle known as Tārakāmaya began between the gods and demons, and it effected the destruction of the world. The gods and the immortals in the Tuṣita heaven survived the destruction and sought refuge with Grandfather Brahmā, the first god.

The Grandfather stopped Uśanas and Śankara, the eldest Rudra, from further fighting, and returned Tārā to Aṅgiras. When he saw that Tārā was pregnant, she whose face shone like the lord of the moon, the learned Bṛhaspati said, "You shall not give birth to that embryo!"

"I shall bear this embryo in my body, in my womb, no matter what!" she answered, refusing to abort the boy who was to become a

*I.e., constellations.

mighty devastator of Dasyus,* like fire raging through a thicket of reeds. And as soon as he was born, that god began to strike down the bodies of the gods.

Filled with concern, the gods asked Tārā, "Who is the father of this boy—Soma or Bṛhaspati? Tell us the truth!"

Ashamed, she said nothing to the gods, good or bad, at which her Dasyu-slaying son began to curse her. Brahmā restrained the boy and asked Tārā, "There is much suspicion about Soma here. Tell us the truth. Whose son is this?"

Reverently folding her hands, she told the beneficent lord Brahmā that her great-souled Dasyu-destroying child was Soma's son. Thereupon the magnanimous progenitor Soma kissed his wise son and named him Budha. Then he arose, along with the sages, to depart, as he had done before.

Ilā, the daughter of a king, bore a son to Budha—the magnificent Purūravas, who had six sons, all mighty heroes, by his wife Urvaśī. Later Soma, the orb of the moon, violently overcome by the sickness of kings, began to wane, diminished by disease, so he returned for refuge to his father Atri. The famous Atri rid him of his evil, and freed from the royal illness, Soma shone forth his glory on all sides as the moon.

# Prahlāda and Hiraṇyakaśipu

O Maitreya, hear the story of Prahlāda the wise, that great-souled one of noble deeds. Long ago Hiraṇyakaśipu, the heroic son of Diti, emboldened by a boon from Brahmā, brought the triple world under his control. That great demon Daitya himself took over Indra's functions; he became the sun, the wind, the fire, Varuṇa who protects the waters, and Soma, the moon. He also became Kubera, lord of wealth, and Yama, lord of death. That demon kept for himself all the shares of the sacrifice. The thirty gods, fine seer, deserted heaven and roamed around the earth, disguised as men.

After conquering all three worlds, Hiraṇyakaśipu grew arrogant because of his power over the triple world. Hymned by the Gandharvas, he indulged himself in his favorite sensual pleasures. All the Siddhas, Gandharvas and Snakes waited upon the great-souled Hiraṇyakaśipu as he enjoyed his drink. The Siddhas performed joyfully before the Daitya king; some made music, others sang, while

*Enemies of the Āryans in the *Ṛg Veda*.

others shouted "Victory!" In his magnificent crystalline cloud palace where enchanting Apsarases danced, the happy demon quaffed his wine.

He had an illustrious son, a young boy named Prahlāda who had gone to live with his *guru,* and recited the verses of a child. Once that boy of virtuous soul, in the company of his teacher, went before his father as he was drinking his wine and prostrated himself. Making his son stand up, Hiraṇyakaśipu addressed Prahlāda, saying, "Dear son, recite the most important thing that you have learned from your diligent studies after all this time."

"O father, listen carefully as I tell you the most important thing that is in my mind, as you have asked. 'I bow in reverence before the goal of all beings, the cause of all causes, who is without beginning, middle or end, who is unborn, who neither waxes nor wanes, the Eternal One.'"

The Daitya king grew angry at these words, his eyes inflamed. He looked at his son's teacher and said, his lower lip trembling, "You false brahmin! Wretch! What unfit lesson is this that my son has learned, full of contempt for me?"

"O lord of the Daityas!" exclaimed the teacher, "Don't be angry! For what your son has just said he did not learn from me!"

"Who taught you this, my son? Tell me, Prahlāda, for your teacher has claimed that he did not teach you this."

Prahlāda answered, "Viṣṇu, who lives in the heart, is the teacher of the whole world. O father, who is ever taught by anyone other than the Supreme Soul?"

"Who is this Viṣṇu, you fool, whom you keep bringing up again and again in front of me waen *I* am the lord of the world?"

"Viṣṇu is the supreme lord from whom the universe proceeds, and who is the universe himself. He is the ultimate goal meditated upon by *yogins,* beyond description."

"You fool! Who other than myself may be called the Supreme Lord in my presence? Yet even so, you repeat this over and over again, courting death!"

"O father, Viṣṇu is not only my lord and the lord of all creatures, but also yours! He is one with Brahmā, the creator, and ordainer, the supreme lord. So be gracious! Why are you so angry?"

Hiraṇyakaśipu then exclaimed, "What wicked person has won the heart of this feeble-minded boy, making him speak these unholy words?"

Prahlāda went on, "Viṣṇu is not only in my heart, but he is always near, pervading all the worlds. He is ever-present, impelling me, you and everybody else, O father, in all our actions." . . .

"Let this evil-souled boy be killed!" cried the demon king, "There is no point in his living, for he damages his own side; he has become a burning coal to his family!" At this command, Daityas by the hundreds of thousands grabbed up their mighty weapons and rose up to kill the king's son.

"Viṣṇu dwells in your weapons, in yourselves as well as in me!" said Prahlāda, "If this be true, O Daityas, then your weapons will not strike me!" And although he was attacked by the multitudinous weapons of hundreds of Daityas, he felt not even the slightest prick. Instead his strength was continually renewed. . . .

Then Hiraṇyakaśipu cried out, *"Bhoḥ! Bhoḥ,* you serpents, destroy at once this most hard-souled, unyielding son of mine with your mouths full of fiery poison!" At his orders, the snakes Kuhaka, Takṣaka and the others began to bite him all over his body with their copious poison. But while he was being bitten by the great snakes, Prahlāda's mind was absorbed in Kṛṣṇa, so he felt no pain and remained firmly fixed in the joy of his meditation on the lord.

"Our teeth are shattered!" cried the snakes. "Our jewels have burst open, our hoods are inflamed and there is trembling in our hearts! And yet his skin is not even scratched! O lord of the Daityas, kill him some other way!"

So Hiraṇyakaśipu then said, "Hey, you elephants of the directions, kill Prahlāda with your death-dealing tusks! Kill him who has taken sides with our enemy! Children destroy their parents like fire burns the wood from which it was kindled!"

And so those elephants, huge as mountain peaks, knocked the boy to the ground and beat him with their tusks. But because he recollected Govinda, the elephant's tusks split apart into a thousand pieces when they struck his chest. So Prahlāda said to his father, "The tusks of these elephants, sharp as axe-blades, are not shattered because of my power; this devastating destruction is the result of my concentration on Janārdana."

The king then said, "Dismiss the elephants, O demons, and light a fire. And wind, fan the fire so that this evil-doer will be consumed!" So the Dānavas put the son of the demon king on a pyre of large logs and lit the fire in order to immolate him, as ordered by their master.

"O father," cried out Prahlāda, "even this fire fanned by the wind fails to burn me in any way. All the quarters of the directions are cool to my eyes, and strewn with carpets of lotuses!" At this, the great-souled brahmin priests, descendants of the Bhārgava, praised the lord of the Daityas and addressed him in a conciliatory manner.

"O king," they said, "don't waste your anger on your son when it might bear more fruit directed against the gods! O king, we shall teach your son to kill your enemies! Children make all kinds of mistakes, O Daitya king, so do not be so angry at this little boy! If we cannot persuade him to forsake Hari, then we shall destroy him ourselves with our own magic." At this request of the priests, the Daitya king ordered his son to be taken down from the funeral pyre. . . .

Some time later, when Prahlāda still refused to give up the worship of Viṣṇu, the Dānavas, witnessing his continued efforts, and in fear of their Daitya master, reported it to him. This time Hiraṇyakaśipu summoned his cooks and said, "You cooks, this hard-headed, wicked son of mine is leading others astray. Kill him at once! Give him Halāhala poison in his food without his knowledge. He is to be destroyed without a moment's hesitation!" And so the cooks gave the great-souled Prahlāda the poison at his father's command.

Casting a spell by reciting a prayer to Ananta, O Maitreya, Prahlāda ate the dreadful Halāhala poison in his food. He swallowed it without any effect, and digested that poison with a healthy mind because it had been rendered powerless by his invocation of Ananta. Then the cooks, in fear and trembling at the sight of the mighty poison digested by Prahlāda, went to the Daitya king, prostrated themselves before him and said, "O demon king, we have given horrible poison to your son, but he has digested it along with his food!"

"Hurry, hurry!" exclaimed the king, "Produce magic, Daitya priests, that will destroy him without further delay!" And so the priests went up to the self-disciplined Prahlāda and spoke in a placating manner, "You have been born as the son of Hiraṇyakaśipu, king of the Daityas, who is famous in the triple world, into a long-lived family of twiceborn. What need have you of the gods, of Ananta, or of anyone else? Your father is the refuge of all the worlds, and you shall be the same. Therefore stop praising your enemy! A father should be looked up to as the supreme teacher of all teachers!"

Prahlāda replied, "It is true, illustrious ones, that the mighty family of Marīci is to be honored in all the triple world. No one should say otherwise. And it is true that my father's behavior is beyond reproach in the whole world. I speak no lie in this. And it is entirely true that one's father is the supreme teacher among teachers, to be most zealously honored. Make no mistake about this; I know it well. But when you ask 'What is the use of worshiping Ananta?' who is it that speaks? There is no meaning in this remark." And after saying this, Prahlāda grew silent, restrained by his respect for them.

But then he began to speak again, with a slight smile, " 'What is the use of Ananta?' *Sādhu! Sādhu!* 'What is the use of Ananta?' *Sādhu*, my teachers! Listen to what value there is in Ananta, if you will not be offended! Success, Love, Duty and Release are called the four aims of man. What is the use of the one from whom all four derive? What is the point of further talk! It is from the immortal Ananta that Duty is acquired by everyone, including Marīci, Dakṣa and the other seers. It is from Ananta that Success is learned by some, and Love by others. Still others, versed in his truth, with knowledge, meditation and trance, gain Release, their fetters gone. Only the worship of Hari lies at the root of success, wealth, fame, knowledge, children, actions and deliberations. Why do you ask what is the use of Ananta, O brahmins, when it is of him alone that Success, Love, Duty and even Release are the fruits?

"There is nothing more to say. You, as my teachers, must decide what is right and what is wrong, for I myself know little. Why discuss this further? Viṣṇu is the master of the world, the creator, preserver and destroyer, dwelling in my heart. He is the enjoyer and also that which is enjoyed. He is the lord of the world! Please forgive everything I have been saying since my infancy!"

To this the priests replied, "Child, we protected you when you were in the fire by promising that you would stop talking like this. But we did not know you were so stubborn. If, at our words, you still refuse to give up clinging to your delusion, then, hard-headed child, we shall kill you with magic!"

Prahlāda answered them, "Who can kill a person? By what means? Who can save a person? By what means? It is oneself that kills and saves, depending on his good or evil deeds. Everything that happens to a person is the result of former action. Therefore one should do good deeds with utmost zeal!"

After this speech, the angry priest of the Daitya king produced the apparition of a witch wreathed in a garland of flame. As this ghastly female approached, earth trembled at her tread. Good and mad, she struck him on the breast with her spear. But when that brilliant spear touched the boy's heart, it fell shattered to the ground, broken to a hundred bits. Where the blessed lord Hari is constant in the heart, even a thunderbolt will shatter, let alone a mere spear!

That witch called forth by the Daitya priests to attack the sinless Prahlāda fell on them instead, slew them and quickly vanished. When the great-minded boy saw those priests scorched by the witch, he fell on his knees and cried, "Save them, O Kṛṣṇa! Save them, Ananta! O all-pervader, form of the world, Janārdana, save these brahmins from this unendurable fire caused by their magic spell! If it be true that Viṣṇu, *guru* to the world, pervades all beings, then by this truth let all these priests live! If it be true, O all-pervader, that I think of my enemies even while concentrating on the immutable Viṣṇu, then let these priests live! If it be true that I bear no ill will even towards those who tried to kill me, those who gave me poison, those who set me on fire, the elephants of the directions that trampled me, and the snakes who bit me, then by this truth let the demon priests live!"

At these words, and at Prahlāda's touch, the brahmins rose up again, unscathed, and addressed him with respect, "Dear child, may you have a long and unobstructed life! May you be full of strength and vigor! May you have sons and grandsons, wealth and sovereignty, and may you be supreme!" So speaking, the priests left, great seer, and told everything that had happened to the Daitya king. . . .

When he heard all this, Hiraṇyakaśipu jumped from his seat in anger and kicked his son in the chest. He shouted in a burning rage, as if on fire, crushing his hands together as if eager to destroy the world. "Vipracitta! Rāhu! Lord Bali! Catch him in your powerful snake-nooses and throw him into the sea, at once! Otherwise all the worlds and all the dim-witted Daityas will follow the opinion of this fool! Even though we stop this wicked child, yet still he sings the praises of our foes! He deserves to die!"

And so the Daityas quickly trapped him in their nooses made of snakes, doing just as their master had commanded, and they threw him into the ocean's waters.

At this the mighty ocean began to shake due to the trembling Prahlāda, and at the peak of its quaking it overflowed on all sides. When Hiraṇyakaśipu saw earth completely flooded by the mighty waters, O honorable one, he said to the Daityas, "O Daityas, cover up this hard-headed son of mine with rocks on every side in the watery abode of Varuṇa, and leave no spaces in between! Fire does not burn him; weapons do not cut him; snakes do not pierce his skin; he cannot be killed by wind, by poison, by witchcraft, by magic, by being dropped from a high place, nor by the elephants of the directions! This boy is evil-minded! There is no point in permitting him to live! If he is crushed by huge boulders under the ocean for a thousand years, surely this evil-minded one will die!"

And so the Daityas and the Dānavas covered him with giant rocks, heaping them thousands of leagues high. And the great-minded Prahlāda, piled high with rocks at the bottom of the sea, praised Acyuta daily with one-pointed mind.*

"Praise be to you, lotus-eyed one! Praise be to you, Supreme

*I.e., concentrated.

Person! Praise be to you, Self of the whole world! Praise be to you of the razor-sharp discus! Praise be to you, god of the brahmins, benefactor of cows and brahmins, giver of gifts to the world! To Kṛṣṇa, to Govinda, let there be praise!

"As Brahmā you emit the universe. Then you protect it while remaining in it. And you also take the form of Rudra at the end of time. Praise be to you in these three forms! Gods, Yakṣas, Asuras, Siddhas, Snakes, Gandharvas and Kinnaras, Piśācas, Rākṣasas, human beings and cattle, birds, plants, ants and watersnakes, earth, water, fire, air, wind, sound, touch, taste, form, smell, mind, intelligence, self, time, the *guṇas*—of all these you are the ultimate purpose, O Acyuta! You are it all! . . .

"Praise be to Viṣṇu who is identical with the world, who is to be thought of as the beginning of the world! Let this immortal god be kind to me! He is both the warp and the woof of the universe. He is the imperishable syllable *OṂ*, the support of all creatures. Let Hari be gracious to me! *OṂ*! Praise be to Viṣṇu! Praise be to him again and again! In him everything exists. From him everything originates. He himself is everything, the refuge of all.

"Ananta is omnipresent. Because of this he exists even as myself. I am the source of everything! I am all things. Everything exists in me. I am eternal. I am undecaying. I am immortal. I am the Supreme Self! I am the refuge of all souls. I am known as Brahman, and at the end, I am the Supreme Person!"

Thus did Prahlāda consider himself to be none other than Viṣṇu, O brahman. Attaining complete identity with the lord, he thought himself to be Acyuta. And he forgot himself entirely, knowing of nothing else whatsoever. "I am the immortal, imperishable, Supreme Soul," thought he. And because he possessed the nature of the lord, his evil utterly eradicated, the immortal Viṣṇu who consists of wisdom dwelt in his pure heart.

As soon as the demon Prahlāda had become one with Viṣṇu by the power of Yoga, those fetters made of snakes broke instantly apart, O Maitreya. The ocean shook, heaving with crowds of trembling sea-monsters, and the whole earth quaked, with her mountains and forest groves. The great-minded Prahlāda threw off the pile of rocks heaped on him by the Daityas and emerged from the sea. When he saw once more the world, the sky and so on, he remembered who he was and said, "I am Prahlāda!" And once again he praised the wise Supreme Person, who is without origin, his mind one-pointed, steady, restrained in body, speech and mind. . . .

As he made praise this way, his mind fixed on the lord, Hari heard him and appeared, dressed in yellow robes. Overcome at the sight of the presence of the lord, O brahmins, Prahlāda stammered, "Praise be to Viṣṇu! O god who relieves the distress of his supplicants, be kind, O Keśava! Purify me again by the gift of your glance, O Acyuta!"

"I am pleased with your practice of unfailing devotion!" said the lord, "Now choose a boon from me, Prahlāda, whatever you desire!"

"O protector, may I always be unshakably loyal to you, for a thousand lifetimes, wherever I am born! And may the pleasure taken by the unenlightened in the objects of the senses always live in my heart as I concentrate on you!"

Hari replied, "You are devoted to me now, and you shall continue to be so. O Prahlāda, choose whatever else your heart desires!"

"My father constantly resented me when I was determined to praise you, O god. Now take away his evil! Weapons have been loosed at my body; I have been thrown into the fire, bitten by snakes, and given poison in my food. I have been tied up and tossed into the sea, and buried under a pile of rocks. All these and other unholy things as well my father ordered done to me. O lord, by your kindness, free my father from the sin he has committed by hating me!"

"O Prahlāda," answered Hari, "all this shall be done, by my grace. And I shall grant you still another boon, O demon's son. What shall it be?"

"I am content with the boon you have already given me, my lord, that my devotion to you shall never waver, by your kindness. What is the use of Success, Love or Duty for one in whose hand Release already rests? My loyalty to you is firm, you who are the root of the whole world!"

"If it be true that your mind is unwavering, and that you are filled with devotion to me, then by my grace, you shall receive supreme *nirvāṇa!*" So speaking, Viṣṇu vanished from Prahlāda's sight, O Maitreya, and the boy returned home where be worshiped his father's feet.

Kissing his head, his father embraced him tightly, crying, "You are alive, my son!" his eyes wet with tears, O brahmin. That mighty demon, regretting what he had done, became well-disposed toward his son, while Prahlāda, like a dutiful son, became obedient to his teacher and his father.

When Hiraṇyakaśipu was put to death by Viṣṇu in the form of Narasiṃha, O Maitreya, Prahlāda became the king of the Daityas. After receiving the kingship for the purity of his deeds, O brahmins, he had many sons and grandsons and a glorious reign. And at the end of his rule, free from the fruits of good and evil deeds, because of his meditation on the lord, he attained supreme *nirvāṇa*. Such was the majesty of the great-minded and loyal Prahlāda who became the king of the demons, O Maitreya, that you asked me to relate.

The sins of whoever hears this story of the great-souled Prahlāda are annihilated at once. A man who hears or recites the story of Prahlāda discards whatever evil he has done, by day or night; there is no doubt about this. Whoever recites this on the full-moon or new-moon day, or on the eighth or twelfth of the month, gets the same fruit as from the gift of a cow, O brahmin. And just as Hari protected Prahlāda in all his trials, so does he always protect whoever hears his story.

# Indra and the Ants

When Indra had grown arrogant after killing Vṛtra and Viśvarūpa, he ordered Viśvakarman to construct a magnificent palace for him. After this a brahmin boy appeared before him and said, "My friend, I know Kaśyapa the progenitor and the ascetic hermit Marīci, who are both your friends. And I have praised Brahmā, the lord creator who sprang from Viṣṇu's navel, and the supreme protector Viṣṇu, endowed with the quality of *sattva,* and also the vast single ocean of the dissolution, devoid of creatures and most horrifying. And now I ask you, Śakra, how manifold is creation? How manifold indeed is the Eon? How many are the eggs of Brahmā; how many are the Brahmās, Viṣṇus and Śivas within the eggs; how many the Indras? Who can attain them? If motes of dust and drops of rain can be numbered, O overlord of the gods, still there shall be no number to the Indras, as the wise know well. An Indra's life and office lasts seventy-one Ages, and one day and night of Brahmā encompasses the span of time of twenty-eight Indras. And Brahmā's life lasts 108 years, so what number is there of Indras when even Brahmās cannot be counted? How many are the eggs of Brahmā, with their Brahmās, Viṣṇus and Śivas, encased as they are in the pure sweat that springs from a single pore of the mighty Viṣṇu? Just as the eggs of Brahmā are innumerable, as are the drops of the sweat of existence, so are the eggs of Brahmā as countless as his hairs. How many gods are there in one egg of Brahmā? And how many of the likes of you?"

Meanwhile the Supreme Person saw a swarm of ants moving in a file a hundred bow-lengths long. He said nothing, but remained there silent like the deep ocean. When he saw the brahmin boy's mirth and heard his song, Indra asked him in utter astonishment, his throat dry, "Why are you laughing, great brahmin? Tell me why at once? Who are you, ocean of virtues hidden behind illusion, bearing the shape of a child?"

When he heard Indra's words, the brahmin boy replied with this superb speech that treats of the soul and contains the quintessence of the good life, a veritable kernel of wisdom: "I have witnessed this swarm of ants; its reason for existence remains hidden. Don't question me, for your ignorance gives rise to grief. The matchless torch of knowledge that cuts at the root of the tree of rebirth for those enwrapped in it is hidden in the darkness of ignorance. Concealed in all the Vedas, it is well-nigh inaccessible even to the perfected ones. Equal to the breath of *yogins*, it shatters the arrogance of the fool."

So speaking, that bull among brahmins stood there smiling, until Indra spoke again, "Reveal quickly, brahmin boy, that ancient torch of knowledge! I do not know who you are, child; you appear to be a mass of wisdom in human form!"

In reply, Kṛṣṇa, who bore the shape of the young brahmin, began to expound the wisdom that even great *yogins* find most difficult to attain: "That swarm of ants that I observed, each one following the one ahead, have every one been Indras in the world of the gods by virtue of their own past action. And now, by virtue of their deeds done in the past, they have gradually fallen to the state of ants." . . .

After so speaking, Hari in the guise of a boy disappeared on that very spot. Indra, however, stood there astonished, as though he had seen a vision in a dream. The supreme lord no longer cared a straw about his riches. Indra of a hundred sacrifices summoned Viśvakarman, spoke affectionately to him and, presenting him with jewels, sent him home with full honor. Entrusting everything to his son, he prepared to seek refuge, abandoning his wife Śacī and the fortune of his kingship, desiring death now that he had found insight.

When Śacī saw that her beloved husband had found wisdom, she went, grievous and trembling, to the shelter of the *guru*. She summoned Bṛhaspati and told him everything; she made him acquaint Śakra with the essentials of worldly wisdom. That teacher himself composed a special text which dealt with the pleasure of married couples, and affectionately and joyfully caused Śakra to recite it aloud. Bṛhaspati, the lord of speech, revealed the text on worldly wisdom. So Indra resumed his kingship, with all its duties, O woman who sports in Vṛndāvana!

This is the story of how Indra lost his pride.

# RIVERS AND SACRED FORDS

## The Descent of the Ganges River

Nārada asked, "How was the Ganges brought down? What great *tapas* did Bhagīratha perform to ensure that his ancestors would have the proper obsequies? Tell me all, you are true to your vows, O ocean of compassion!"

Mahādeva replied, "The seer Bhagīratha went to the Snowy Mountain to rescue his ancestors, and having gone there did *tapas* for ten thousand years. The primeval god who is without taint became graciously disposed and gave him the Ganges, which came from the sky. God Śarva saw the Jāhnavī coming where he, the lord of the universe, always resides, and he caught her in his twisted hair-tuft and held her there for ten thousand years; because of the power of the lord the Ganges did not come out. Bhagīratha wondered where his little mother had gone, and through meditation discerned that she had been caught by the lord. The powerful man thereupon betook himself to Kailāsa, O best of hermits, and having gone there he practiced abundant *tapas*.

"Placated by him I gave him the river; relinquishing one hair I released the stream of the three courses. He took the Ganges and went to the netherworld Pātāla, where his ancestors lay. The first name of the Ganges is known as Alakanandā. When it descends to Haridvārā it becomes the Water of Viṣṇu's Foot which is a pre-eminent ford hard to attain even for the gods. When a man bathes there and visits Hari (in particular), and performs the circumambulation, he will not know suffering. Multitudes of evil deeds including brahmin murders, however many, all vanish from a mere visit to Hari.

"Once I myself went to Haridvārā, which is the sanctuary of Keśava, and because of the power of that ford I took on the form of Viṣṇu. The good people who go there find good health—men, women, the four-cornered worlds themselves. From merely visiting Hari they all go to the heaven Vaikuṇṭha. Beautiful Haridvārā is also a grand pilgrimage place of mine. This best of all fords bestows the four goals of life in the Kali Age; it gives Dharma to people, and release and success as well, there where the lovely and pure Ganges flows perennially."

This little tale, called Haridvārā, is holy and fine. They who listen to the great fame of the place obtain the same fruit as offering up a Horse Sacrifice or giving away a thousand cows. Such blessing does the wise man receive from just visiting Hari, be he a cow killer, a brahmin murderer, or a parricide; even such sins, however numerous, O brahmin, all disappear from seeing Hari.

# The Hermitage of Atri

Once there was a noble brahmin named Purūravas living in a brahmin village on the bank of a river. He had been the mighty king of Madra in his former life. Called Purūravas in this birth, O ever-faultless one, he performed the twelfth-night fast and worshiped Janārdana in order to gain a kingdom. During his fast he oiled his body after bathing. From the fast, he won the peerless kingdom of Madra, but because he had oiled his limbs while fasting, he became ugly.

That lord of earth abounded in all kingly virtues, but his people did not love him because he was so hideous. Anxious to restore his beauty, the king of Madra resolved to do *tapas*. And so he made his minister the ruler and went off to the Himālaya mountain. Accompanied by his own determination, that famous king went on foot to see the river which is the seat of sacred fords. At the edge of his territory, he saw that enchanting river called Irāvatī.

The king, whose fame was pure as snow, saw that river, a mighty torrent, flowing swiftly down from the frosty mountain top with icy water that sparkled like sunbeams on the snow, silvery like frost. He saw that holy, shining, heavenly river honored by Śakra and crowded with Gandharvas, sparkling on all sides, sprinkled with the ichor of the elephants of the gods and bridged by rainbow-hued spray in the sunlight. When the great King Purūravas saw that golden river dotted with ascetic's hermitages and visited by mighty brahmins, adorned with rows of snowy geese as if covered with shining chowrie plumes or jasmine flowers, he became supremely happy. The sight of the lovely, cool, and holy river that waxed and waned like the moon brought joy to his heart.

Her icy waters tumble swiftly. She is frequented by truthful brahmins. This magnificent daughter of Mount Himālaya sparkles with rippling waves, and her waters are as sweet as honey. Ascetics adorn her banks, and from her a ladder rises to heaven. She destroys all evil. She is the supreme queen of the seas, adored by hosts of great seers, this lovely river that grants the wishes of the whole world.

This beautiful river, free of weeds, is the benefactress of the entire earth. Her banks are teeming with herds of cows, and she shows the way to heaven. Resonant with flocks of geese and cranes, she is adorned with lotus flowers. Her navel is a deep whirlpool, and her thighs broad sandy islands. Blue lotuses are her eyes, and a red lotus blossom her mouth. Clothed in snow-white foam, her lower lip is a *cakravāka* bird. Rows of cranes are her teeth, and her eyebrows shoals of wriggling fish. Her breasts are the beautiful frontal mounds of elephants rising out of her own waters. She tinkles with anklets of geese, and her bangles are lotus stalks.

Smitten by her beauty, crowds of Apsarases followed by Gandharvas continually cavort in the middle of the day. Flowing onward, she is perfumed with pure saffron dropped by the Apsarases and by other fragrant scents wafting from the trees along her shores. She is most difficult to look at due to the sun's reflection on her dancing waves. Her banks are gouged out by the blows of elephant's tusks. And six-footed bees seek out her waters, scented by the sandal perfume of the women of the gods, and fragrant with ichor from the cheeks of the gods' elephants.

Trees growing on her shores, bent down by sweet-smelling blossoms, are alive with the buzzing of bees swarming there, attracted by the fragrance. Deer, enraptured, continually make love along her banks where there are seers, rich in *tapas,* gods and Apsarases. Here women, bodies freshly bathed, mostly celestials, with faces like lotus blossoms and the moon, are honored by the gods. The river flows continually onward, undisturbed by hosts of gods, kings, and barbarians, untroubled by troops of tigers. After seeing her whose waters are dotted with lotuses by day, but spotless as the starry sky by night, that river which grants all wishes and desires to the virtuous, the king went on.

After he had seen that holy river, his fatigue dispelled by the breeze, the king went on to see the mighty blessed Mt. Himālaya that abounds with many sky-scraping white peaks, the holy goal of the Siddhas, far beyond the range of birds. That ruler of men saw the handsome mountain wearing a lower garment of pine trees and wrapped in clouds above. One peak was turbaned with white clouds and crowned with the sun and moon, while another was blanketed in snow and layered with minerals. Covered with sandal and *pañcāngula* trees, the mountain's bulk bestows coolness even in summer.

In some places it is strewn with huge boulders, and in others it is marked by the lac-reddened footprints of Apsarases. Some places are bright with sunlight, while others are in shadow. In some places there is copious water quaffed by the fearsome mouths of caves.

Other places are brightened by troops of playful Vidyādharas, or made resonant with songs from the mouths of the most beautiful of Kinnara women.

Some spots are beautifully decorated with the heavenly flowers of the *santānaka* and other trees that have fallen on the ground where Gandharvas and Apsarases have been drinking. A lovely place, bestrewn with beds of flowers freshly crushed by the sleeping Gandharvas, that mountain abounds in lush green grass, with winds becalmed, made utterly magnificent with flowers.

This mountain is the refuge of ascetics, a rare gift for lovers. It is grazed by deer, and its mighty trees are cracked by the blows of elephants, which can be seen, a restless confused herd, along with the awful cries of creatures fearful of the lion's roar. The mountain slopes are sprinkled with ascetics and with grassy swards, and its treasury of jewels beautifies the triple world. This mountain is a never-failing refuge, frequented by important men. The king saw this great mountain, lacking nothing, rich in wealth and precious stones, where ascetics gain their goal with just a little *tapas,* by the mere sight of which all stains are washed away.

Some places are filled with wind-whipped waters that cascade down the precipices to join into a mighty waterfall. Other places, with lofty, rugged peaks, contain lakes that are warmed by continual sunshine, beautiful beyond imagination. The mountain is adorned with spots filled with stands of bamboo that are intertwined with the branches of groves of tall pine trees. Its lofty horn has a parasol of snow, hundreds of waterfalls, dangerous thundering torrents, and caves hidden by the snow.

After seeing this mountain with its beautiful flanks, that noble king of Madra continued his journeying until he reached a special place. There the king rested for a while on the beautiful mountainside, where even the thorns are as sweet as nectar, where all the female buffalo and she-goats guard the heavenly milk, and the rocks are filled inside and out with milk and curds. At the sight of the divine ponds and rivers of pure water, the king rejoiced.

Here there were hot springs, there chilly waters, and enchanting mountain dells at every step. For five leagues on every side there was no snow, and one could not see the mountain's foot. Aloft, O king, soared the white mountain peak where massive clouds continually make snow. On that rare mountain, fat clouds full of water rain without ceasing on its peerless craggy peaks.

On that mountain there is a charming hermitage where all desires are granted and whose trees drop fruit fit for the chief of gods. That supreme hermitage, where black bees are always buzzing, encircles the mountain like a necklace. Visited by the wives of the gods, it destroys all sins. There, heaps of snow, shining like the orb of the moon, are piled up here and there by playful monkeys. The hermitage is surrounded on all sides by valleys filled with snow and rocky caves always hidden from mankind.

After worshiping Bhava, the mighty King Purūravas, lord of Madra, reached that hermitage, by the grace of the god of gods, the lovely hermitage that allays fatigue. Adorned with hundreds of beautiful flowers, radiant, brilliant, conferring bliss, it was built by the sage Atri himself. Between two huge and variegated mountain peaks rises a third lofty and cloudless mountain whose icy waters are always freezing cold, with clumps of trees below it on the western slope. There, full of curiosity at the sight, the king entered a cavern, lovely to behold, surrounded by jasmine trees and creepers. . . .

In the middle of it the ascetic Atri had built a temple whose approach was a blazing golden causeway, studded with all kinds of gems. That temple shone luminous like moonlight, its staircases of fine beryl, its walls of purest coral, its lofty pillars of sapphire and its altar made of emerald, glittering with a lattice of diamond chips. It was lovely and magnificent to see!

In this sanctuary sat Janārdana, god of gods, reclining on the coils of a serpent, adorned with all sorts of ornaments. One of the knees of the discus-bearing god was bent, its foot resting on the serpent king. The second foot, O faultless one, lay on the lap of Lakṣmī, as the god reposed on the coils of the snake. His arm, adorned with an upper-arm bracelet, lay on another coil of the chief of snakes. And a second arm of the god of gods was extended, supporting his head on the back of his fingers. The hand of his third arm, resting on his bended knee, decorated with a jewelled bracelet, lay near his navel, slightly curved. And now hear about the fourth hand. It curved upward, toward his nose, holding a *santāna* blossom. Lakṣmī massaged his foot, with hands like lotus petals, while, adorned with anklets, he wore a chaplet of *santāna* flowers on his head.

The king greeted that god of mysterious deeds who was adorned with upper-arm bracelets and rings, his head lustrous with precious stones, as he lay on the hoods of the king of snakes. This image of the god, fashioned by Atri, is to be revered by the Siddhas and worshiped with *santāna* flowers. His limbs are to be anointed with heavenly perfumes and scents, and he is to be perfumed with divine incense while sweet juicy fruits are to be offered him by Siddhas.

After looking intently at his face, the king greeted that god whose right side shimmered, whose face resembled a blue lotus bloom. He fell to the ground on his knees, bowing his head, by the rule, and hymned Madhusūdana with his thousand names. Then he stood up and circumambulated him again and again. After this visit to the lovely sanctuary, the king remained there in the hermitage.

Taking refuge in a beautiful cave, out of the rain, the king did *tapas* while worshiping Madhusūdana with various kinds of flowers, fruits, roots and incense. He bathed three times a day and concentrated on fire worship. Living only on pond water, and renouncing all food, that lord born of men, the king, passed his time lying on the bare ground. Amazingly, his body did not weaken as he went without food, subsisting only on water. Thus the king enjoyed his *tapas*. Worshiping the supreme god without pause, he lived for some time at that heavenly hermitage, feeling no pain.

# The River Sarasvatī and Kurukṣetra

What is the source of the blessed Sarasvatī, supreme among rivers, that flows through Kurukṣetra? Upon reaching this lake and creating shrines along her banks, how does this lovely river flow out again toward the west, her course now seen, now unseen? Relate in detail the ancient tradition of the sacred fords.

This magnificent immortal river, the mere thought of which always effaces evil, springs from the sacred fig tree. That mighty river of holy waters, having cleft a thousand mountains, enters the forest called Dvaita. When the great seer Mārkaṇḍeya saw the Sarasvatī flowing from the fig tree, he bowed his head and praised her.

"O goddess, you are the mother of all the worlds, the radiant fire-drilling block of the gods. You are, O goddess, whatever is and is not. O granter of release, every meaningful word is connected with you and is established in you, as a Yogin, O goddess. The universe is rooted in the supreme syllable *OṂ*, which is Brahman, the root of everything that perishes. As fire dwells in wood and fragrance in earth, so in you, O goddess, rests this whole world, and Brahman too.

"The knowledge of whatever has parts and whatever is partless, as well as the knowledge of Brahman, who has the condition of both duality and non-duality, comes from you, O goddess, and also what is eternal and what dies, the gross and the subtle, everything that exists on earth, or in the heavens, or anywhere else. Whatever is formless and whatever has form, every single thing on earth, whatever can be distinguished and differentiated, all these are related to your vowels and consonants."

Thus praised, the goddess Sarasvatī, the tongue of Viṣṇu, answered the great-souled seer Mārkaṇḍeya, "Wherever you lead, O brahmin, there I shall untiringly follow!"

Originally this place was the holy lake of Brahmā. Then it was called Rāma's pool. Ploughed by the seer Kuru, it was named Kurukṣetra, or Kuru's field. Carrying holy water, the holy Sarasvatī now flows deep underneath the middle of this field.

Listening to the instructions of the wise seer Mārkaṇḍeya, that river entered Kurukṣetra in a continuous stream. After reaching Rantuka, the Sarasvatī flooded Kurukṣetra with her holy waters and swept off toward the west, where there are a thousand sacred fords frequented by seers. These I shall celebrate, by the grace of the supreme lord.

The memory of those shrines brings merit; the sight of them destroys evil; bathing at them brings release even for wicked men. Those who call to mind the sacred fords, those who please the gods there, those who bathe in them and those who have faith in them gain the supreme goal. Whoever remembers Kurukṣetra, no matter whether he is clean or unclean, is purified both inside and out.

Whoever utters these words, "I shall go to Kurukṣetra! I shall live in Kurukṣetra!" is released from all evils. To know Brahman, to perform *śrāddha* in Gayā, to die in Gogṛha and to live in Kurukṣetra—these are said to be the four means of liberation for mankind.

This place, built by the gods, which lies between the two heavenly rivers, the Sarasvatī and the Dṛṣadvatī, is called Brahmāvarta. Whoever always says, "Even though I am far away, I shall go to live in Kurukṣetra!" is freed from his sins. Whoever lives on the bank of the Sarasvatī, bathing in its waters, shall gain the knowledge of Brahman, without a doubt.

Gods, seers and Siddhas frequent this place of the Kurus. Whoever visits it continually sees Brahman within himself. Even criminals with a fickle human nature, if they control themselves out of a desire for release and frequent this place, are freed from the impurities which have accrued to them in many previous lifetimes, and witness and spotless deity eternally dwelling in the heart.

Men who continually attend the altar of Brahman, the holy field of Kurukṣetra, and lake Sannihita, gain the ultimate goal. For in time, even planets, constellations and stars may fall from the sky, but those who die in Kurukṣetra will never fall at all.

Brahmā and the other gods, seers, Siddhas and Cāraṇas live there, as well as Gandharvas, Apsarases and Yakṣas who want to maintain their place. A man who goes there filled with faith and who bathes in the great pool Sthāṇu, wins whatever his heart desires; of this there is no doubt. A man should practice self-control, circumambulate the lake, go to Rantuka to seek forgiveness again and again, bathe in the Sarasvatī, observe and salute the Yakṣa,* offer flowers and incense and food to the god, and recite the following: "By your grace, O chief Yakṣa, I shall make a pilgrimage to whatever sacred fords, forest and rivers there may be. Make my way ever clear!"

# The River Yamunā

Once the great-souled upholder of the earth, the serpent Śeṣa, after accomplishing some great task, was roaming around the forest with the cowherds in the guise of the man Baladeva. In order to reward him with great pleasure, Varuṇa said to his wife, "O Madirā (Wine), that mighty hero Ananta will find you desirable and beneficent. Go in joy, pure woman, and make him happy!" At his words, Vāruṇī materialized in the hollow of a *kadamba* tree that grew in Vṛndāvana.

The handsome Baladeva, wandering around in the forest, smelled the exquisite aroma of Madirā and conceived a thirst for the wine. When the plough-bearer saw a stream of wine flowing from the tree, Maitreya, he was delighted. And filled with joy, he drank it up, in the company of the cowherd men and women who, skilled in the ways of singing and music-making, sang sweetly to him.

When he was drunk and disoriented, covered with drops of perspiration that shone like pearls, he shouted to the river Yamunā, "Come over here! I want to take a bath!" Ignoring the words of the drunken man, the river refused to come, at which the furious plough-bearer snatched up his plough. Crazed with drink, he grabbed her and dragged her after him with the edge of his plough, exclaiming, "You refused to come to me, wicked woman. Now escape if you can!"

Hauled around by him, the river left her course at once and flooded the forest where Balabhadra was. Then she approached Rāma in human form, eyes rolling in terror, and said to him, "Have mercy on me, club-wielder! Let me go!" The plough-weaponed hero answered her sweet words, "You would not respect my bravery and strength, O river, so I shall pull you in a thousand different directions with the thrust of my plough!" But after the Yamunā had flooded that part of

*Rantuka.

the earth, Baladeva was moved by the words of that river, who was so afraid, and set her free.

After the great-souled Baladeva had bathed, the goddess Lakṣmī appeared and gave him a lovely lotus-blossom earring, a never-fading garland of lotus flowers sent by Varuṇa, and two garments deep blue like the sea. Thus adorned with a beautiful earring, dark blue robes, and a lovely garland, he shone forth in radiant beauty.

# The Virtues of Vārāṇasī

The city of Vārāṇasī is my place of utmost mystery, said Śiva, which conveys all creatures across the ocean of existence. There dwell great-souled devotees of mine, keeping their vows to me, great goddess, observing supreme self-control. Pre-eminent among all sacred fords, the best of places, superior to all knowledge, is this my place, the supreme Avimukta.

Within this area are to be found sanctuaries, purifying fords, and shrines in cremation grounds surpassing those in other divine spots in earth. This abode of mine floats in the sky, unattached to the earth. Those without Yoga cannot see it, but *yogins* witness it with their minds. This is the famous burning ground known as Avimukta.

Becoming Time, there I destroy the world, O lovely woman. This is my most favored place among all mysteries, O goddess. My devotees who go there enter into me. There gifts, prayers, offerings, oblations, *tapas* and all other acts, meditation, Vedic study and knowledge become indestructible. All the evil accumulated in a thousand previous lives is destroyed for one who enters Avimukta.

Brahmins, kṣatriyas, vaiśyas and śūdras, people of mixed caste, women, foreigners and others born from impure wombs, all these together, as well as worms and ants, game and fowl, after dying in Avimukta, O lovely-faced woman, are reborn as men in my auspicious city, O goddess, with a crescent moon on their heads, three eyes, and mounted on great bulls.

If a sinner dies in Avimukta, he does not go to hell because everyone favored by the lord gains the highest goal. Recognizing that release is most difficult to attain, and that rebirth is most horrible, a man should crush his own feet with a stone in order to remain in Vārāṇasī. That goal, supreme mistress, is hard to attain even by *tapas* for a pure man who dies anywhere else. This benefit springs from my kindness, O delight of the king of the mountains; those who remain unenlightened, still deluded by my Māyā, do not see it. Those fools, wrapped in ignorance, who do not visit Avimukta, are reborn again and again into semen, urine and excrement.

A wise man, even if beset by a hundred obstacles, gains that supreme goal which ends suffering if he should live here, and goes to the supreme abode of Śiva where there is no birth, old age or death. For those who seek release, this is the only place to go to escape rebirth. Having reached it, one's task is done, so think the wise. Not by gifts, nor by *tapas,* nor even by sacrifices or knowledge is the marvelous goal attained which can be found in Avimukta. People of various castes, outcastes, disgusting Caṇḍālas and others, those whose bodies are filled with impurities, and those who are covered with crimes, for these the only remedy is Avimukta. This the wise know.

Avimukta is supreme wisdom! Avimukta is the final goal! Avimukta is ultimate reality! Avimukta is matchless well-being! To those who live in Avimukta, who dedicate themselves to me, I grant supreme knowledge and, in the end, the highest goal.

The river Ganges which flows through heaven, earth and the netherworld, enters Vārāṇasī in particular, and there she destroys the evil accumulated in a hundred life-times. Anywhere else but in Vārāṇasī it is most difficult to find easy access to the Ganges, or to perform *śrāddha,* gifts, *tapas,* prayer and vows. A man who lives in Vārāṇasī should continually make sacrifices, give gifts and worship the gods, while living on air. Whether one be a sinner, a crook or a wicked person, one is wholly purified by a visit to Vārāṇasī. . . .

One can acquire the ultimate truth called Avimukta, O goddess, in a single life-time in Vārāṇasī. This Avimukta lies between the eyebrows in the center of the navel, in the heart, in the head, in the sun, and also in Vārāṇasī. This city lies between the Varaṇa and the Asi rivers; here dwells the true and eternal Avimukta. There is not now nor shall there ever be a place superior to Vārāṇasī where both Nārāyaṇa and Mahādeva, lord of the heaven, are to be found. There gods and Gandharvas, Yakṣas, Snakes and Rākṣasas always honor me, as the Grandfather, god of gods. Those who have committed a major crime, and men even more wicked than they, gain the supreme goal by going to Vārāṇasī.

## Vārāṇasī and the Yakṣa

Pūrṇabhadra had a famous son named Harikeśa, an illustrious Yakṣa who was both pious and virtuous. From the time of his birth he was supremely loyal to Śarva.* He worshiped him devoutly, making Śarva his final goal. Whether walking, standing still or roaming around, whether eating or drinking, sitting or lying down, his thoughts were always on Rudra.

That preoccupied Yakṣa was addressed by his father Pūrṇabhadra, who said, "You are a misbegotten child! I think you must not be my son, for you do not act like one born into a Yakṣa family. We Guhyakas are by nature cruel of heart; we eat anything, including flesh; we are habitually violent. Little son, stop acting the way you do; for your conduct is not acceptable to the great-souled Svayambhū, if the way of life that he ordained for you is to be upheld. Householders should not act in ways appropriate to other stages of life! You are now on the wrong path, for you act as though you were a human being. Give up this human behavior and behave like us. Your actions are appropriate to one born into the human race. Surely you should observe instead the duties I assign to you!"

After speaking in this manner to his son, the eminent Pūrṇabhadra left, saying, "Leave now, my son, and do as you please!"

So Harikeśa went forth, leaving his house and family. Reaching Vārāṇasī, he practiced intense *tapas*. He stood there motionless, like a pillar, unblinking, like a rock or a piece of dead wood, his senses under control, constantly devoted to Śiva, while a thousand divine years went by. Eventually he was overgrown by an anthill and nibbled at by the ants who pierced him with cruel mouths as sharp as diamond needles. Bloodless, fleshless and skinless, he grew as white as a conch-shell, jasmine, or the moon, as he continued to concentrate on the god Śiva until only his bones remained. . . .

Meanwhile, the goddess said to her husband Śankara, "I would like to see your garden once again. I am always interested in hearing about the glory of that place, O god, and the rewards it offers, O supreme one, because it is so dear to you."

At Śarvāṇī's request, the supreme lord god Śarva began to describe it, as she had asked. Śankara, the lord of the gods, bearer of the Pināka, went forth with the goddess Pārvatī to show her the garden, saying, "This is Vārāṇasī, my place of greatest mystery. It brings release at all times to all creatures. In it, goddess, live the perfected ones who continually observe my vows. Perpetually carrying various *lingas*, they long for my heaven. With senses conquered and minds released, they practise the highest Yoga. This is my lovely garden, filled with all kinds of trees, resonant with the songs of a variety of birds, adorned with ponds full of blue and red lotuses, ever attended

*Śiva.

by hosts of Apsarases and Gandharvas. Any devotee of mine whose actions are always loyal to me, whose mind is concentrated on me, gains release here and nowhere else; that is why living here always delights me. This is my great, divine mystery of mysteries. Brahmā and the other gods and Siddhas who seek release all recognize that this place is most beloved. Because of this, it is dear to me. I have never deserted this place; nor shall I ever do so, and hence it is known as 'Avimukta' or 'Not-Deserted.'

Henceforth, my lovely goddess, those who live here, whether householders or *linga*-bearers loyal to me, whose final goal is me, shall enjoy supreme release, so hard to win, by my favor. Even a man whose mind is not free from doubt, who has abandoned the love of the law, if he dies here, will not be reborn again. All wise men with subdued senses who abide in truth, without egotism, who are loyal to me, abstaining from ritual, free from attachments, when they reach death, they shall attain supreme release, by my grace, O devoted woman! He who dies here gains the same release as the *yogin* who does Yoga for a thousand lifetimes! This that I have told you, in brief, is the ultimate mystery of this place, O goddess, the great reward of Avimukta!"

When the god saw the Yakṣa Harikeśa doing *tapas*, he said to his mistress, the daughter of the mountain, "Lovely woman, I must give a boon to this Yakṣa, out of kindness! He is a devotee of mine, O fair-hipped one, whose stains have been removed by *tapas*. Aho! He deserves a reward from me, mistress of the world!" So speaking, the god who is the master of the world went with the goddess to where the zealous Yakṣa stood, so emaciated that his veins stood out like cords.

When the goddess saw at a glance that fleshless Guhyaka, a white skeleton held together by bones and sinews, she exclaimed to the god, "O Śankara, the gods call you cruel, and you are rightly named! For you have not rewarded with a boon the ascetic prowess of this one who serves you in this holy place, O Mahādeva. Why has this young Yakṣa gone to such pains? By your grace, supreme lord, give him a boon at once! The Manus, the supreme seers and the other celestials say, O god, that whether offended or pleased, Śiva should grant success, the attainment of happiness and sovereignty, and in the end, release."

Thus addressed, the god who is the master of the world, who bears a bull on his banner, went with the goddess to where Yakṣa sat. There he witnessed Harikeśa reduced to skin and bones, prostrate in devotion. The bull-bannered god then granted divine sight to Harikeśa, with which he beheld Śankara. Slowly opening his eyes on command, the Yakṣa saw the bull-bannered god standing there with his *gaṇas*. The god of gods said, "I give you a boon, as in times past: the power to see me without hindrance in the triple world, and a body of the same color as mine."

Upon receiving this boon, with his whole body prostrate at the god's feet, and making obeisance with his head, the Yakṣa spoke. Prompted by the god's words, namely, "I give you a boon," the Yakṣa answered, "O lord, give me unwavering devotion to you and to no other! Make me the giver of food to the world. And bestow on me *gaṇapati**-hood forever. And may I always behold your shrine Avimukta. This is what I desire, O lord of gods, this matchless boon from you!"

And the god of gods replied, "You shall be a Gaṇeśa, a leader of my troops. You shall be free from birth, death and all disease. And you shall be the giver of bounty, honored by everyone. You shall be invincible among all others, and you shall be skilled in the highest Yoga. You shall give food to people, and always protect this holy place. You shall be most mighty, full of truth, brahminic, and dear to me, a great *yogin* with three eyes and a staff in your hand. Udbhrama and Saṃbhrama shall be your two attendants who will act on your orders in the world with eagerness and zeal.

Thus Vāmadeva, the blessed lord of the immortals, made that Yakṣa a Gaṇeśvara, lord of the *gaṇas*, and they left Vārāṇasī together.

## The Pilgrimage of Śiva to Vārāṇasī

When that ghastly skull remained stuck to the palm of his hand,† Rudra grew disturbed, O brahmin, his mind upset at the thought. Then that dreadful, terrifying female called Brahmahatyā, or Brahmin-Murder, black as a heap of collyrium, with flaming red hair, approached Hari. When he saw that ghastly apparition coming, he said to her, "Who are you, gruesome woman? Why have you come?"

The horrible Brahmahatyā answered that skull-carrying god, "I am Brahmin-Murder. Accept me, three-eyed one!" And so speaking, Brahmahatyā entered the trident-bearer Rudra, setting his body afire. . . .

That cloud-bannered god Śarva, although yoked to Yoga, was

*Master of the *gaṇas*.
†See "The Skull-Bearer," Ch. 4.

weighed down by Brahmahatyā wherever he went. Not at ponds, fords or hermitages, nor at the holy shrines of the gods could he find release from the burden of his crime. Finally the desperate Śankara went to Kurukṣetra where he found the god whose banner bears the bird, discus in hand. . . .

"Praise be to you, immortal god who bears the discus! Glory be to you, Mādhava, in the form of a fish! I know you have compassion for the world, so set me free, Keśava, from the bondage of this sin! Destroy the evil which has lodged in my body and which overpowers me because of brahmin murder!

"I am on fire! I shall perish! I have acted heedlessly! Purify me! You yourself are a sacred shrine. Praise be to you!"

So honored by the great-souled Śankara, the blessed discus-bearer answered this, in order to destroy Brahmahatyā, "Listen to my sweet speech, Maheśvara; it shall annihilate Brahmin-Murder, confer purity and increase merit. There is a certain one who lives in the holy east, born of a portion of myself, who is known as Yogaśāyin. He inhabits Prayāga, and from his right foot flows the beautiful, pure and sin-destroying river famed as the Varaṇa. From his left foot streams another river renowned as the Asi. Both these fine rivers have been venerated in the world.

"The area which lies between these two rivers is the field of Yogaśāyin, the ultimate sacred ford in the three worlds, which gives release from all evil. It has no equal anywhere in heaven, on earth or in the netherworld. Here there is a pure and holy city celebrated as Vārāṇasī, in which even people devoted to pleasure gain absorption in you, O lord, and where the elders, hearing the jingling belts of playful women mingled with the sound of the Veda chanted by the bulls of brahmins commend them both with good humor, over and over again. In this city, when the moon sees lac-reddened footprints at the crossroads where women have strayed, it wonders if a pond of rosy lotuses has just passed by. At night in Vārāṇasī, lofty temples hide the moon, and they conceal the sun by day, with their fine long pennants waving in the breeze.

"Here black bees ignore their flower-cups, lured instead by the shining faces of painted women which are reflected in the moonstone walls. Here men grow fatigued, worn out by bewitching play, O Śambhu, no one enters the fine houses by force, except for dice, and no one attacks women violently, except in the play of love.

"O lord of gods, in this great shrine of Vārāṇasī, such as I have just described, dwells the blessed Lola Ravi who removes all sins. If you go to the place called Daśāsvamedha where Keśava, a portion of myself, resides, O excellent god, you shall gain release from your crime."

Thus addressed by the eagle-bannered Viṣṇu, the bull-bannered Śiva bowed with bent head, and sped swift as an eagle to Vārāṇasī to rid himself of evil. When he reached that holy city full of shrines, he visited Lola and Daśāsvamedha, bathed in the sacred fords, and with his sins cleansed, he sought out Keśava.

When he found Keśava, Śankara prostrated himself before him and said, "By your grace, O Hṛṣīkeśa, Brahmahatyā has been destroyed. But this skull still sticks to my hand, O lord of gods. Please tell me why, for I don't know!"

At Mahādeva's words, Keśava replied, "There is a reason, Rudra, which I shall tell you. This holy pool full of lotuses in front of me is the best of the sacred fords, revered by gods and Gandharvas. As soon as you have taken a ritual bath in this supreme ford, O Śambhu, the skull shall fall off. Thereafter you shall be called Kapālin, or Skull-Bearer in the world, O Rudra, and this sacred ford shall be known as Kapālamocana, or Skull-Releaser."

Thus addressed by Keśava, lord of the gods, Maheśvara duly bathed at Kapālamocana, by the Vedic rule, O seer. And after the destroyer of Tripura had taken a ritual bath at that ford, the skull fell from the palm of his hand. And so, by the grace of the lord, that choicest of fords was named Skull-Releaser.

# Gayā

Listen, O Vyāsa, as I relate the magnificent glory of Gayā, holiest of the holy, that gives both happiness here and release hereafter. Once upon a time there was a demon named Gaya, who practiced such intense *tapas* that all creatures were disturbed. Heated by his *tapas*, the gods went for refuge to Hari seeking the demon's death. Hari told them, "People's souls will be safe only when his huge body has been felled." To this the gods replied, "So be it."

One day that mighty demon, bearing lotuses from the ocean of milk for the worship of Śiva, stopped for the night in the country of Kikaṭa. There Viṣṇu deluded him with his magic and killed him with his mace. Ever since then, the mace-bearer Viṣṇu has lived there in Gayā, dispensing release, while the demon's body has remained in that place in the form of a *linga*. Living together in that holy spot are Janārdana, Śiva the lord of Time and Brahmā, the Great-Grandfather too.

Since Viṣṇu declared this to be a holy place, a man who performs sacrifices and *śrāddhas* here, who gives *piṇḍas** to the ancestors, bathes, and so on, goes to heaven and Brahmaloka, not to hell. Knowing the sacred form of Gayā to be the best, the Grandfather made a sacrifice and honored the brahmins who went there to be priests. Pouring forth the mighty river that is always full of water, and the lakes and ponds, he produced delicious foods, fruits and Kāmadhenu, the wishing cow. And the lord gave to the brahmins five acres of land around Gayā.

Those brahmins who lived in Gayā grew greedy, and began to take money and goods for the practise of Dharma. So Viṣṇu cursed them: "You shall have neither knowledge nor wealth for three generations! This water-bearing river shall be only a pile of rocks for you!" But the accursed brahmins beseeched Lord Brahmā until he took pity on them, and said, "Virtuous people who perform *śrāddha* at Gayā, who honor you, and who always worship me, shall go to Brahmaloka."

There are four means of release for mankind: knowing Brahman, performing funeral ceremonies at Gayā, dying at Gogṛha, and living in Kurukṣetra. O Vyāsa, even the oceans, ponds, tanks and wells go to the sacred ford at Gayā, eager to bathe. Of this there is no doubt. By performing *śrāddha* at Gayā, all the evils born from greed, brahmin-murder, drinking liquor, theft, having intercourse with a teacher's wife, or associating with those who do these things, are annihilated. Those who die without having performed life-rites, those who are killed by wild animals or robbers, those who are bitten by snakes—all these are released and go to heaven if their funeral rites are performed at Gayā. The fruit a man obtains by giving the gift of *piṇḍas* to his ancestors at Gayā I could not describe in a million years!

# Prayāga

After the Bhārata war, King Yudhiṣṭhira, son of Pṛthā-Kuntī, won the kingdom. Overcome with grief at the death of his kinsmen, he thought over and over again, "King Duryodhana was the general of eleven armies. After causing us much pain, they are all dead, and only we five Pāṇḍavas remain, because we turned for help to Vāsudeva.

"We have slain Bhīṣma, Droṇa and the mighty Karṇa, King Duryodhana and all their sons and brothers. All these kings who

*Offerings in the form of rice balls.

considered themselves brave have been killed. O Govinda, what is the use of having a kingdom now? How can we be happy? What is the point of living?" Thinking, "This is shameful and wicked" the king grew despondent. He stood there listless, without moving, with his face downcast.

When the king recovered, he asked himself over and over again, "Is there some ritual duty, some vow, or pilgrimage which will remove the stain of this great crime—one which will conduct a man to Viṣṇu's matchless heaven? How can I ask Kṛṣṇa what to do; he is the one who made me do all this in the first place! And how can I ask Dhṛtarāṣṭra after I have killed his hundred sons?" And so Yudhiṣṭhira, king of Dharma, fell into despair. And all the great-souled men known as the Pāṇḍavas, overcome by their brother's grief, wept too. And others who had gathered there, along with Kuntī and Draupadī, all fell crying to the ground.

Meanwhile in Vārāṇasī, the sage Mārkaṇḍeya knew that Yudhiṣṭhira was sorrowful and crying, overwhelmed by grief. Shortly thereafter that great ascetic arrived at Hāstinapura and stood at the king's gate. "Mārkaṇḍeya the seer is standing at the door, anxious to see you," announced the gate-keeper, at which the son of Dharma went at once to the door.

"Welcome, great seer! Welcome, illustrious one! Now my life bears fruit and my family is saved! At the sight of you my Fathers are gratified, great seer, and my body is purified by your presence!" Seating that seer on his lion throne, the great-souled Yudhiṣṭhira worshiped him with water for his feet and other offerings. Pleased and honored, Mārkaṇḍeya said to the king, "Tell me at once, O king, why you are weeping! What has made you so despondent? What troubles you? What causes you such distress?"

"Remembering everything we have done in order to win this kingdom, great seer, causes me continual anguish!" he replied.

"Hear, mighty king, the established Dharma of the kṣatriyas. There should be no guilt for a wise man who must fight in battle, especially for a kṣatriya under the law of kingship. Take this to heart, and stop feeling guilty!"

At his words King Yudhiṣṭhira bowed his head to the seer and asked his visitor to remove all his crimes, saying, "I beg you, most wise one, you who understand the triple world at all times, tell me how a person is released from his sins!"

"Hear, mighty king," said the seer, "for people who do meritorious acts, the most effective way to annihilate sins is to go to Prayāga."

Yudhiṣṭhira then said, "I want to hear the story of the last Eon, blessed seer, as related by the mouth of god Brahmā! I want to know how and why man should go to Prayāga, where people go when they die in Prayāga, and what is the benefit of living in Prayāga. Tell me all this!"

"I shall tell you, my son" replied Mārkaṇḍeya, "the supreme benefit as I heard it long ago from Brahmā. The area that extends from Pratiṣṭhāna to Prayāga and from the pool of Vāsuki to that city, which includes the sanctuaries of the Snakes Kambala, Aśvatara and Bahumūlaka, is known in the three worlds as the field of Prajāpati. Those who bathe there go to heaven; those who die there are not reborn. There Brahmā and the other gods all together give protection. And there are also many other holy shrines that remove all sins, O king, so many that I could not describe them in many hundreds of years. Now I shall relate in brief the glory of Prayāga.

"Sixty thousand bows there are that guard the river Ganges. And the sun with its seven horses continually protects the Yamunā. Indra watches over Prayāga in particular, at all times. And Hari guards its boundaries, along with the celestials. The trident-bearing lord Śiva protects the banyan tree, and the gods guard the holy shrine that removes all evil.

"One who is immersed in wickedness does not go there at all; but when one's crime is small, or rather small, O lord of mankind, it is destroyed by just the thought of Prayāga. A man is released from evil just by visiting the shrine, by saying its name, or by getting some clay from it, O king! At Prayāga there are beautiful lakes through which flows the Ganges river. Evil is instantly destroyed at the entrance of the city.

"An evil-doer who only thinks of the Ganges, even from a distance of a thousand miles, gains the supreme goal. By reciting its name, one is released from evil. By visiting it, one finds riches. Bathing in it, drinking it, or washing in it, one purifies one's family to the seventh generation.

"One who bathes at the confluence of the Ganges and Yamunā rivers, who speaks the truth, controls his anger, practices non-injury, follows Dharma, knows the elements of existence and is bent upon the well-being of cows and brahmins, is released from stains. With his mind concentrated, he gains his desires. One who goes to Prayāga, which is guarded by all the deities, and lives there as a celibate *brahmacārin* for a month, satisfying the Fathers and the gods, gets all his wishes and desires wherever he is born again.

"Famed in the three worlds as the divine daughter of the sun, the illustrious river Yamunā meets with the Ganges at Prayāga where the god Maheśvara is always present in person. After going to holy Prayāga, most difficult to attain by humans, O Yudhiṣṭhira, the gods, Dānavas and Gandharvas, the seers, Siddhas and Cāraṇas, after touching water here, O chief among kings, gained heaven."

# SUPERNATURALS

## The Fathers

Long ago the progenitor Ruci roamed around earth, indifferent to the world and without desires, sleeping wherever he found himself at sunset. When his departed Fathers saw this seer who had neither hearth nor home, who ate a single meal a day, freed from attachment, without even a hermitage, they said, "Son, you are lacking in virtue, for you have not taken a wife. Why is this? Marriage is a bridge to heaven and release; without it one is fettered, as by eating raw meat. A householder who honors all the gods, the departed Fathers, the seers and the needy gain heaven! One should share with the gods by uttering 'Svāhā,' with the Fathers by saying 'Svadhā' and with one's servants and guests by gifts of food. O seer among men, you increase your bondage every day by your debt to the gods, to us and to all creatures. How do you hope to reach heaven, even by gratifying the gods and ancestors, without begetting sons before shaving your head and renouncing the world? Because of your misconduct, O son, you shall endure unhappiness here, hell after death, and after leaving hell you shall be miserable in yet another life!"

"Family life entails degradation into grief and evil!" he replied, "That is why I have not taken a wife. Because of a moment's weakness, one risks one's Self. And release is not guaranteed by marriage! It is better that the Self remain unencumbered through daily purification in the waters of knowledge, even though mired in the mud of egotism. The Self, marked by the mud of deeds done in many previous lives, should be cleansed by the waters of the knowledge of truth by the wise who control their faculties!"

"I am old now," Ruci continued. "Who would give me a wife, O Fathers? It is difficult for a poor man to marry."

"Our fall and your own degradation," they replied, "shall come to pass because of this, if you do not heed our words!" And saying this, his Fathers suddenly vanished from sight like lamps blown out by the wind.

And so the brahmin seer roamed the world in search of a maiden. Failing to find a bride, he was kindled to great worry by the words of his Fathers and became terribly depressed. "What shall I do? Where shall I go? How shall I find a wife? I must quickly find a way to assure the happiness of my Fathers and myself!"

As the great-souled seer pondered these things, an idea came to him. "I shall propitiate the lotus-born Brahmā for a boon by my *tapas*!" And so the great-minded Ruci practiced *tapas* for a hundred divine years. Self-controlled, he stood in the woods for a long long time, maintaining his self-restraint, to please the god.

Finally the Grandfather Brahmā appeared and said, "I am pleased with you. Tell me what you want!"

Prostrating himself, he said to Brahmā, the goal of the world, that he wanted to do as his Fathers had instructed him. Brahmā replied, "You shall become a progenitor by whom offspring shall be produced. After you have had progeny, that is, your own sons, O brahmin, repeat the proper rituals. Then after having done your duty, you shall win success. Take a wife, as your Fathers told you to do. Honor your Fathers by taking to heart their wishes. When they are satisfied, the Fathers will grant you your desire, namely a wife and children. Indeed, is there anything your ancestors will not give to you when they are satisfied?"

When he heard the words of Brahmā whose origin is hidden Ruci performed water libations to the Fathers on the beautiful bank of a river. The respectful brahmin worshiped his Fathers with this hymn, fixed in attention, and bowed in devotion. . . .

"I praise the Fathers who are embodied in heaven, who enjoy the Svadhā offering, who grant the desires of those who offer a desiderative sacrifice, and who grant release to those who have no desires. Let all the Fathers be satisfied who fulfill the needs of their followers—godhood, Indraness and still more, elephants, horses, jewels and palaces—those Fathers who dwell in white mansions in the moonbeams and rays of the sun. May these Fathers be satisfied here with food and drink, and may they be nourished by offerings of perfume and other pleasing things! . . .

"Worthy of honor by brahmins are those Fathers who are white as a lotus or a moonbeam, by the kṣatriyas those Fathers who have the color of fire or the sun, by the vaiśyas those Fathers who are bright gold, and by the śūdras those Fathers who are dark blue. By my offering of flowers, perfumes, incense, water, food and other goods, and with the *agnihotra*, may they be satisfied. I am always bowed low before these Fathers!" . . .

Thus praised so fervently by Ruci, O excellent seers, the Fathers appeared one by one, illuminating the ten directions. And he saw them standing in front of him adorned with the flowers, perfume and oil that he had offered them. Prostrate with devotion, the reverent Ruci folded his hands once again and cried out to each in turn, "Praise be to you!" At which the placated Fathers said to that fine seer, "Choose a boon!" With head bowed, he replied, "Brahmā has ordered me to produce children. I want a wife who is wealthy, fecund and divine!"

And so the Fathers answered, "Here and now you shall have a beautiful wife, and she shall bear you a son, excellent seer! He shall be a wise Manu, famous and distinguished, O Ruci. And he shall become famous in the three worlds as Raucya, the son of Ruci. And he shall have many strong, valiant, and great-souled sons who shall rule earth. After you have become a progenitor, and after you have created the four kinds of creatures, knowing Dharma, at the end of your reign, you shall attain your final goal!" . . .

Then near at hand, from the middle of that river arose a lovely, slender Apsaras named Pramloca. The beautiful nymph addressed the great-souled Ruci in melodious tones, showing him much kindness, "By my grace, there has been born to me a lovely daughter of fine form, the child of the great-souled Puṣkara, son of Varuṇa. Take this lovely girl for your wife, as a gift from me. She shall bear you a wise Manu as your son."

When he agreed, she lifted her lovely daughter named Mālinī from the water. That seer led her to the bank of the river where he took her hand in marriage, excellent seers. And she bore him a son, a heroic, magnificent child named Ruci, as I told you before.

# The Mothers

Once there was a demon named Andhaka, who was as black as a pile of collyrium. Yoked in mighty *tapas,* he was invincible to the gods. When he saw lord Mahādeva playing with his wife Pārvatī, he set out to abduct the goddess. And so a ferocious battle began between Andhaka and Śambhu.

As that awful battle raged in the region of Avanti, near the Mahākāla forest, Rudra was harassed by Andhaka. When Rudra loosed the dreadful arrow Pāśupata, the blood of Andhaka gushed from the hole it made, and from that hole sprang up Andhakas by the hundreds and thousands. From their blood as they were torn asunder arose still more, until the whole world was filled with ghastly Andhakas.

When the god had seen the demon's magical powers, he poured forth the Mothers in order to drink up the blood of the Andhaka—Maheśvarī, Brāhmī, Kaumārī, Mālinī and hundreds more. . . . These horrible females became gorged with Andhaka blood, but when they had drunk their fill, still more creatures arose from the Andhakas. Further tormented by these creatures with spikes and clubs in their hands, lord Śankara, utterly confounded by them, went for refuge to the unborn lord god Vāsudeva.

Lord Viṣṇu emitted the dry river Revatī, who gulped down in an instant all the blood of those Andhakas. The more she drank their gushing blood, the drier grew the goddess, O lord of creatures. As she lapped up the Andhakas' blood, they were all laid low by the foe of Tripura.

When Śarva, upholder of the three worlds, attacked the original demon Andhaka, instantly impaling him on the points of his trident, the great and brave hero Andhaka began to sing Śankara's praises. Bhava was pleased, and so he granted him the boon of always being near the god, and the office of a Gaṇeśa.

Then all the hosts of Mothers said to Śankara, "O lord, now we are going to devour the gods, demons and human beings—the whole world—by your grace. Give us your permission!" But Śankara replied, "Surely it is your duty to protect all beings, not to destroy them. So give up this awful plan at once!" But those ferocious Mothers ignored Śankara's words and began to gobble up the three worlds with their moving and unmoving beings.

As the triple world was being eaten by the hosts of Mothers, lord Śiva concentrated on the lord of the gods in the form of a Man-Lion, the god who has neither beginning nor end, the origin of the existence of all the worlds. In his form as a Man-Lion his long sharp claws are smeared with the blood from the chest of the Daitya king, and his tongue is like lightning; he has enormous fangs and a prickly, bristling mane. His fierce claws are as sharp as diamonds and his mouth stands agape from ear to ear. He blazes forth like Mt. Meru, eyes shining like the morning sun.

Shaped like the peak of the Himālaya mountain, his mouth glistens with striking fangs, and he is garlanded with a mane of flame made from the fire of the anger that sprang from his claws. His upper armlets are of diamonds and he wears a magnificent crown, necklace and bracelets, and glitters with a great golden belt. Wearing a pair of blue garments dark as lotus petals, he fills the entire chamber of the egg of Brahmā with his brilliance. Like a whirlwind he stirs the flames of the offering fires into circles like the whorls of his body hair. And he sports an enormous wreath of many-colored flowers.

At the mere thought of him, lord Viṣṇu granted Rudra a vision of himself in this very form as a Man-Lion, so difficult for even the gods to behold, on which Rudra was concentrating. Then Śankara prostrated himself before the lord of gods and praised him saying, "Glory be to you, Jagannātha, in the form of a Man-Lion! You are sated with the blood of the Daitya, your pointed claws ablaze, your body a tawny gold; you are utterly resolute!

"I bow before you, navel-lotused god! You are Śakra among gods. You are the *guru* of the world. Roaring like the clouds at the end of the Eon, you shine forth like ten million suns! You have the rage of a thousand Yamas, the energy of a thousand Indras, the bulk of a thousand Kuberas; your soul consists of a thousand Varuṇas! You are made of a thousand Kālas; your senses are controlled in a thousand ways; you are steadfast as a thousand earths, and embodied in a thousand fires. You have the luster of a thousand moons, the power of a thousand planets, the brilliance of a thousand Rudras, and you are praised by a thousand brahmins. You appear ferocious, with a thousand sets of arms; you look out from a thousand faces; you churn with a thousand devices, and you are the liberator from a thousand deaths!

"The Mothers whom I created to destroy Andhaka are now ignoring my orders and devouring the world. I cannot destroy them because I made them. How can I annihilate those whom I myself created?"

Thus addressed by Rudra, the god Hari, in the form of a Man-Lion, emitted the goddess of speech Vāṇīśvarī from his tongue, Māyā from his heart, Bhavamālinī from his genitals and Kālī from his bones. These were created first by the great-souled god. . . . Thirty-two mighty and powerful goddesses in all arose from the god's body, and they were fully capable of both the creation and destruction of the triple world.

As soon as these goddesses emerged from the gods, great king, they were furious at the host of Mothers and began to attack them, their eyes wide with rage. The fire from the eyes of those dreadful females was unbearable to behold. When they went to the Man-Lion for refuge, he exclaimed, "Just as people and cattle protect their offspring for a long time, and just as the hosts of celestials promptly take care of those they conquer, so must you goddesses protect the world, at my urging, and worship the slayer of Tripura along with the gods and humans. Do not harass those who are loyal to the slayer of Tripura, but always be the guardians of those who remember me.

"Grant the desires of those who always pay you tribute, those who recite prayers and do other things that I command, and protect those people and my seat as well. Mahādeva will confer on you a supremely gruesome form and you shall be at the head of all the great goddesses if you keep to what I say.

"Now that you hosts of Mothers whom I created have ceased your depredations, O large-eyed women, you shall be my lovers for all time. You shall receive worship from mankind, along with me, and when worshiped by yourselves alone, you shall grant all desires. Those who adore the dry river Revatī, desirous of a son, shall receive a son, without a doubt." Exclaiming this, his body wreathed in flame, the lord vanished then and there, along with the host of Mothers.

And on that very spot sprang up the sacred ford called Kṛtaśauca, where lives the primeval god Hara who takes away the suffering of the world. After he bestowed a set of supremely horrible bodies on that group of ghastly Mothers, he stayed there at that ford, in their midst. And having placed seven of the goddess Mothers into his shrine as Rudra, Śiva—half woman and half man—also disappeared. Now whenever Hara and the host of Mothers reappear, the enemy of Tripura and Andhaka worships the lord of the gods in the form of a Man-Lion.

# Garuḍa

Long ago when the bird Garuḍa, the son of Vinatā, had crawled out of his egg, he was immediately hungry for a meal, and he said to his mother, "Give me something to eat!" His stately mother, seeing the powerful, mountainlike Garuḍa, her son, said cheerfully, "Son, I cannot assuage your kind of hunger at all. Your father is doing *tapas* on the northern bank of the Lauhitya. He is the law-minded grandfather of the world named Kaśyapa. Go to your father and tell him your desire. At his advice your hunger shall be stilled."

At her words Garuḍa went to his father in an instant, for he was as fast as the wind. Seeing his father, greatest of seers, blazing like fire, the bird bowed his head and said to him, "I am your son, great-souled one, I have come hungry. Give me something to eat, lord protector."

That best of seers sank into contemplation, recognized his son and out of affection said, "There are a hundred thousand evil Niṣādas* living on the ocean shore. Eat them and be happy. They are like crows at a place of pilgrimage, devastating it, and they are dangerous. But spare the brahmin who lives there in concealment."

Thus the bird went and devoured them. But he also swallowed the brahmin, who was unidentifiable. The brahmin stuck in his craw, and he could neither swallow him nor spit him out. He went to his father and said, "What has happened to me, father? Some creature is stuck in my craw and I cannot do anything about it!" Kaśyapa replied, "I told you, son; it is a brahmin, didn't you know?"

*Aborigines.

Then the wise and law-minded seer spoke to the brahmin, "Come to me, I shall tell you what is good for you." The brahmin replied to that bull among seers, "These Niṣādas have always been my friends, They are all dear fathers and brothers-in-law with their children and other good people as well. I shall go with them to either hell or heaven!"

Hearing his words Kaśyapa was surprised and said, "Born in a family of brahmins you have fallen among Caṇḍāla brood. These men are sure to go to hell. There will be no atonement for them for a long time. They are all evil and criminal Caṇḍālas. A man can only be happy after he has sworn off his vices, whether he has committed his heinous crimes from ignorance or delusion. He who practices Dharma comes to a good end; a criminal does not observe Dharma, but sets his mind on more crime. Having committed all those crimes he goes to perdition, as one drowns in the sea if he boards a boat made of stone. Later he will expiate his sin."

The brahmin replied to that sagacious seer, "If this bird does not let go of me and all my relatives, I shall give up the ghost inside this bird which has gnawed at my entrails. That is my solemn promise!"

Thereupon, out of fear of brahmin-murder, the seer said to Garuḍa, "Spit out all those Mlecchas* with their brahmin!" And the bird, which knew he was at fault, at his father's behest spat out all the Niṣādas over forests and mountain tracts in all directions. . . .

Again the bird said, "I am terribly hungry." Compassionately Kaśyapa said to Garuḍa, "Somewhere in the ocean there are two mighty creatures, a giant elephant and a tortoise, who are trying to kill each other. They will quickly still your hunger in the waters."

At his father's word the mighty and fast bird flew off and found the tortoise and the elephant, gripped them in his talons, and flew up to the sky with the speed of lightning. As Mt. Mandara and other mountains were unable to hold him, he flew two hundred thousand leagues with the speed of a gale, and finally the mighty bird perched on a branch of a huge rose-apple tree. The branch snapped and the powerful king of birds, fearful of killing cows and brahmins, caught the falling branch.

Viṣṇu Hari, assuming the form of a man, saw the great bird speeding through the sky with all he carried, and he said, "Who are you and why are you circling in the sky, king of birds, carrying a huge branch and a giant elephant and tortoise?" The bird replied to Hari in his human form, "I am Garuḍa, great-armed one, wearing the form of a bird because of my *karman*, the son of Kaśyapa and Vinatā. Look,

*Non-Āryan tribal people.

I am carrying these two to eat them somewhere, but neither earth nor trees nor mountains can support me. From aloft I saw a rose-apple tree many leagues away. I perched on a branch of it so I could eat them, but it snapped and now I am roaming around holding it. I am fearful of killing thousands of millions of brahmins and cows, and am close to despair. What am I to do? Where can I go? Who can support my weight?" Hari replied, "Perch on my arm and eat your elephant and tortoise!"

"Oceans and the greatest mountains cannot hold me, so how will you carry this big creature? Who but Nārāyaṇa can carry me? What man in the three worlds could bear my impact?"

"A wise man should carry out his task, so carry out yours now. When you have done so you will surely know me."

Looking at the great being, the bird thought it over, and saying, "So be it then," perched on the mighty arm. The arm did not tremble at the giant bird's alighting, and perched there he dropped the branch in the mountains. No sooner did the branch fall than the earth with forests and all creatures, as well as the oceans quaked.

Soon the elephant and tortoise were eaten, but he was not filled and still hungry. Knowing this, Govinda said to the bird, "Eat the flesh of my arm and you shall be happy." He ate the plentiful flesh of the arm hungrily, and not a wound showed. Thereupon the wise bird said to Hari, lord of creation, "Who are you? What favor can I do in return?"

Said Nārāyaṇa, "Know that I am Nārāyaṇa, come to do you a kindness." To convince him he showed him his real form, yellow-robed, cloud-dark, enchanting with four arms, carrying conch, discus, mace and lotus, sovereign over all gods. When he saw it, Garuḍa bowed his head to Hari, "What favor can I do for you? Tell me, Supreme Person."

Majestic Hari, lord of the gods of gods, said, "Be my mount, heroic friend, for all time to come." And that best of birds replied, "I am graced, O lord of gods. My existence has borne fruit, protector, now that I have set eyes on you, my lord!"

## Denizens of the Netherworlds

There are those who hold that ten thousand leagues below the sun Rāhu circles like a star. He gained immortality and the power of eclipse by the grace of the lord, although as the son of a lioness and an outcast among the demons he did not deserve it. Later we shall describe his birth and deeds. They also say that the solar orb, which spreads warmth, is 10,000 leagues in diameter, while that of the moon is 12,000 and that of Rāhu 13,000. On set days Rāhu storms upon the sun and moon because of a long-lasting feud, and eclipses them. When the blessed lord perceives an eclipse of either one, he employs for their protection his discus called Sudarśana, his favorite weapon which, because of its refulgence, is irresistible and always spinning. Rāhu stays for a while, and then, atremble and with heart beating, withdraws to a distance; that is what people call "eclipse."

Ten thousand leagues below Rāhu are the seats of the Siddhas, Cāraṇas, and Vidyādharas. Below these are the pleasure grounds of the Yakṣas, Rākṣasas, Piśācas, ghosts and wandering spirits; they comprise the atmosphere that stretches as far as the wind blows and clouds are seen. At a distance of a hundred leagues below them lies this earth, which stretches as far as the principal birds can fly. The various parts of earth and their locations have been described. Below the earth there are seven cavities, separated by distances of ten thousand leagues, and of the same width and length, to wit: Atala, Vitala, Sutala, Talātala, Mahātala, Rasātala, and Pātāla. In these unearthly holes, which contain palaces, gardens and playgrounds filled with pleasures, luxuries and riches surpassing even heaven, the Daityas, Dānavas and Nāgas lead householder lives, with wives, children, relatives, friends and dependents. They play their magic tricks, are at all times happy and loving, and their pleasures are unimpeded even by the lord himself.

In these worlds there are cities built by the artificer Maya which shine forth adorned with palaces, ramparts, towers, halls, sanctuaries, squares, temples etc., colorfully constructed with the choicest of many precious stones and with the mansions of the lords of the netherworlds, whose floors are teeming with loving couples of Snakes and Asuras, doves, parrots and mynah birds. Their gardens outshine the beauty of the world of the Immortals with the totally captivating splendors of lovely trees bending under their blossoms, fruits, buds and enchanting flowers, intertwined with the limbs of vines, and of ponds dwelt upon by couples of various birds, filled with crystalline waters, which inhabit beds of water lilies and all kinds of lotuses in water that is alive with jumping fish, with the enchanting songs that arise from their continuous sport—it is a feast for the senses! No fear that might be inspired by the divisions of time like day and night is found here, for the jewels in the hoods of the great Snakes dispel all darkness.

The inhabitants of these worlds know no sickness and disease on account of food, drink, bathing and so on, being suffused with the alchemy of the juices of divine herbs. Nor do they suffer wrinkles, gray hair, old age, nor other conditions of aging with their attendant discolorations, fatigue and exhaustion. Death from any cause holds no power over these fortunate beings, except from the punishment of the discus of the lord's refulgence; when that penetrates the netherworlds, male embryos of the Asura wives are miscarried out of fear.

In Atala dwells the Asura Bala, son of Maya, who has created the 96 magic tricks, some of which magicians possess even now, and from whose yawning mouth issued the three groups of women called self-willed, lustful and whorish. They intoxicate a man who has entered their netherworld with an aphrodisiac potion and freely make love to him with coquetry, sly glances, caresses, smiles, sweet talk and embraces. The potion makes the man think he is lord and master, and deeming himself as strong as a myriad elephants he boasts like a drunk.

In the world of Vitala below that one, Hara-Bhava, lord of Hāṭaka, dwells locked in copulation with Bhavānī, amidst his attendant ghosts and *gaṇas,* in order to support Brahmā's creation. From the seminal juices of Bhava and Bhavānī wells forth the river called Hāṭakī. Fire, fanned by the wind, drinks that fluid, and when he spits it out it becomes the gold named Hāṭaka, which men and women in the harems of the demon lords wear as their ornament.

Below that is Sutala. The widely renowned and famous Bali, son of Virocana, was made to enter this realm by the blessed lord; to do Indra a favor, Bali was born from Aditi and in the form of a dwarf robbed Viṣṇu of the three worlds, but then took pity on him. Now he dwells here endowed with such opulent wealth as is not even found with Indra, and according to his Dharma he worships the adorable lord Viṣṇu. Even today he dwells there without fear. . . .

Below this world, in Talātala, glories the Dānava prince Maya, overlord of Tripura, whose city was burned by lord Śiva to benefit the three worlds. By the god's grace he gained the rank of master magician and, being under the protection of the Great God, he has no fear of Sudarśana.

Below that is Mahātala. There live the many-headed Snakes born of Kadrū, the band named Krodhavaśa (Irascible), headed by Kūhaka, Takṣaka, Kāliya, Suveṇa and others, with magnificent coils. They live in constant fear of the king of birds Garuḍa, Viṣṇu's mount, although they sometimes foolishly venture out to play out of affection for their wives, children, friends and households.

Below that, in Rasātala, live the Dānavas born of Diti, called Paṇis, as well as the Nivātakavacas and Kāleyas who inhabit Hiraṇyapura, enemies of the gods, by nature most powerful and violent. But their pride in strength was humbled by the refulgence of lord Hari, whose majesty pervades all the worlds, and they live there like moles and fear Indra because of the spells uttered by his ambassadress Saramā.

Below that is Pātāla, where dwell the lords of the race of Snakes led by Vāsuki: for example, Śankha, Kūlika, Mahaśankha, Śveta, Dhanaṃjaya, Dhṛtarāṣṭra, Śankhacūḍa, Kambala, Aśvatara and Devadatta of mighty coil and fury, who have five, seven, ten, a hundred and a thousand heads; and the brilliant jewels in their hoods dispel the dense darkness of that netherworld. . . .

At the root of Pātāla, at a distance of 30,000 leagues, lies the *tamas* portion of the lord called Ananta, whom they also call Saṃkarṣaṇa inasmuch as he represents the "pulling together" of the subject and object of experience. The orb of the earth is held upon a single head of the thousand-headed lord who is embodied in Ananta, and thus it functions. When in due time the lord wishes to annihilate the world, there arises between his eyebrows, which are moving and knitted in wrath, the Rudra named Saṃkarṣaṇa, his eleventh manifestation, three-eyed, three-tufted, brandishing his trident. In the circles of the gemlike nails, reddish and shining, of his lotus feet the lordly Snakes, when they bow down in devotion with prominent Bhāgavatas, see joyously mirrored their own faces whose cheeks are embellished with the glow of their glistening earrings. The Snake princesses, hoping for blessings, while anointing with a paste of aloe, sandal and saffron the silvery pillars of his wide, white, lovable, translucent and handsome arms that sparkle with the reflected play of his beautiful bracelets, gaze bashfully upon his lotuslike countenance. He glances at them with tenderly compassionate eyes and grimaces with the happy intoxication of his affection for them; they in turn display the lovely wanton smiles betokening the entrance of the god of love into hearts made turbulent from touching him.

The blessed lord Ananta, ocean of infinite qualities, the primeval god, dwells there for the well-being of the worlds, the fury of his wrath withdrawn, contemplated by hosts of gods, Asuras, Snakes, Siddhas, Gandharvas, Vidyādharas and seers, his eyes joyous, distorted and unfocused with ceaseless inebriation, causing the leaders of the deities of his entourage to swell with the elixir of his enchanting loquacity. Intoxicating with the drops of fragrant honey from his fresh *tulasī* flower, whose color never fades, a swarm of bees that bursts into sweet song, he wears, robed in blue, sporting a single earring and his lovable arm cradling the pole of his plough, his wild flower garland Vaijayantī in play, as Indra's elephant wears its golden harness.

# Glossary

Only terms and proper names of recurrent importance to Purāṇic mythology are included in this glossary.

*Acyuta* lit. "the unfallen one," name of Viṣṇu-Kṛṣṇa.

*Adharma* lawlessness.

*adhvaryu* principal priest of the Yajur Veda at fire sacrifices.

*Aditi* a goddess, mother of the group of gods named Ādityas.

*Ādityas* a group of gods of varying numbers, including Indra and Viṣṇu, but especially the sun god who is the Āditya par excellence.

*Agastya* a Vedic seer.

*Agni* the fire god.

*agnihotra* a milk oblation to the sun performed at dawn and dusk.

*agniṣṭoma* basic form of the Soma sacrifice.

*Agrya* one of the seven netherworlds.

*ahaṃkāra* lit. "ego-factor," the organ of subjectification of experience in Sāṃkhya philosophy.

*aho* expression of surprise.

*ahorātra* period of a day and night.

*Airāvata* Indra's elephant.

*Ājagava* Śiva's bow.

*Akrūra* uncle of Kṛṣṇa and early devotee.

*Alakā* city of Kubera.

*Amarāvatī* city of the gods.

*Ambikā* lit. "little mother," one of the names of the Goddess.

*Anakadundubhi* other name of Kṛṣṇa's father Vasudeva.

*Ananga* lit. "the bodiless one," other name of Kāma, the god of love.

*Ananta* lit. "endless," one of the names of the snake that supports the earth, also a name of Viṣṇu.

*Anasūyā* wife of the seer Atri.

*Andhaka* a demon, enemy of Śiva.

*Aṅgāraka* the planet Mars.

*Aṅgiras* name of a seer particularly associated with the Atharva Veda.

*Āṅgirasa* a lineage of brahmins.

*anuṣṭubh* Vedic meter; see *śloka*.

*Apsaras* semicelestial dancing girl of the gods.

*Āraṇyaka* lit. "forest book," a division of Vedic texts.

*Ardhanarīnara* lit. "half woman, half man," a manifestation of Śiva, also called Ardhanarīśvara.

*arghya* gift offered to a guest upon arrival.

*Arundhatī* wife of the seer Vasiṣṭha.

*Āryan* a member of one of the three twice-born classes; often used in the sense of "noble."

*Āryāvarta* area in northern India famous for its holiness.

*Asuras* demons, antagonists of the Devas, or gods.

*aśvamedha* Horse Sacrifice.

*aśvattha* the tree *ficus religiosus*.

*Aśvins* Vedic twin gods associated with healing.

*Atala* one of the seven netherworlds.

*Atharva Veda* the last of the four Vedas, containing many magic spells.

*ātman* lit. "Self" or "soul," the Self as supramundane entity.

*Atri* one of the seven seers.

*Auttami* one of the fourteen Manus; name of a Manvantara.

*avatāra* lit. "descent," an incarnation of a god, especially Viṣṇu.

*Avimukta* a place of pilgrimage in or about Vārāṇasī.

*ayana* lit. "course," viz. of the sun, the northern course between winter and summer solstice, the southern during the rest of the year.

*Āyurveda* the traditional medical science.

*Baladeva* name of Rāma, the elder brother of Kṛṣṇa.

*Balarāma* name of Rāma, the elder brother of Kṛṣṇa.

*Bali* a demon defeated by Viṣṇu in his Dwarf *avatāra*.

*Bhadrakālī* a name of the Goddess.

*Bhairava* a name of Śiva in his fierce aspect.

*bhakti* religious devotion to a supreme god, especially Kṛṣṇa.

*Bharata* an ancient king who has given his name to the land of India (see Bhāratavarṣa); founder of the dynasty of the Bhāratas.

*Bhāratavarṣa* classical designation of the Indian subcontinent.

*Bhārgava* an important lineage of brahmins, descended from Bhṛgu.

*Bhauma* the planet Mars.

*Bhautya* one of the fourteen Manus; name of a Manvantara.

*Bhava* name of Śiva.

*Bhavānī* name of the Goddess as wife of Bhava, or Śiva.

*bhoḥ* interjection, lit. "you, sir."

*Bhṛgu* eponym of a clan of brahmins; one of the Seven Seers.

*Bhūrloka* name of the earth in a vertical stratification of seven worlds.

*Bhūtas* a class of dangerous spirits, especially the restless dead.

*Bhuvarloka* name of the atmosphere.

*Brahmā* the creator god, priest of the gods, often called the Grandfather.

*brahmacārin* a student of the Veda who practices *brahmacarya*, "continence."

*Brahmahatyā* personified brahmin murder.

*Brahmaloka* the domain and dwelling of the god Brahmā.

*Brahman* the supreme creative principle from which the world emanates and to which it returns; substratum and substance of existence; frequently identified with any one of the chief gods.

*Brahmán* name of the principal priest belonging to the Atharva Veda at the fire sacrifice.

*Brāhmaṇa* a division of Vedic texts dealing with ritual.

*Brahmā-Sāvarṇi* one of the fourteen Manus; name of a Manvantara.

*brahmin* the highest, or priestly, class in the four-class system.

*Bṛhaspati* the priest of the gods, often identified with Brahmā; also the planet Jupiter.

*Buddha* in Hinduism an *avatāra* of Viṣṇu.

*Budha* the planet Mercury.

*Cākṣusa* one of the fourteen Manus; name of a Manvantara.

*Cāmuṇḍa* a name of the Goddess in her fierce aspect.

*Caṇḍāla* an outcaste.

*Caṇḍī, Caṇḍikā* lit. "the fierce one," a ferocious aspect of the Goddess.

*Cāraṇas* a class of heavenly musicians.

*Dadhi* lit. "curds," name of a circular ocean.

*Dadhīci* a seer from whose bones

Indra's thunderbolt was fashioned.

*Daityas* a class of demons.

*Dakṣa* name of a creator god (Prajāpati), best known from his insult to Śiva, who thereupon disrupted his sacrifice.

*Dakṣa-Sāvarṇi* one of the fourteen Manus; name of a Manvantara.

*dakṣiṇā* stipend paid to priests in remuneration for their ritual services.

*Dāmodara* lit. "rope-belly," one of the epithets of Viṣṇu-Kṛṣṇa.

*Dānavas* a class of demons.

*Devakī* Kṛṣṇa's mother.

*Devas* a class of gods, antagonists of the Asuras, or demons.

*Devī* lit. "goddess," the Goddess.

*Dharma* metaphysically based system of laws, duties, rites and obligations incumbent on a Hindu according to his class and stage of life.

*Dharmaśāstra* a class of prescriptive texts dealing with Hindu Dharma.

*Dharma-Sāvarṇi* one of the fourteen Manus; name of a Manvantara.

*Dhenukā* a demoness destroyed by Kṛṣṇa.

*Dhruva* the pole star.

*Diti* the progenitrix of the class of demons called Daityas.

*Durgā* lit. "the inaccessible one," name of a ferocious aspect of the Goddess.

*Durvāsas* a sage notorious for his bad temper and madness.

*Dvāpara* the third Age in the four-Yuga system.

*Dvārakā* Kṛṣṇa's city on the Arabian Gulf.

*Gabhastimat* one of the seven netherworlds.

*Gaṇapati* lit. "lord of *gaṇas*," other name of Gaṇeśa.

*gaṇas* attendants of the god Śiva.

*Gandhamādana* a mythical mountain range.

*Gandharvas* heavenly musicians.

*Gaṇeśa* lit. "lord of *gaṇas*" (q.v.), particularly a name of the elephant-headed son of Śiva.

*Gangā* the river Ganges, also personified.

*Garuḍa* a giant bird, devotee and mount of Viṣṇu.

*Gaurī* lit. "the white one," a beneficent aspect of the Goddess.

*Gayā* a place of pilgrimage, particularly for funerary rites.

*Gāyatrī* a verse held to be the most sacred of the Ṛg Veda.

*ghī* clarified butter, also *ghee.*

*Ghṛta* lit. "*ghī*" (q.v.), one of the circular oceans.

*Gokula* the village of Kṛṣṇa's youth.

*Goloka* Kṛṣṇa's heaven.

*Govardhana* the mountain lifted up by Kṛṣṇa to protect the cowherds.

*Govinda* lit. "cow-finder," name of Viṣṇu-Kṛṣṇa.

*guṇas* cosmological constituents and determining characteristics of all phenomena: *sattva, rajas,* and *tamas* (q.v.).

*guru* any elder person commanding respect, especially a teacher.

*Halāhala* the poison that came up at the Churning of the Ocean and was swallowed by Śiva.

*Hara* name of Śiva.

*Hari* name of Viṣṇu-Kṛṣṇa.

*Hari-Hara* the combined personalities of Viṣṇu and Śiva.

*Hariścandra* name of a much afflicted king.

*Harivarṣa* one of the subcontinents of earth.

*Himālaya, Himavat* lit. "the domain of snow," the mountain range; also personified as father of the Goddess.

*Hiraṇmaya* name of a continent.

*Hiraṇyakaśipu* Viṣṇu's demon antagonist in the Man-Lion *avatāra*.

*hotar* name of the principal priest belonging to the Ṛg Veda at the fire sacrifice.

*Hṛṣīkeśa* lit. "of the bristling hair," name of Kṛṣṇa.

*Ikṣurasa* lit. "sugar-cane juice," name of one of the circular oceans.

*Ilā* name of a woman who was turned into a man.

*Ilāvṛta* name of a continent.

*Indra* chief of the gods in the Vedic pantheon, also called Śakra.

*Īśa* lit. "the lord," a name of Śiva.

*Īśāna* lit. "the lord," a name of Śiva.

*Īśvara* lit. "the lord," a name of Śiva.

*Jagannātha* lit. "protector of the world," often an epithet of Viṣṇu-Kṛṣṇa.

*Jamadagni* name of a seer, the father of Paraśurāma.

*Jambūdvīpa* name of the continent that includes the Indian subcontinent.

*Janārdana* a name of Viṣṇu-Kṛṣṇa.

*Janarloka* one of the seven heavens.

*Kaca* a young brahmin who as his student received from Śukra the secret of immortality for the gods.

*Kailāsa* a plateau in the Himālayas where Śiva dwells.

*Kaiṭabha* name of a demon.

*Kāla* lit. "time," Time and Death personified.

*Kālanemi* name of a demon.

*Kali* the fourth and worst Age in the four-Yuga system.

*Kālī* name of the Goddess in her destructive aspect.

*Kāliya* the snake demon in the river Yamunā, made innocuous by Kṛṣṇa as a child.

*Kalkin* name of the last *avatāra* of Viṣṇu tiding over the transition from the Kali to the Kṛta Age.

*kalpa* translated as "Eon," a thousand periods of four *yugas,* or "Ages."

*Kāma* the god of love.

*Kāmadhenu* the Wish-granting Cow.

*Kaṃsa* uncle of Kṛṣṇa and his deadly enemy.

*Kaṇḍu* name of an immortal seer.

*Kapālin* name of Śiva as skull-bearer.

*karman* lit. "act," usually the consequences of acts in one's life that determine one's fate in the next.

*Kārttikeya* lit. "son of the Kṛttikās (Pleiades)," name of the son of Śiva's semen, also called Skanda, Guha and Kumāra.

*Kāśī* another name for Vārāṇasī.

*kāṣṭhā* a unit of time.

*Kātyāyanī* name of the Goddess.

*Kaustubha* Viṣṇu's jewel that originated at the churning of the ocean.

*Keśava* lit. "long-haired one," name of Viṣṇu-Kṛṣṇa.

*Kinnaras* semicelestial beings living in mountains, sometimes depicted as horse-headed, also called Kiṃpuruṣas.

*koṭi* a large number, usually ten million.

*Kratu* one of the Seven Seers.

*Krauñca* name of a continent.

*Kṛṣṇa* epic and Purāṇic hero who became an *avatāra* of Viṣṇu.

*Kṛta* the first and best Age in the four-Yuga system.

*Kṛttikas* the Pleiades; the wives of the Seven Seers, considered to be the mothers of Kārttikeya.

*kṣatriya* the second, martial class in the four-class system.

*Kṣīra* lit. "milk," one of the circular oceans.

*Kubera* the god of wealth, leader of Yakṣas, residing in the city Alakā.

*Kubjā* lit. "hunch-backed," name of a hump-backed girl straightened by Kṛṣṇa.

*Kūrma* lit. "tortoise," the Tortoise *avatāra* of Visnu and eponym of a Purāṇa.

*Kurukṣetra* a country in northern India famed as the battle field of the *Mahābhārata* war and a place of pilgrimage.

*Kuśa* name of a continent.

*lakh* the number 100,000.

*Lakṣmī* the goddess of beauty and good fortune, born at the Churning of the Ocean and consort of Viṣṇu, also named Śrī.

*linga* lit. "mark"; ithyphallic symbol of Śiva.

*loka* lit. "world," the domain or estate of certain gods, or a layer in a vertically stratified universe.

*Mādhava* tribal name of Viṣṇu-Kṛṣṇa.

*Madhu* name of a demon.

*Madhusūdana* lit. "slayer of Madhu," name of Viṣṇu-Kṛṣṇa.

*Mahābhārata* the epic of the war between the Pāṇḍavas and Kauravas.

*Mahādeva* lit. "great god," name of Śiva.

*Mahākāla* lit. "great destructive time," name of Śiva.

*Mahākālī* the Goddess in her destructive aspect.

*Mahākhya* one of the seven netherworlds.

*Mahāmāyā* lit. "great illusion," name of the Goddess as progenitrix of the illusory universe.

*Maharloka* one of the seven heavens.

*Mahat* in Sāṃkhya philosophy the first evolute of Prakṛti, identified with *buddhi*, "resolution."

*Mahātala* one of the seven netherworlds.

*Mahāyogin* lit. "great Yogin," name of Śiva as ascetic.

*Maheśa* lit. "great lord," name of Śiva.

*Maheśvara* lit. "great lord," name of Śiva.

*Mahiṣa* the buffalo demon, destroyed by Durgā.

*Maitreya* name of a seer who serves as interlocutor in some Purāṇas.

*maṇḍala* circular geometric figure representing the cosmos.

*Mandara* the mountain used to churn the ocean.

*Māndehas* a class of demons.

*Manmatha* name of Kāma, the god of love.

*mantra* a line of the *Ṛg Veda,* often used in the sense of "spell."

*Manu* a progenitor especially associated with the Fish *avatāra* of Viṣṇu.

*Manus* fourteen regents of Manvantaras in a scheme of historical time divergent from the four-Yuga system.

*Manvantara* lit. "period of a Manu," in a scheme of historical time divergent from the four-Yuga system.

*Marīci* one of the Seven Seers.

*Mārkaṇḍeya* a seer, survivor of the end of time and eponym of a Purāṇa.

*Maruts* Vedic storm gods and attendants of Indra.

*mātṛkas* the Mothers.

*Matsya* lit. "fish," the Fish *avatāra* of Viṣṇu and eponym of a Purāṇa.

*Maya* a demon famed for his artistry.

*Māyā* lit. "wizardry, illusion," the creative power of a god personified, often as his wife.

*Meru* central mountain of the earth and abode of gods.

*Mīmāṃsā* one of the schools of philosophy concerned mainly with the canons governing Vedic ritual.

*Mitra* a Vedic god of contracts.

*Mlecchas* non-Indian barbarians.

*Mohinī* lit. "bewitching woman," name of Viṣṇu as the woman who seduced the Asuras to regain the nectar of immortality for the gods in the Churning of the Ocean.

*mokṣa* release from transmigration.

*muhūrta* a unit of time.

*Nāgas* a class of semidivine snakes.

*nakṣatra* a constellation in the lunar zodiac.

*Nandin* the bull which is Śiva's mount.

*Nārada* a seer who is a frequent

intermediary between gods and men.

*Naraka* hell.

*Narasiṃha* lit. "man-lion," name of one of Viṣṇu's *avatāras*.

*Nārāyaṇa* name of Viṣṇu, especially during the period of dissolution after a Yuga or Kalpa.

*nimeṣa* lit. "eye-blink," the shortest unit of time.

*Nirṛti* Vedic goddess of death and corruption.

*nirvāṇa* state of final bliss, lit. "extinction."

*Nitala* one of the seven netherworlds.

*Nyāya* one of the schools of philosophy mainly concerned with the canons of logic.

*Parameṣṭhin* lit. "he who stands on high," name of Brahmā or any other of the great gods.

*parārdha* unit of time; all of elapsed time in the history of the universe.

*Paraśurāma* lit. "the Rāma with the axe," one of Viṣṇu's *avatāras*.

*Parikṣit* ancient king who ruled at the end of the Mahābhārata war.

*Pārvatī* lit. "she from the mountain," name of the Goddess as daughter of the Himālaya and spouse of Śiva.

*Paśupati* lit. "lord of cattle," name of Śiva.

*Pātāla* one of the seven netherworlds.

*Pināka* name of Śiva's weapon.

*Piśācas* class of demons, sometimes attendants of Śiva.

*pitṛs* lit. "fathers," deceased ancestors.

*Plakṣa* name of a continent.

*Pradhāna* in Sāṃkhya the original germinal matter from which the material universe evolves; synonym of Prakṛti.

*Pradyumna* Kṛṣṇa's son by Rukminī, sometimes identified with the god of love.

*Prahlāda* a demon, son of Viṣṇu's adversary Hiraṇyakaśipu, but a devotee of Viṣṇu.

*Prajāpati* lit. "lord of creatures," frequent appellation of Brahmā and other major gods.

*Prakṛti* in Sāṃkhya the original germinal matter from which the material universe evolves; synonym of Pradhāna.

*Pramāthas* a class of attendants of Śiva.

*Prayāga* place of pilgrimage at the confluence of the rivers Ganges and Yamunā, modern Allahabad.

*Pretas* ghosts of the dead to whom no sacrifices have been offered, attendants of Śiva.

*Pṛthivī* lit. "the wide one," name of the earth.

*Pṛthu* a legendary king who milked the earth for beneficial products.

*pūjā* a form of iconic worship.

*Pulaha* one of the Seven Seers.

*Pulastya* one of the Seven Seers.

*Purūravas* a legendary king who married and lost the nymph Urvaśī.

*Puruṣa* a name of Viṣṇu as the sacrificial substance from which the world was created; in Sāṃkhya the principle of consciousness which interacts with Prakṛti.

*Puṣkara* name of a continent; also a famed place of pilgrimage.

*Pūtanā* a demoness killed by Kṛṣṇa as a child.

*Rādhā* lover of Kṛṣṇa in his youth.

*Rāhu* a demon whose immortal and bodiless head is responsible for solar and lunar eclipses.

*Raivata* name of a mountain range.

*rajas* the second of the three *guṇas* or cosmological constituents governing dynamics, passion and strife.

*Rājasūya* a Vedic ritual of royal consecration.

*Rākṣasas* name of a class of demons.

*Rāma* a prince who became an *avatāra* of Viṣṇu.

*Rāmāyaṇa* epic romance of the exile of Rāma, the abduction of his wife by a demon, and her recovery by battle.

*Rāsa* the special circular dance at which Kṛṣṇa dallied with the cowherd women.

*Rāsalīlā* the sport of the Rāsa dance.

*Rasātala* one of the seven netherworlds.

*Rati* lit. "sexual pleasure," name of the wife of Kāma, the god of love.

*Raucya* one of the fourteen Manus; name of a Manvantara.

*Reṇukā* the wife of the seer Jamadagni and mother of Paraśurāma, who killed her at his father's behest.

*Ṛg Veda* first of the four Vedas consisting of hymns (*ṛc-s*) to Vedic gods and utilized at the ritual.

*Rudra* Vedic name of the god Śiva.

*Rudra-Sāvarṇi* one of the fourteen Manus; name of a Manvantara.

*Rukmiṇī* wife of Kṛṣṇa as an adult.

*Śacī* wife of the Vedic god Indra.

*sadasya* a concelebrant of the Vedic sacrifice.

*sādhu* lit. "good," an interjection of approbation.

*Sādhyas* a class of semidivine beings.

*Śāka* name of a continent.

*Śakra* synonym of the Vedic god Indra.

*śakti* lit. "power," the creative force of a god, especially Śiva, personified as his wife and semi-independent of him.

*Śakuntalā* a heroine, daughter of Viśvāmitra, wife of King Duṣyanta and mother of Bharata.

*Śalmāla* name of a continent.

*Sāma Veda* third of the four Vedas consisting of *sāmans* or melodies to Ṛg Vedic verses that were chanted at the fire sacrifice.

*Śaṃbhu* lit. "the benefactor," name of Śiva in his benign aspect.

*śāmī* a tree from which was taken the wood for the drilling of the fire for the sacrifice.

*Saṃkarṣaṇa* older brother of Kṛṣṇa, synonym for Baladeva, etc.

*Sāṃkhya* a school of philosophy stressing the dualism of material nature and consciousness.

*saṃsāra* transmigration of the soul.

*Saṃvartaka* the cloud that floods the world with water at the end of time.

*Śanaiścara* the planet Saturn.

*Sanatkumāra* an eternally youthful son of Brahmā.

*Śankara* lit. "the benefactor," name of Śiva in his benign aspect.

*Sarasvatī* name of a river associated with learning, and wife of Brahmā.

*Śārnga* Viṣṇu's bow.

*Śarva* lit. "hunter," name of Śiva.

*Satī* lit. "the good woman," daughter of Dakṣa and wife of Śiva, who cremated herself because of a slight done Śiva by her father.

*sattva* first of the three *guṇas* or cosmological constituents governing light, wisdom and serenity.

*Satyaloka* one of the seven heavens.

*Saubhari* an ascetic who indulged and conquered his senses.

*Sauri* the planet Saturn.

*Śauri* a patronymic of Kṛṣṇa.

*Śeṣa* name of the snake that bears the earth; also a synonym of Kṛṣṇa's elder brother Balarāma.

*Siddhas* semi-celestial perfected beings.

*Sītā* abducted but recovered wife of Rāma.

*Śiva* the destroyer god; other common appellations include Bhava, Hara, Īśvara, Kapālin, Mahādeva, Mahākala, Mahāyogin, Maheśvara, Paśupati, Śankara.

*Śivā* name of Śiva's wife.

*Skanda* name of Śiva's son, synonymous with Kārttikeya.

*śloka* Vedic and Sanskrit meter of thirty-two syllables, principally used in epic and Purāṇa; the *anuṣṭubh*.

*smṛti* a class of Sanskrit texts containing traditional teachings.

*Soma* the pressed-out juice of a plant imbibed at the fire sacrifice; also identified with the moon which contains it.

*śrāddha* a commemorative ritual for the deceased ancestors.

*Śrī* name of the goddess of beauty and good fortune, wife of Viṣṇu, synonymous with Lakṣmī.

*Śrīvatsa* the whorl of hair on the chest of Viṣṇu-Kṛṣṇa.

*śruti* a class of Sanskrit texts, especially Vedic, which are regarded as self-authenticating revelation.

*Sthāṇu* name of Śiva, lit. "pillar."

*Sudarśana* name of Viṣṇu's discus.

*śūdra* fourth and lowest class in the four-class system.

*Sudyumna* name of the woman Ilā when she was changed into a man.

*Śukra* the planet Venus; also a seer.

*Surā* lit. "liquor," name of one of the circular oceans.

*Sūrya* the sun god.

*Sutala* one of the seven netherworlds.

*svadhā* a ritual addressed to the deceased ancestors.

*Svādu* lit. "sweet," name of the fresh-water ocean.

*svāhā* a cry uttered at the fire sacrifice.

*Svarloka* heaven in a vertically stratified universe.

*Svārociṣa* one of the fourteen Manus; name of a Manvantara.

*Svayambhū* lit. "the self-existent," appellation of Brahmā and other major gods.

*Svāyambhuva* one of the fourteen Manus; name of a Manvantara.

*svayaṃvara* a form of marriage in which the bride selects her husband.

*Syamantaka* name of a jewel of Viṣṇu-Kṛṣṇa.

*Talātala* one of the seven netherworlds.

*tamas* last of the three *guṇas* or cosmological constituents governing inertness, indolence and ignorance.

*Tāmasa* one of the fourteen Manus; name of a Manvantara.

*Taparloka* one of the seven heavens.

*tapas* the ascetic self-restraint and self-mortification to which one voluntarily subjects oneself in order to gain uncommon powers.

*Tārakā* enemy of Viṣṇu.

*tattva* in Sāṃkhya a principle in the structure of the evolved universe.

*tejas* the personal power or prestige of a person or god that emanates from him like a nimbus.

*tilaka* mark affixed between the eyebrows to ward off evil.

*tīrtha* lit. "ford," a place of pilgrimage usually found by a river.

*Tiṣya* synonym for the Kṛta Age.

*Tretā* the second Age in the four-Yuga system.

*Trilocana* lit. "three-eyed," name of Śiva.

*Tripura* a triple city which Śiva destroyed by fire.

*Tripurāri* lit. "enemy of Tripura," name of Śiva.

*Tryambaka* name of Śiva.

*Tvaṣṭar* a god, patron of architecture.

*Udaya* name of a mountain over which the sun rises.

*udgātar* the principal priest belonging to the Sāma Veda at the fire sacrifice.

*Umā* name of the Goddess as the wife of Śiva.

*Upaniṣads* a division of Vedic texts concerned chiefly with metaphysical teachings.

*Upendra* lit. "lesser Indra," a somewhat pejorative name of Viṣṇu.

*Urvaśī* an Apsaras who was temporarily married to the mortal King Purūravas.

*Uśanas* the priest of the demons, synonymous with Śukra and Kāvya; also the planet Venus.

*Uttarakuru* name of a mythical country north of the Himālayas.

*Vaikuṇṭha* Viṣṇu's heaven.

*vaiśya* the third class of agriculturalists and artisans in the four-class system.

*Vaitaraṇī* the river of hell.

*Vaivasvata* one of the fourteen Manus; name of a Manvantara.

*Vālakhilyas* a class of sages.

*Vāmana* lit. "dwarf," the Dwarf *avatāra* of Viṣṇu.

*Varāha* lit. "swine," the Boar *avatāra* of Viṣṇu.

*Vārāṇasī* sacred city, present Banaras.

*Varuṇa* Vedic god, in later times god of ocean and water.

*Vāsava* name of Indra.

*Vasiṣṭha* one of the Seven Seers characterized by infinite patience.

*Vasudeva* the father of Kṛṣṇa.

*Vāsudeva* patronymic of Kṛṣṇa.

*Vāsuki* the king of the Snakes.

*Vasus* a group of Vedic gods.

*Vāyu* the wind god; eponym of a Purāṇa.

*Veda* collective, or any one, of the four Vedas, the Ṛg, Yajur, Sāma and Atharva.

*Vedānta* the texts of Upaniṣads and the school of philosophy based on them.

*Virāj* name of an androgynous creative Vedic deity.

*Viṣṇu* the preserver god, closely identified with Kṛṣṇa; other common appellations include Acyuta, Hari, Jagannātha, Keśava, Mādhava, Madhusūdana, Nārāyaṇa.

*Viśvakarman* a Vedic god, the god architect.

*Viśvāmitra* a seer who was originally a kṣatriya and notorious for his bad temper.

*Viśvedevas* a group of Vedic gods.

*Vitala* one of the seven netherworlds.

*Vivasvat* name of the sun god.

*Vraja* one of the villages of Kṛṣṇa's childhood.

*Vṛndāvana* one of the villages of Kṛṣṇa's childhood.

*Vṛtra* a Vedic demon defeated by Indra.

*Vyāsa* reputed author of the *Mahābhārata* and inspirer of the Purāṇas.

*Yādava* tribe, and tribal name, of Kṛṣṇa.

*Yajur Veda* second of the four Vedas containing brief sacrificial formulæ *(yajus)*.

*Yakṣas* semi-divine chthonic spirits, guardians of wealth.

*Yama* the god of death.

*Yamunā* name of a river, place of pilgrimage.

*Yaśodā* Kṛṣṇa's substitute mother.

*Yoga* a method of physical and mental self-control, productive of magical and mystical powers, which in the end reunites the practician with the supreme being.

*yogin* a practician of Yoga.

*yoni* female organ, womb and source of creation.

*yuga* one of the four Ages (Kṛta, Tretā, Dvāpara and Kali) through which the universe consecutively moves; translates as "Age."

# Notes on Sources

The "Invocations and Prayers" are from the following sources. "*OṂ*" (Ch. 1) is from Mārkaṇḍeya 39.6–16; "To Viṣṇu" (Ch. 2) is from Mārkaṇḍeya, Invocation 1, 2; "Song of the Cowherd Women to Kṛṣṇa" (Ch. 3) is from Bhāgavata 10.31.1–7, 14; "To Śiva" (Ch. 4) is from Kūrma 1.10.43–45; 50–51; 53–57; 65–70; and "To the Goddess" (Ch. 5) is from Mārkaṇḍeya 88.2–5, 23–28, 34.

In Chapter 1, "Origins," "The Origin of Brahmā from the Lotus in Viṣṇu's Navel" is from Kūrma 1.9.6–29; "Prakṛti and Puruṣa" is from Mārkaṇḍeya 42.61–73; "The Cosmic Egg" is from Vāmana Saromāhātmya 22.17–22, 30–39; "The Origin of the World from Brahmā" is from Kūrma 1.7.30–58; "The Four Heads of Brahmā" is from Matsya 3.1–12, 30–47; "Puruṣa, the Cosmic Person" is from Bhāgavata 2.5.34–42; "The Origin and Nature of Time" is from Mārkaṇḍeya 43.3–44; "The Four Ages" is from Kūrma 1.27.16–57; 28.1–7; "The Kali Age" is from Viṣṇu 4.24.70–97; "The Dissolution of the World in Viṣṇu" is from Viṣṇu 6.3.14–41; 4.1–10; "The Dissolution into Prakṛti and Puruṣa" is from Kūrma 2.44.1–24; "The Shape of Space" is from Viṣṇu 2.9.1–7; 11.21–26; 12.1–15, 21–28; "The Seven Heavens" is from Kūrma 1.39.1–12, 27–41, 45; "The Seven Netherworlds" is from Viṣṇu 2.5.1–27; "The Hells" is from Vāmana 11.50–58; 12.1–42, 55, 56; "The Regions of Earth" is from Kūrma 1.43.1–19; 44.1–30, 35; 45.1–21, 43–45; "The Origin of the Seers and the Manus" is from Mārkaṇḍeya 47.1–18; 50.3–12; "The Manvantaras" is from Viṣṇu 3.2.2–14, 45–53.

In Chapter 2, "Viṣṇu," "The Four Forms of Viṣṇu" is from Mārkaṇḍeya 4.44–58; "The Twelve *Avatāras* of Viṣṇu" is from Matsya 47.32–52; "The Twenty-Two *Avatāras* of Viṣṇu" is from Garuḍa 1.12–35; "The *Avatāras* of Viṣṇu and the Story of Anasūyā" is from Garuḍa 142.1–29; "Matsya, the Fish" is from Matsya 1.11–35; 2.1–37; "Kūrma, the Tortoise" is from Agni 3.1–22; "Varāha, the Boar" is from Śiva Vāyavīya 1.11.10–13, 18–36; "Narasiṃha, the Man-Lion" is from Śiva Rudra 2.5.4–43; "Aditi and the Birth of

Vāmana, the Dwarf" is from Vāmana Saromāhātmya 7.7–15; 8.1–5, 9–18, 28; 9.12–16; "Vāmana, the Dwarf, and Bali" is from Vāmana Saromāhātmya 10.1–9, 33–66, 85–87, 91; "Paraśurāma, Rāma with the Axe" is from Bhāgavata 9.15.16–20, 23–41; 16.1–27; "Rāma in the Rāmāyaṇa" is from Garuḍa 143.1–51; "Kṛṣṇa in the Mahābhārata" is from Garuḍa 145.1–43; "Vaikuṇṭha, Viṣṇu's Celestial City" is from Kūrma 1.47.49–69; "Sudarśana, Viṣṇu's Discus" is from Vāmana 56.16–46; "Bali and Sudarśana the Discus" is from Vāmana 67.1–19; "The Churning of the Ocean" is from Viṣṇu 1.9.2–116; "Viṣṇu and Śrī" is from Viṣṇu 1.8.17–35.

In Chapter 3, "Kṛṣṇa," "The Conception of Kṛṣṇa" is from Viṣṇu 5.1.5–33; 56–86; 2.1–6; "The Birth of Kṛṣṇa" is from Viṣṇu 5.3.1–29; "Pūtanā, the Child-Killer" is from Viṣṇu 5.5.1–23; "The Naughty Children Rāma and Kṛṣṇa; the Move to Vṛndāvana" is from Viṣṇu 5.6.1–35; "Kāliya, the Snake" is from Viṣṇu 5.7.1–25; 43–49; 54–57; 70–72; 76–83; "Mount Govardhana" is from Viṣṇu 5.11.1–25; "Conversation with the Cowherds" is from Viṣṇu 5.13.1–13; "Kṛṣṇa and Rādhā" is from Brahmavaivarta 4.16.1–16; 25–40; 48–49; 54–65; 123–78; "The Theft of the Clothes" is from Brahmavaivarta 4.27.52–58; 60–78; 80–98; "The Rāsalīlā Dance" is from Viṣṇu 5.13.14–62; "Rādhā and the Dance" is from Brahmavaivarta 4.27.217–21; 224–42; 28.5–24; 46–48; 52–53; 59–64; 71–79; 100–109; 112–131; "The Departure of Kṛṣṇa" is from Brahmavaivarta 4.69.12–20; "The Plotting of Kaṃsa" is from Viṣṇu 5.15.1–24; "The Invitation to Rāma and Kṛṣṇa" is from Viṣṇu 5.17.18–26; 18.1–12; "The Hunchbacked Girl" is from Viṣṇu 5.20.1–13; "The Death of Kaṃsa" is from Viṣṇu 5.20.14–93; 105; "The Building of Dvārakā" is from Viṣṇu 5.23.1–28; 24.1–7; "The Longing of the Cowherd Women for Kṛṣṇa" is from Viṣṇu 5.24.8–21; "The Abduction of Rukmiṇī" is from Viṣṇu 5.26.1–12; 28.1–5; "Pradyumna and the Fish" is from Viṣṇu 5.27.3–32; "The End of the Yādavas" is from Viṣṇu 5.37.1–76.

In Chapter 4, "Śiva," "The Origin of Rudra, the Howler" is from Kūrma 1.10.1–38; "The Birth of Pārvatī" is from Vāmana 25.1–75; "The Test of Pārvatī's *Tapas*" is from Śiva Śatarudra 33.1–63; "The Betrothal of Śiva and Pārvatī" is from Vāmana 26.1–71; "The Wedding of Śiva and Pārvatī" is from Vāmana 27.1–62; "Dakṣa's Insult" is from Śiva Vāyavīya 1.18.4–59; "The Destruction of Dakṣa's Sacrifice" is from Kūrma 1.14.4–97; "Gaṇeśa" is from Śiva Rudra 13.15–39; 14.1, 2, 7–10, 57–63; 15.1–20; 16.7–13, 18–35; 17.3–59; "Kārttikeya" is from Vāmana 31.2–56; "Śukra" is from Vāmana 43.20–46; "The Burning of Tripura" is from Matsya 128.3–28; 129.1–20; 130.1–19, 37–50; 131.1–18; 132.5–22, 70, 71; 137.30–38, 42–54; 139.1–17, 44–58, 65–75, 85–87; "Sunartaka the Dancer" is from Śiva Śatarudra 34.1–37; "The

Tāṇḍava Dance of Śiva" is from Linga 106.2–28; "The Dance of Śiva in the Sky" is from Kūrma 2.5.1–11, 22–27, 40–42; "The Sages of the Pine Forest" is from Śiva Koṭirudra 12.6–54; "Brahmā, Viṣṇu, and the Linga of Śiva" is from Kūrma 1.25.64, 67–69, 88–95; "The Skull-Bearer" is from Vāmana 2.20–37; Kūrma 2.31.67–104; "Kāmadeva, the God of Love," is from Vāmana 6.25–44, 58–77, 82–87, 94–97, 103–107; "The Illusions of Śiva" is from Śiva Umā 4.11–39; "The Weapons of Śiva" is from Śiva Umā 1.12–41, 57–64; "The Origin of Women" is from Śiva Śatarudra 3.1–31; "Hari-Hara" is from Vāmana 36.1–9, 19–31.

In Chapter 5, "The Goddess," "The Blazing Tower of Splendor" is from Śiva Umā 49.1–43; "Śiva and *Śakti;* the Great Goddess" is from Kūrma 1.11.1–47, 63–75, 211–220, 326; "The Demons Madhu and Kaiṭabha" is from Mārkaṇḍeya Devīmāhātmya 78.45–53, 61–77; "The Origin of the Goddess from the Gods" is from Mārkaṇḍeya Devīmāhātmya 79.1–70; "The Death of Mahiṣa, the Buffalo Demon" is from Mārkaṇḍeya Devīmāhātmya 80.21–44; "The Birth of Kālī and the Final Battle" is from Mārkaṇḍeya Devīmāhātmya 84.1–25; 89.29–37; "Bhadrakālī and the Thieves" is from Bhāgavata 5.9.12–20; "Sarasvatī and King Navaratha" is from Kūrma 1.23.13–27.

In Chapter 6, "Seers, Kings and Supernaturals," "Mārkaṇḍeya and the Cosmic Ocean" is from Matsya 165.1–22; 166.13–67; "Nārada" is from Bhāgavata 1.6.5–39; "Kaṇḍu" is from Brahma 1.69.7–28; 43–101; "Śukra and Kaca" is from Matsya 25.8–66; "Agastya and Vasiṣṭha" is from Matsya 60.21–31; "Vasiṣṭha and Viśvāmitra" is from Mārkaṇḍeya 9.1–31. "Pṛthu and the Milking of the Earth" is from Matsya 10.3–35; "Ilā and Sudyumna" is from Bhāgavata 9.18–42; "Purūravas and Urvaśī" is from Viṣṇu 4.6.35–93; "Hariścandra and his Son" is from Bhāgavata 9.7.7–25; "Hariścandra and Viśvāmitra" is from Mārkaṇḍeya 7.1–61; 8.1–130, 174–194, 217–221, 239–254, 258–262, 268–278; "Parikṣit" is from Bhāgavata 1.18.24–50; 19.1–6, 18; "Yayāti" is from Bhāgavata 9.18.1–51; 19.1–25; "Vidūratha" is from Mārkaṇḍeya 113.10–76; "Saubhari" is from Bhāgavata 9.6.37–55; "Śakuntalā" is from Bhāgavata 9.20.1–31; "The Māndehas at Twilight" is from Viṣṇu 2.8.49–59; "The Battle between the Gods and Demons" is from Vāmana 47.1–51; 48.1–15; "Indra and Vṛtra" is from Bhāgavata 6.9.1–19; "Dadhīci's Bones" is from Śiva Śatarudra 24.11–32; "Diti and the Maruts" is from Vāmana 45.20–42; "The Seers' Wives and the Maruts" is from Vāmana 46.3–23; "Soma" is from Vāyu 2.28.1–47; "Prahlāda and Hiraṇyakaśipu" is from Viṣṇu 1.17.1–26, 31–34, 37–53; 18.1–46; 19.50–69, 82–86; 20.1–8, 15–39; "Indra and the Ants" is from Brahmavaivarta 4.47.100–160; "The Descent of the Ganges River" is from Padma 6.22.9–28; "The Hermitage of Atri" is from Matsya 114.10–13, 16–19; 115.1–21; 116.1–21; 117.66–76; 118.1–3, 25–45; "The River Sarasvatī and Kurukṣetra" is from Vāmana Saromāhātmya 11.1–8, 20–24; 12.1–21; "The River Yamunā" is from Viṣṇu 5.25.1–17; "The Virtues of Vārāṇasī" is from Kūrma 1.29.22–54, 60–65; "Vārāṇasī and the Yakṣa" is from Matsya 179.5–23, 47–54, 70–75, 80–100; "The Pilgrimage of Śiva to Vārāṇasī" is from Vāmana 3.1–5, 11–13, 23–36, 40–51; "Gayā" is from Garuḍa 82.1–18; "Prayāga" is from Matsya 102.2–25; 103.1–19; "The Fathers" is from Garuḍa 88.2–12, 25–27; 89.2–12, 29–31, 36–38, 49, 61–71; 90.1–7; "The Mothers" is from Matsya 178.2–9, 33–64, 73–89; "Garuḍa" is from Padma 5.44.40–70, 79–110; "Denizens of the Netherworlds" is from Bhāgavata 5.24.1–18, 28–31; 25.1–7.

# Bibliography of Sanskrit Purāṇas

Agni Purāṇa. *Ānandāśrama Sanskrit Series*, 1900.
Bhāgavata Purāṇa. Bombay: Nirnayasagar Press, 1950.
Brahma Purāṇa. Bombay: Śrī-Venkaṭeśvara Steam Press, 1906.
Brahmavaivarta Purāṇa. *Ānandāśrama Sanskrit Series*, 1937.
Garuḍa Purāṇa. Varanasi: Paṇḍitapustakālaya, 1963.
Kūrma Purāṇa. Varanasi: All-India Kashiraj Trust, 1972.
Linga Purāṇa. Bombay: Śrī-Venkaṭeśvara Steam Press, 1906.
Mārkaṇḍeya Purāṇa. Bombay: Śrī-Venkaṭeśvara Steam Press, 1910.
Matsya Purāṇa. Calcutta: Sarasvatī Press, 1876.
Padma Purāṇa. *Ānandāśrama Sanskrit Series*, 1819; 1893.
Śiva Purāṇa. Bombay: Śrī-Venkaṭeśvara Steam Press, 1906.
Vāmana Purāṇa. Varanasi: All-India Kashiraj Trust, 1969.
Vāyu Purāṇa. Bombay: Śrī-Venkaṭeśvara Steam Press, 1895.
Viṣṇu Purāṇa. Gorakhpur: Gītā Press, n.d.

# Index

Only names and terms of significant importance to this volume are included in this index.

# HINDU TRADITION SERIES

**1 .THE MAHĀBHĀRATA AND GREEK MYTHOLOGY**—
FERNANDO WULFF ALONSO

This book, based on a previous publication in Spanish, defends that in the Mahābhārata – one of the most profound, captivating and richest stories of human history and, without a doubt, the most vivid of the world's epics – Greek mythological and epic materials were systematically employed. The employment of these materials by no means takes away from the work's authenticity, instead quite the contrary.
[978-81-208-3791-1]

**2. VIRAHA-BHAKTI** :The Early History of Kṛṣṇa Devotion—FRIEDHELM HARDY

The present work is a detailed study of the multifarious of origins of viraha-bhakti in South India and its developments up to the point at which it entered the pan-Indian scene. The study suggests a revision of the monolithic image of Indian religion implied in much scholarly literature. It differentiates a great variety of interacting traditions and milieux, and demonstrates the dynamism of Indian culture. By identifying a specific type of religion and reflecting on its significance, the author attempts, at the same time, to go beyond purely textual and historical considerations. Thus the book will be of interest to any student of Indian religion and culture.
[978-81-208-3616-1]

**3. CLASSICAL HINDU MYTHOLOGY** : A Reader in the Sanskrit Purāṇas— *Edited and Translated by* CORNELIA DIMMITT and J.A.B. VAN BUITENEN

The Mahāpurāṇas embody the received tradition of Hindu mythology. This anthology contains fresh translations of these myths, only a few of which have ever been available in English before, thus providing a rich new portion of Hindu mythology.
[978-81-208-3972-4]

**4. MYTHOLOGY OF BRAHMA**— GREG BAILEY
[Forthcoming]